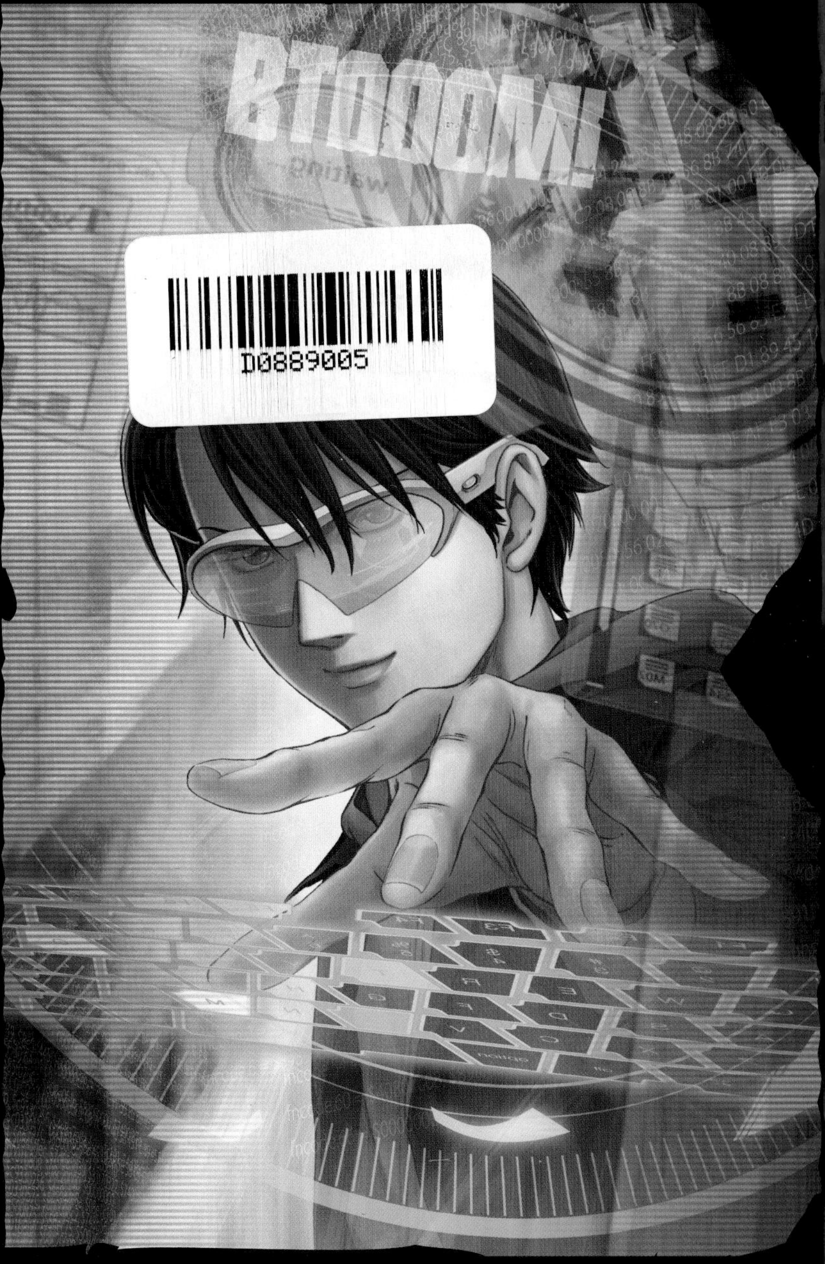
BTOOOM!

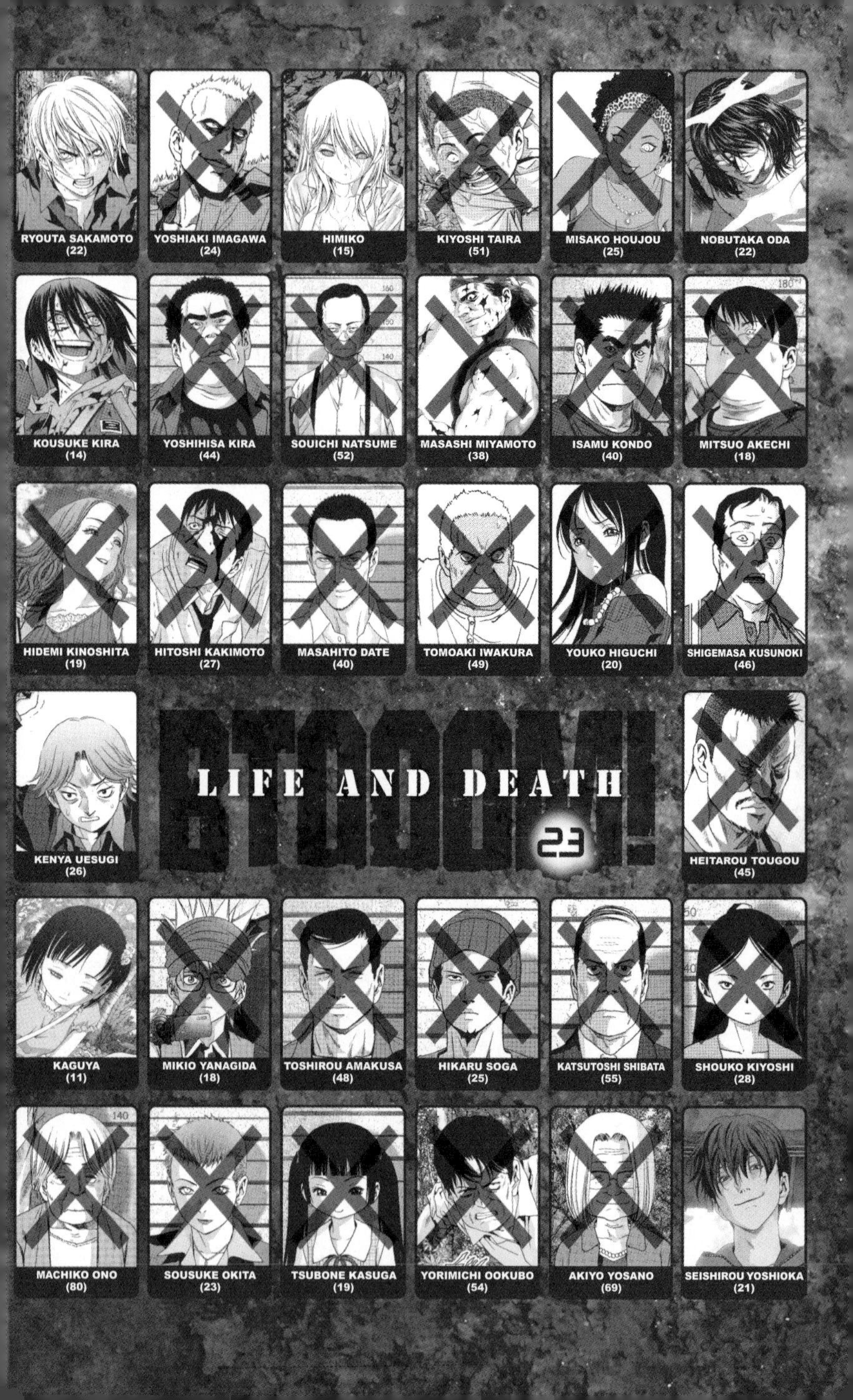
RYOUTA SAKAMOTO (22)
YOSHIAKI IMAGAWA (24)
HIMIKO (15)
KIYOSHI TAIRA (51)
MISAKO HOUJOU (25)
NOBUTAKA ODA (22)
KOUSUKE KIRA (14)
YOSHIHISA KIRA (44)
SOUICHI NATSUME (52)
MASASHI MIYAMOTO (38)
ISAMU KONDO (40)
MITSUO AKECHI (18)
HIDEMI KINOSHITA (19)
HITOSHI KAKIMOTO (27)
MASAHITO DATE (40)
TOMOAKI IWAKURA (49)
YOUKO HIGUCHI (20)
SHIGEMASA KUSUNOKI (46)
KENYA UESUGI (26)
BTOOOM!
LIFE AND DEATH
23
HEITAROU TOUGOU (45)
KAGUYA (11)
MIKIO YANAGIDA (18)
TOSHIROU AMAKUSA (48)
HIKARU SOGA (25)
KATSUTOSHI SHIBATA (55)
SHOUKO KIYOSHI (28)
MACHIKO ONO (80)
SOUSUKE OKITA (23)
TSUBONE KASUGA (19)
YORIMICHI OOKUBO (54)
AKIYO YOSANO (69)
SEISHIROU YOSHIOKA (21)

BTOOOM!

JUNYA INOUE

CHARACTER

NOBUTAKA ODA

GENDER: Male
AGE: 22
BLOOD TYPE: AB
JOB: Restaurant manager
HOME: Tokyo

Sakamoto's biggest rival and an old classmate of his from high school. His elaborate plans and surprisingly daring athleticism have helped him procure chips at a rapid pace as he plans for his own departure from the island. Engaging in life-or-death battles with his former best friend Sakamoto, he has demonstrated himself to be an unequaled master at combat.

HIMIKO

GENDER: Female
AGE: 15
BLOOD TYPE: B
JOB: High school student
HOME: Tokyo

A foreign high school girl who has teamed up with Sakamoto. She harbors a deep resentment against men after a sordid experience in her past, but after surviving some battles thanks to Sakamoto, she begins to trust him. Her character in the online version of "BTOOOM!" is actually married to Sakamoto's character, and she has fallen in love with the real Sakamoto too.

RYOUTA SAKAMOTO

GENDER: Male
AGE: 22
BLOOD TYPE: B
JOB: Unemployed
HOME: Tokyo

After spending every day cooped up in his home gaming online, he suddenly finds himself forced to participate in "BTOOOM! GAMERS," a killing game taking place on a mysterious uninhabited island. As a world ranker in the online third-person shooter "BTOOOM!," he uses his experience and natural instincts to survive and concoct a plan to get off the island with his comrades, only for it to end in failure. At the Sanctuary, he teams up with Kaguya and Soga to beat Torio.

KAGUYA

GENDER: Female
AGE: 11
BLOOD TYPE: AB
JOB: Grade schooler
HOME: Tokyo

A mysterious little girl who came across Sakamoto when he washed ashore. She doesn't speak and uses a tablet to communicate. She's the figurehead of the Order of Moonlight, a religious cult, and can see dead people. In the Sanctuary, she worked with Sakamoto and Soga to defeat the real villain behind the tragedies, Torio.

KENYA UESUGI

GENDER: Male
AGE: 26
BLOOD TYPE: AB
JOB: Office worker
HOME: Tokyo

A cowardly and easily flattered young man who used to dream of becoming an actor. He was almost killed by Kira, but he escaped thanks to Higuchi's lie-detecting ability. He was previously a part of Tougou's team.

KOUSUKE KIRA

GENDER: Male
AGE: 14
BLOOD TYPE: AB
JOB: Junior high student
HOME: Tokyo

This junior high student harbors a dark, brutal, murderous past. On the island, he blew up his own father and is genuinely enjoying this murderous game of "BTOOOM!". He's always been a big fan of the online version of the game, and his dream is to defeat "SAKAMOTO," a top world ranker. Unfortunately, he keeps failing at it. Tougou's death makes him realize for the first time ever how precious life is.

BTOOOM! 23

LONGER SCHWARITZ

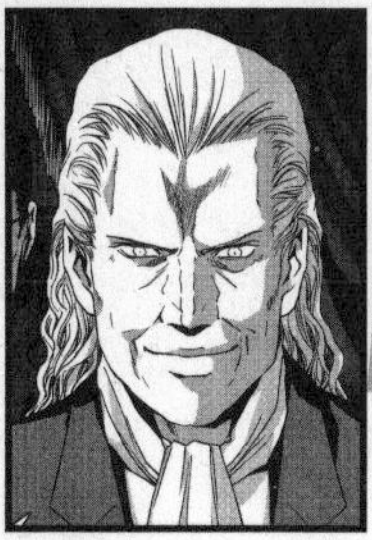

GENDER: Male
AGE: 77
BLOOD TYPE: O
JOB: Capitalist
HOME: New York

A descendant of European aristocracy, he is a man of power who controls the world behind the scenes with his considerable capital. In order to more thoroughly control the online realm, he founds the THEMIS project and has high hopes for "BTOOOM! GAMERS."

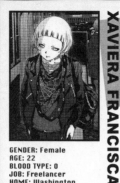

XAVIERA FRANCISCA

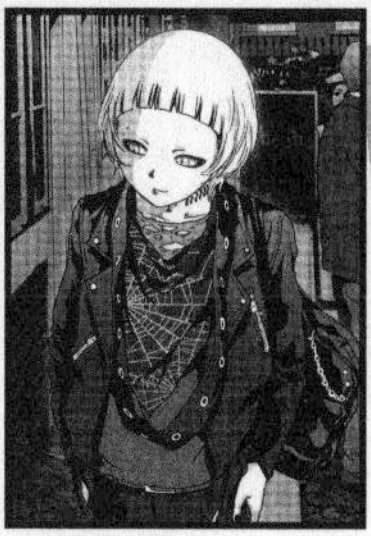

GENDER: Female
AGE: 22
BLOOD TYPE: O
JOB: Freelancer
HOME: Washington

The operator of the drone that dropped the medicine case down on the island. Instead of BIMs, she attacks the players with a machine gun. Her skill is universally acknowledged and in the online version of "BTOOOM!", she is the reigning world champion. However, she's never beaten Sakamoto, so she's obsessed with doing so.

SEISHIROU YOSHIOKA

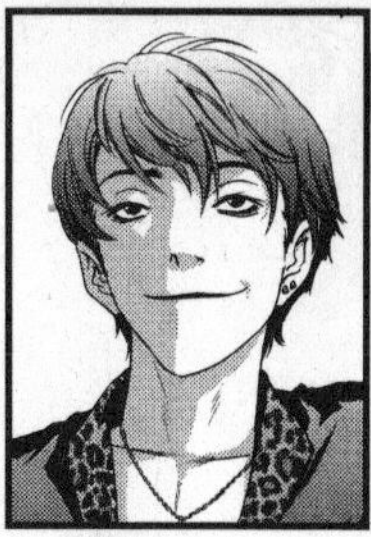

GENDER: Male
AGE: 21
BLOOD TYPE: A
JOB: Musician
HOME: Tokyo

Himiko's childhood friend and the lead vocalist of a popular band. He and his bandmates lured their fans—Himiko's classmates—into his apartment and raped them. He was later arrested. He is the reason behind both Himiko's distrust of men and her nomination for the island.

HISANOBU

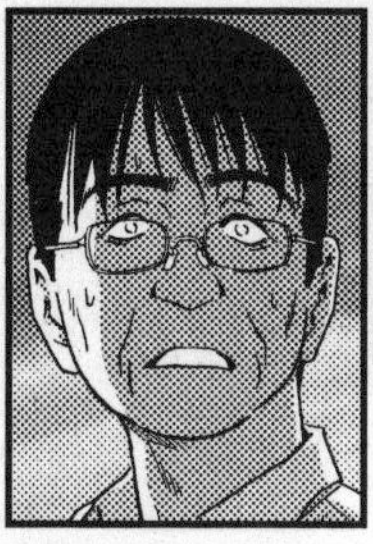

GENDER: Male
AGE: 55
BLOOD TYPE: A
JOB: Unemployed
HOME: Tokyo

Yukie's new husband and Sakamoto's stepfather. He's worried about how much time his stepson spends up in his room and scolds him, only to be attacked. Having just been laid off, he racks up debt because of his praiseworthy efforts to preserve his family's lifestyle. However, Yukie is frail in body and mind and attempts to kill herself. Fate has dealt him an unfair card in life.

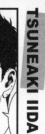

TSUNEAKI IIDA

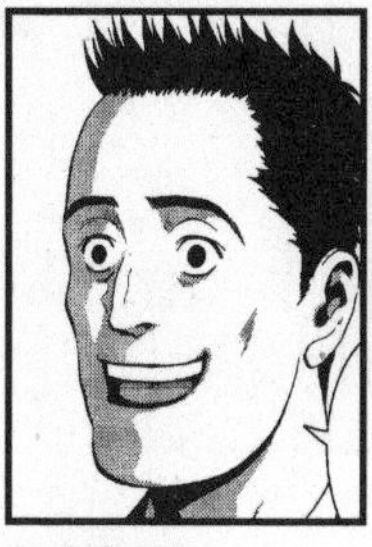

GENDER: Male
AGE: 24
BLOOD TYPE: A
JOB: Programmer
HOME: Tokyo

An employee at Tyrannos Japan and Sakamoto's senpai from college. He's an excellent programmer and works under Takanohashi on the development of "BTOOOM! GAMERS." But he doesn't agree with the inhumane nature of the game and approached Sakamoto with the proposal and strategy to put a stop to the game's development, only for the plan to fall apart.

MATTHEW PERRIER

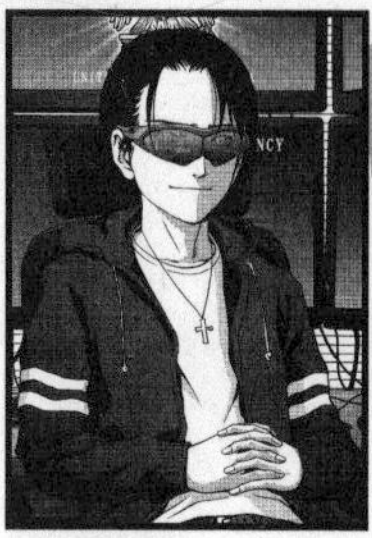

GENDER: Male
AGE: 27
BLOOD TYPE: O
JOB: Ex-NSA programmer, political refugee
HOME: Washington (location unknown after exile)

A former programmer with the NSA (U.S. National Security Agency), he's a capable hacker and curbed a number of cyber-crimes while with the NSA. But after learning about the government's darker side, he made off with sensitive data about the THEMIS project—in a way, the evidence of their nefarious plans—and defected to another country.

CONTENTS

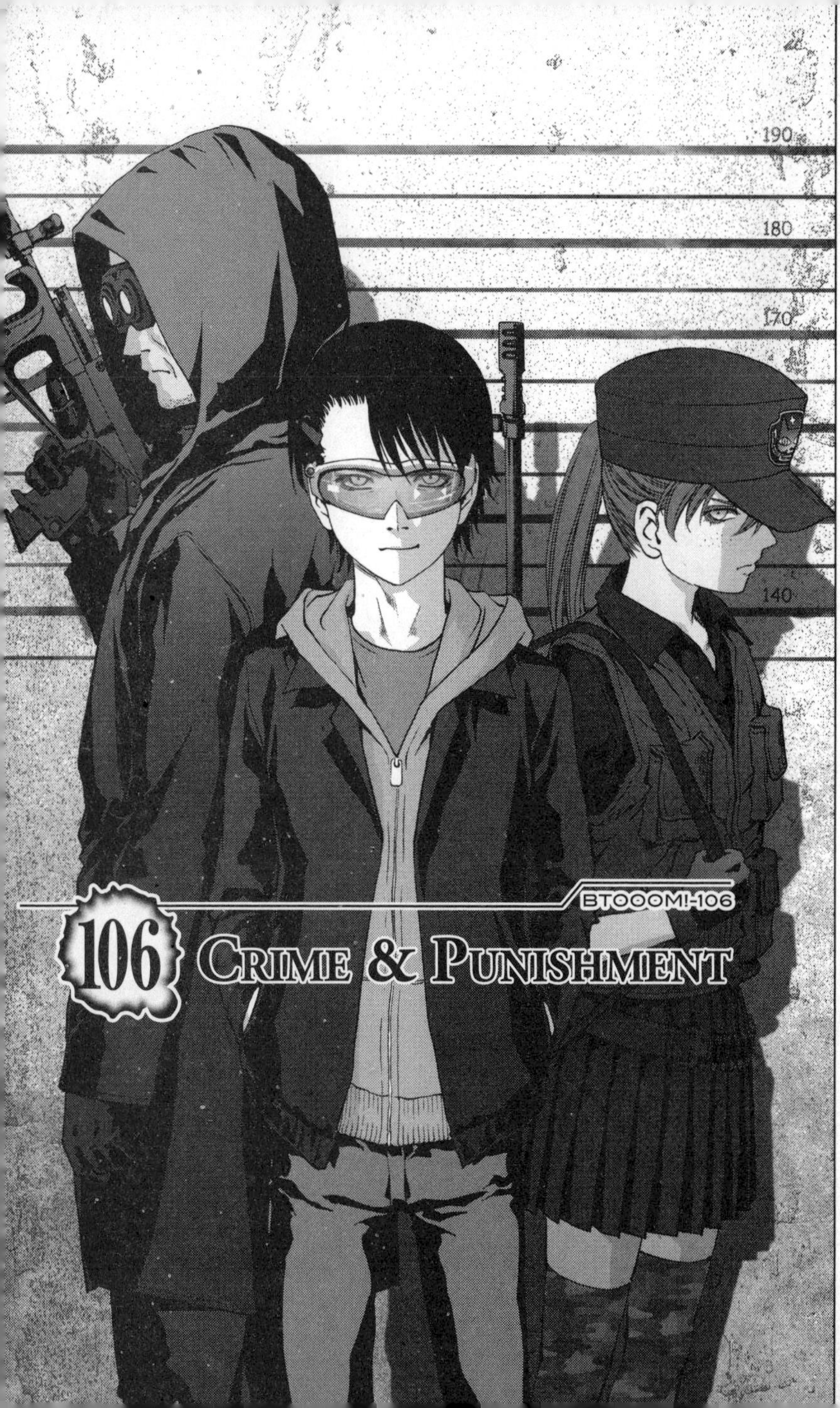
190
180
170
140
BTOOOM!-106
106
CRIME & PUNISHMENT

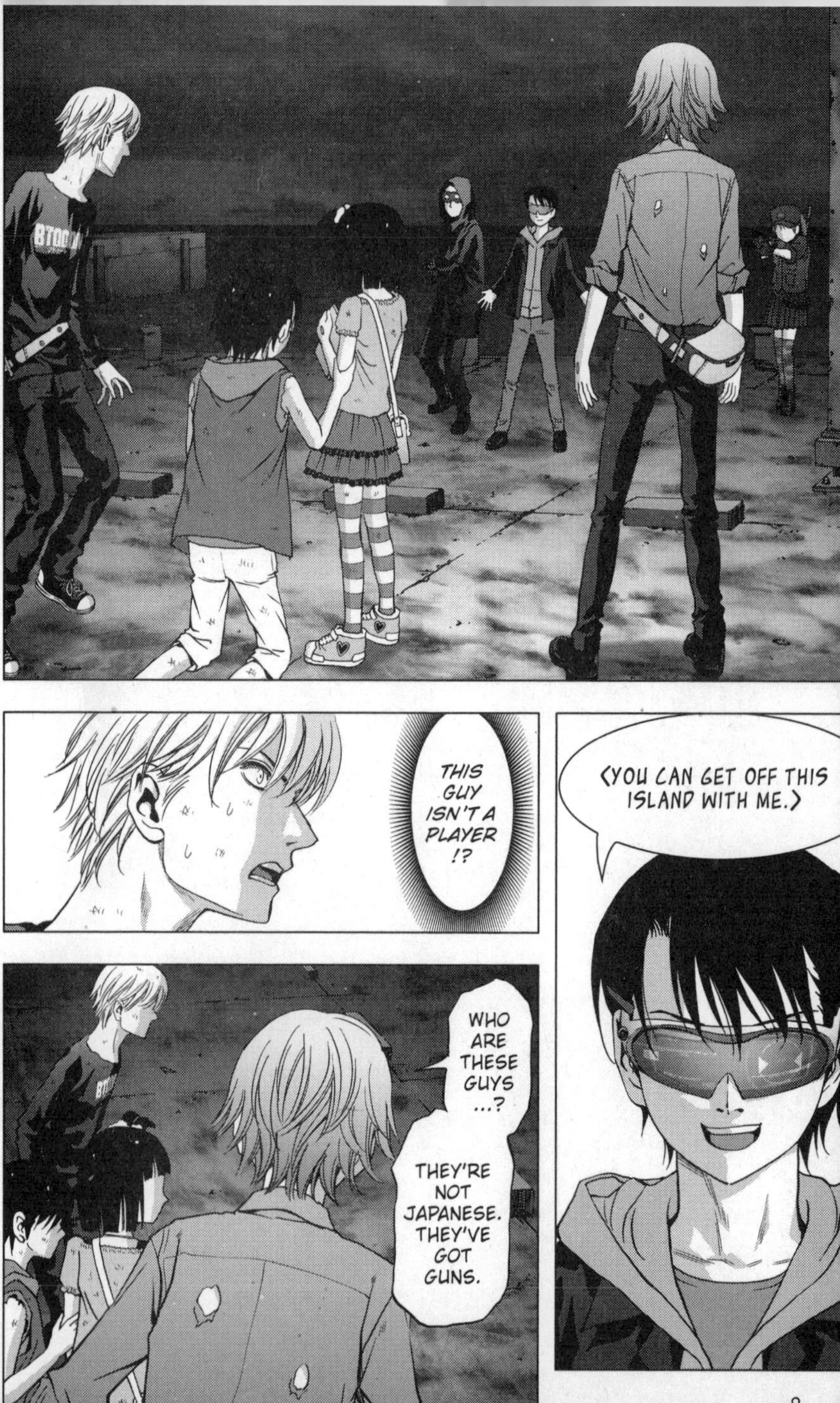

〈YOU CAN GET OFF THIS ISLAND WITH ME.〉
THIS GUY ISN'T A PLAYER!?
WHO ARE THESE GUYS...?
THEY'RE NOT JAPANESE. THEY'VE GOT GUNS.

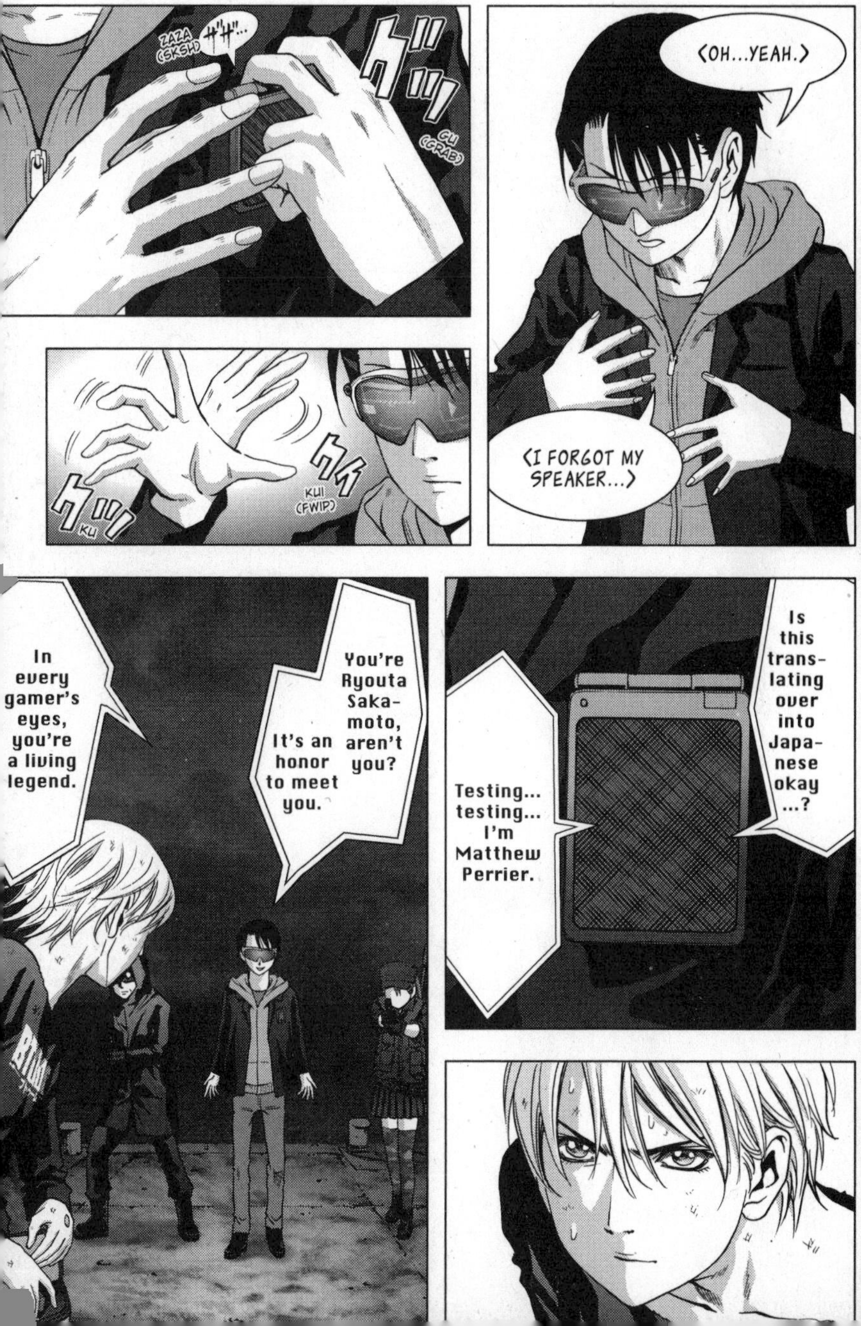
〈OH...YEAH.〉
〈I FORGOT MY SPEAKER...〉
ZAZA (SKSH)
ザザ...
GU (GRAB)
KUI (FWIP)
KU
Is this trans-lating over into Japa-nese okay ...?
Testing... testing... I'm Matthew Perrier.
You're Ryouta Saka-moto, aren't you?
It's an honor to meet you.
In every gamer's eyes, you're a living legend.

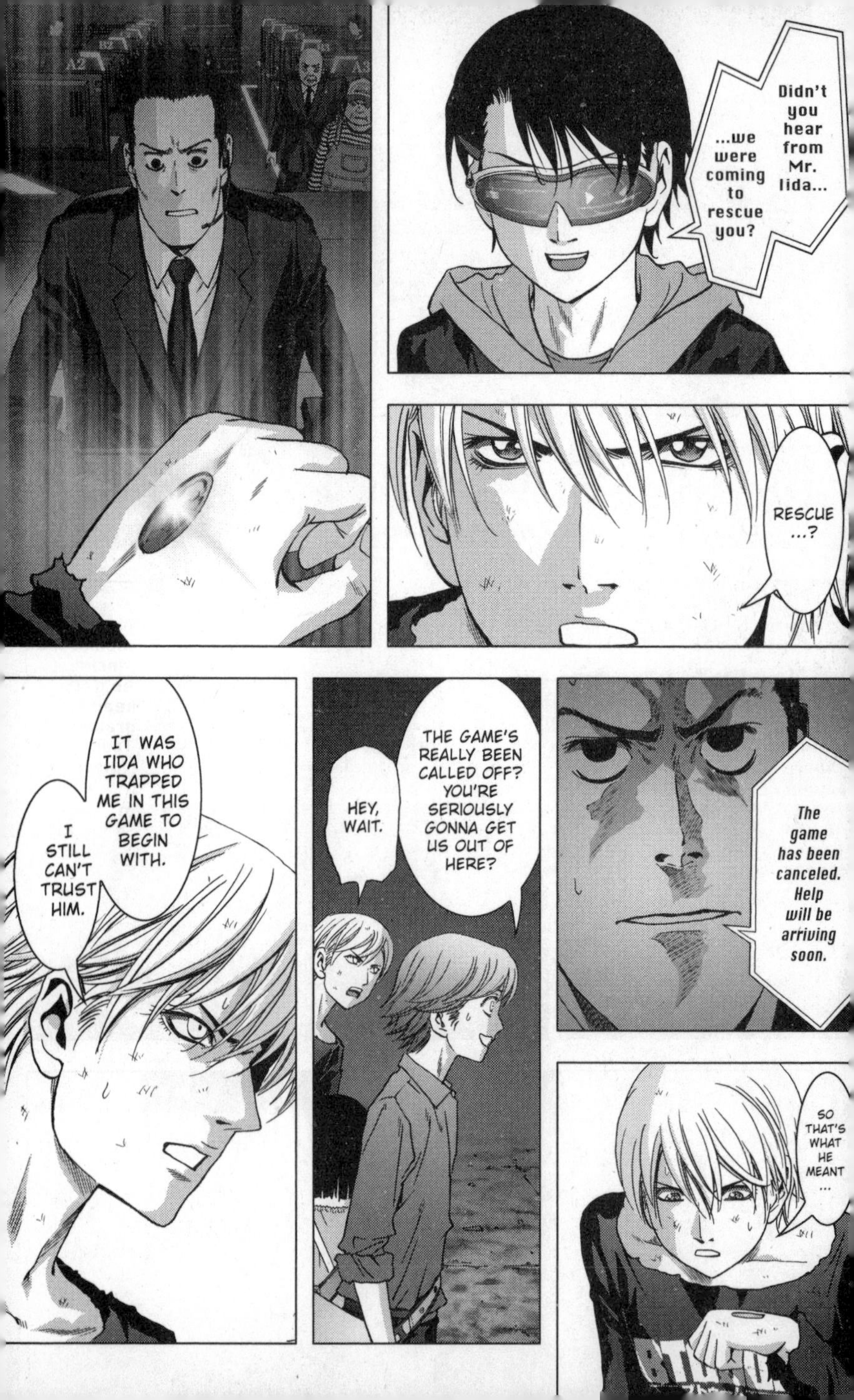
Didn't you hear from Mr. Iida...
...we were coming to rescue you?
RESCUE ...?
The game has been canceled. Help will be arriving soon.
SO THAT'S WHAT HE MEANT ...
THE GAME'S REALLY BEEN CALLED OFF? YOU'RE SERIOUSLY GONNA GET US OUT OF HERE?
HEY, WAIT.
IT WAS IIDA WHO TRAPPED ME IN THIS GAME TO BEGIN WITH.
I STILL CAN'T TRUST HIM.

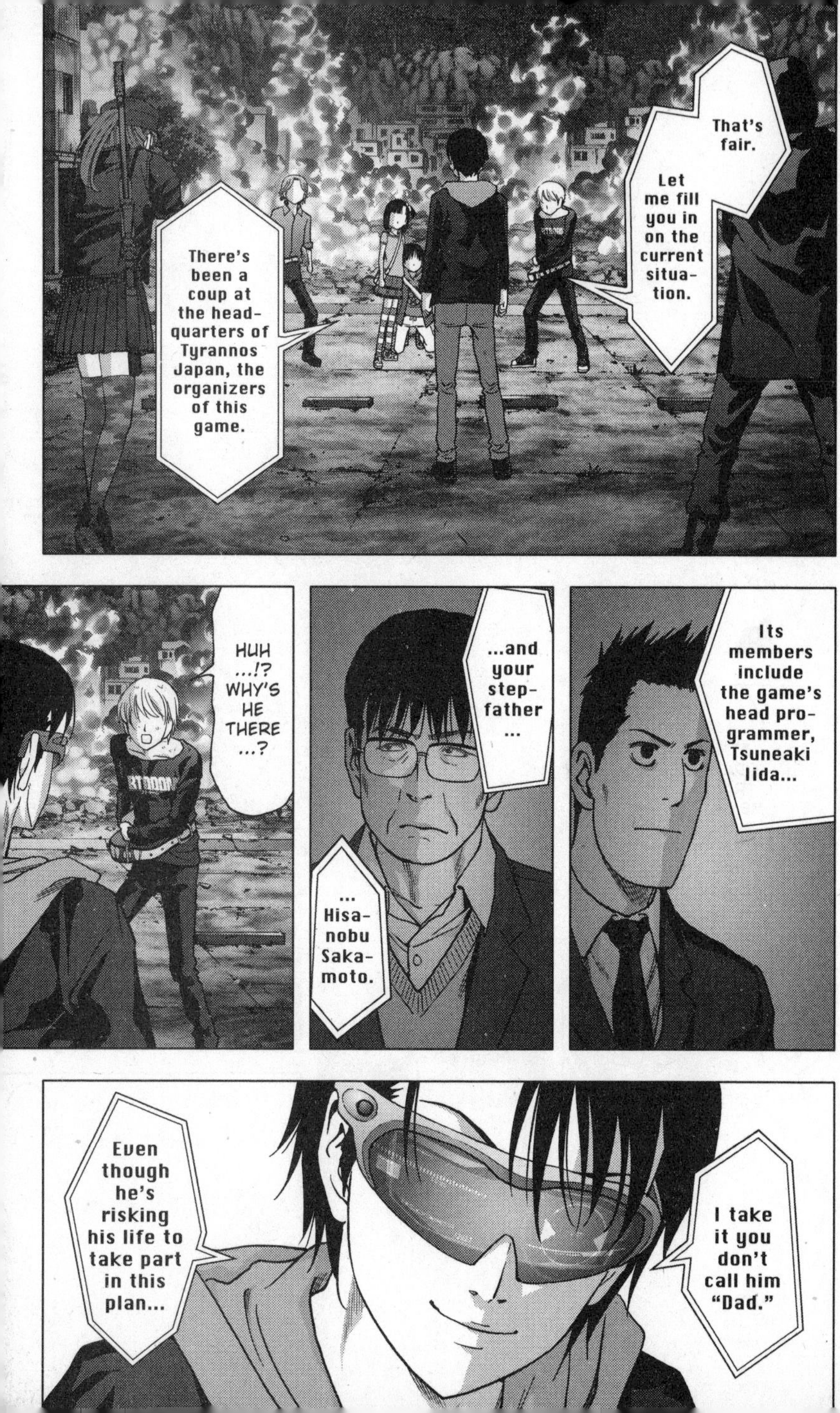
That's fair.
Let me fill you in on the current situation.
There's been a coup at the headquarters of Tyrannos Japan, the organizers of this game.
Its members include the game's head programmer, Tsuneaki Iida...
...and your stepfather...
...Hisanobu Sakamoto.
HUH...!? WHY'S HE THERE...?
I take it you don't call him "Dad."
Even though he's risking his life to take part in this plan...

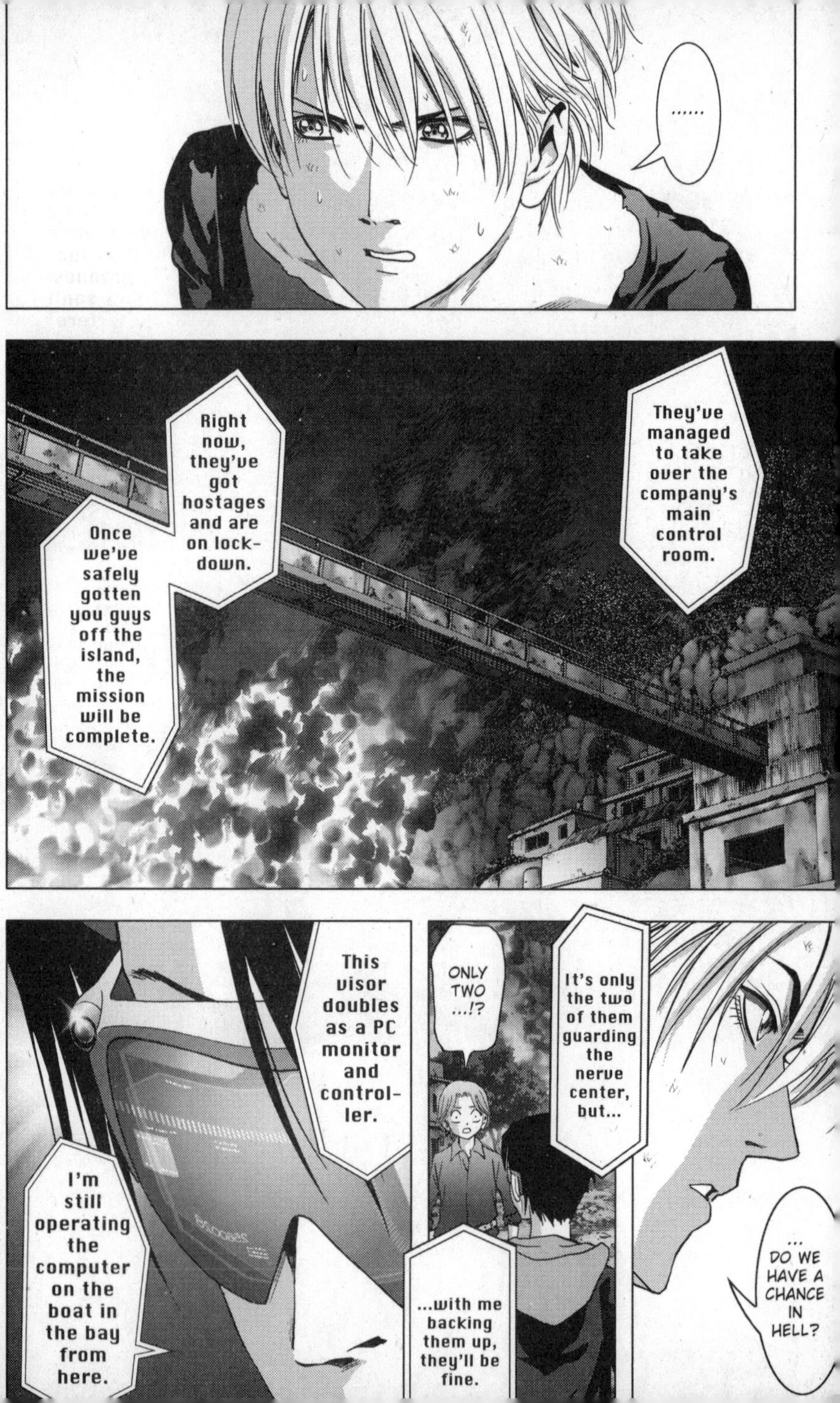
......
They've managed to take over the company's main control room.
Right now, they've got hostages and are on lock-down.
Once we've safely gotten you guys off the island, the mission will be complete.
It's only the two of them guarding the nerve center, but...
... DO WE HAVE A CHANCE IN HELL?
ONLY TWO ...!?
...with me backing them up, they'll be fine.
This visor doubles as a PC monitor and controller.
I'm still operating the computer on the boat in the bay from here.

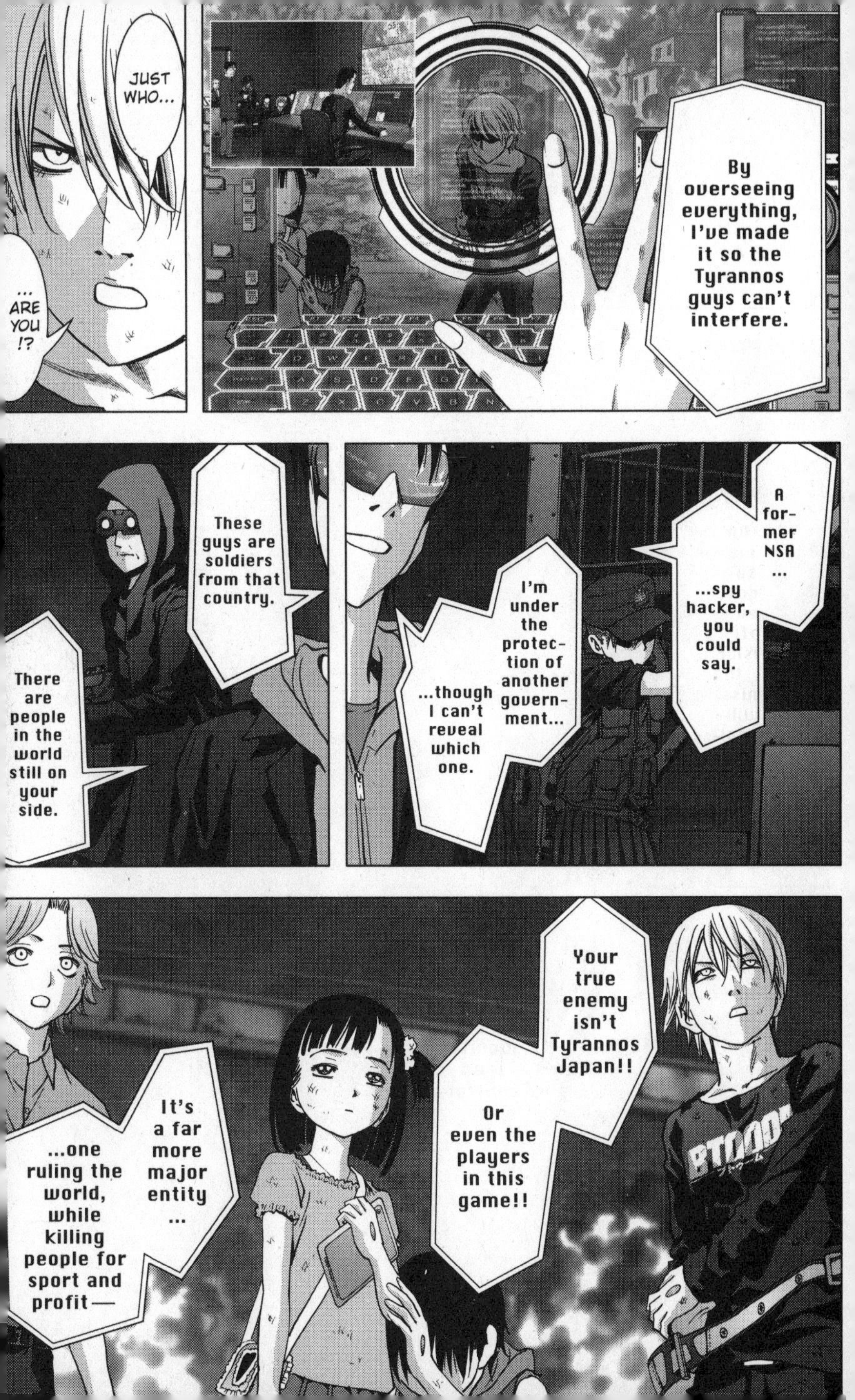
By overseeing everything, I've made it so the Tyrannos guys can't interfere.
JUST WHO...
...ARE YOU !?
A former NSA ...
...spy hacker, you could say.
I'm under the protection of another government...
...though I can't reveal which one.
These guys are soldiers from that country.
There are people in the world still on your side.
Your true enemy isn't Tyrannos Japan!!
Or even the players in this game!!
It's a far more major entity ...
...one ruling the world, while killing people for sport and profit—

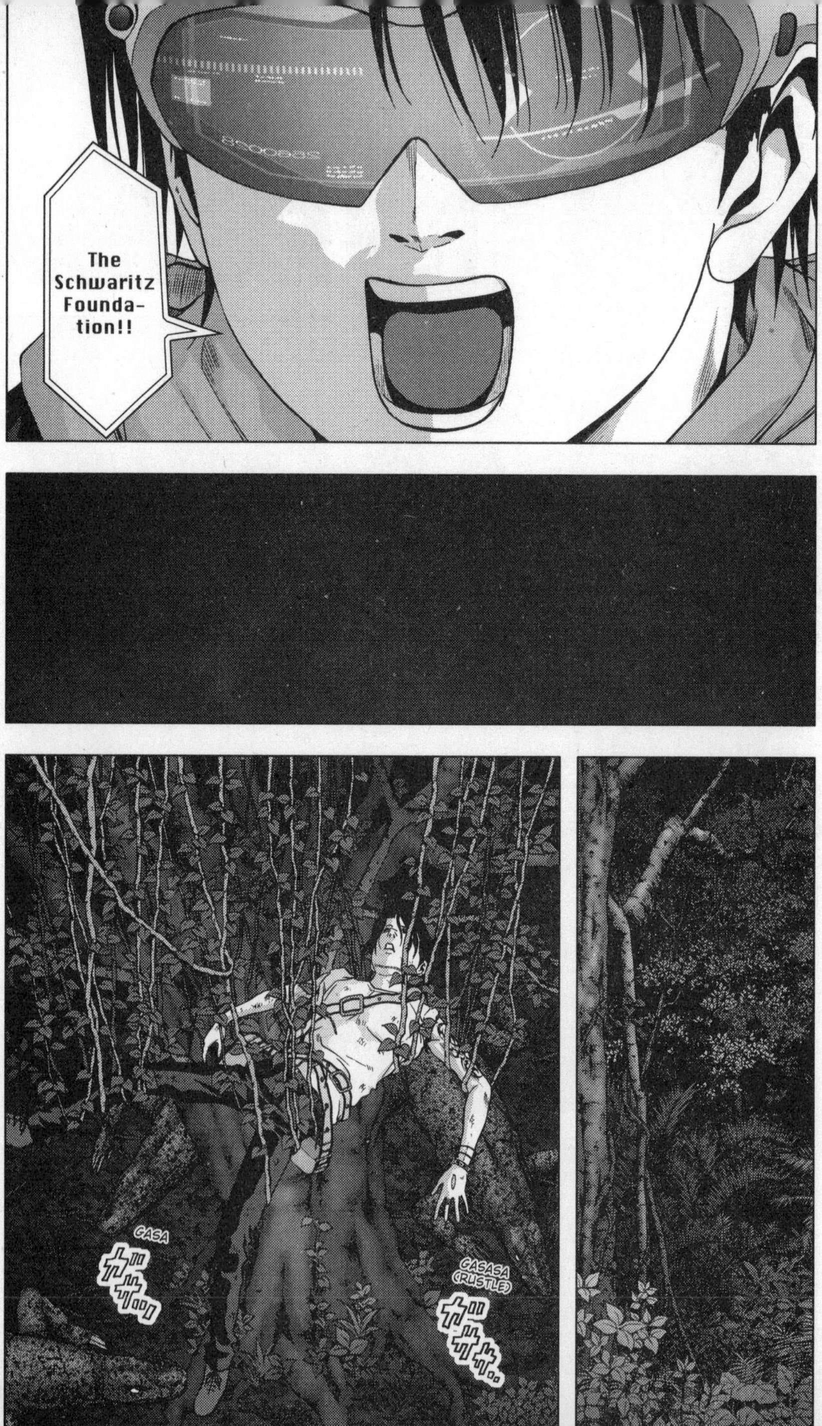
The Schwaritz Foundation!!
GASASA (RUSTLE)
GASA

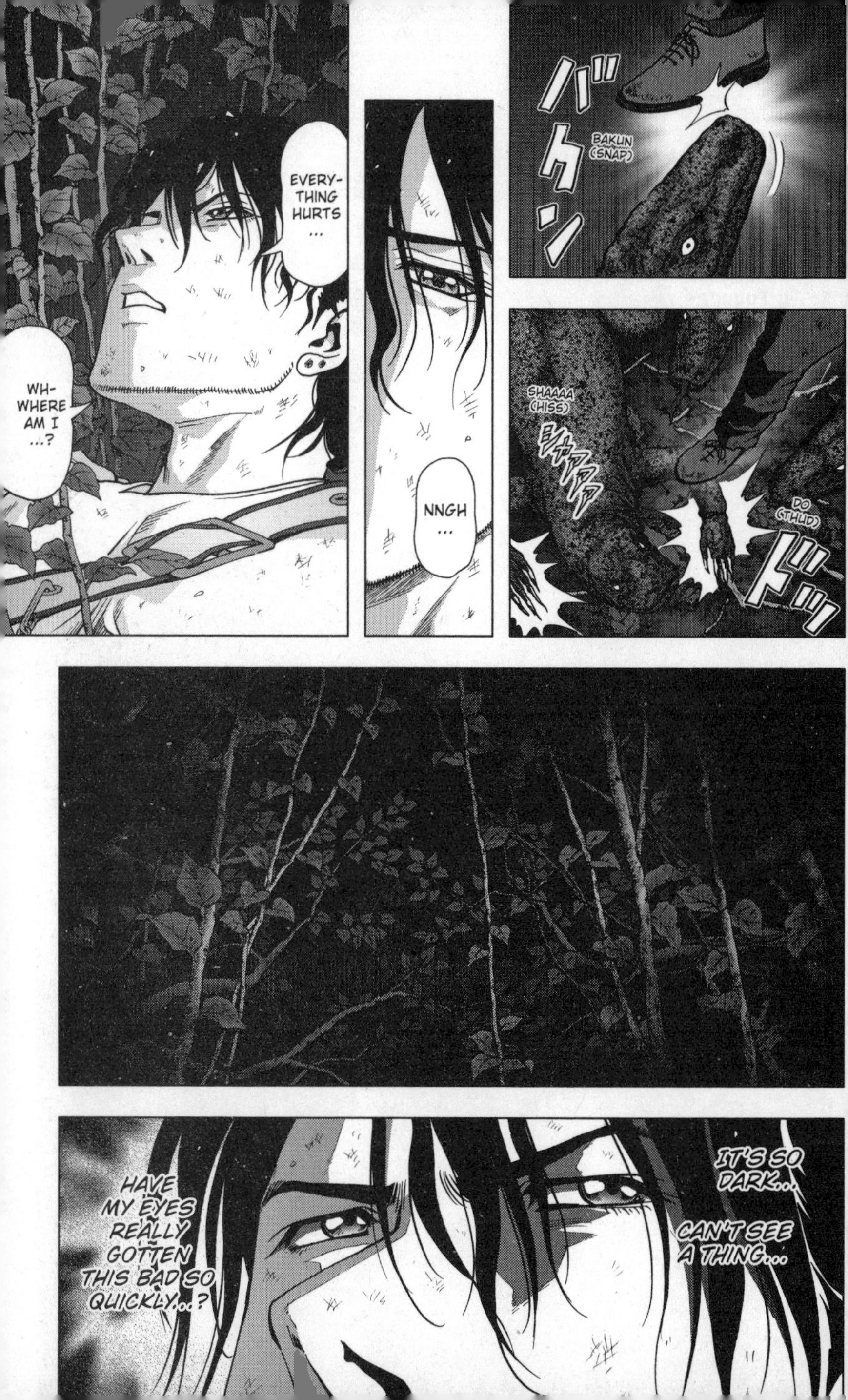
バクン
BAKUN (SNAP)
シャアア
SHAAAA (HISS)
DO (THUD)
ドッ
NNGH ...
EVERY-THING HURTS ...
WH- WHERE AM I ...?
IT'S SO DARK...
CAN'T SEE A THING...
HAVE MY EYES REALLY GOTTEN THIS BAD SO QUICKLY...?

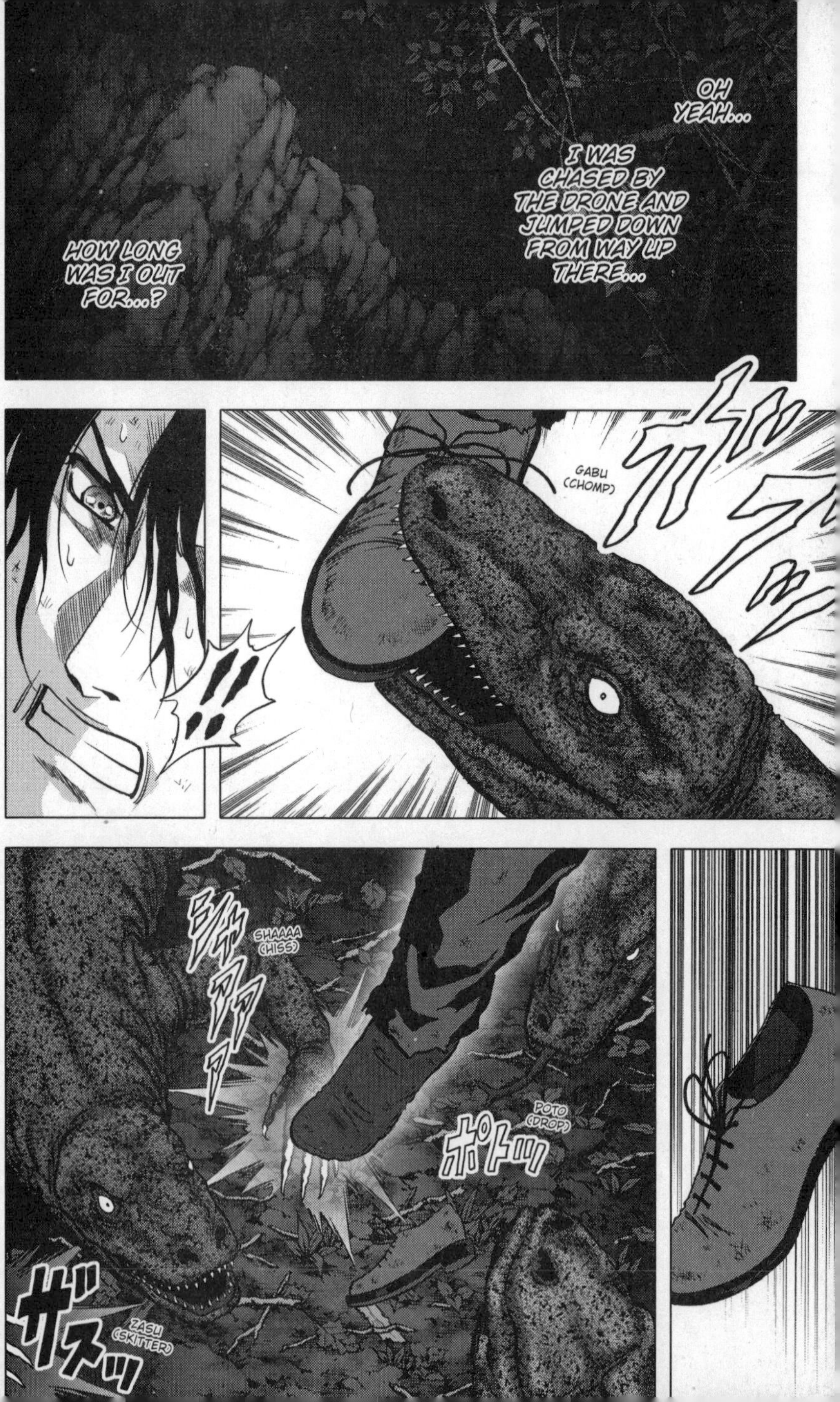
OH YEAH...
I WAS CHASED BY THE DRONE AND JUMPED DOWN FROM WAY UP THERE...
HOW LONG WAS I OUT FOR...?
GABU (CHOMP)
!!
SHAAAA (HISS)
POTO (DROP)
ZASU (SKITTER)

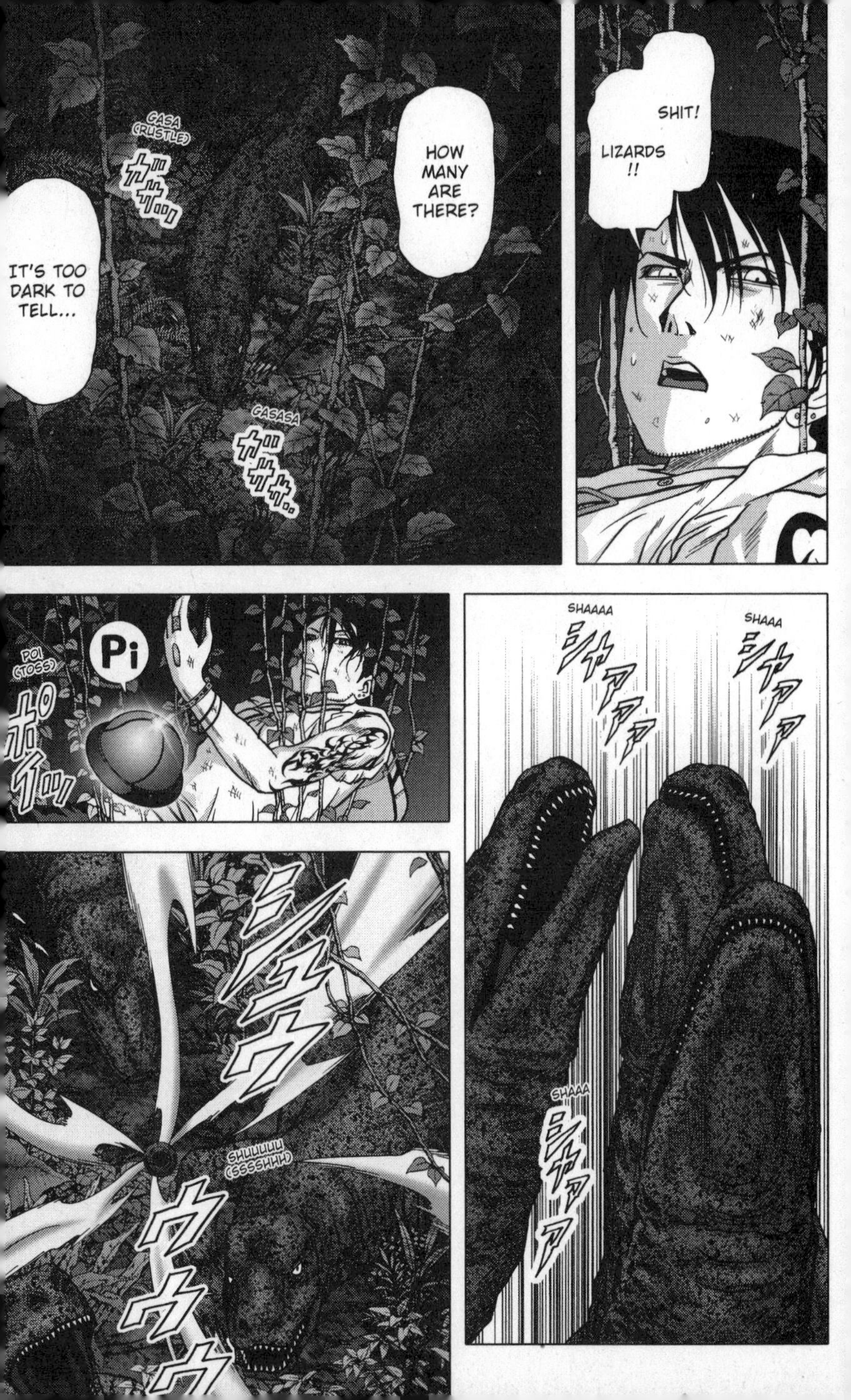

SHIT!
LIZARDS !!
HOW MANY ARE THERE?
GASA (RUSTLE)
IT'S TOO DARK TO TELL...
GASASA
SHAAAA
SHAAA
SHAAA
Pi
POI (TOSS)
SHUUUUU (SSSSHHH)

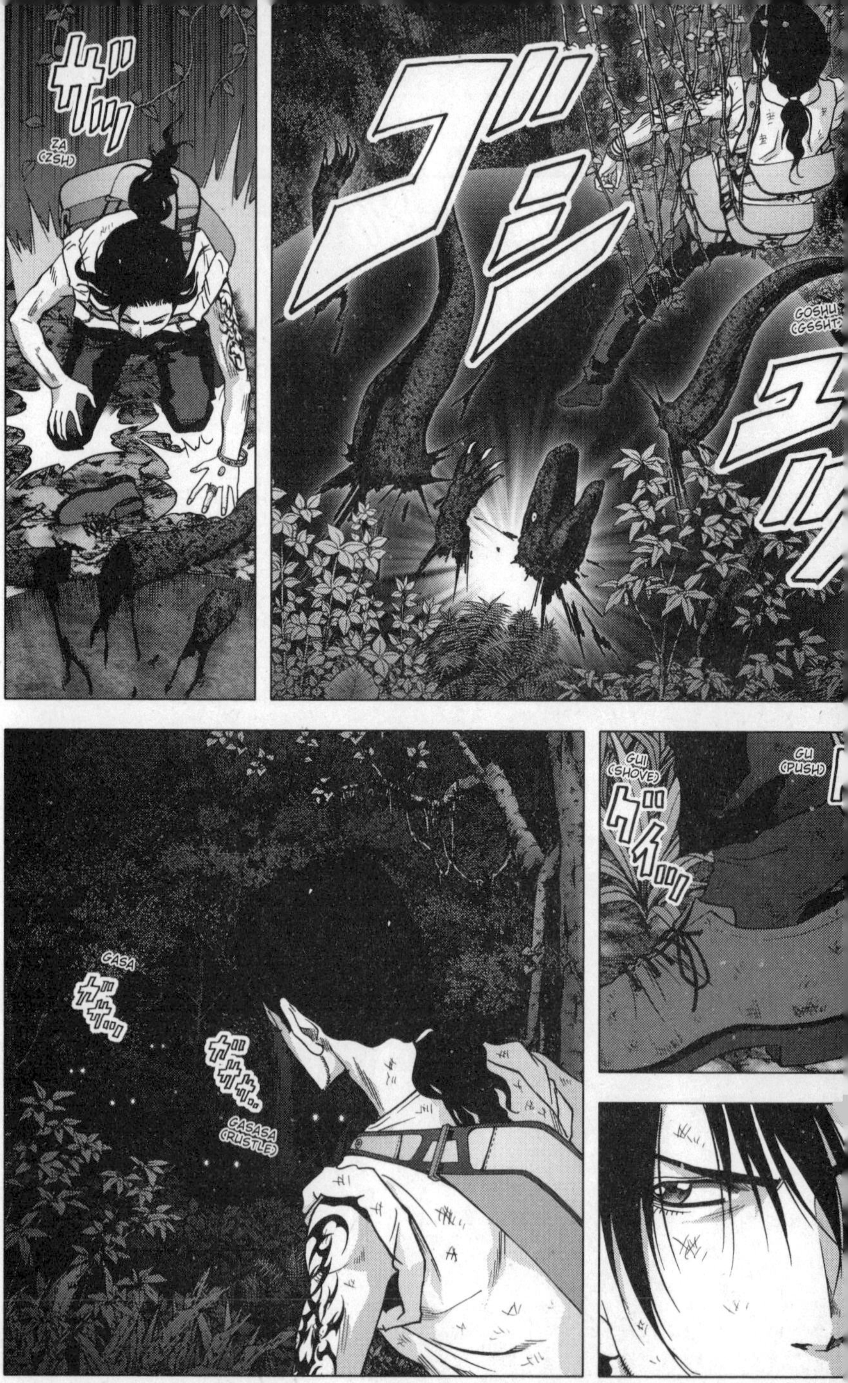
GOSHU (GSSHT)
ZA (ZSH)
GU (PUSH)
GUI (SHOVE)
GASA
GASASA (RUSTLE)

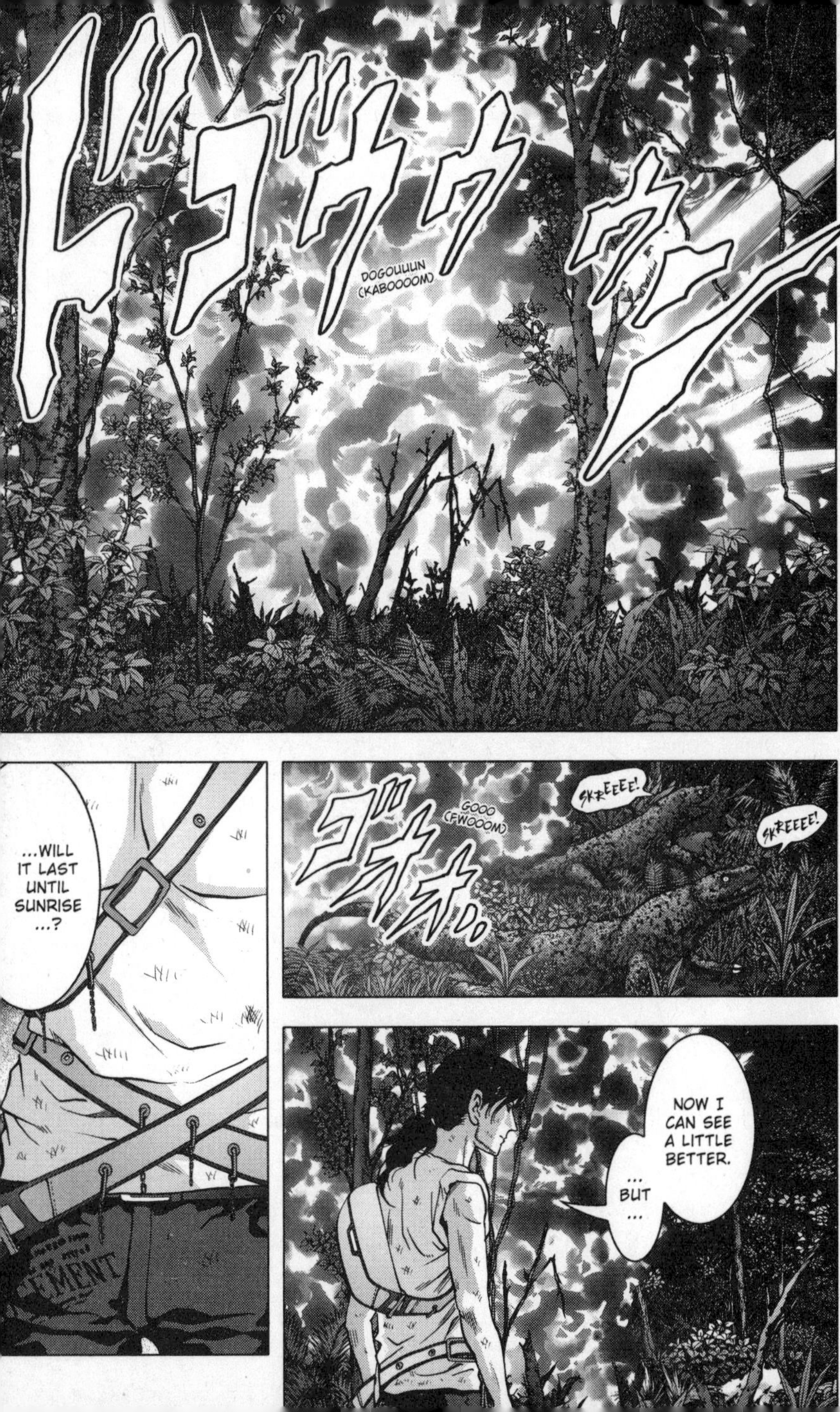
DOGOUUUN (KABOOOOM)
SKREEEE!
SKREEEE!
GOOO (FWOOOM)
NOW I CAN SEE A LITTLE BETTER.
... BUT ...
...WILL IT LAST UNTIL SUNRISE ...?

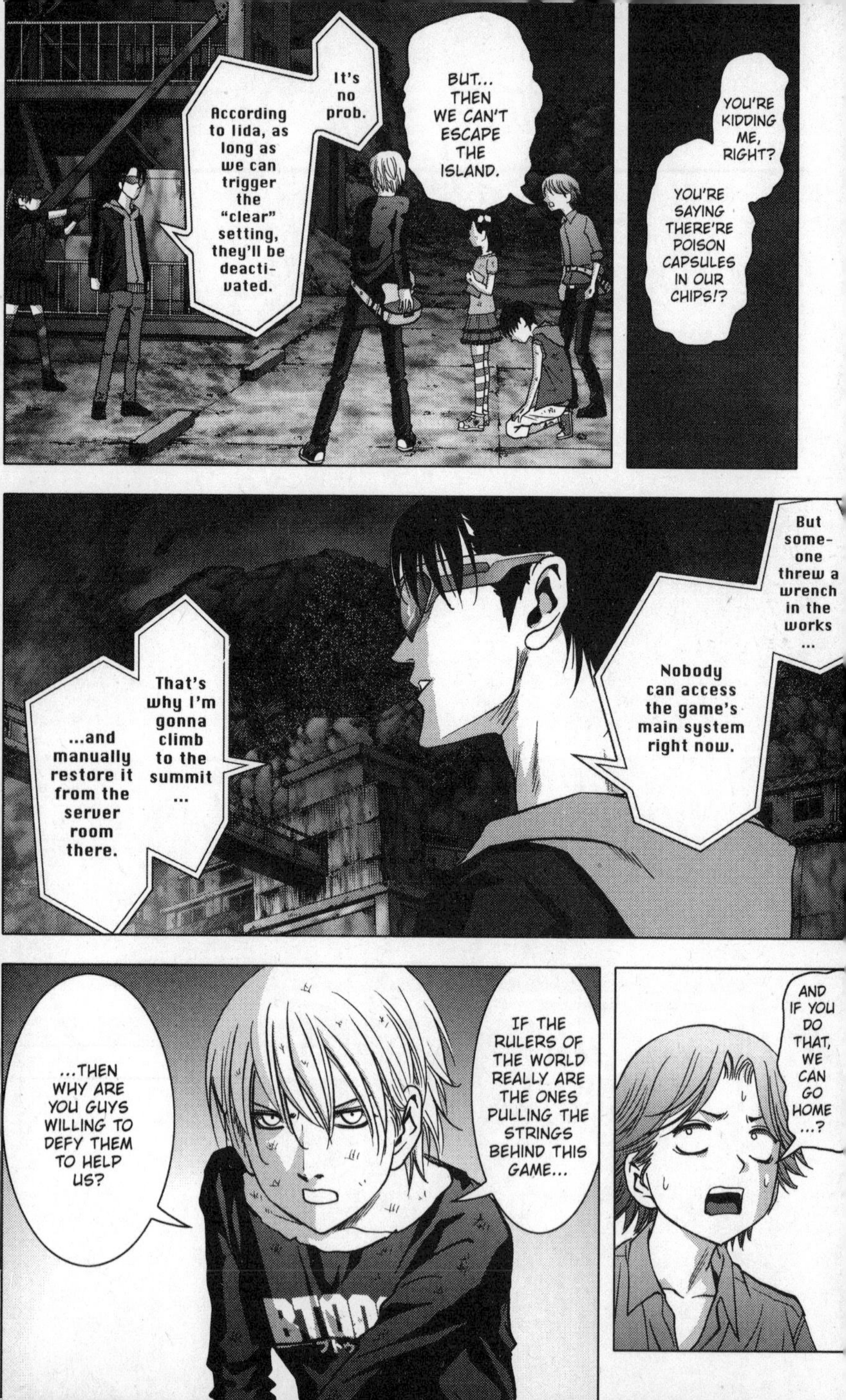
YOU'RE KIDDING ME, RIGHT?
YOU'RE SAYING THERE'RE POISON CAPSULES IN OUR CHIPS!?
BUT... THEN WE CAN'T ESCAPE THE ISLAND.
It's no prob.
According to Iida, as long as we can trigger the "clear" setting, they'll be deactivated.
But someone threw a wrench in the works...
Nobody can access the game's main system right now.
That's why I'm gonna climb to the summit...
...and manually restore it from the server room there.
AND IF YOU DO THAT, WE CAN GO HOME...?
IF THE RULERS OF THE WORLD REALLY ARE THE ONES PULLING THE STRINGS BEHIND THIS GAME...
...THEN WHY ARE YOU GUYS WILLING TO DEFY THEM TO HELP US?

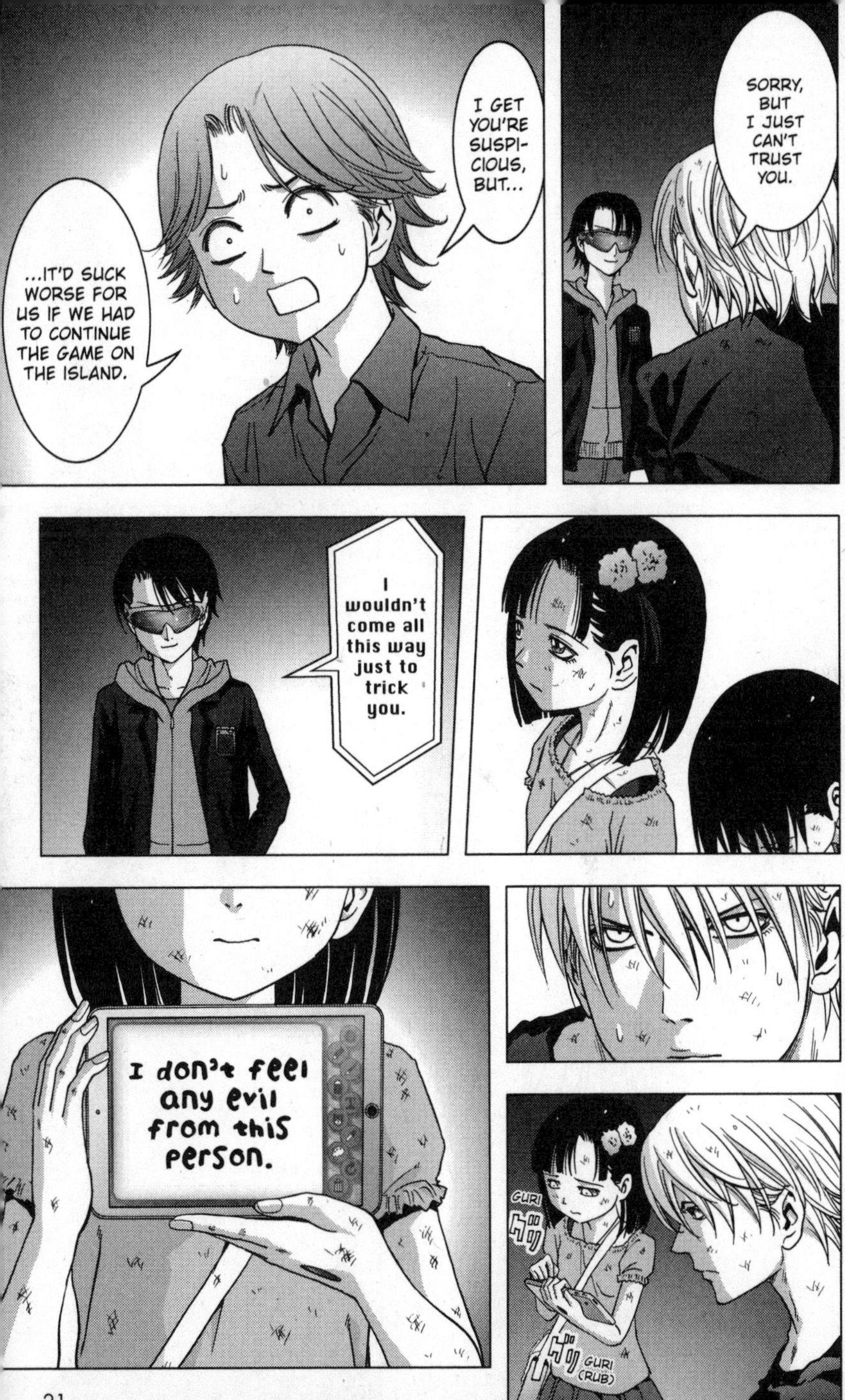
SORRY, BUT I JUST CAN'T TRUST YOU.
I GET YOU'RE SUSPICIOUS, BUT...
...IT'D SUCK WORSE FOR US IF WE HAD TO CONTINUE THE GAME ON THE ISLAND.
I wouldn't come all this way just to trick you.
GURI
GURI (RUB)
I don't feel any evil from this person.

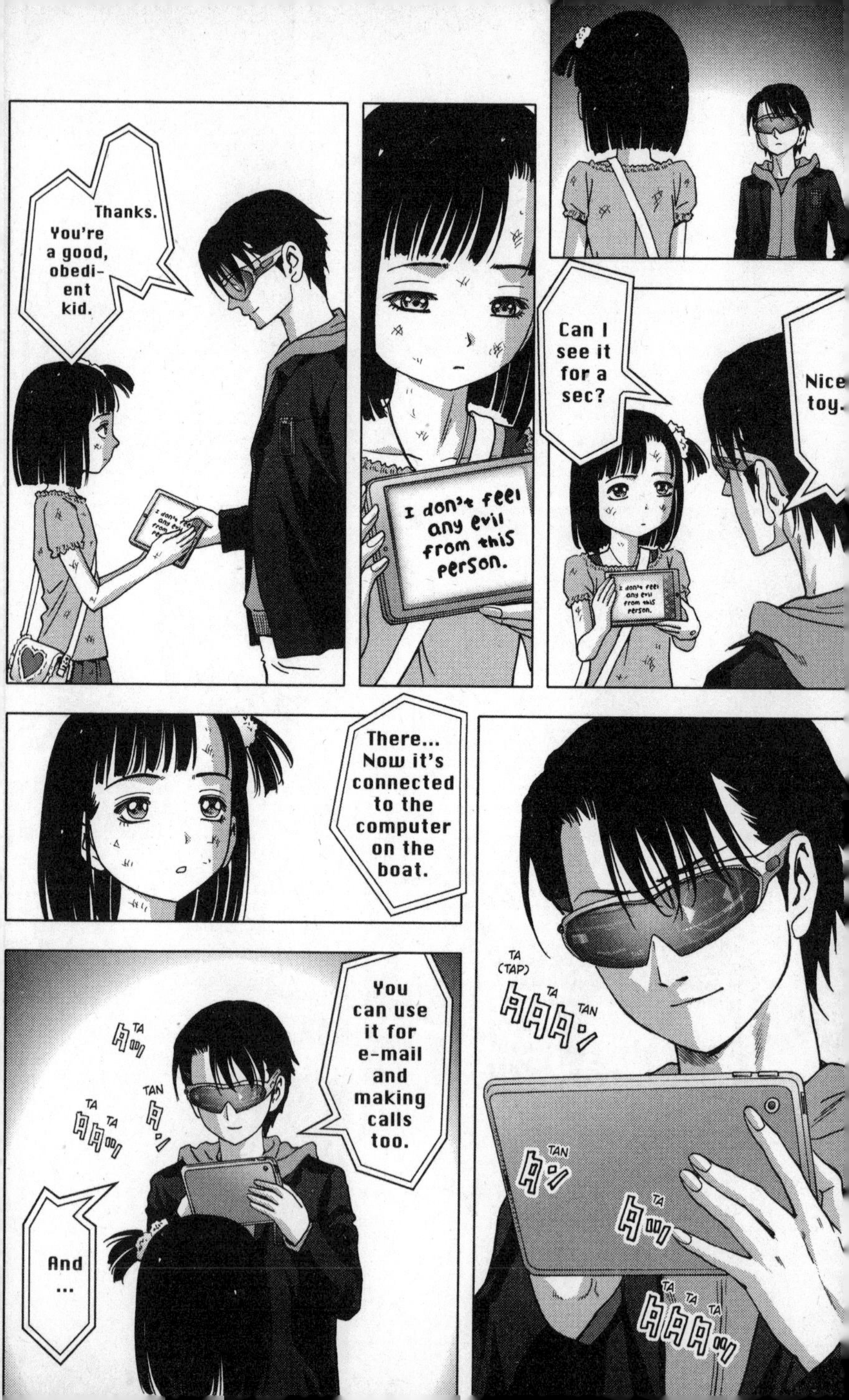
Nice toy.
Can I see it for a sec?
I don't feel any evil from this person.
I don't feel any evil from this person.
Thanks. You're a good, obedient kid.
TA (TAP) TA TAN
TAN
TA
TA TA TA
There... Now it's connected to the computer on the boat.
You can use it for e-mail and making calls too.
TA
TAN
TA TA
And ...

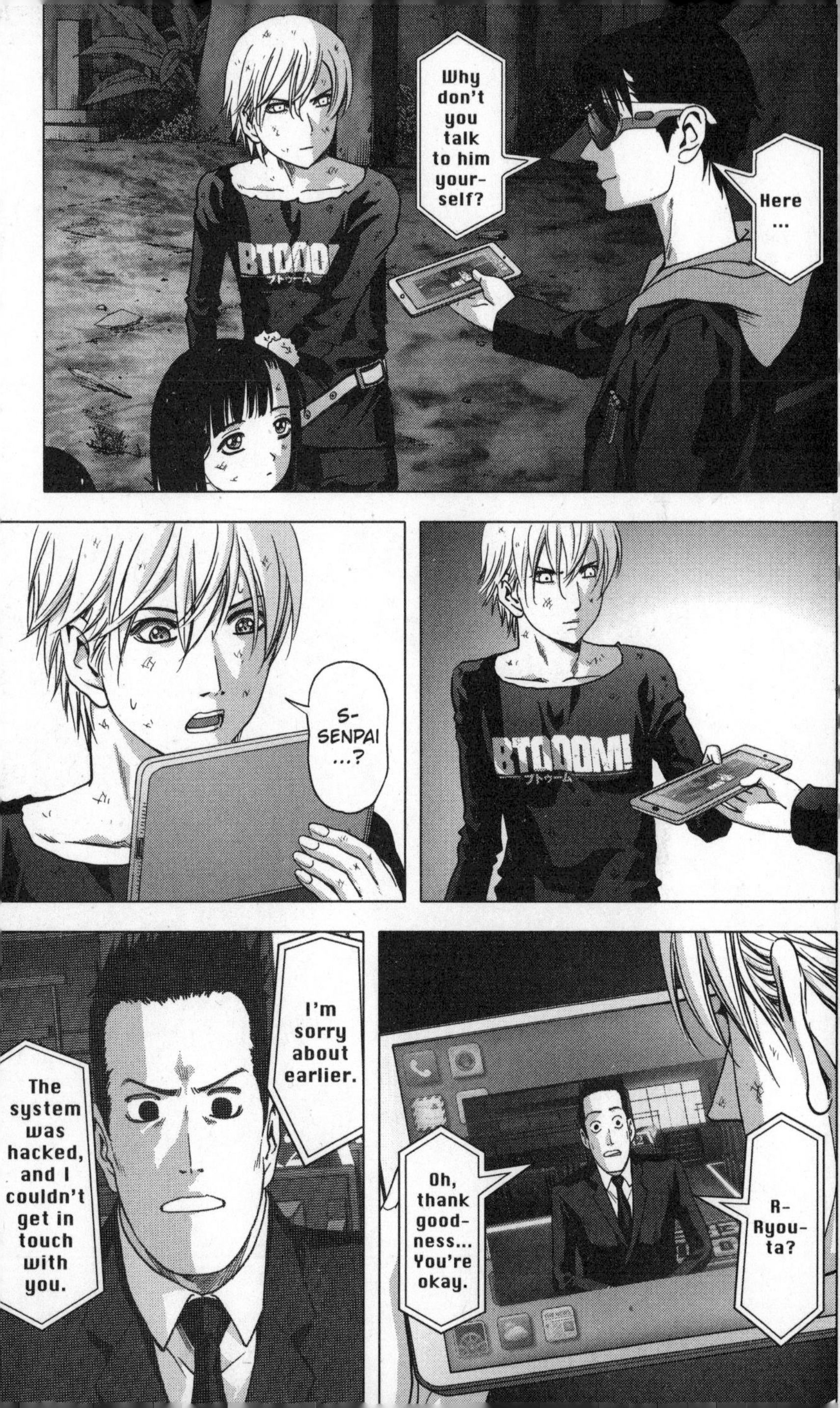
Here...
Why don't you talk to him yourself?
S-SENPAI...?
R-Ryouta?
Oh, thank goodness... You're okay.
I'm sorry about earlier.
The system was hacked, and I couldn't get in touch with you.

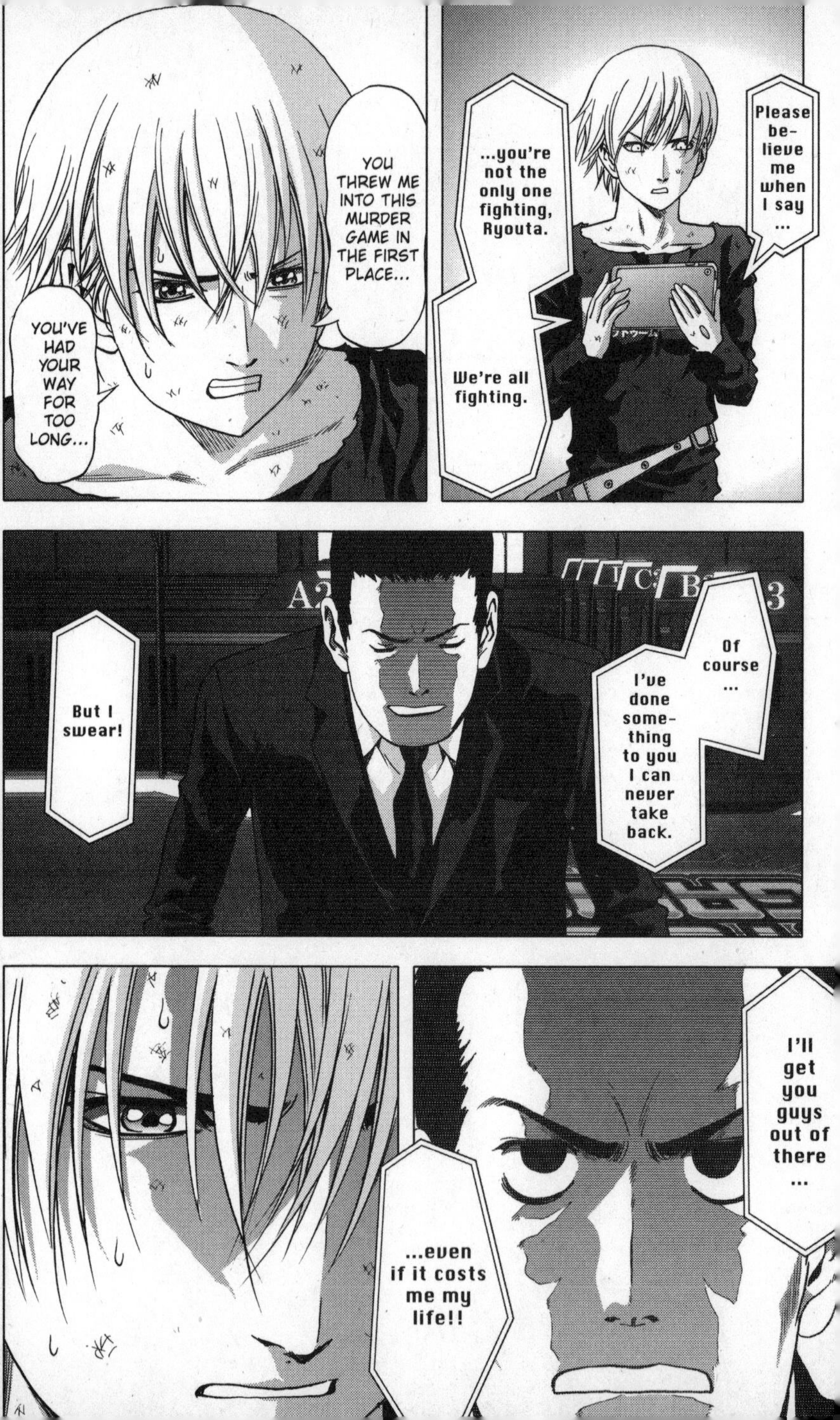
Please be-lieve me when I say ...
...you're not the only one fighting, Ryouta.
We're all fighting.
YOU THREW ME INTO THIS MURDER GAME IN THE FIRST PLACE...
YOU'VE HAD YOUR WAY FOR TOO LONG...
Of course ...
I've done some-thing to you I can never take back.
But I swear!
I'll get you guys out of there ...
...even if it costs me my life!!

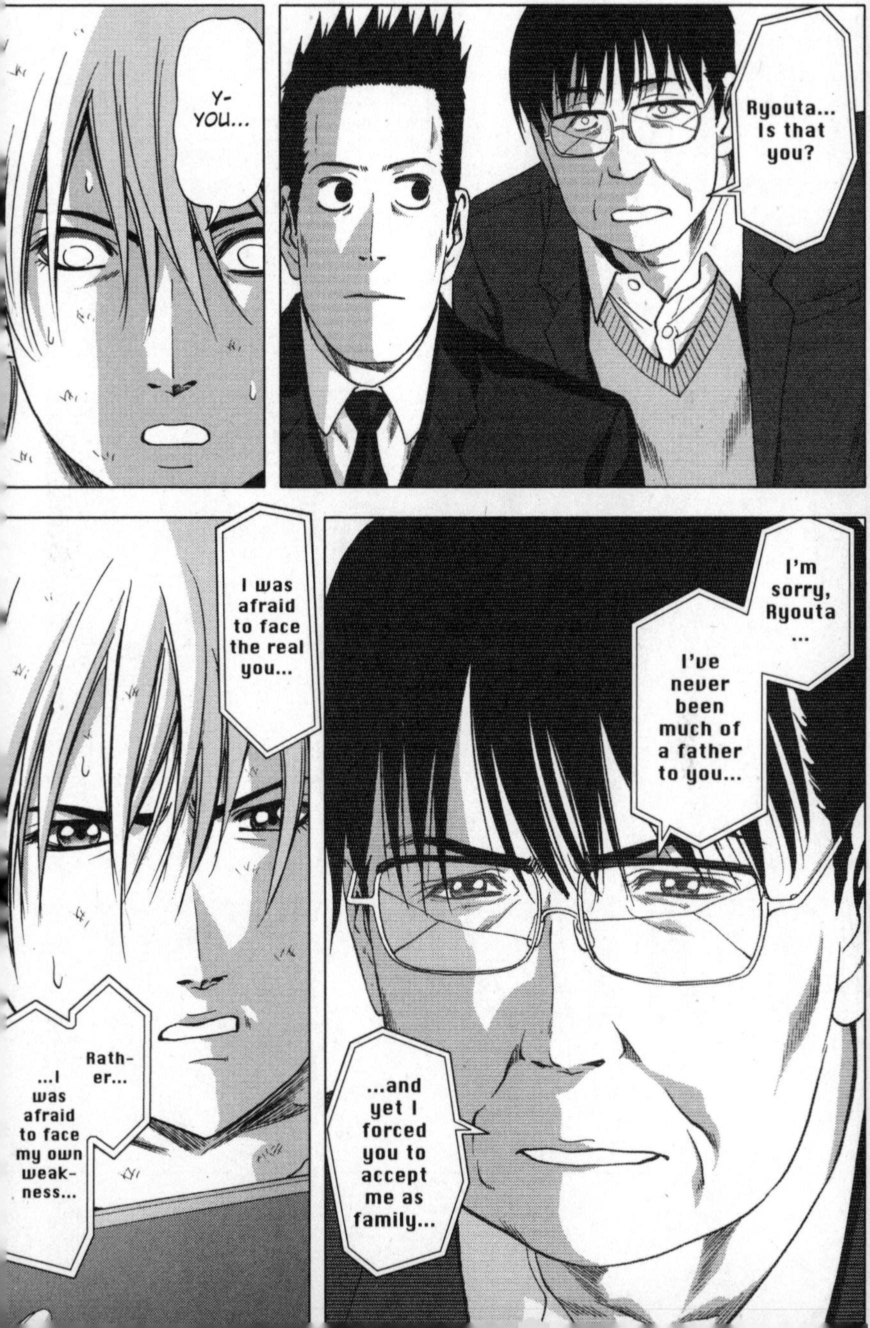
Ryouta... Is that you?
Y-YOU...
I'm sorry, Ryouta ...
I've never been much of a father to you...
...and yet I forced you to accept me as family...
I was afraid to face the real you...
Rath-er... ...I was afraid to face my own weak-ness...

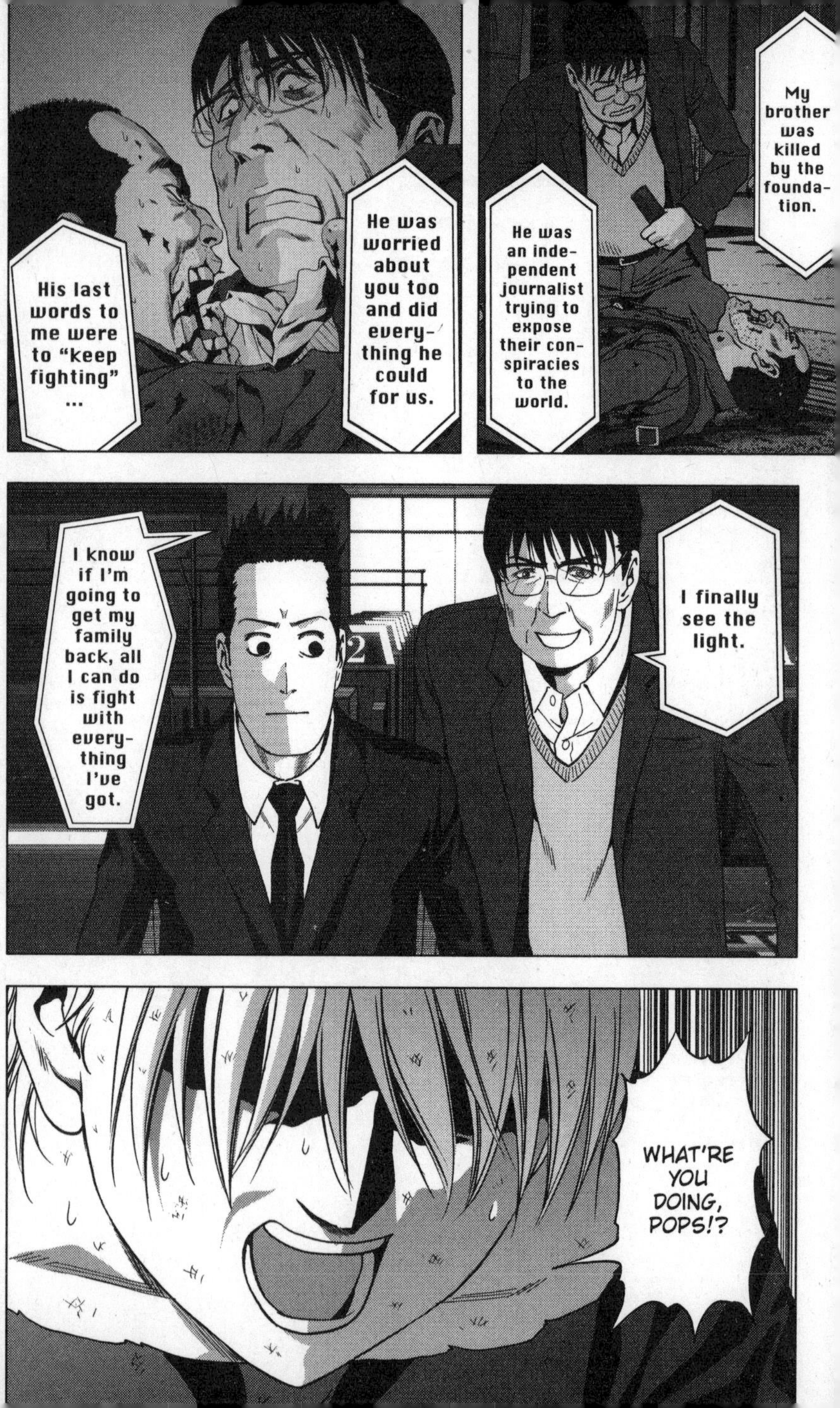
My brother was killed by the foundation.
He was an independent journalist trying to expose their conspiracies to the world.
He was worried about you too and did everything he could for us.
His last words to me were to "keep fighting" ...
I finally see the light.
I know if I'm going to get my family back, all I can do is fight with everything I've got.
WHAT'RE YOU DOING, POPS!?

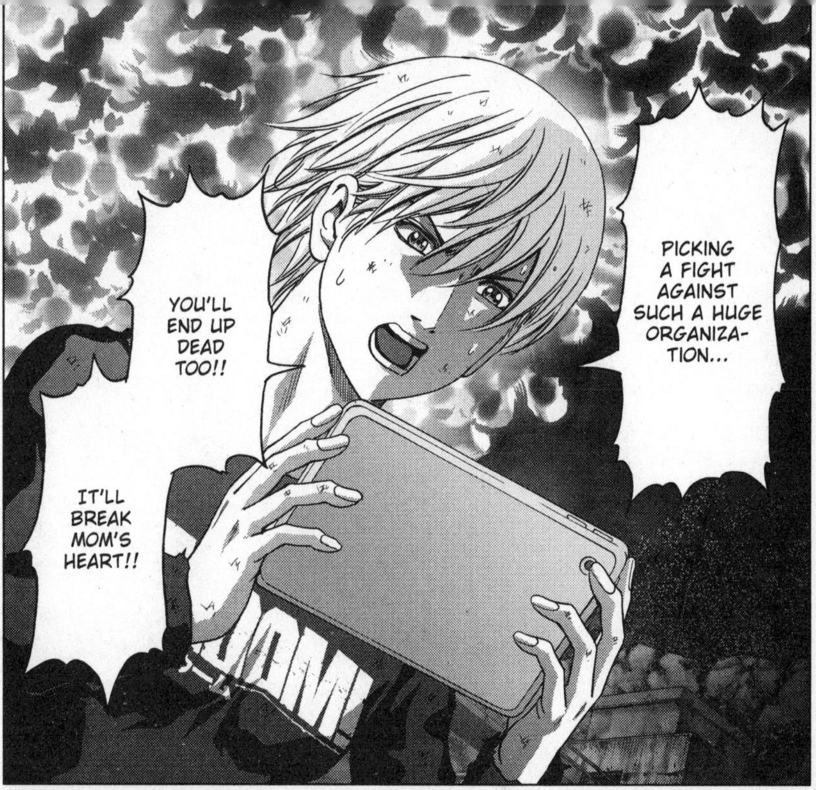
PICKING A FIGHT AGAINST SUCH A HUGE ORGANIZATION...
YOU'LL END UP DEAD TOO!!
IT'LL BREAK MOM'S HEART!!

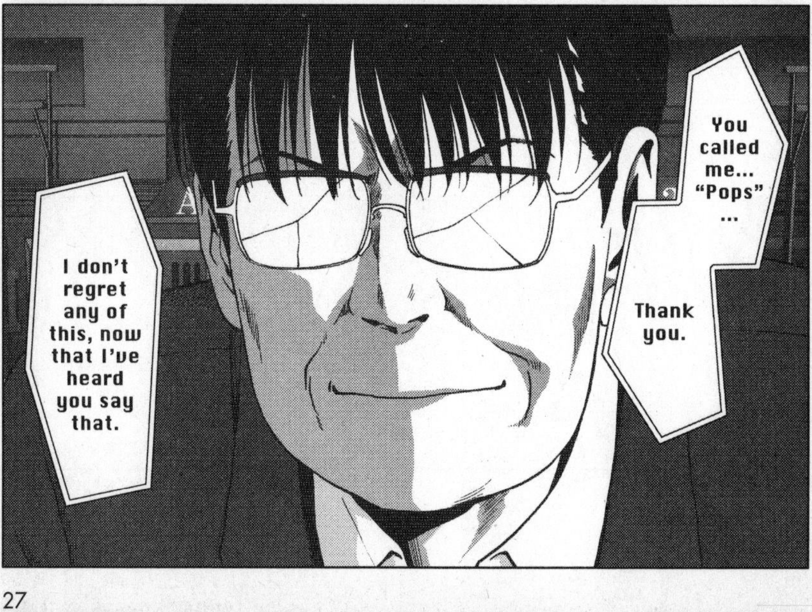
You called me... "Pops"...
Thank you.
I don't regret any of this, now that I've heard you say that.

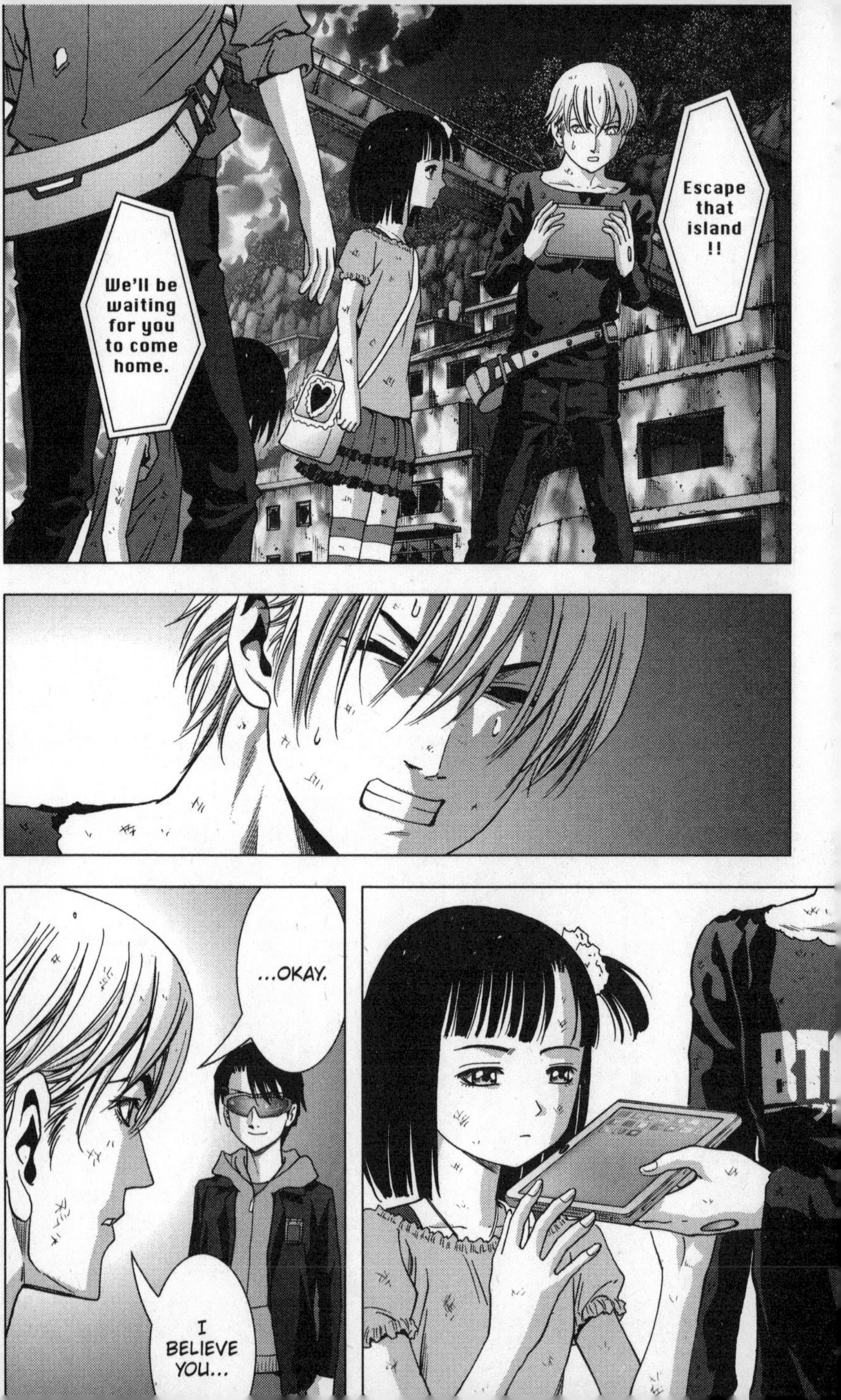
Escape that island !!
We'll be waiting for you to come home.
...OKAY.
I BELIEVE YOU...

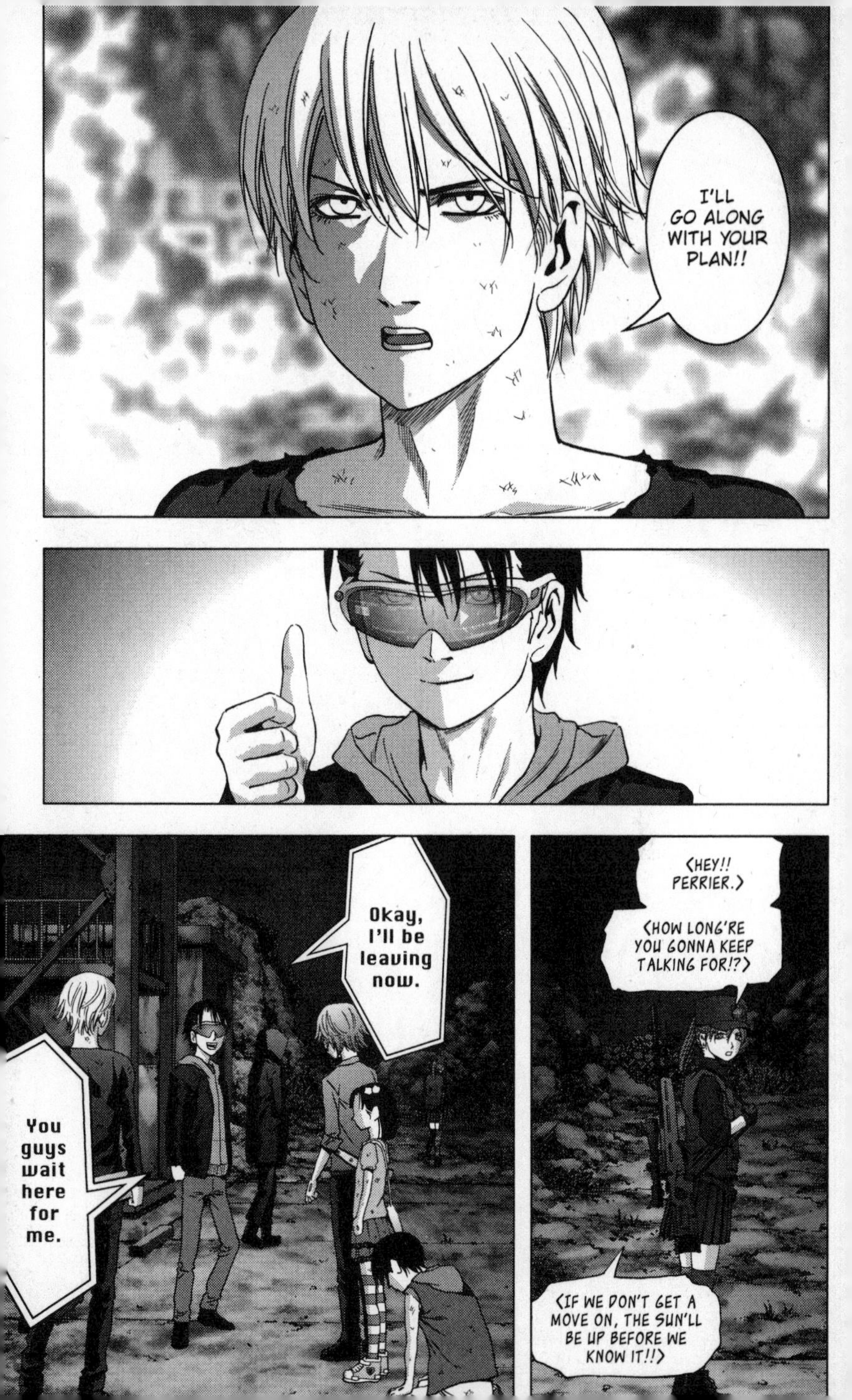
I'LL GO ALONG WITH YOUR PLAN!!
<HEY!! PERRIER.>
<HOW LONG'RE YOU GONNA KEEP TALKING FOR!?>
<IF WE DON'T GET A MOVE ON, THE SUN'LL BE UP BEFORE WE KNOW IT!!>
Okay, I'll be leaving now.
You guys wait here for me.

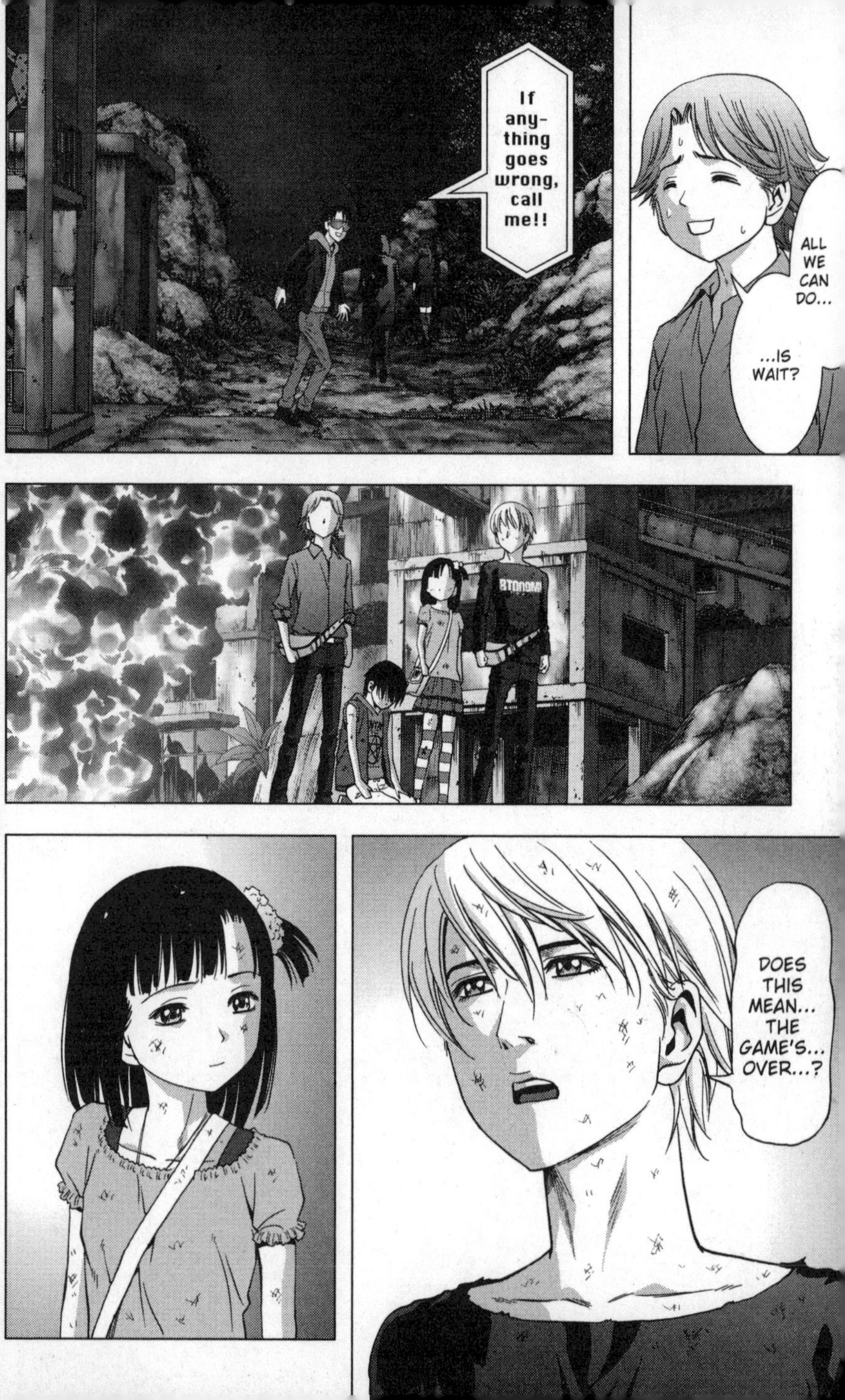
ALL WE CAN DO...
...IS WAIT?
If any-thing goes wrong, call me!!
DOES THIS MEAN... THE GAME'S... OVER...?

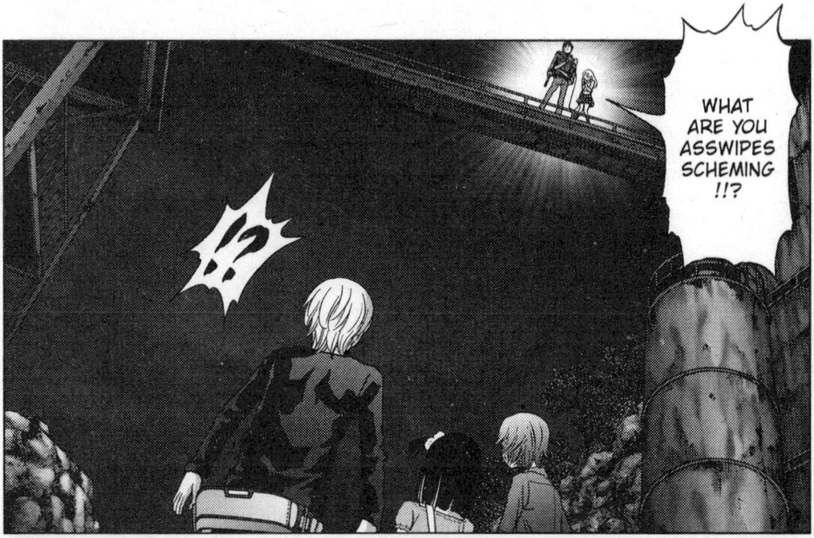
WHAT ARE YOU ASSWIPES SCHEMING !!?
!?
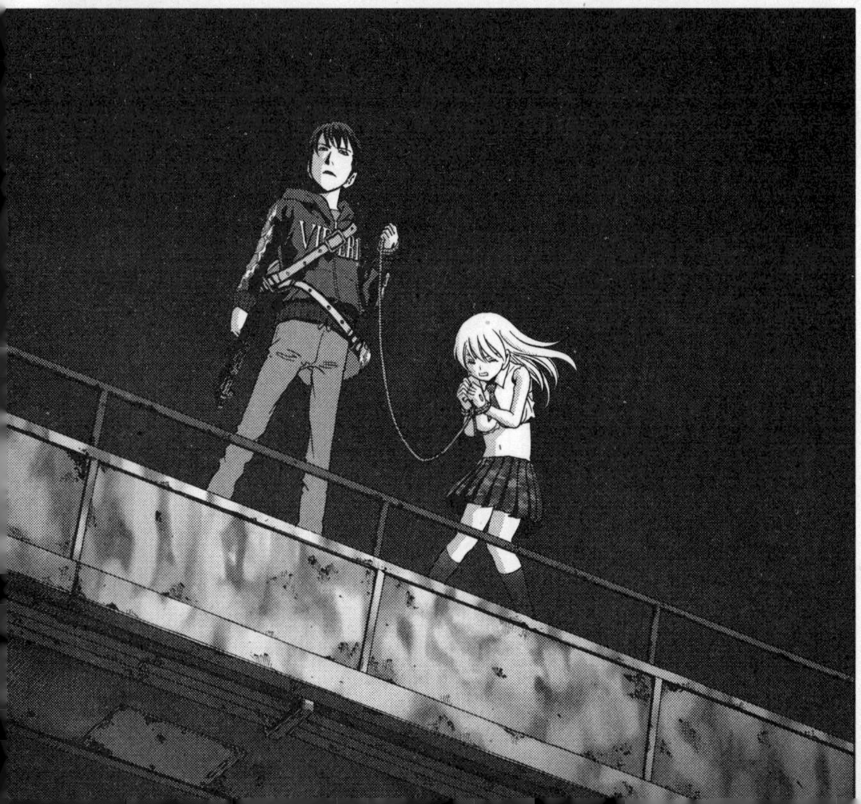

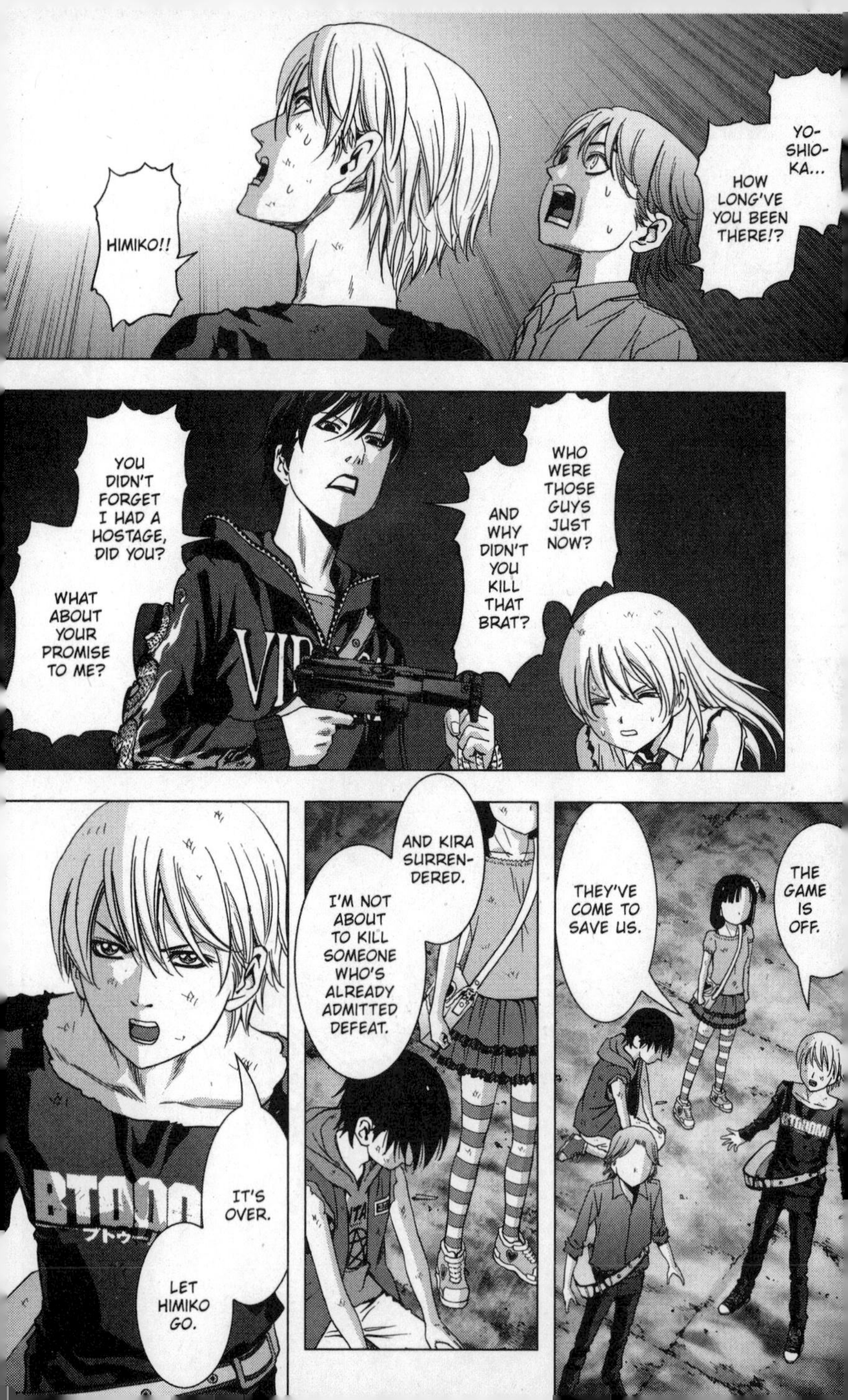
YO-SHIO-KA...
HOW LONG'VE YOU BEEN THERE!?
HIMIKO!!
WHO WERE THOSE GUYS JUST NOW?
AND WHY DIDN'T YOU KILL THAT BRAT?
YOU DIDN'T FORGET I HAD A HOSTAGE, DID YOU?
WHAT ABOUT YOUR PROMISE TO ME?
THE GAME IS OFF.
THEY'VE COME TO SAVE US.
AND KIRA SURREN-DERED.
I'M NOT ABOUT TO KILL SOMEONE WHO'S ALREADY ADMITTED DEFEAT.
IT'S OVER.
LET HIMIKO GO.

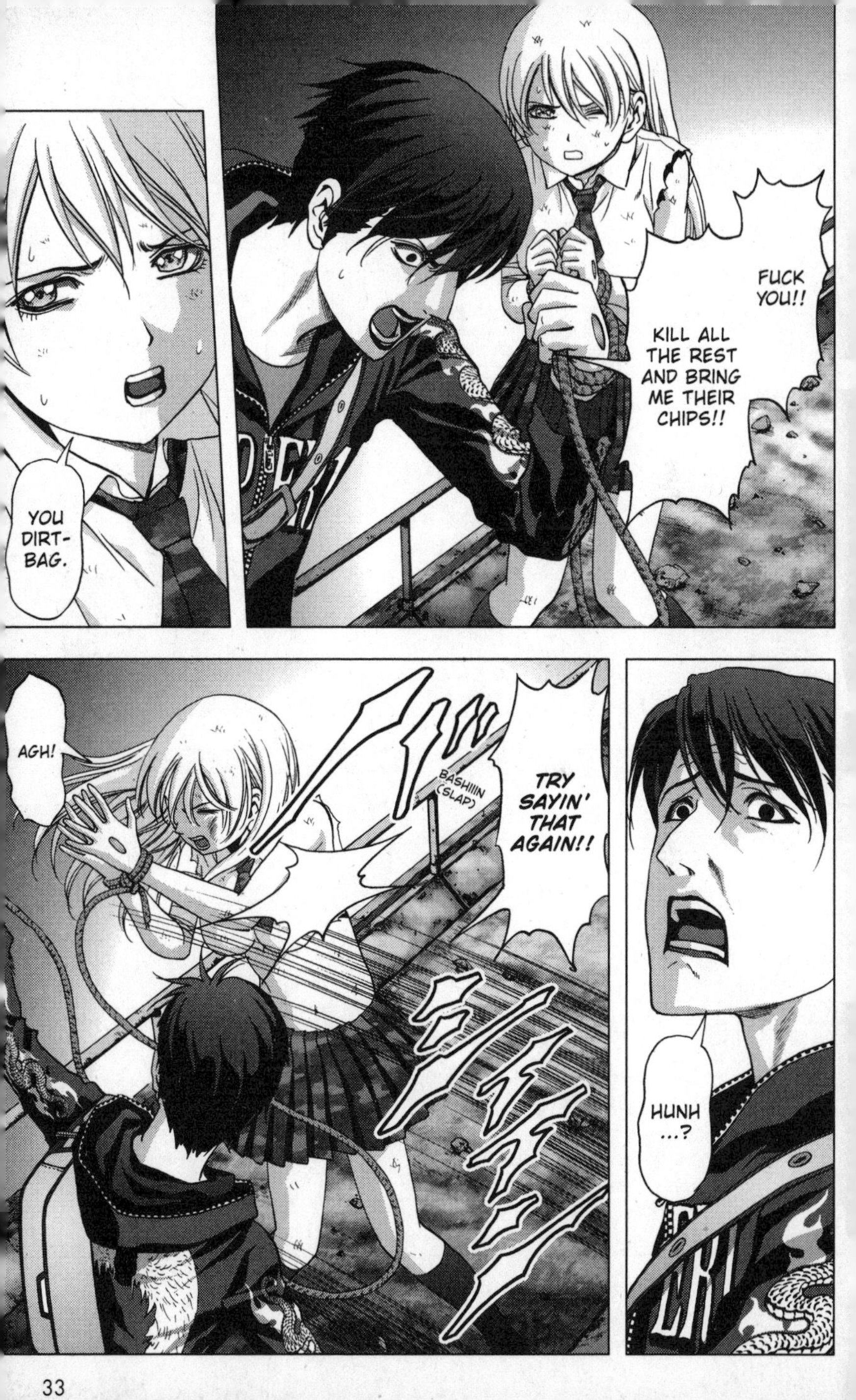
FUCK YOU!!
KILL ALL THE REST AND BRING ME THEIR CHIPS!!
YOU DIRT-BAG.
HUNH ...?
TRY SAYIN' THAT AGAIN!!
BASHIIN (SLAP)
AGH!

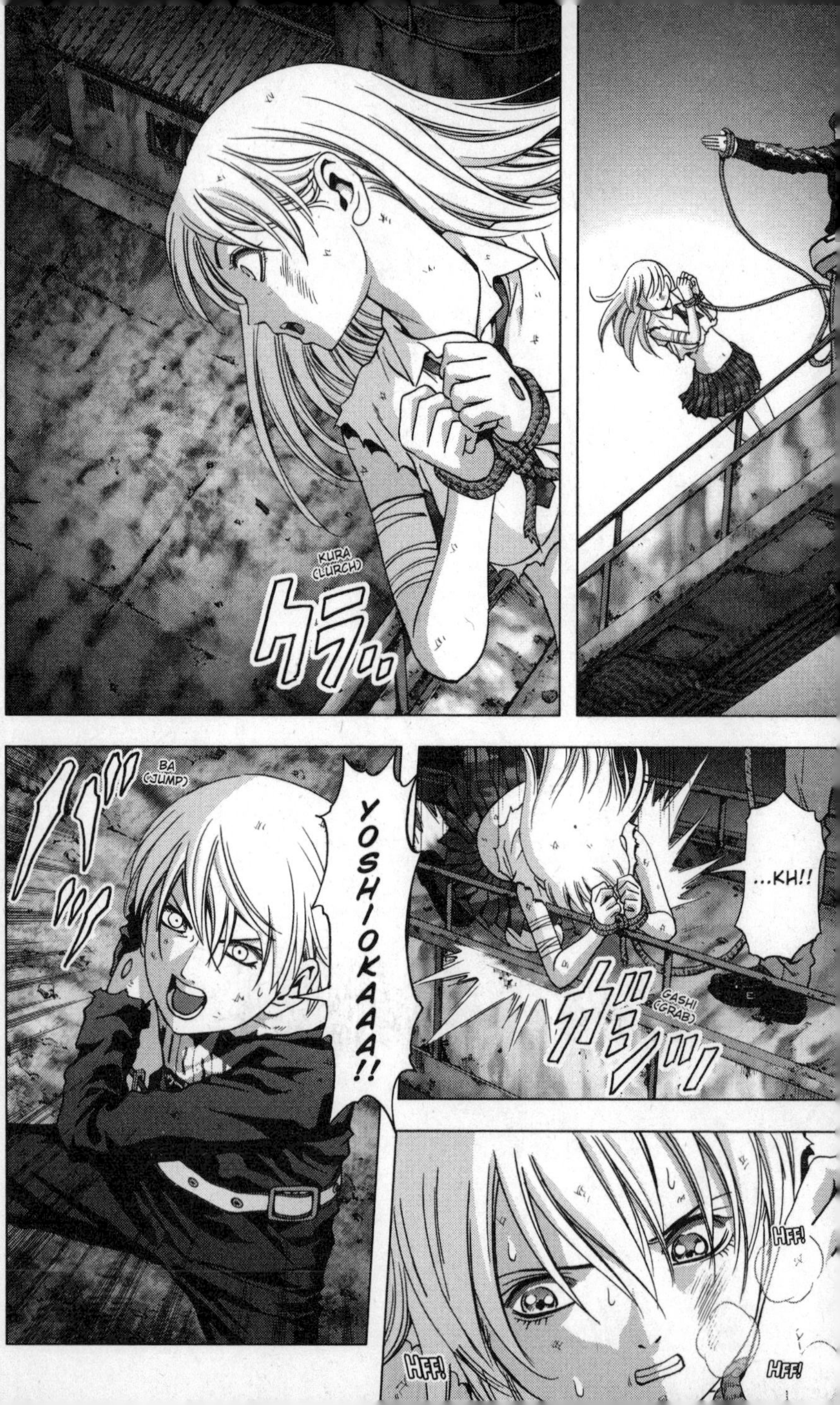
KURA (LURCH)
...KH!!
GASHI (GRAB)
HFF!
HFF!
HFF!
BA (JUMP)
YOSHIOKAAAA!!

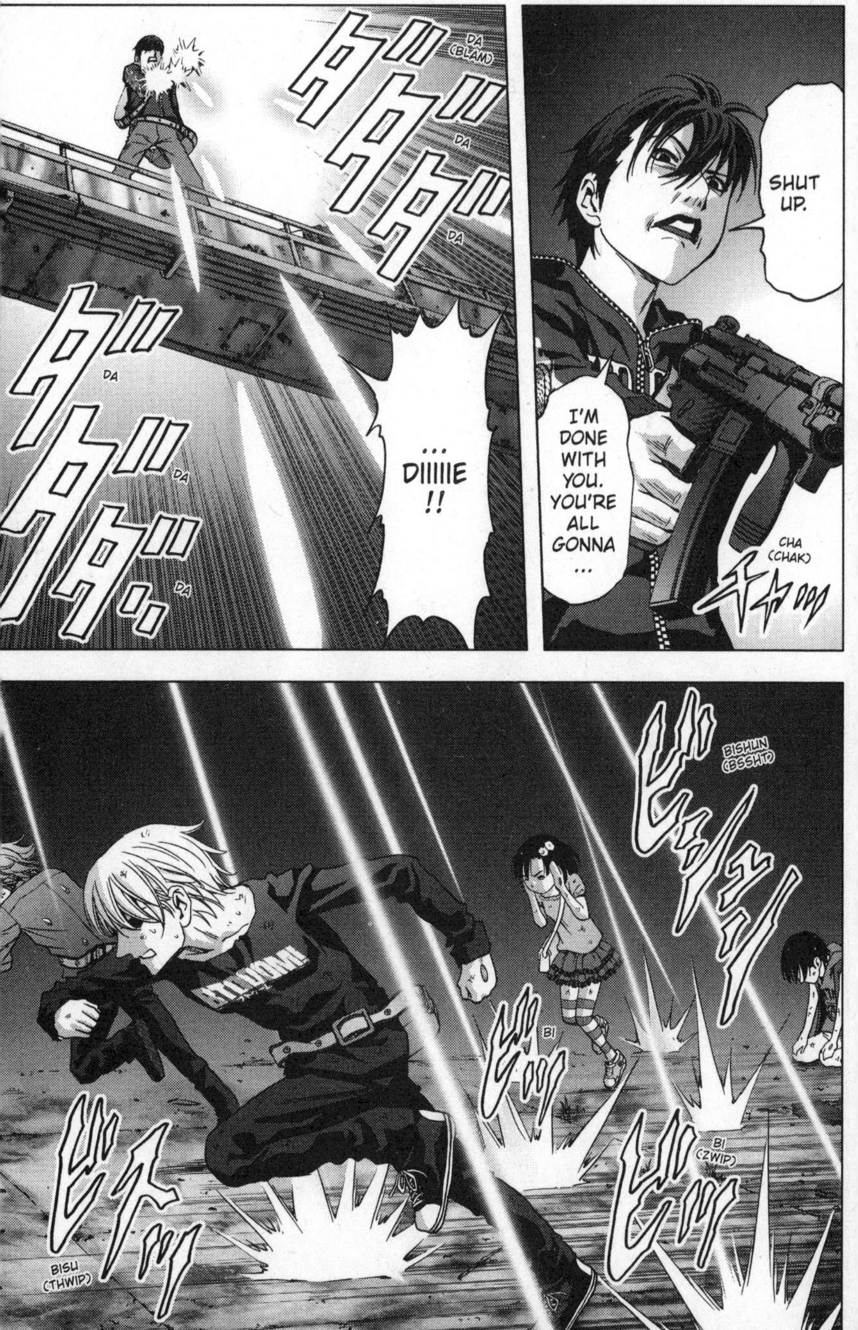
SHUT UP.
I'M DONE WITH YOU. YOU'RE ALL GONNA ...
CHA (CHAK)
DA (BLAM)
DA
DA
DA
DA
DA
... DIIIIIE !!
BISHUN (BSSHT)
BI (ZWIP)
BI
BISU (THWIP)

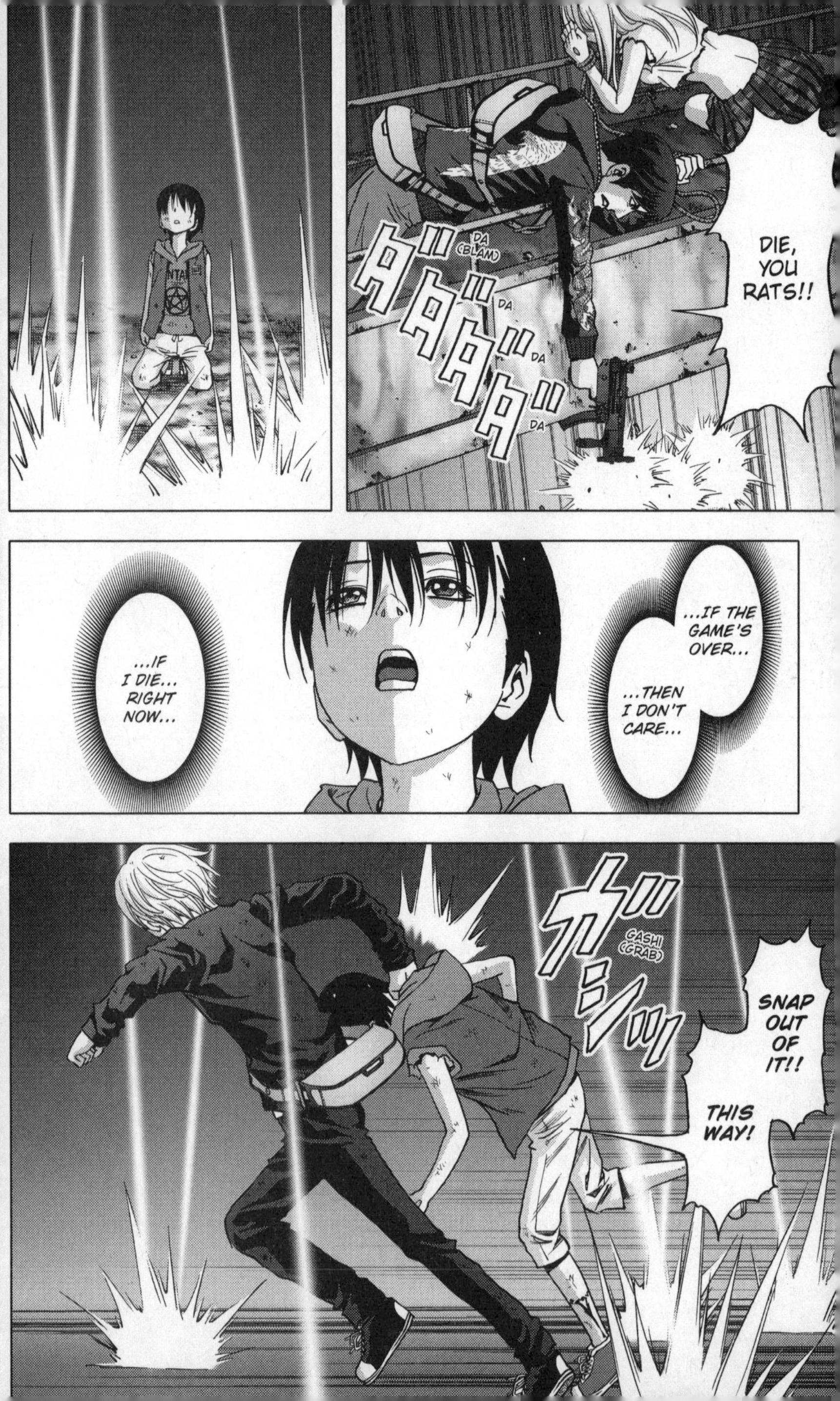
DIE, YOU RATS!!
DA (BLAM) DA DA DA
...IF THE GAME'S OVER...
...THEN I DON'T CARE...
...IF I DIE... RIGHT NOW...
GASHI (GRAB)
SNAP OUT OF IT!!
THIS WAY!

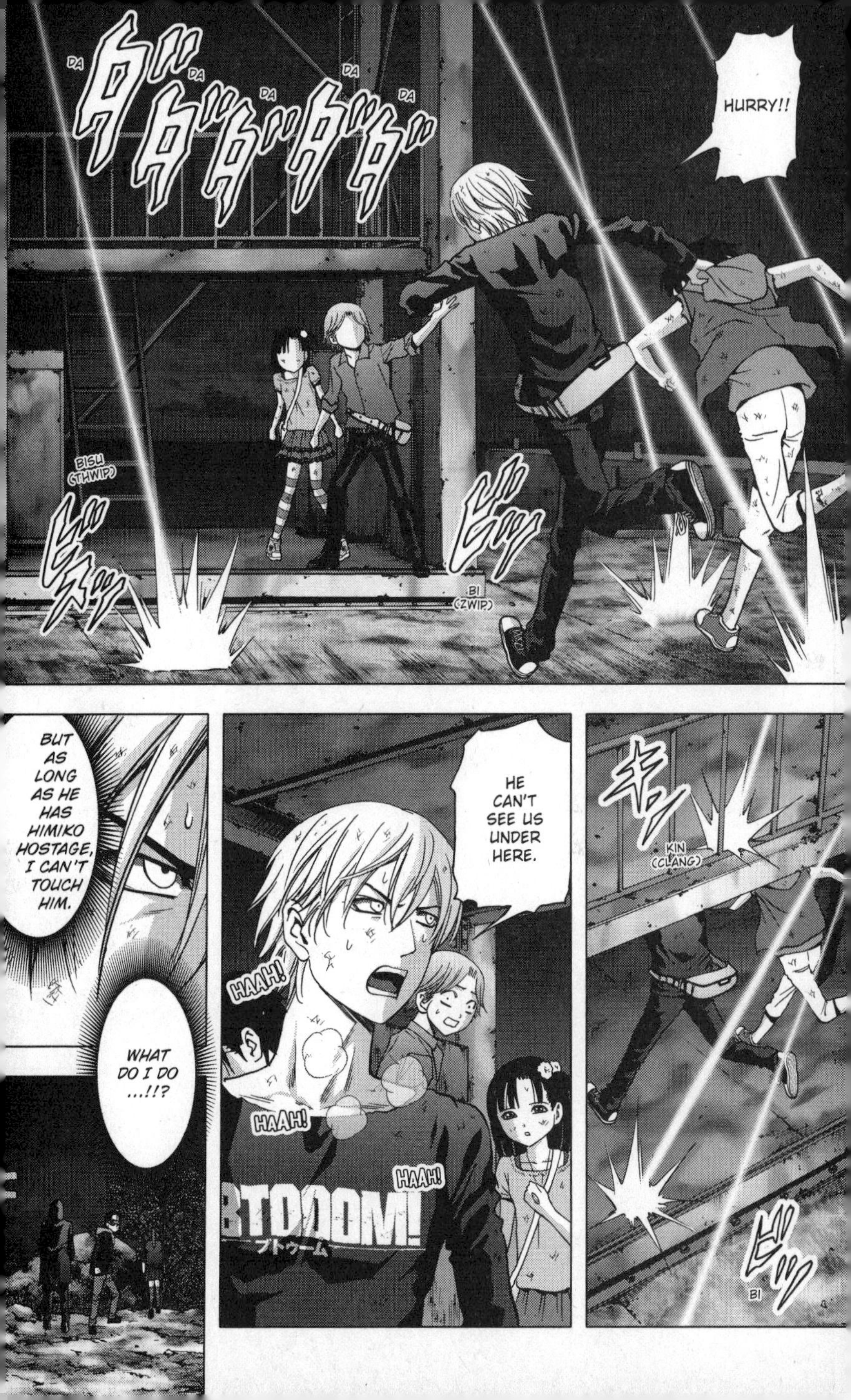
HURRY!!
DA DA DA DA DA
BI (ZWIP)
BISU (THWIP)
KIN (CLANG)
BI
HE CAN'T SEE US UNDER HERE.
HAAH!
HAAH!
HAAH!
BTOOOM!
BUT AS LONG AS HE HAS HIMIKO HOSTAGE, I CAN'T TOUCH HIM.
WHAT DO I DO ...!!?

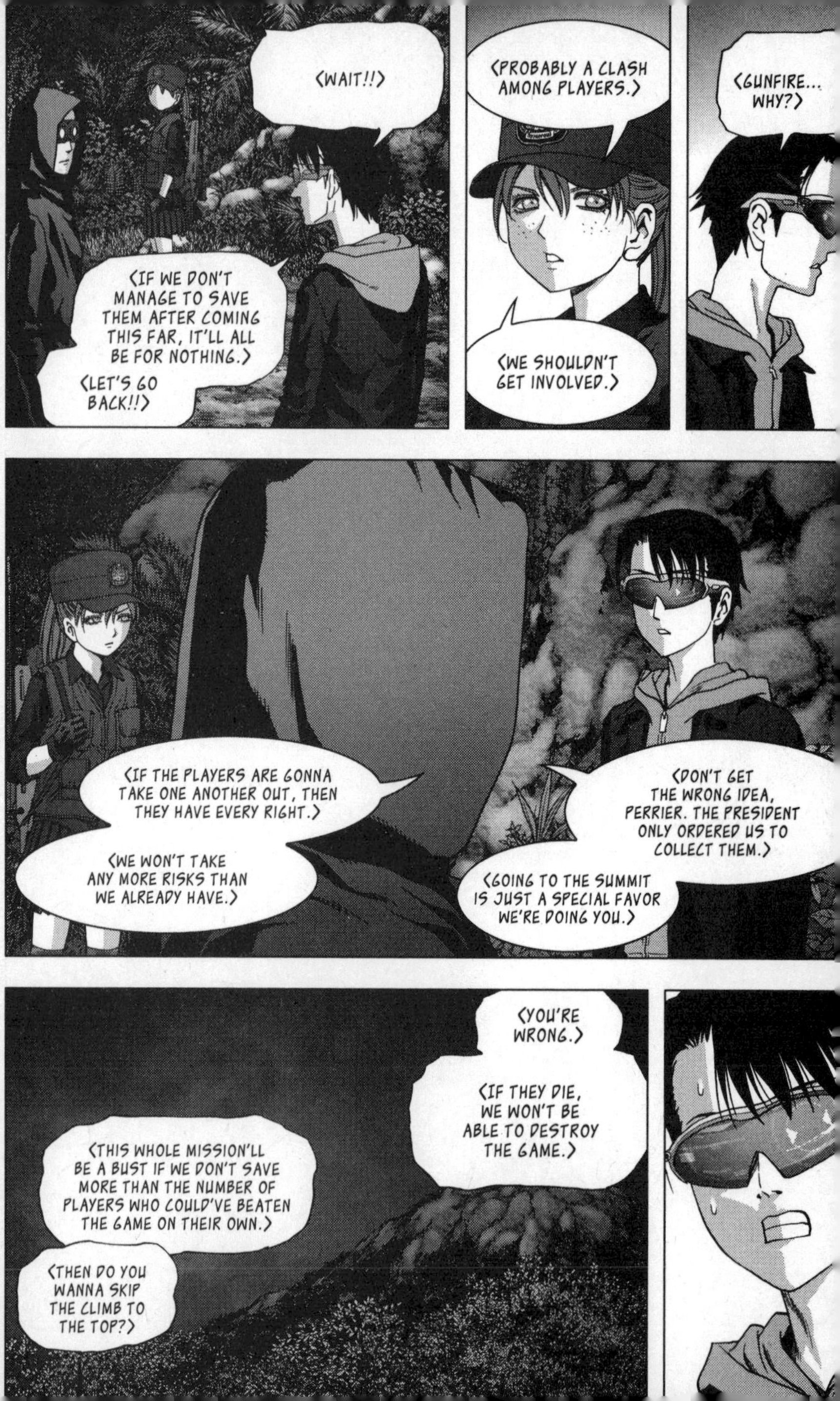
<GUNFIRE... WHY?>
<PROBABLY A CLASH AMONG PLAYERS.>
<WE SHOULDN'T GET INVOLVED.>
<WAIT!!>
<IF WE DON'T MANAGE TO SAVE THEM AFTER COMING THIS FAR, IT'LL ALL BE FOR NOTHING.>
<LET'S GO BACK!!>
<DON'T GET THE WRONG IDEA, PERRIER. THE PRESIDENT ONLY ORDERED US TO COLLECT THEM.>
<GOING TO THE SUMMIT IS JUST A SPECIAL FAVOR WE'RE DOING YOU.>
<IF THE PLAYERS ARE GONNA TAKE ONE ANOTHER OUT, THEN THEY HAVE EVERY RIGHT.>
<WE WON'T TAKE ANY MORE RISKS THAN WE ALREADY HAVE.>
<YOU'RE WRONG.>
<IF THEY DIE, WE WON'T BE ABLE TO DESTROY THE GAME.>
<THIS WHOLE MISSION'LL BE A BUST IF WE DON'T SAVE MORE THAN THE NUMBER OF PLAYERS WHO COULD'VE BEATEN THE GAME ON THEIR OWN.>
<THEN DO YOU WANNA SKIP THE CLIMB TO THE TOP?>

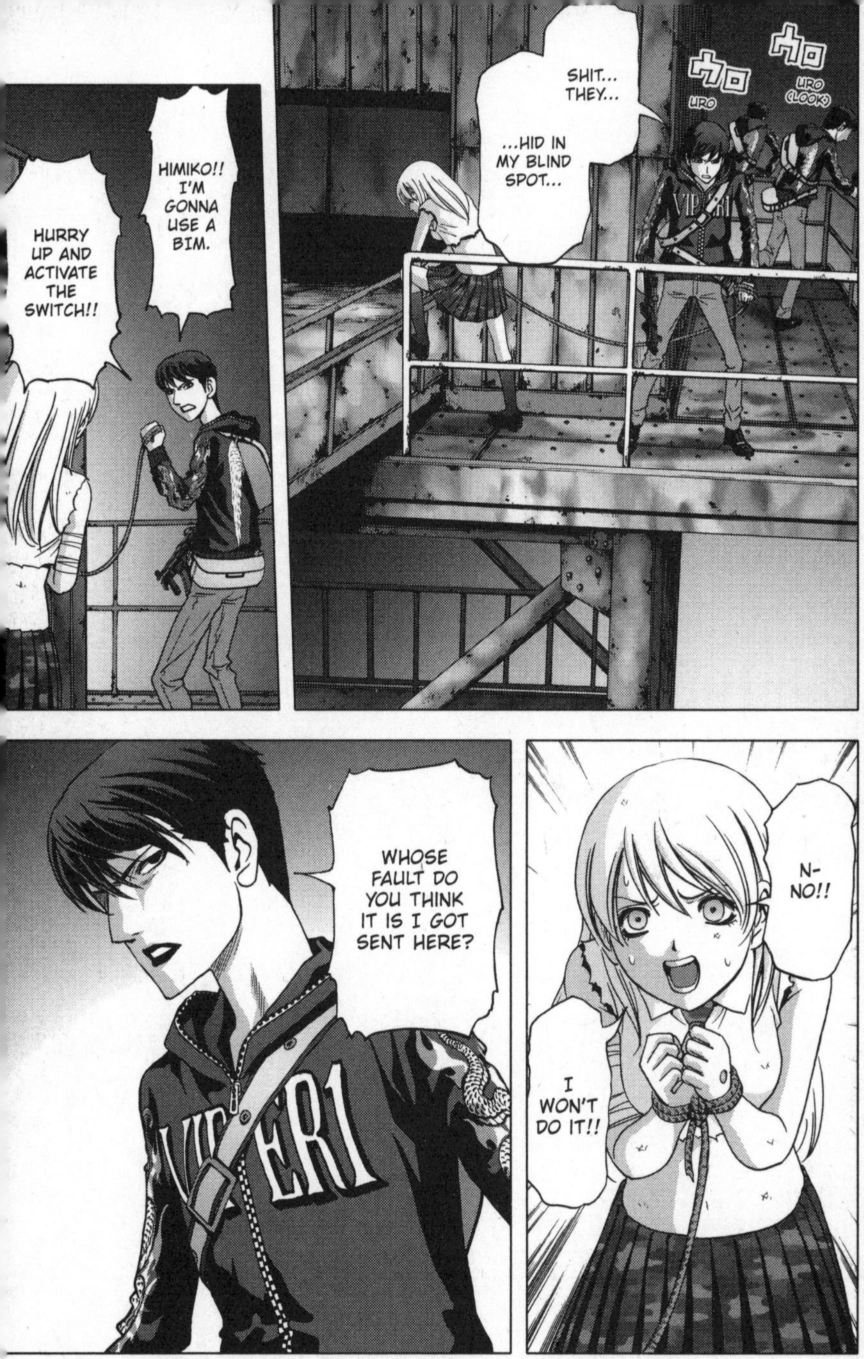
ウロ
URO (LOOK)
ウロ
URO
SHIT... THEY...
...HID IN MY BLIND SPOT...
HIMIKO!! I'M GONNA USE A BIM.
HURRY UP AND ACTIVATE THE SWITCH!!
N- NO!!
I WON'T DO IT!!
WHOSE FAULT DO YOU THINK IT IS I GOT SENT HERE?

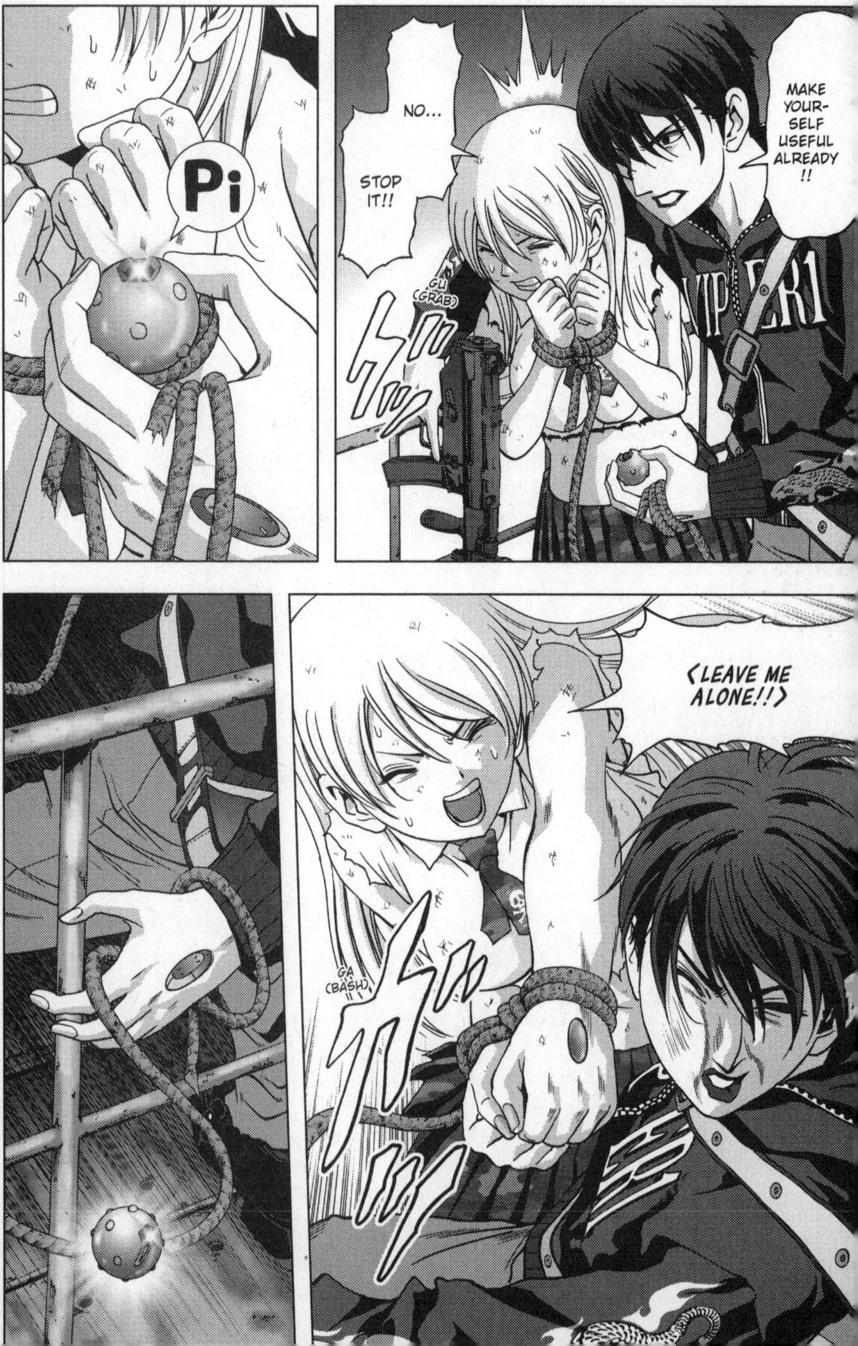
MAKE YOUR-SELF USEFUL ALREADY!!
NO...
STOP IT!!
GU (GRAB)
Pi
<LEAVE ME ALONE!!>
GA (BASH)

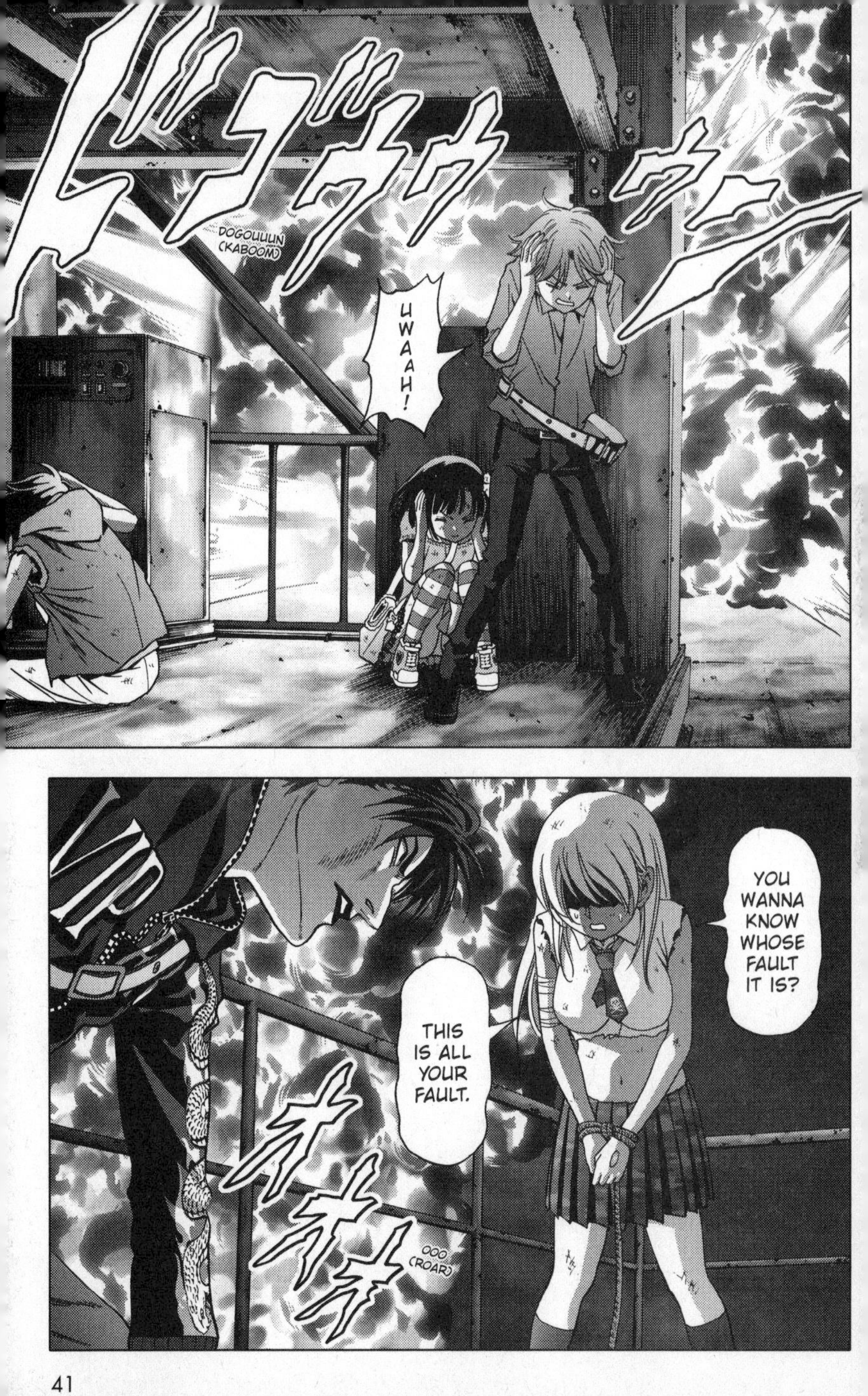
DOGOUUUN (KABOOM)
UWAAAH!
YOU WANNA KNOW WHOSE FAULT IT IS?
THIS IS ALL YOUR FAULT.
OOO (ROAR)

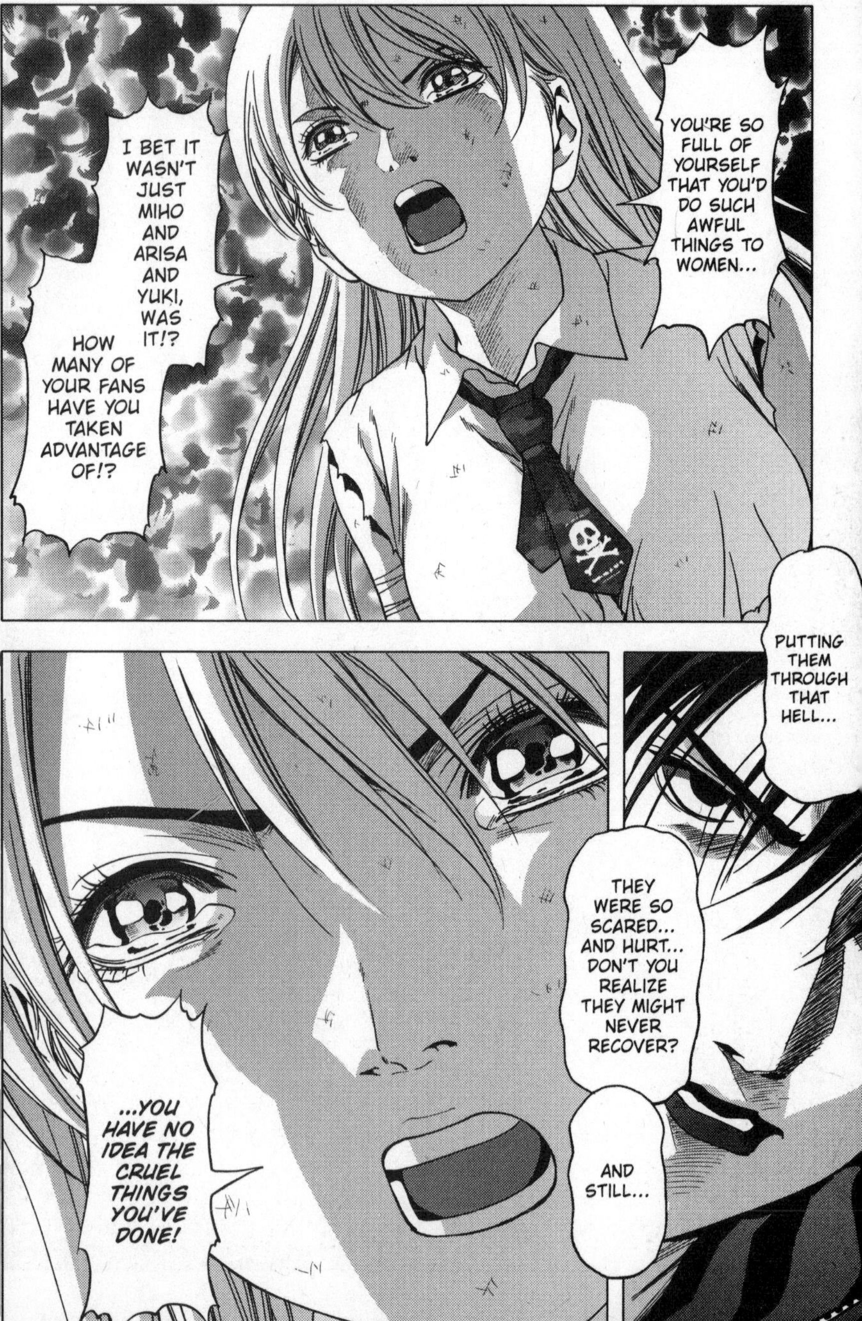
YOU'RE SO FULL OF YOURSELF THAT YOU'D DO SUCH AWFUL THINGS TO WOMEN...
I BET IT WASN'T JUST MIHO AND ARISA AND YUKI, WAS IT!?
HOW MANY OF YOUR FANS HAVE YOU TAKEN ADVANTAGE OF!?
PUTTING THEM THROUGH THAT HELL...
THEY WERE SO SCARED... AND HURT... DON'T YOU REALIZE THEY MIGHT NEVER RECOVER?
AND STILL...
...YOU HAVE NO IDEA THE CRUEL THINGS YOU'VE DONE!

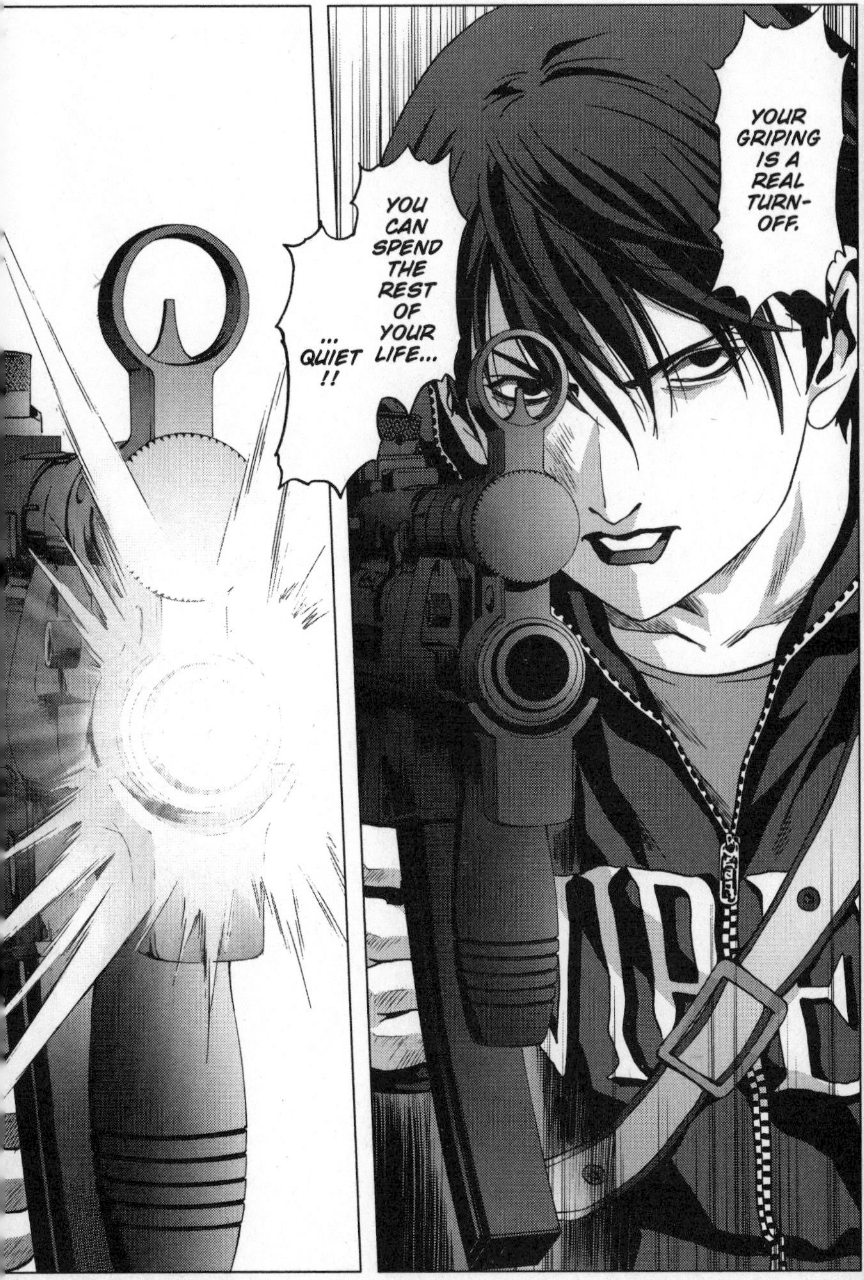
YOUR GRIPING IS A REAL TURN-OFF.
YOU CAN SPEND THE REST OF YOUR LIFE...
...QUIET!!

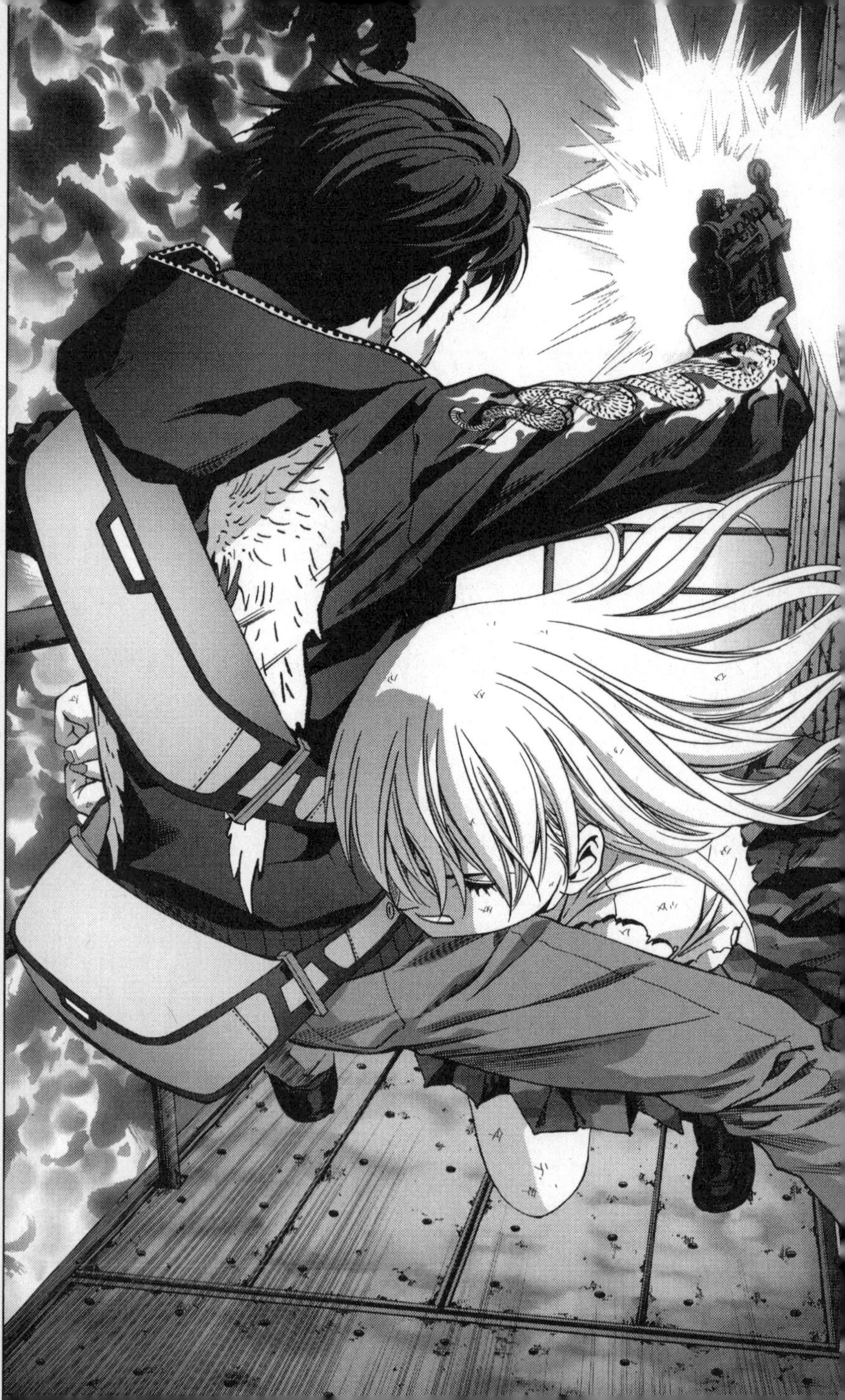

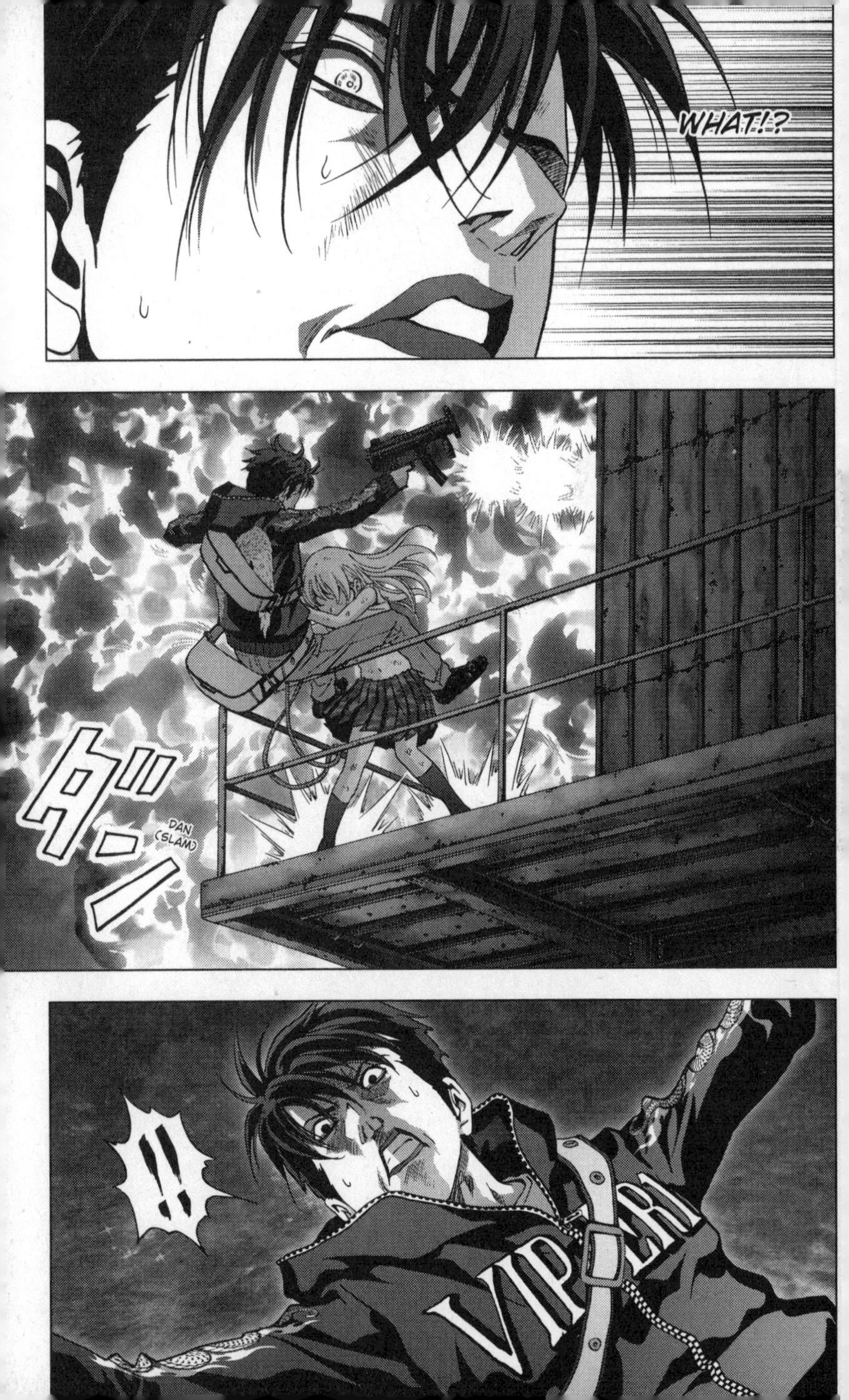
WHAT!?
DAN (SLAM)
!!
VIPER

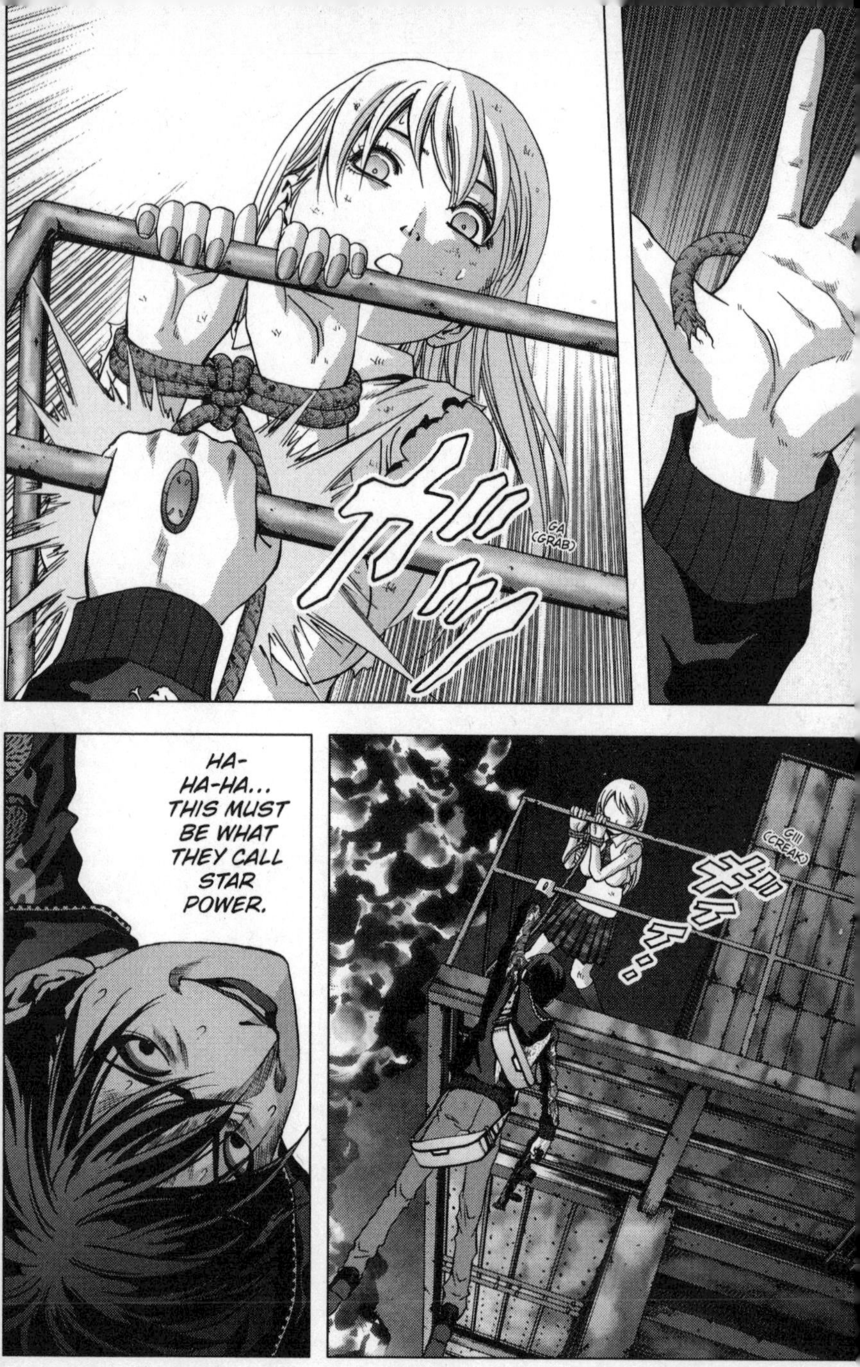
GA (GRAB)
GIII (CREAK)
HA-HA-HA... THIS MUST BE WHAT THEY CALL STAR POWER.

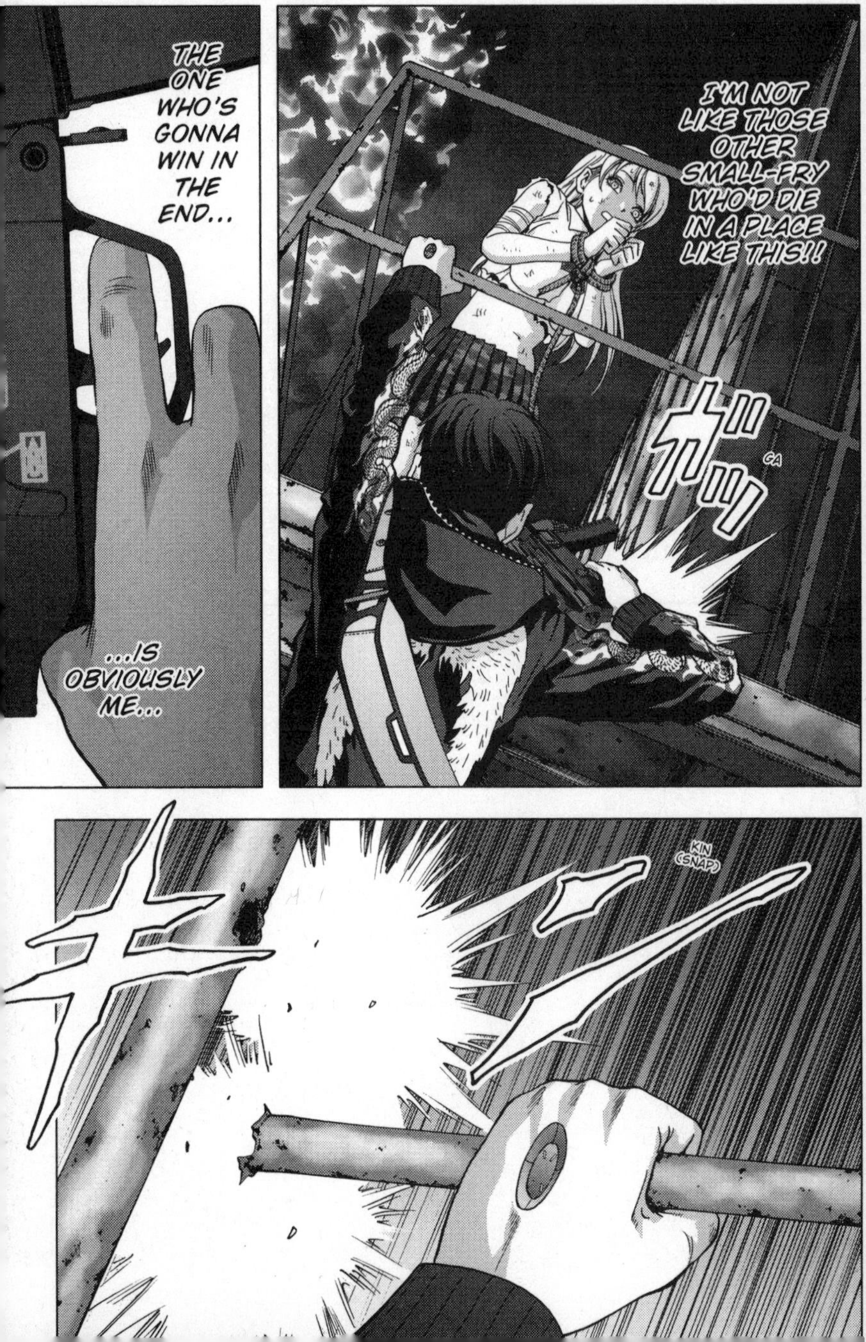
I'M NOT LIKE THOSE OTHER SMALL-FRY WHO'D DIE IN A PLACE LIKE THIS!!
ガッ
GA
THE ONE WHO'S GONNA WIN IN THE END...
...IS OBVIOUSLY ME...
キン
KIN (SNAP)

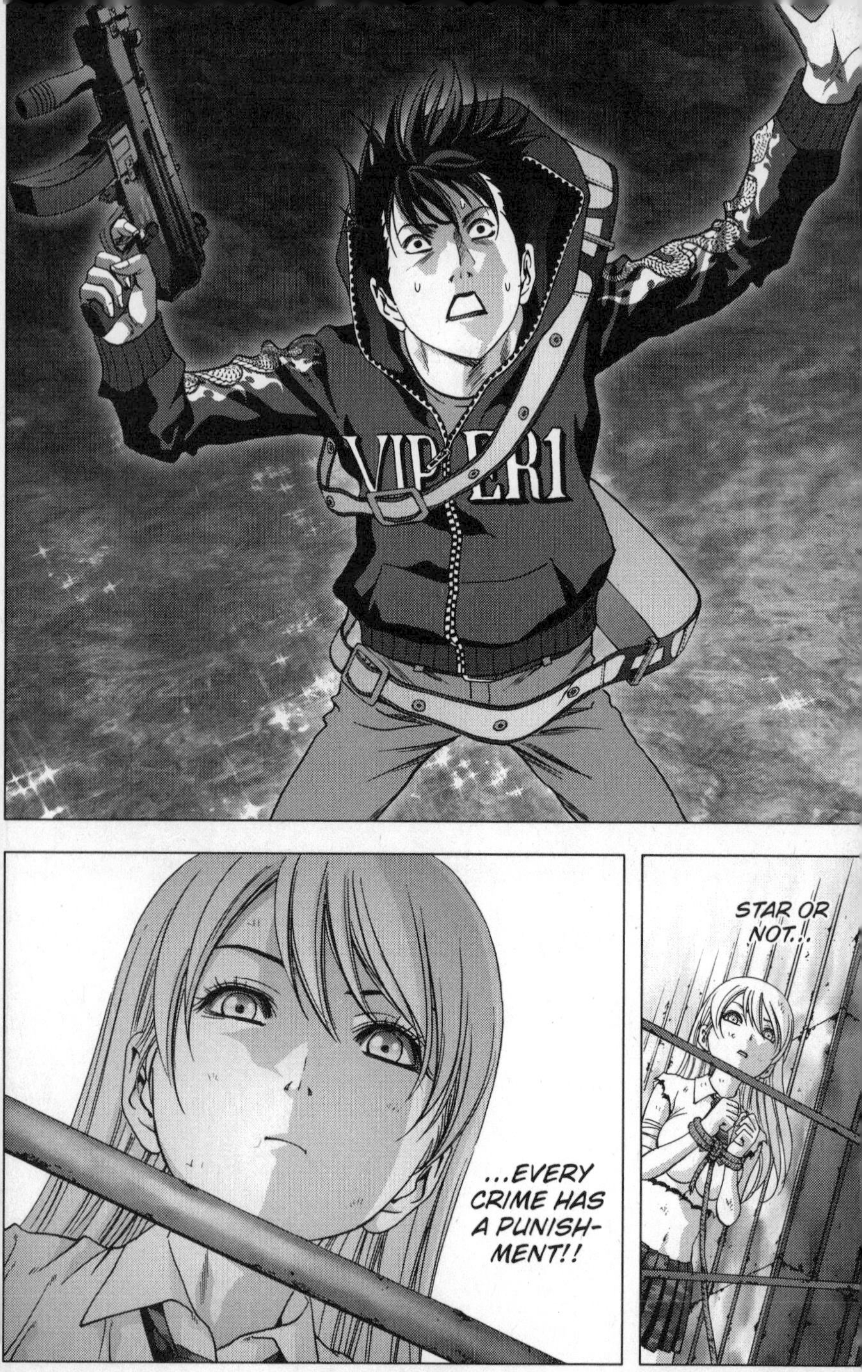
STAR OR NOT...
...EVERY CRIME HAS A PUNISH-MENT!!

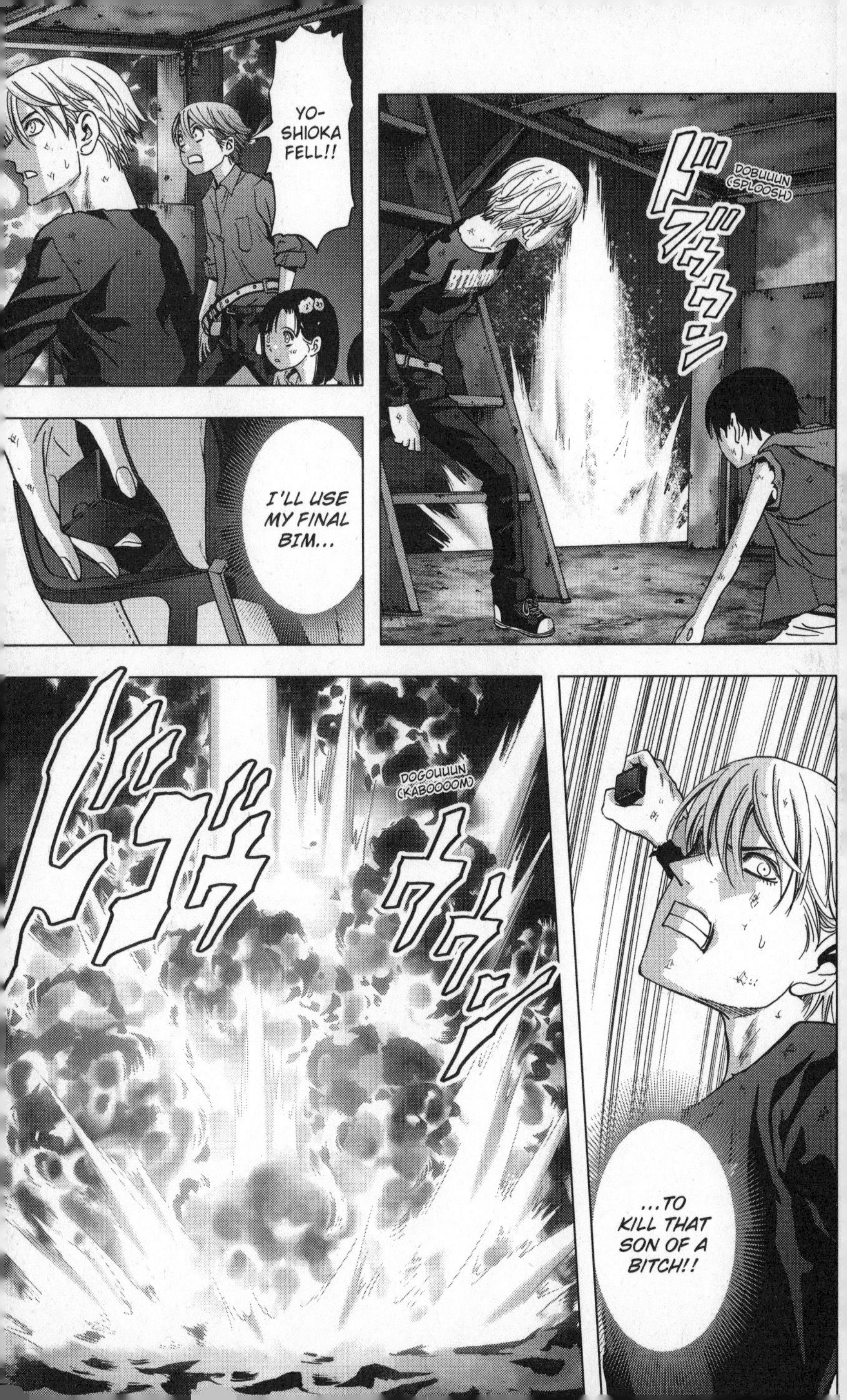

DOBUUUN (SPLOOSH)
YO-SHIOKA FELL!!
I'LL USE MY FINAL BIM...
...TO KILL THAT SON OF A BITCH!!
DOGOUUUN (KABOOOOM)

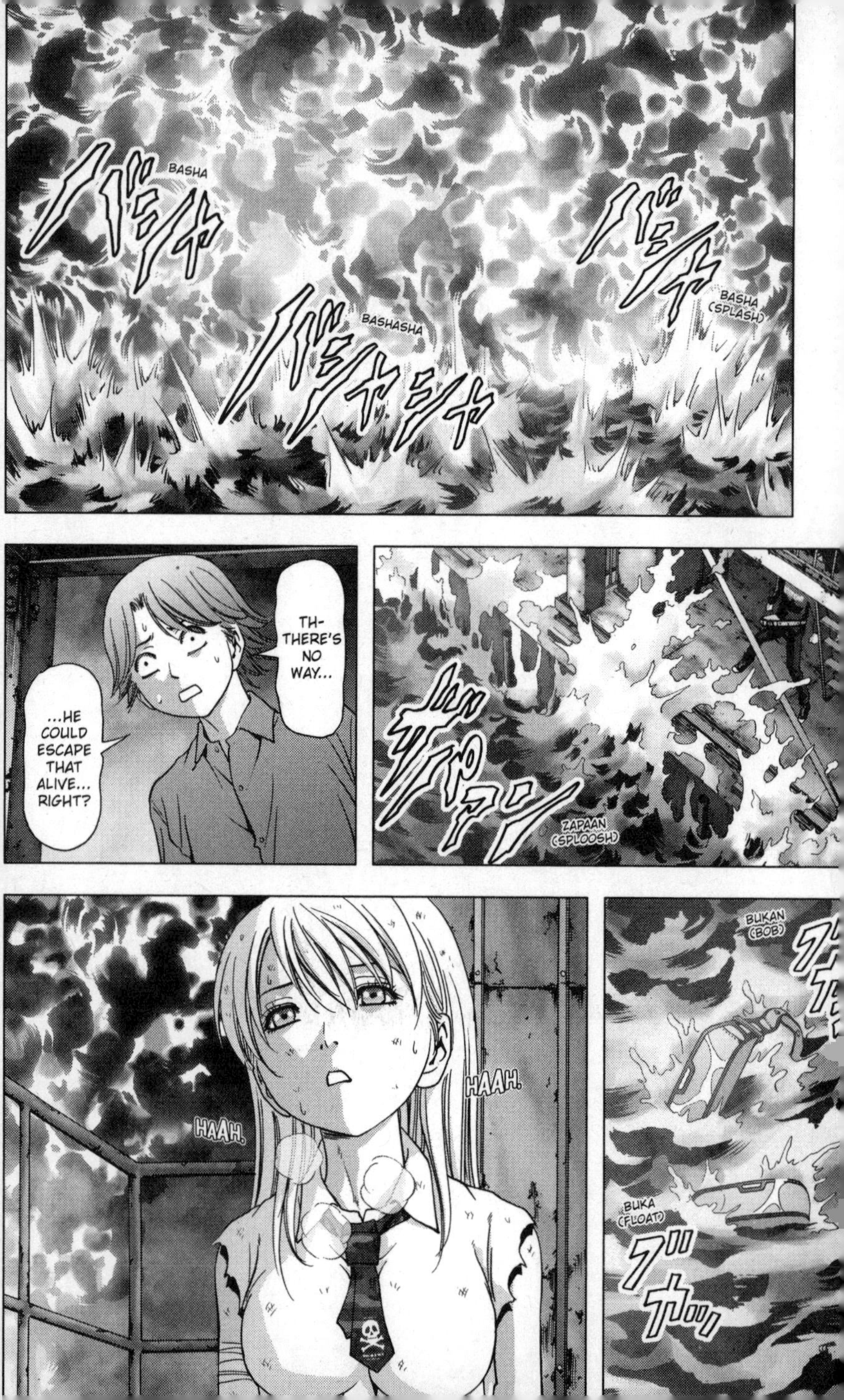
BASHA (SPLASH)
BASHASHA
BASHA
ZAPAAN (SPLOOSH)
TH-THERE'S NO WAY...
...HE COULD ESCAPE THAT ALIVE... RIGHT?
BUKAN (BOB)
BUKA (FLOAT)
HAAH.
HAAH.

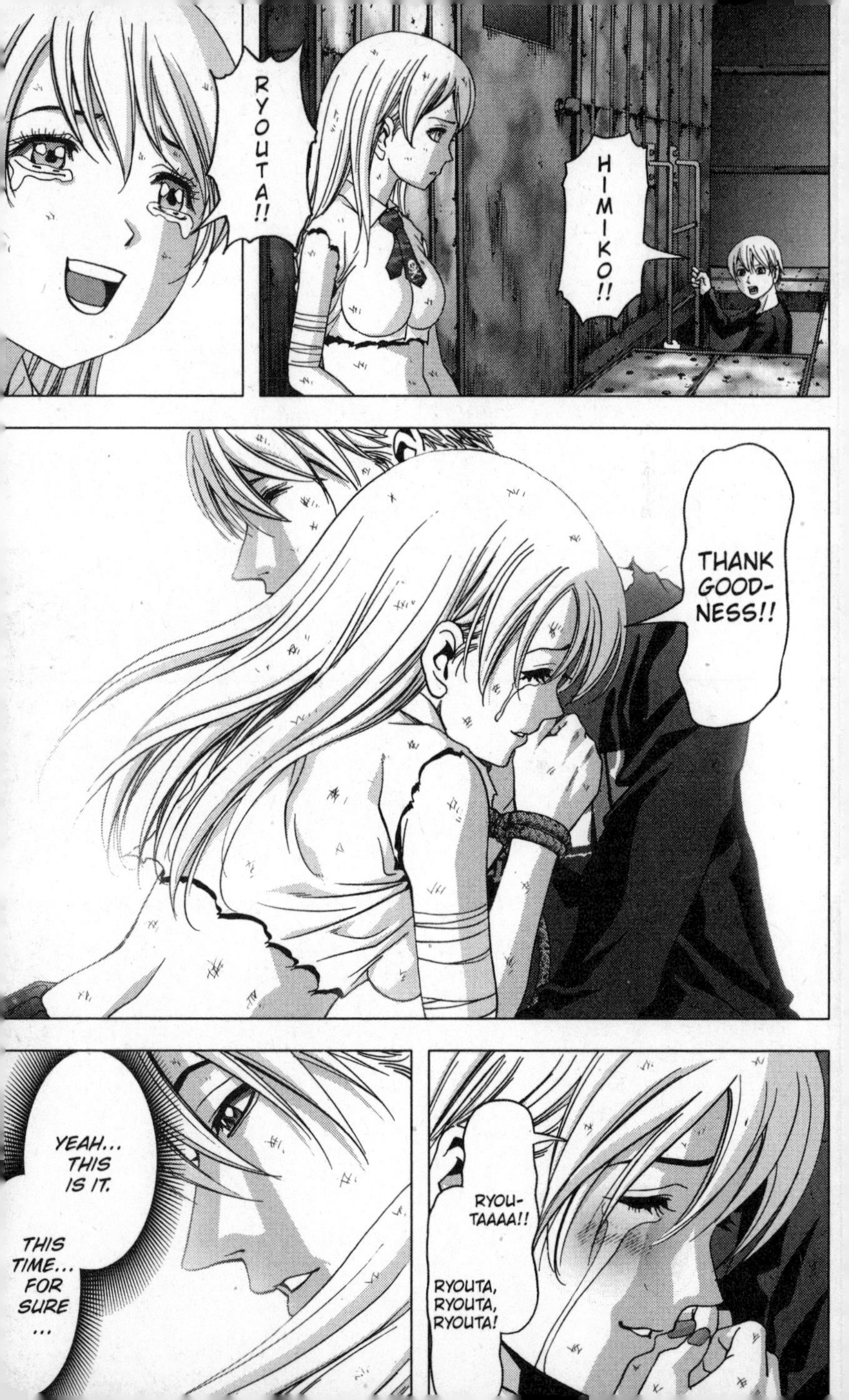
HIMIKO!!
RYOUTA!!
THANK GOODNESS!!
RYOUTAAAA!!
RYOUTA, RYOUTA, RYOUTA!
YEAH... THIS IS IT.
THIS TIME... FOR SURE...

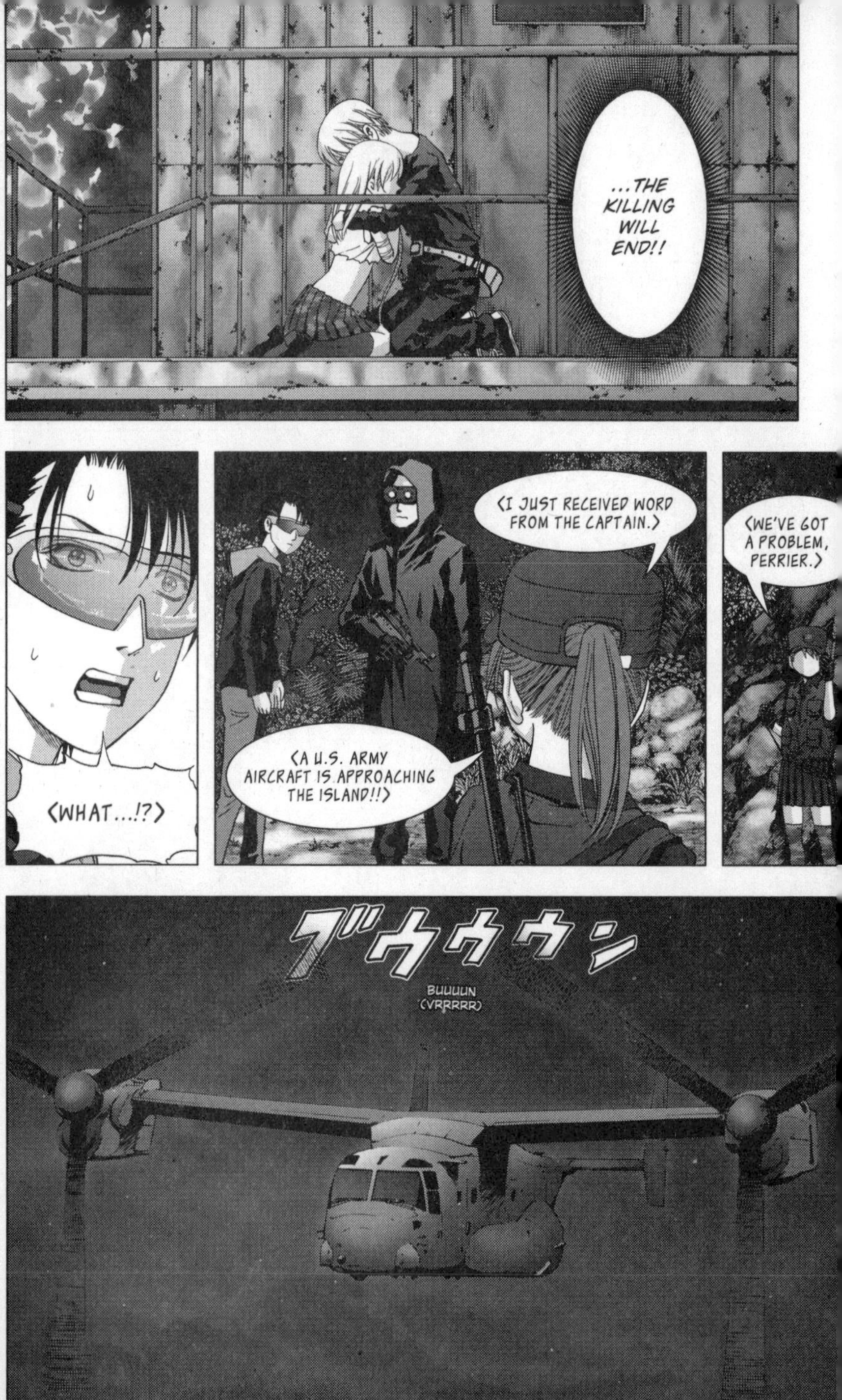
...THE KILLING WILL END!!
⟨WE'VE GOT A PROBLEM, PERRIER.⟩
⟨I JUST RECEIVED WORD FROM THE CAPTAIN.⟩
⟨A U.S. ARMY AIRCRAFT IS APPROACHING THE ISLAND!!⟩
⟨WHAT...!?⟩
ブゥゥゥン
BUUUUN
(VRRRRR)

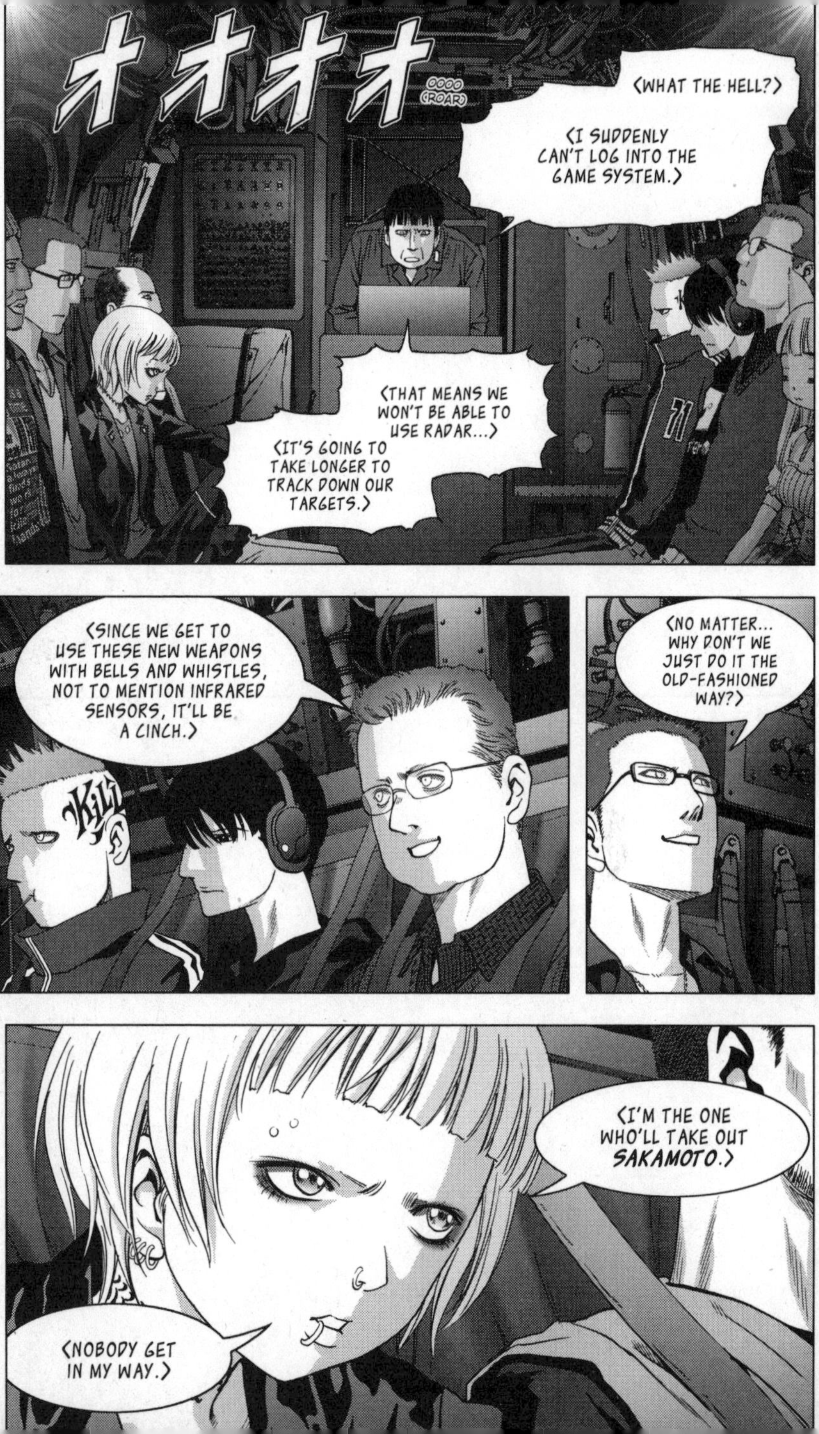
<WHAT THE HELL?>
オオオオ OOOO (ROAR)
<I SUDDENLY CAN'T LOG INTO THE GAME SYSTEM.>
<THAT MEANS WE WON'T BE ABLE TO USE RADAR...>
<IT'S GOING TO TAKE LONGER TO TRACK DOWN OUR TARGETS.>
<NO MATTER... WHY DON'T WE JUST DO IT THE OLD-FASHIONED WAY?>
<SINCE WE GET TO USE THESE NEW WEAPONS WITH BELLS AND WHISTLES, NOT TO MENTION INFRARED SENSORS, IT'LL BE A CINCH.>
<I'M THE ONE WHO'LL TAKE OUT SAKAMOTO.>
<NOBODY GET IN MY WAY.>

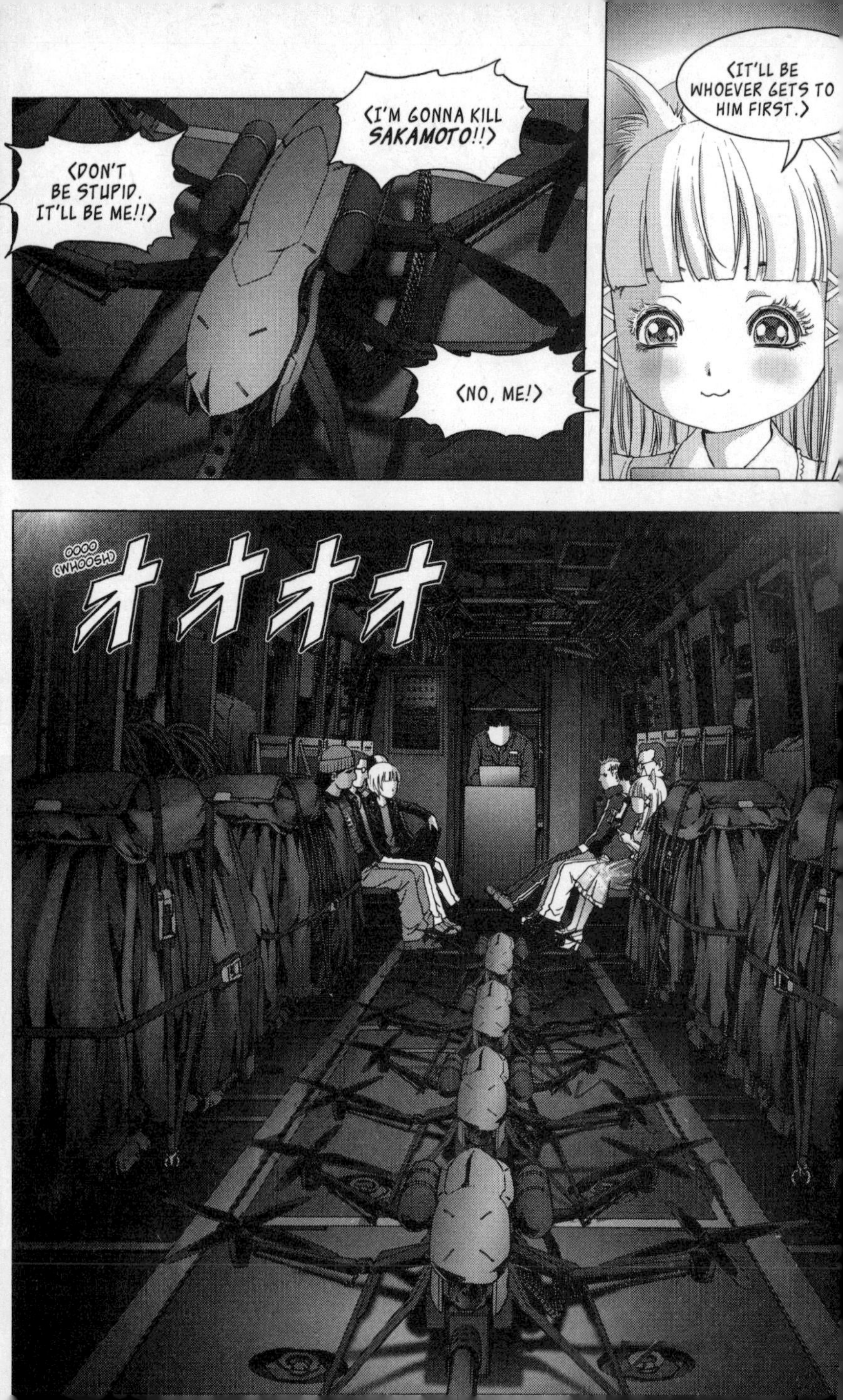
‹IT'LL BE WHOEVER GETS TO HIM FIRST.›
‹I'M GONNA KILL SAKAMOTO!!›
‹DON'T BE STUPID. IT'LL BE ME!!›
‹NO, ME!›
OOOO (WHOOSH)
オオオオ

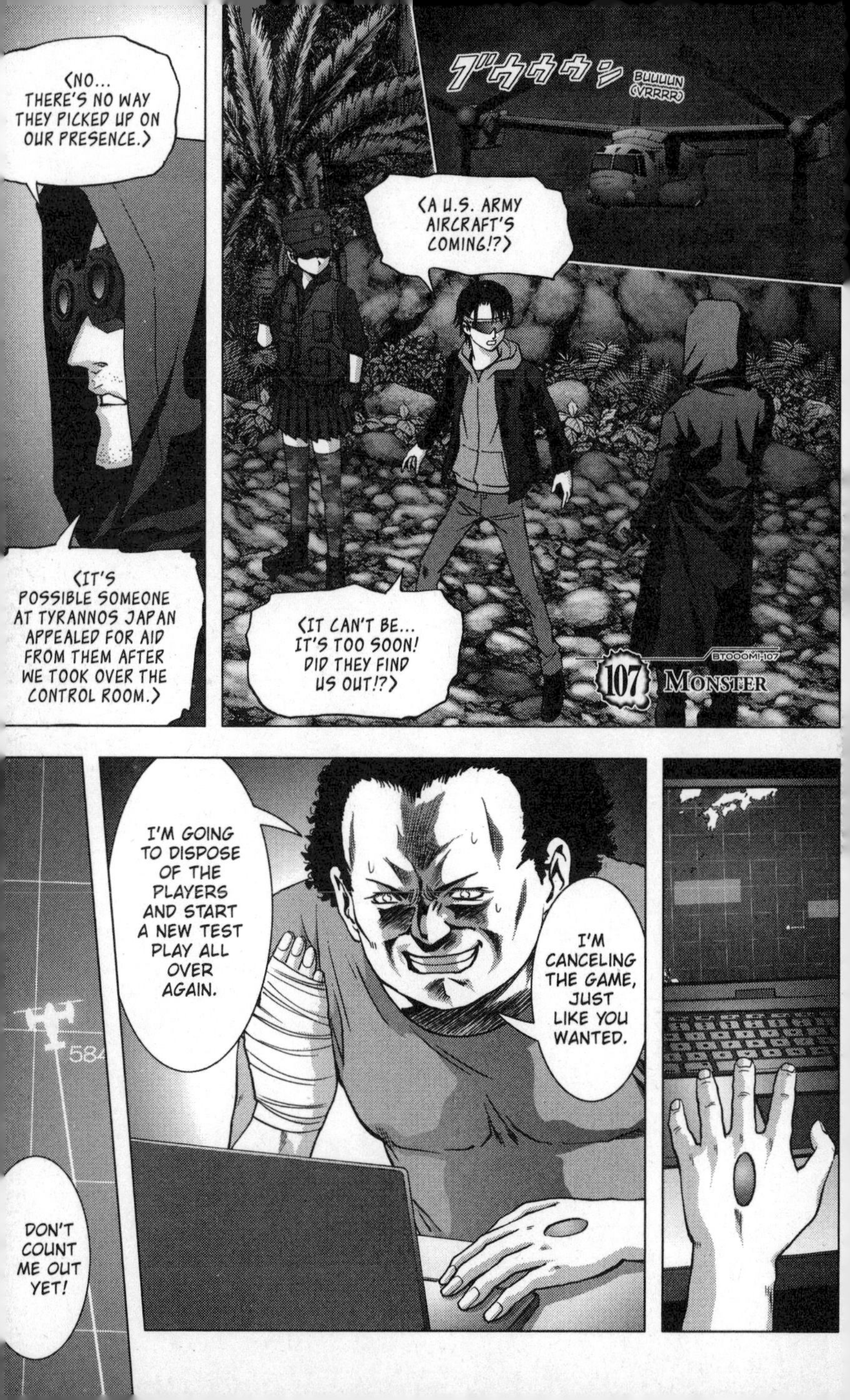
ブウウウン
BUUUUN (VRRRR)
<A U.S. ARMY AIRCRAFT'S COMING!?>
<IT CAN'T BE... IT'S TOO SOON! DID THEY FIND US OUT!?>
BTOOOM!-107
107 MONSTER
<NO... THERE'S NO WAY THEY PICKED UP ON OUR PRESENCE.>
<IT'S POSSIBLE SOMEONE AT TYRANNOS JAPAN APPEALED FOR AID FROM THEM AFTER WE TOOK OVER THE CONTROL ROOM.>
I'M CANCELING THE GAME, JUST LIKE YOU WANTED.
I'M GOING TO DISPOSE OF THE PLAYERS AND START A NEW TEST PLAY ALL OVER AGAIN.
584
DON'T COUNT ME OUT YET!

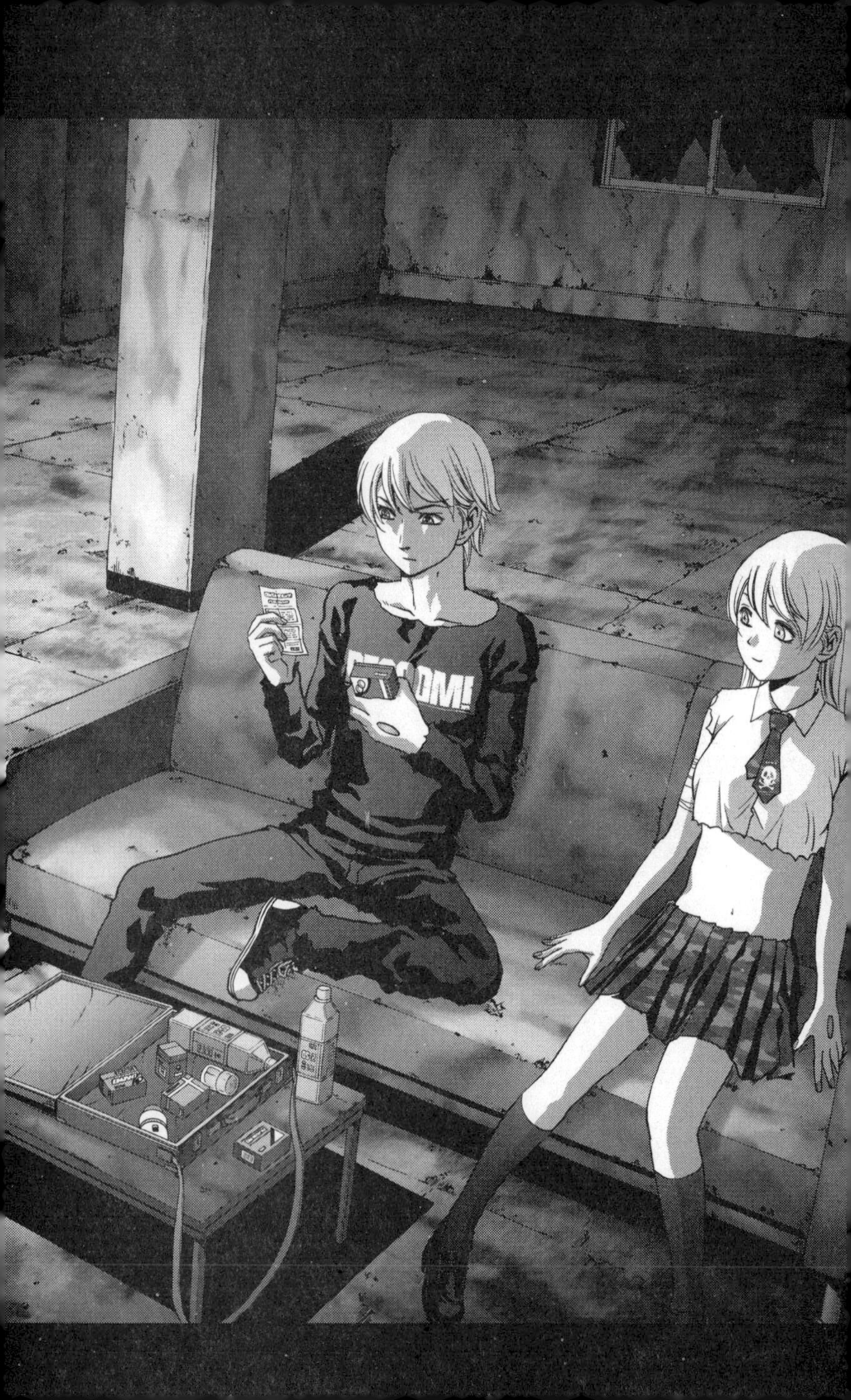

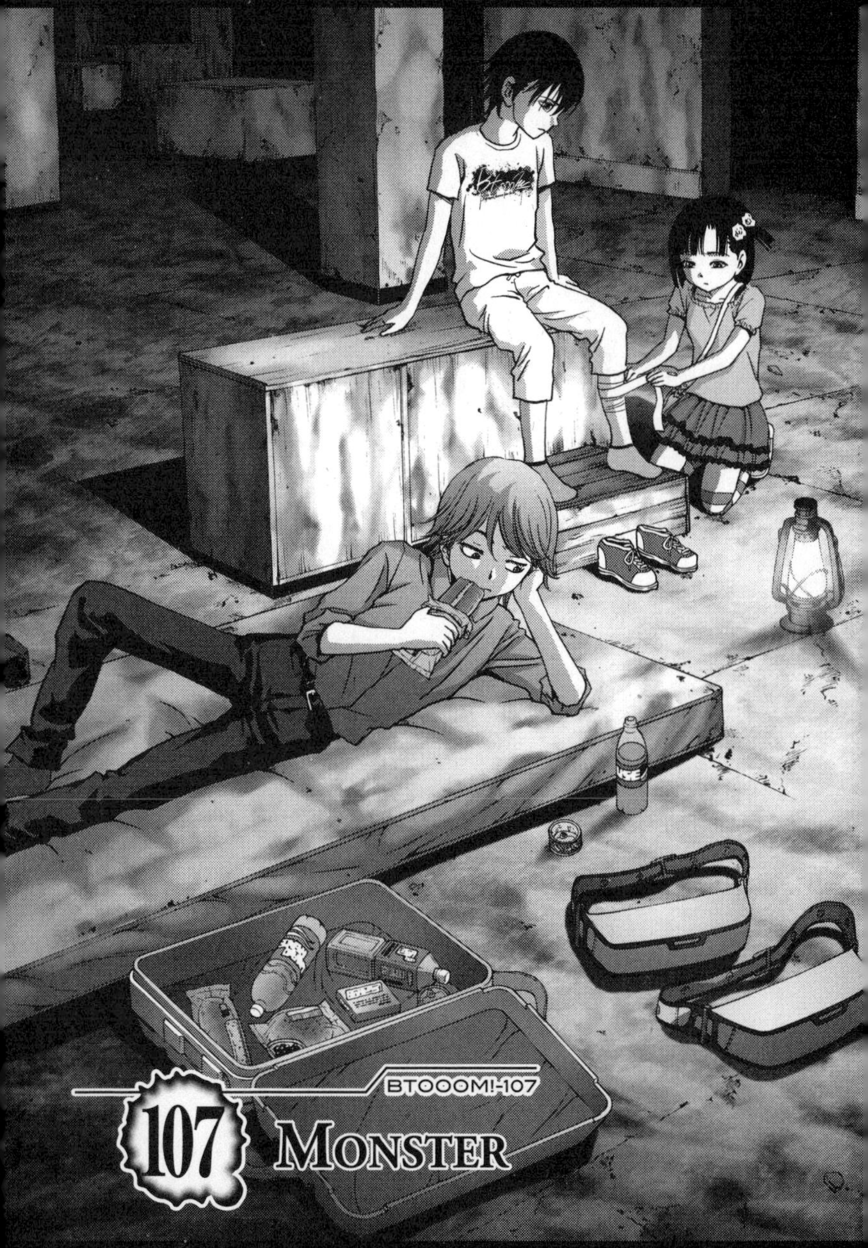
BTOOOM!-107
107
MONSTER

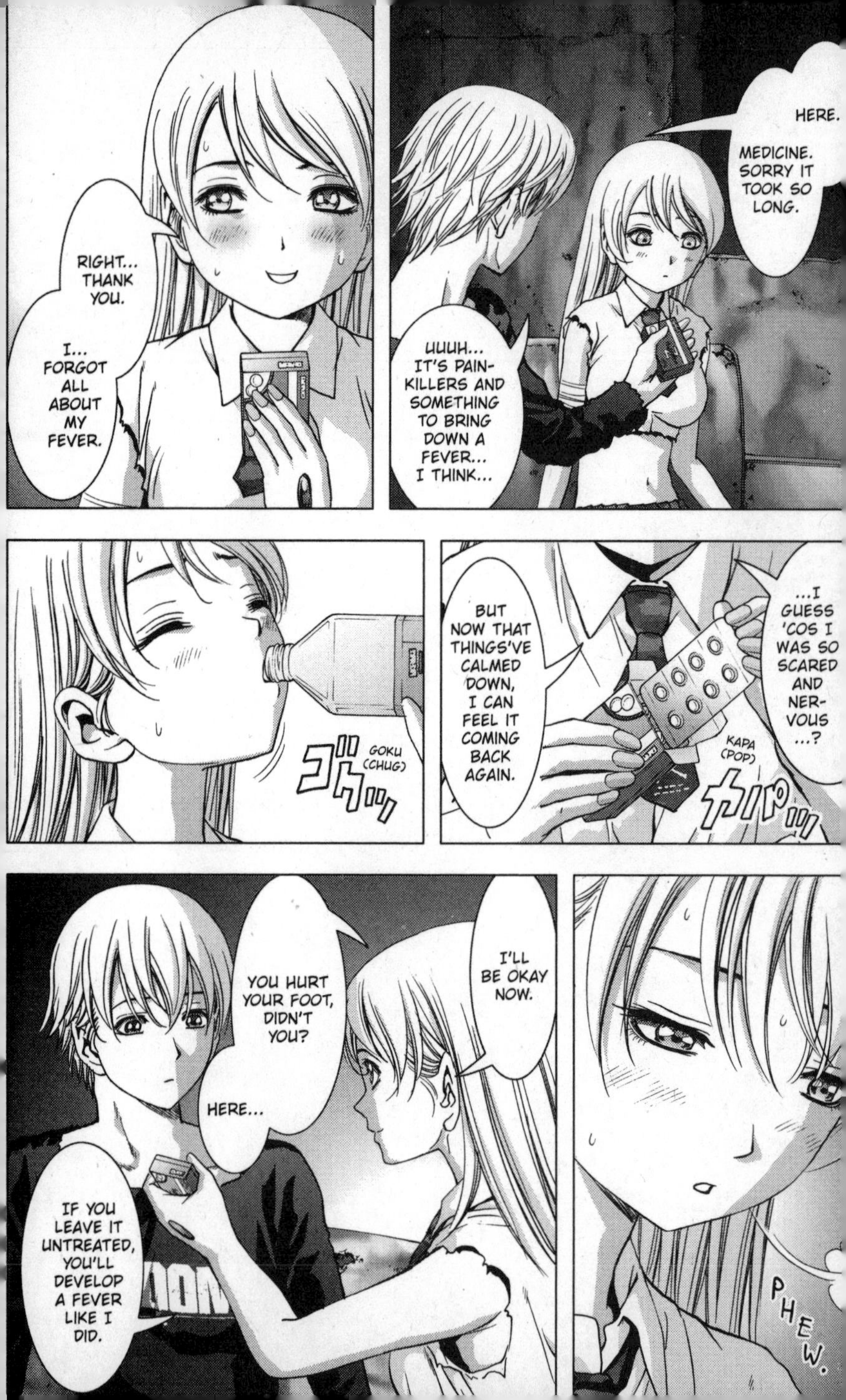
HERE.
MEDICINE. SORRY IT TOOK SO LONG.
UUUH... IT'S PAIN-KILLERS AND SOMETHING TO BRING DOWN A FEVER... I THINK...
RIGHT... THANK YOU.
I... FORGOT ALL ABOUT MY FEVER.
...I GUESS 'COS I WAS SO SCARED AND NER-VOUS...?
BUT NOW THAT THINGS'VE CALMED DOWN, I CAN FEEL IT COMING BACK AGAIN.
KAPA (POP)
GOKU (CHUG)
PHEW.
I'LL BE OKAY NOW.
YOU HURT YOUR FOOT, DIDN'T YOU?
HERE...
IF YOU LEAVE IT UNTREATED, YOU'LL DEVELOP A FEVER LIKE I DID.

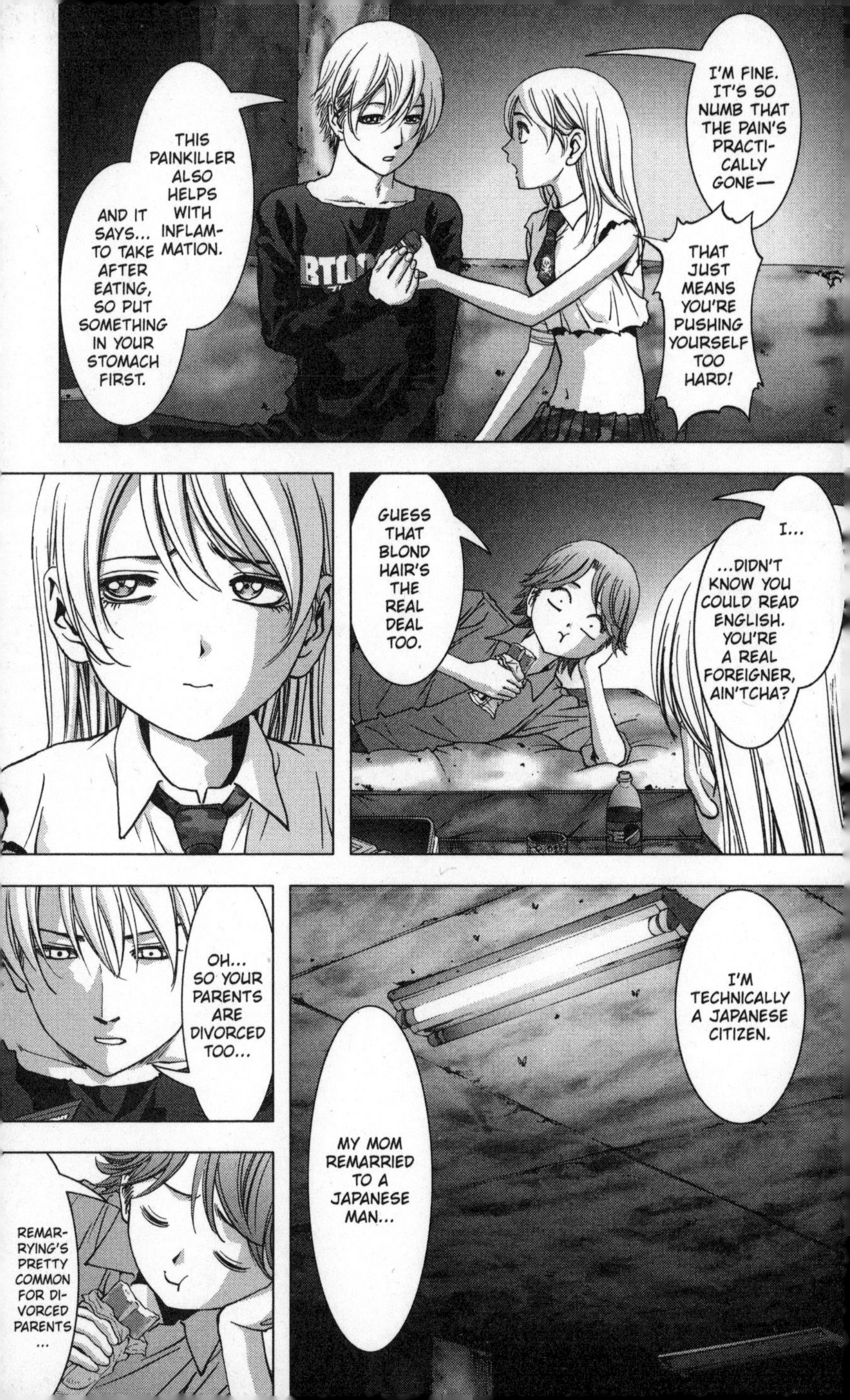
I'M FINE. IT'S SO NUMB THAT THE PAIN'S PRACTICALLY GONE—
THAT JUST MEANS YOU'RE PUSHING YOURSELF TOO HARD!
THIS PAINKILLER ALSO HELPS WITH INFLAMMATION.
AND IT SAYS... TO TAKE AFTER EATING, SO PUT SOMETHING IN YOUR STOMACH FIRST.
I... ...DIDN'T KNOW YOU COULD READ ENGLISH. YOU'RE A REAL FOREIGNER, AIN'TCHA?
GUESS THAT BLOND HAIR'S THE REAL DEAL TOO.
I'M TECHNICALLY A JAPANESE CITIZEN.
MY MOM REMARRIED TO A JAPANESE MAN...
OH... SO YOUR PARENTS ARE DIVORCED TOO...
REMARRYING'S PRETTY COMMON FOR DIVORCED PARENTS...

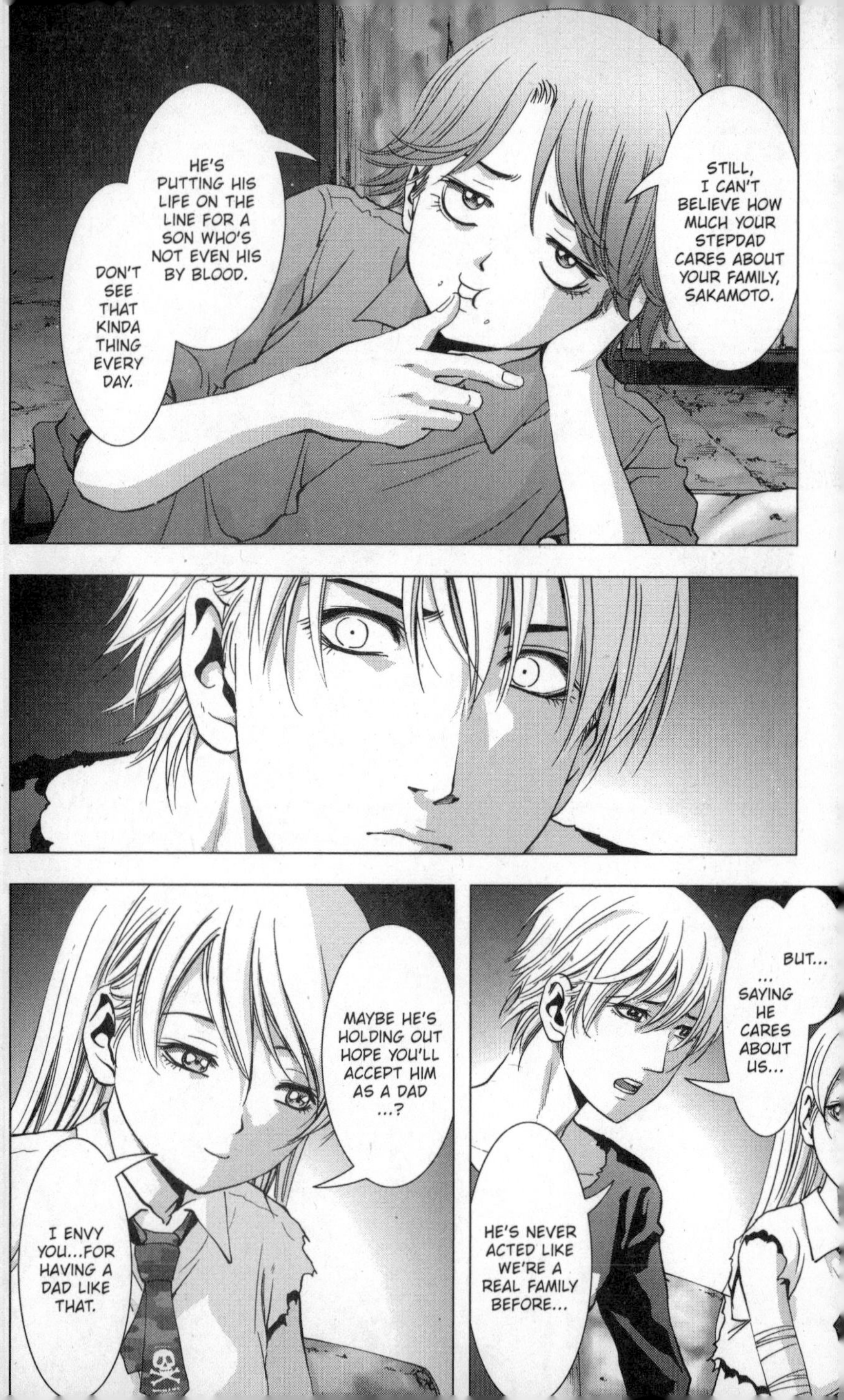
STILL, I CAN'T BELIEVE HOW MUCH YOUR STEPDAD CARES ABOUT YOUR FAMILY, SAKAMOTO.
HE'S PUTTING HIS LIFE ON THE LINE FOR A SON WHO'S NOT EVEN HIS BY BLOOD.
DON'T SEE THAT KINDA THING EVERY DAY.
BUT...
...SAYING HE CARES ABOUT US...
HE'S NEVER ACTED LIKE WE'RE A REAL FAMILY BEFORE...
MAYBE HE'S HOLDING OUT HOPE YOU'LL ACCEPT HIM AS A DAD ...?
I ENVY YOU...FOR HAVING A DAD LIKE THAT.

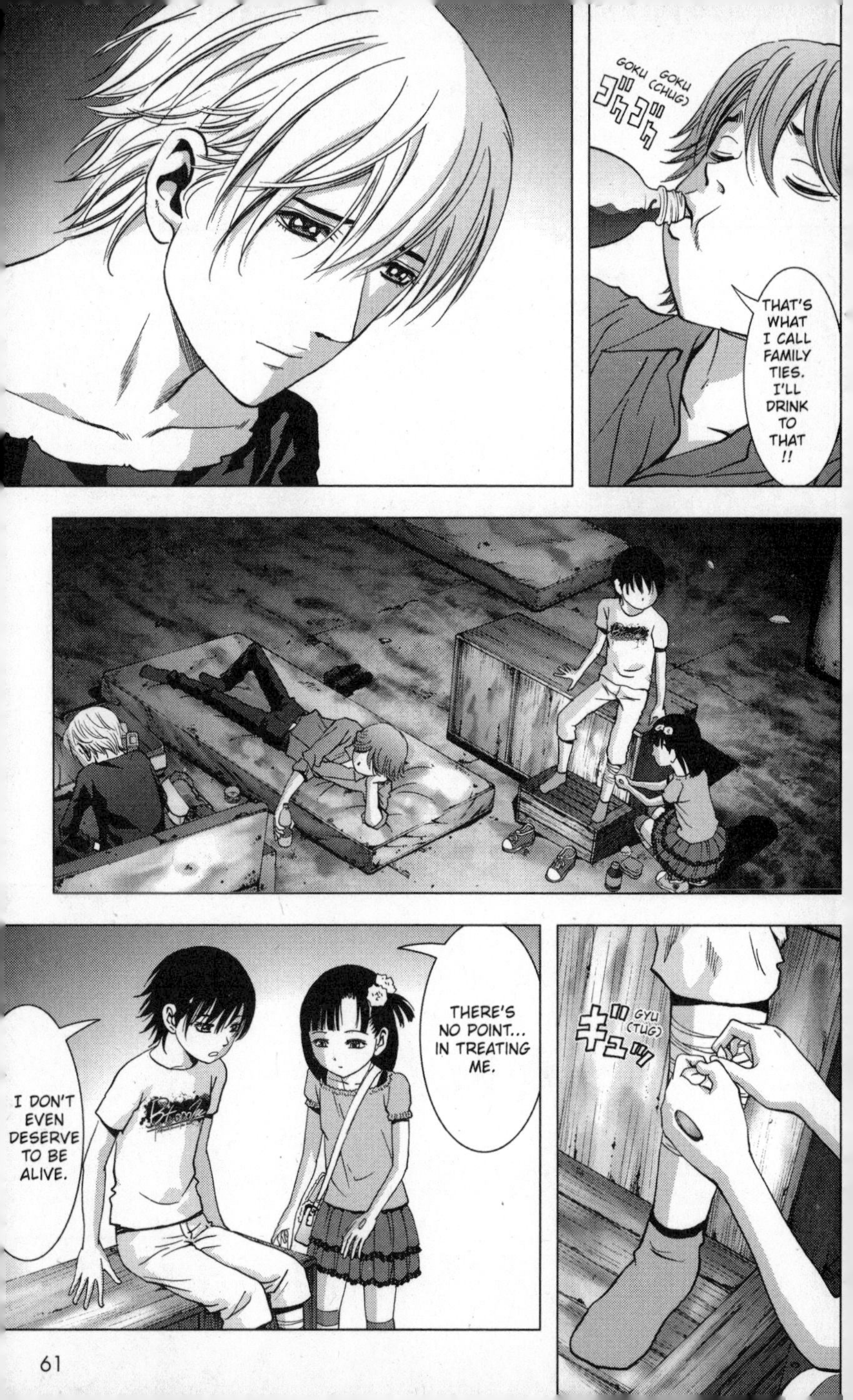
GOKU GOKU (CHUG)
ゴクゴク
THAT'S WHAT I CALL FAMILY TIES. I'LL DRINK TO THAT !!
GYU (TUG)
キュッ
THERE'S NO POINT... IN TREATING ME.
I DON'T EVEN DESERVE TO BE ALIVE.

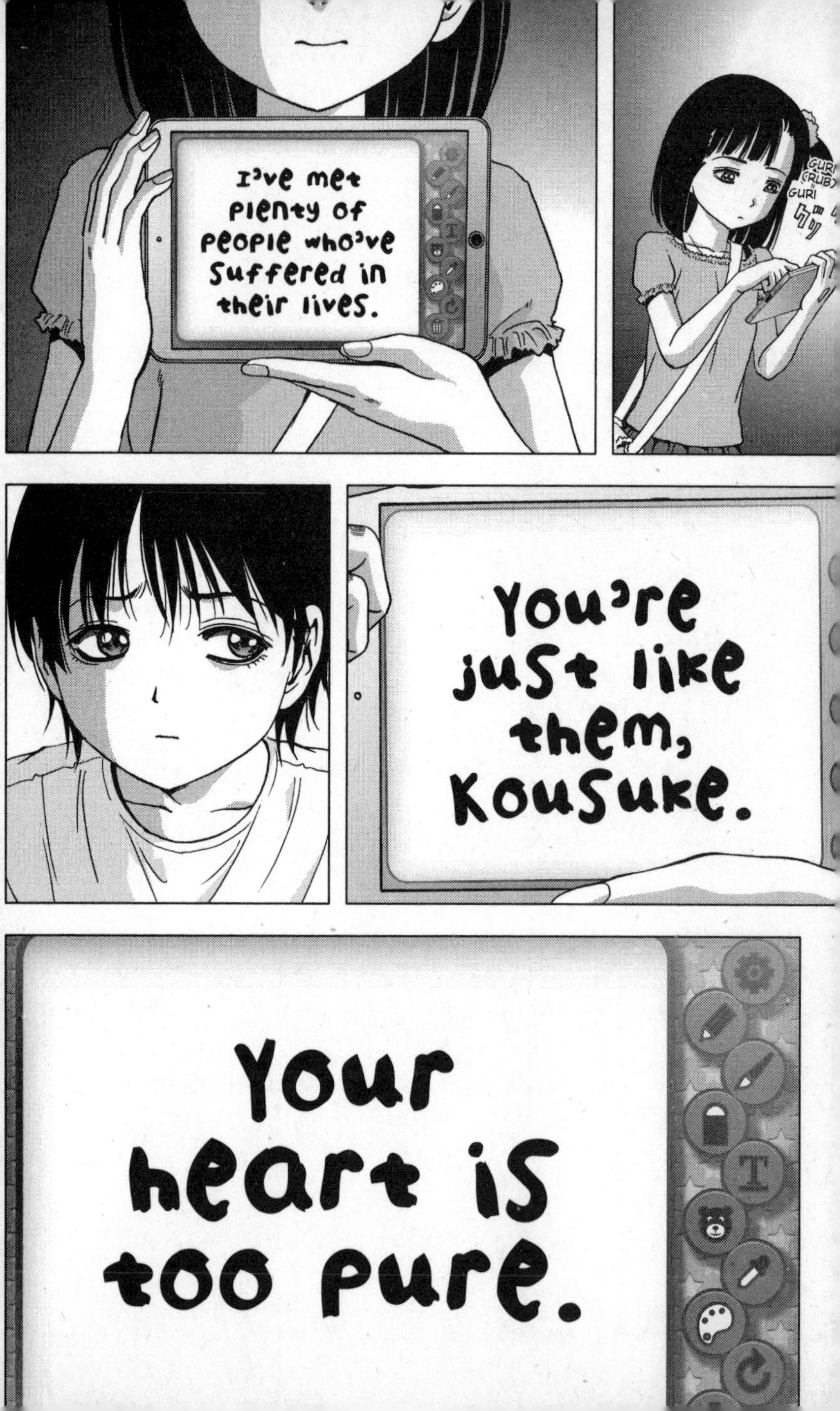
GURI (RUB) GURI
I've met plenty of people who've suffered in their lives.
You're just like them, Kousuke.
Your heart is too pure.

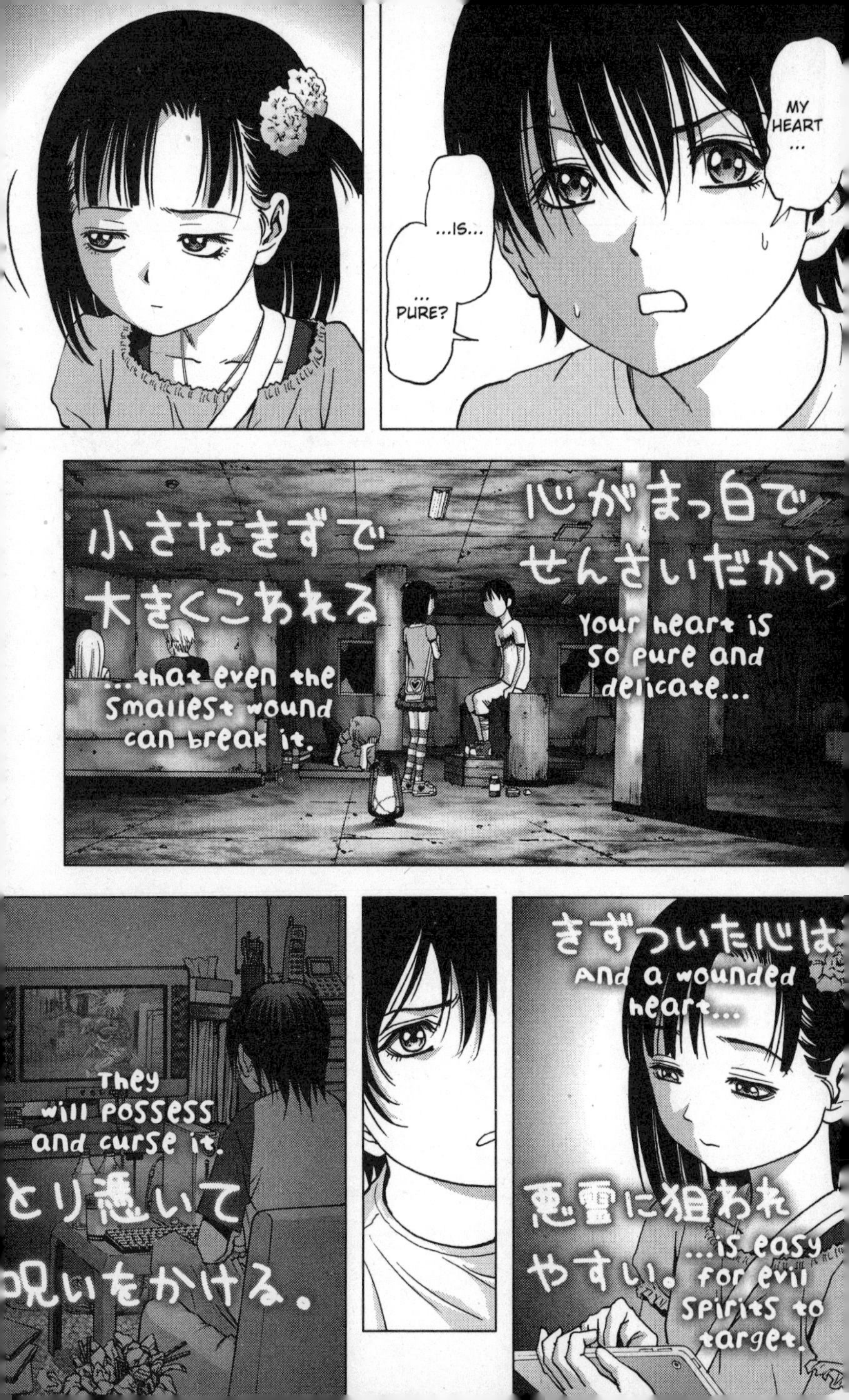
MY HEART ...
...IS...
... PURE?
心がまっ白で せんさいだから
Your heart is so pure and delicate...
小さなきずで 大きくこわれる
...that even the smallest wound can break it.
きずついた心は
And a wounded heart...
悪霊に狙われやすい。
...is easy for evil spirits to target.
とり憑いて 呪いをかける。
They will possess and curse it.

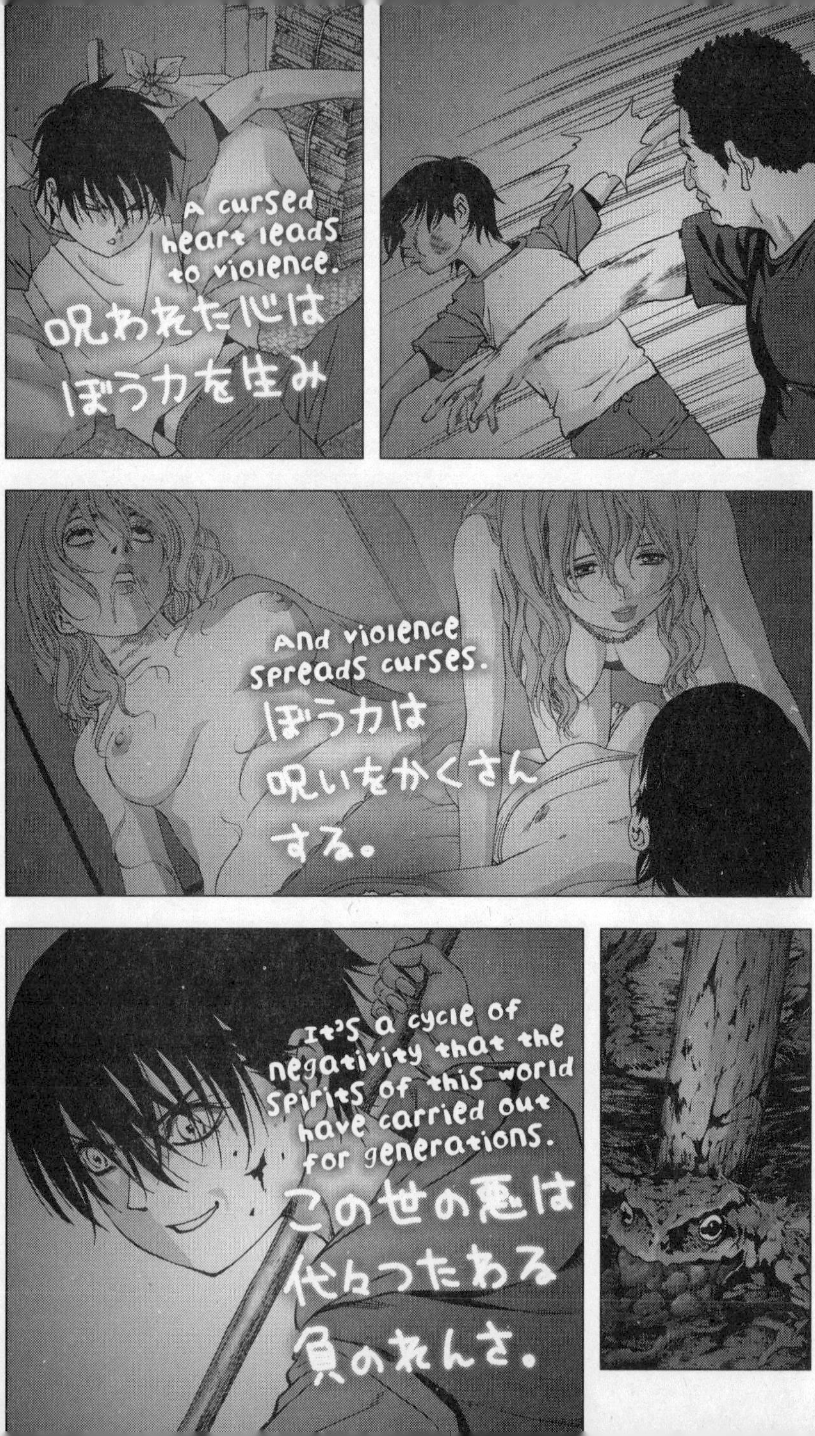
A cursed heart leads to violence.
呪われた心は
ぼう力を生み
And violence spreads curses.
ぼう力は
呪いをかくさん
する。
It's a cycle of negativity that the spirits of this world have carried out for generations.
この世の悪は
代々つたわる
負のれんさ。

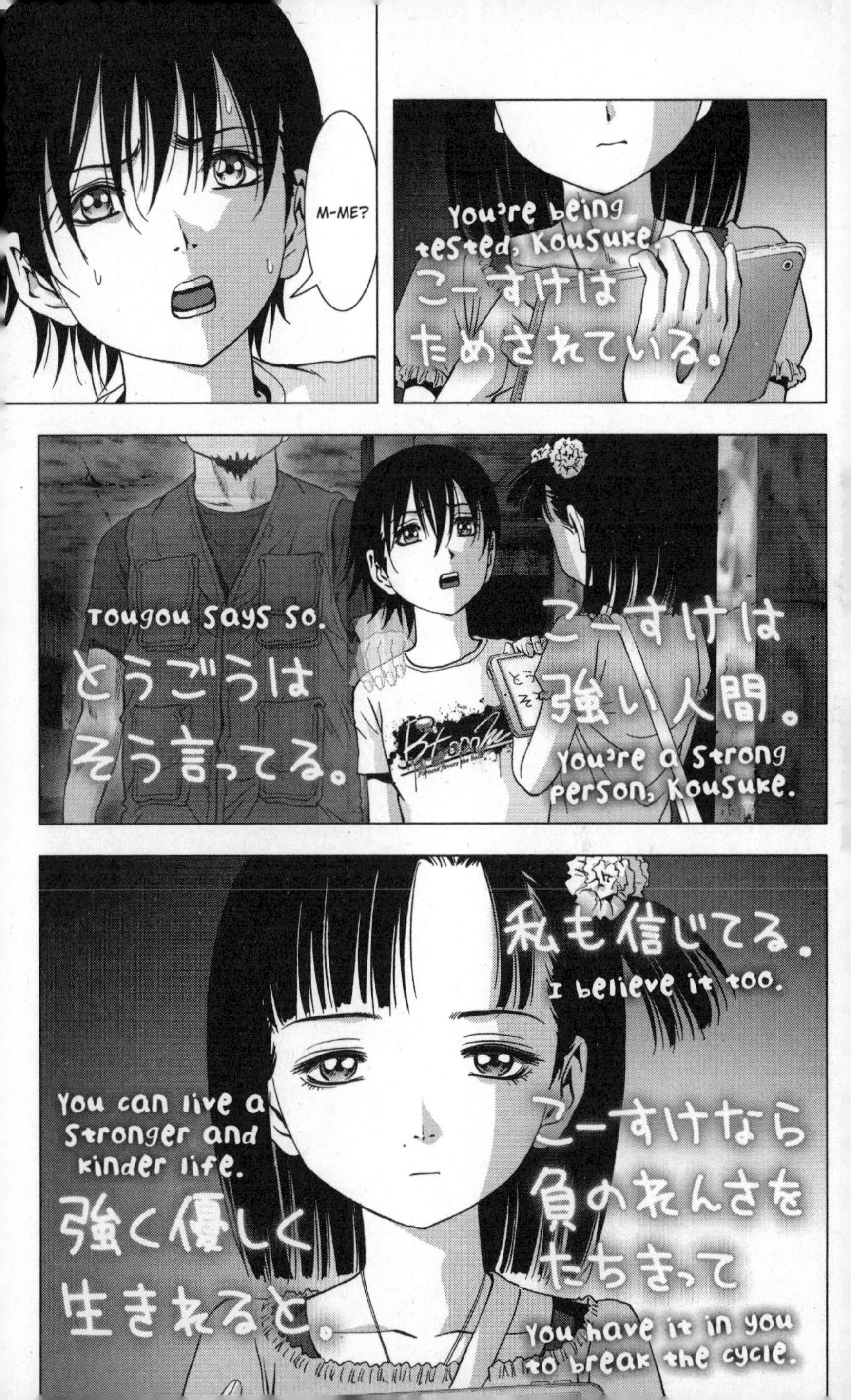
You're being tested, Kousuke.
こーすけはためされている。
M-ME?
こーすけは強い人間。
You're a strong person, Kousuke.
Tougou says so.
とうごうはそう言ってる。
私も信じてる。
I believe it too.
こーすけなら負のれんさをたちきって
You have it in you to break the cycle.
You can live a stronger and kinder life.
強く優しく生きれると。

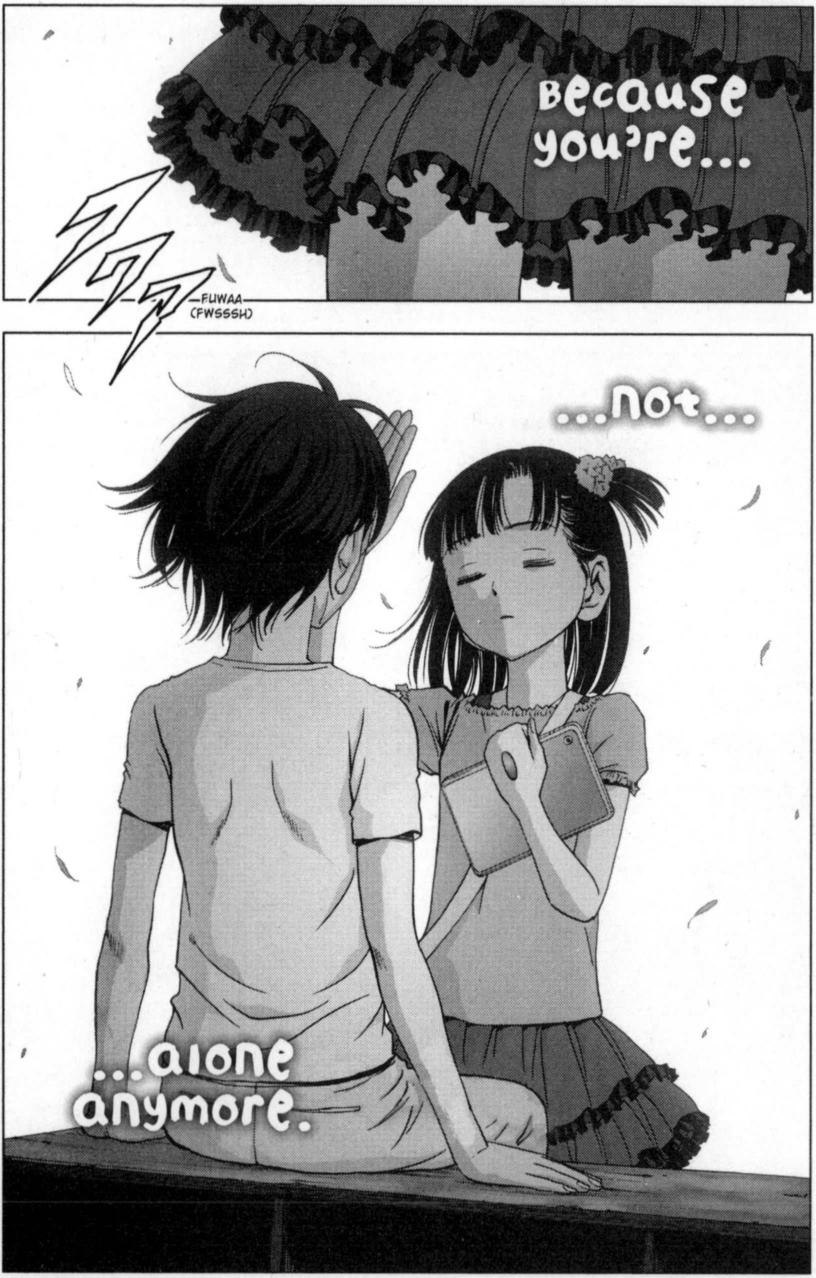
Because you're...
FUWAA (FWSSSH)
...not...
...alone anymore.

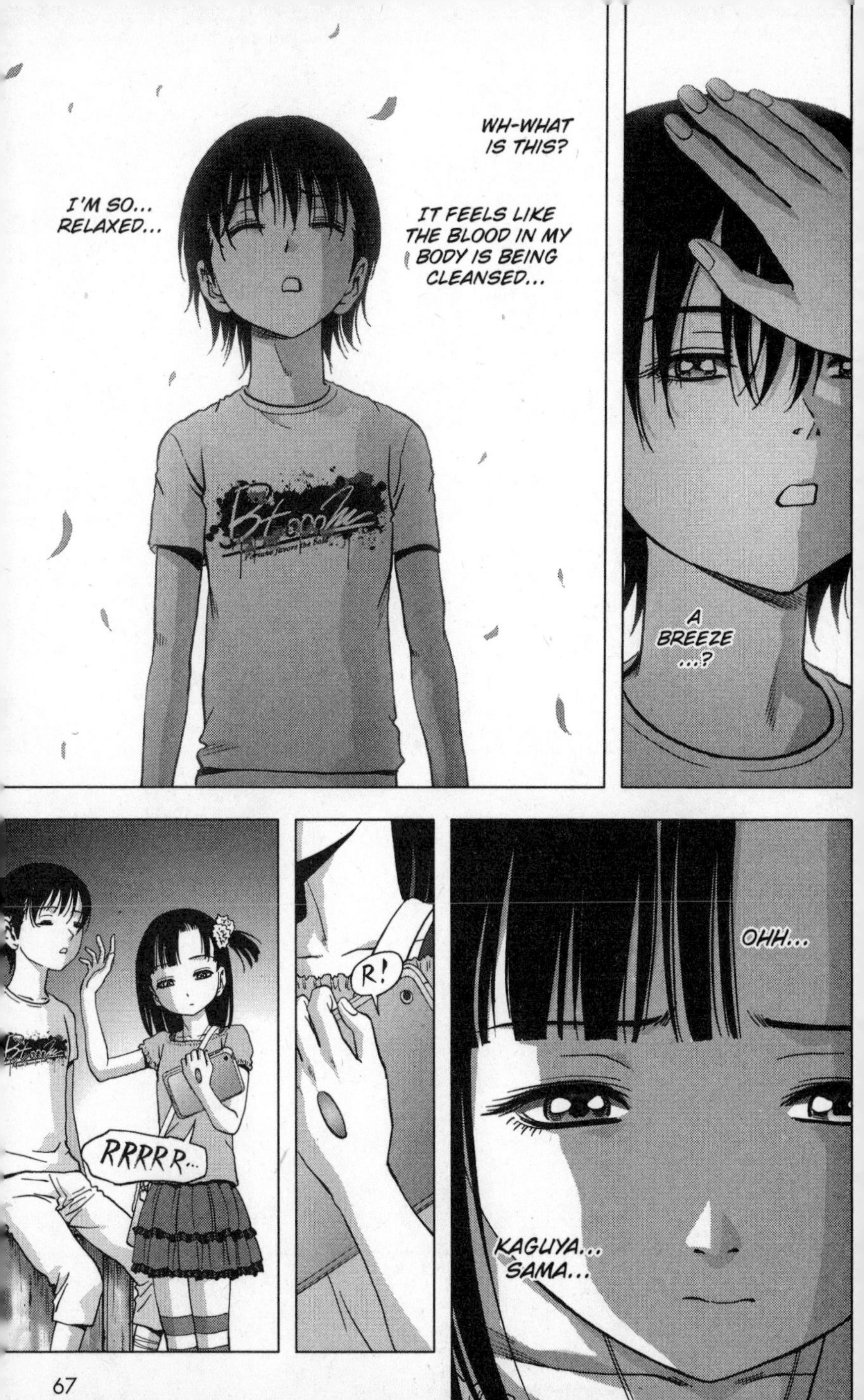
A BREEZE ...?
WH-WHAT IS THIS?
IT FEELS LIKE THE BLOOD IN MY BODY IS BEING CLEANSED...
I'M SO... RELAXED...
OHH...
KAGUYA... SAMA...
R!
RRRRR...

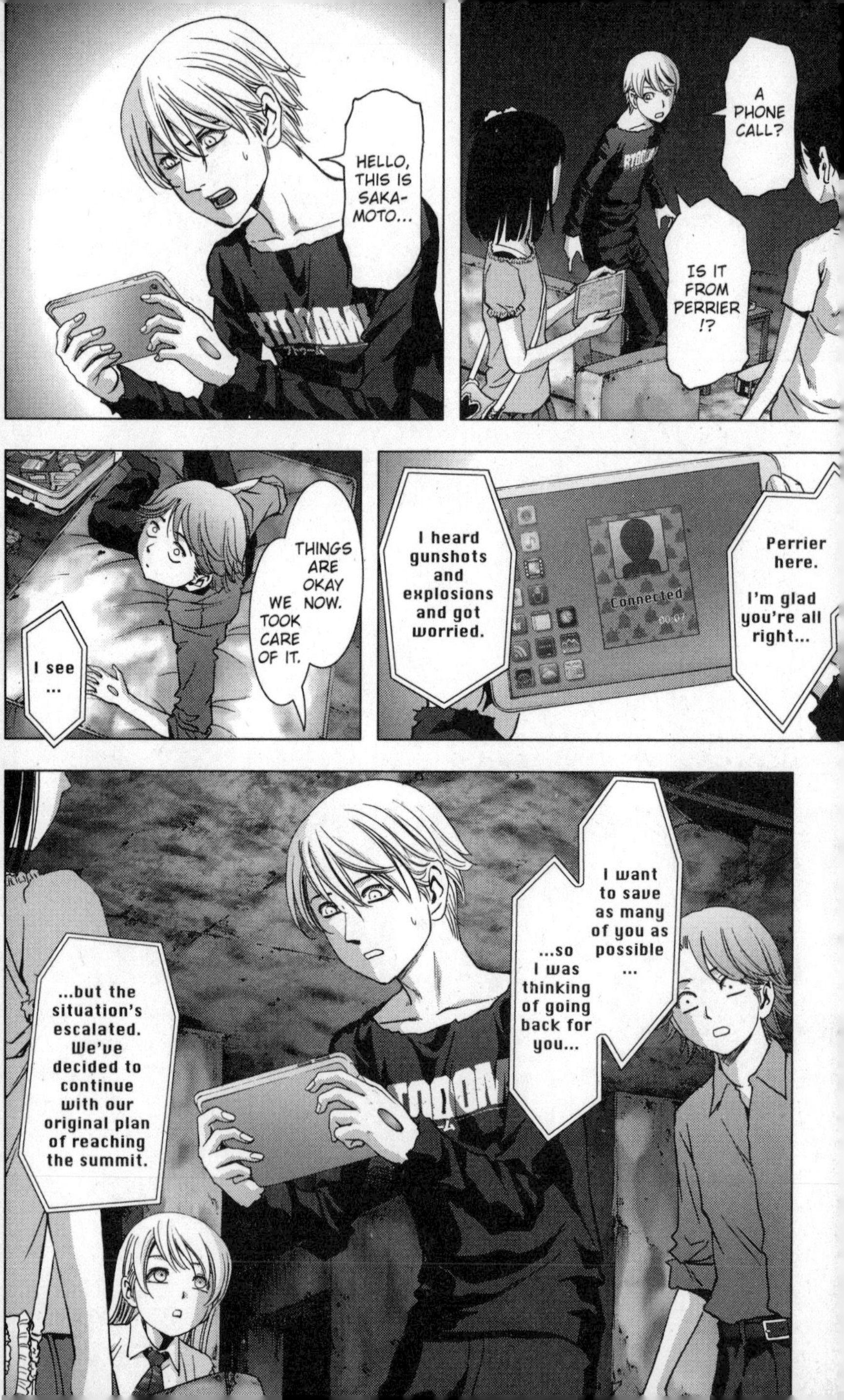
A PHONE CALL?
IS IT FROM PERRIER !?
HELLO, THIS IS SAKA-MOTO...
Perrier here. I'm glad you're all right...
I heard gunshots and explosions and got worried.
THINGS ARE OKAY NOW. WE TOOK CARE OF IT.
I see ...
I want to save as many of you as possible ...
...so I was thinking of going back for you...
...but the situation's escalated. We've decided to continue with our original plan of reaching the summit.

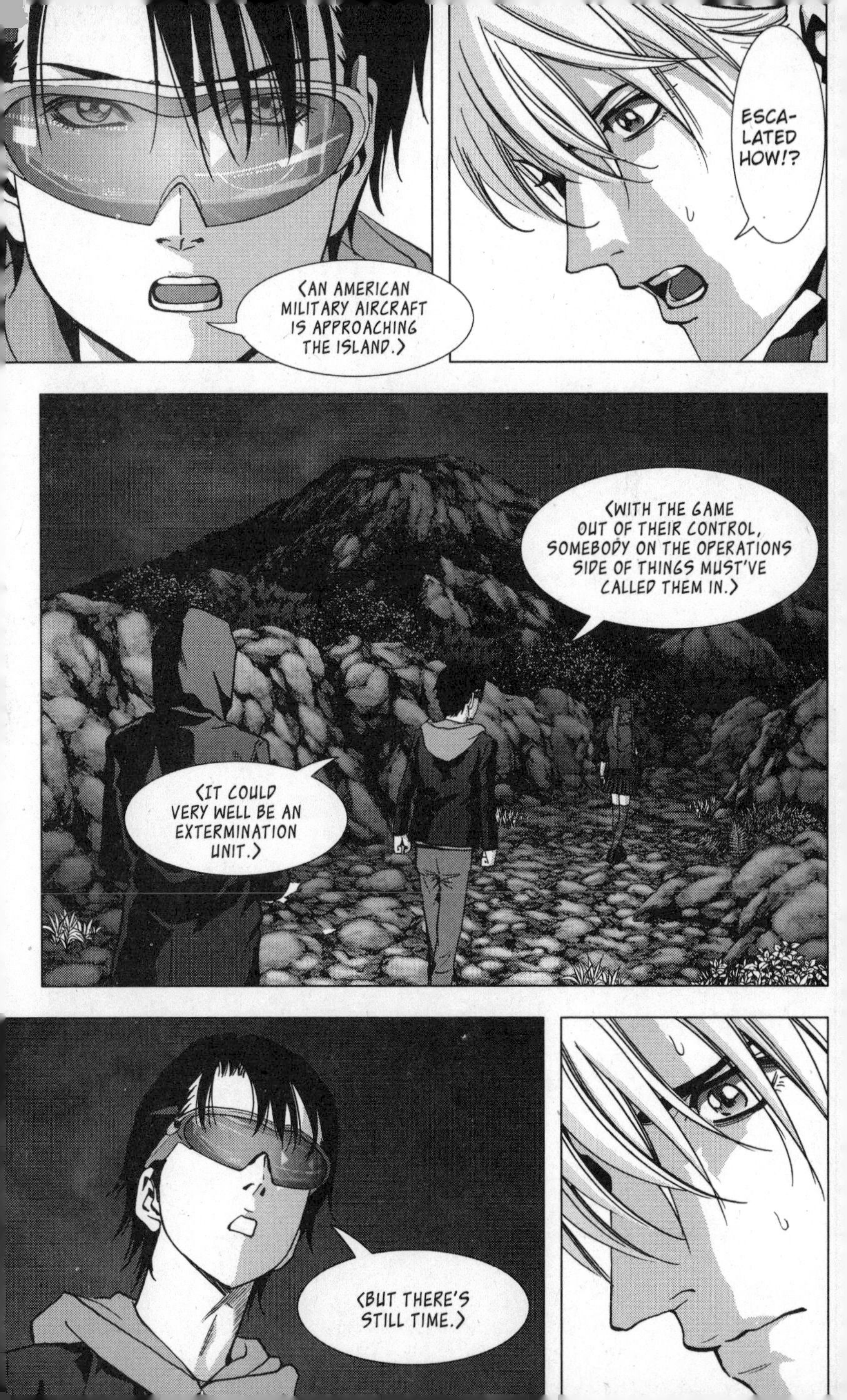
ESCA-LATED HOW!?
‹AN AMERICAN MILITARY AIRCRAFT IS APPROACHING THE ISLAND.›
‹WITH THE GAME OUT OF THEIR CONTROL, SOMEBODY ON THE OPERATIONS SIDE OF THINGS MUST'VE CALLED THEM IN.›
‹IT COULD VERY WELL BE AN EXTERMINATION UNIT.›
‹BUT THERE'S STILL TIME.›

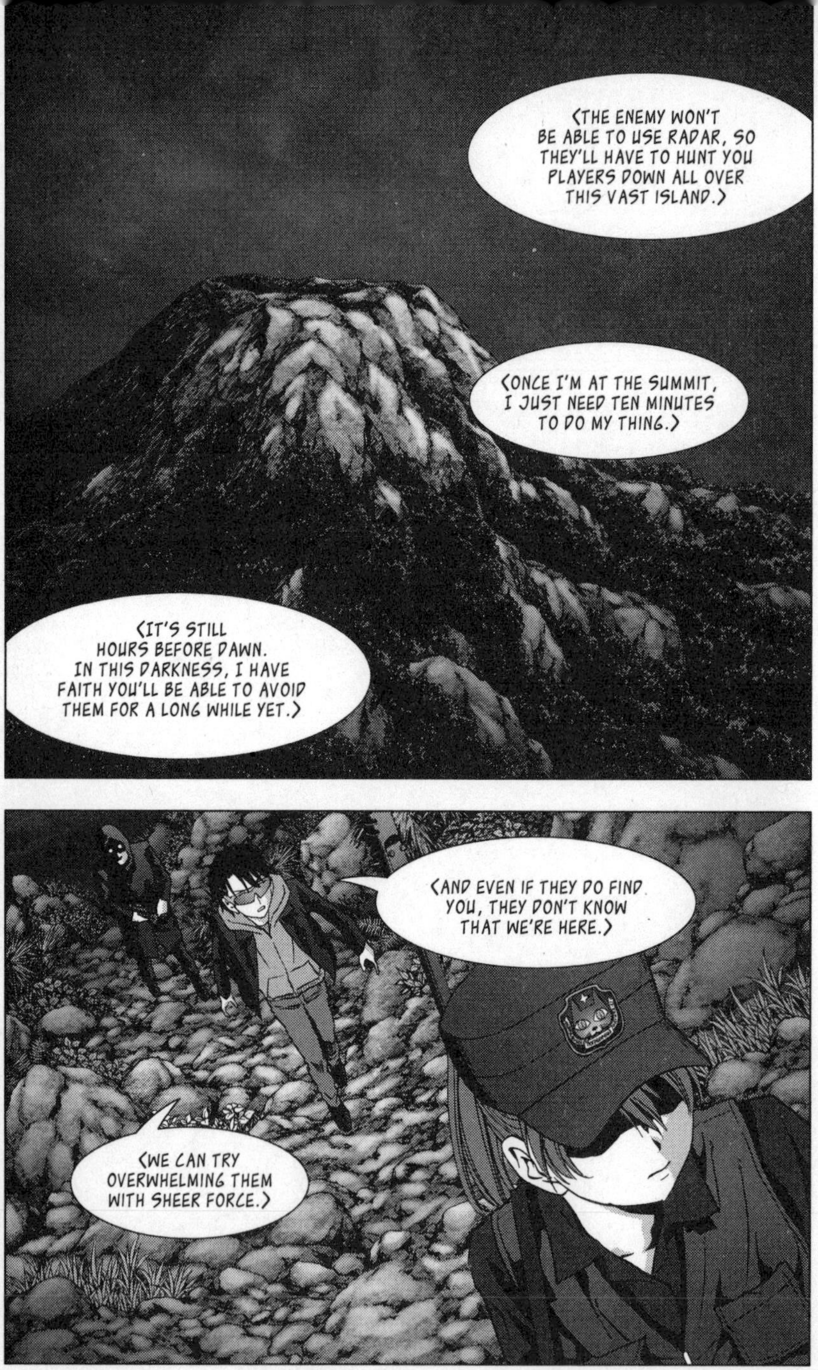
‹THE ENEMY WON'T BE ABLE TO USE RADAR, SO THEY'LL HAVE TO HUNT YOU PLAYERS DOWN ALL OVER THIS VAST ISLAND.›
‹ONCE I'M AT THE SUMMIT, I JUST NEED TEN MINUTES TO DO MY THING.›
‹IT'S STILL HOURS BEFORE DAWN. IN THIS DARKNESS, I HAVE FAITH YOU'LL BE ABLE TO AVOID THEM FOR A LONG WHILE YET.›
‹AND EVEN IF THEY DO FIND YOU, THEY DON'T KNOW THAT WE'RE HERE.›
‹WE CAN TRY OVERWHELMING THEM WITH SHEER FORCE.›

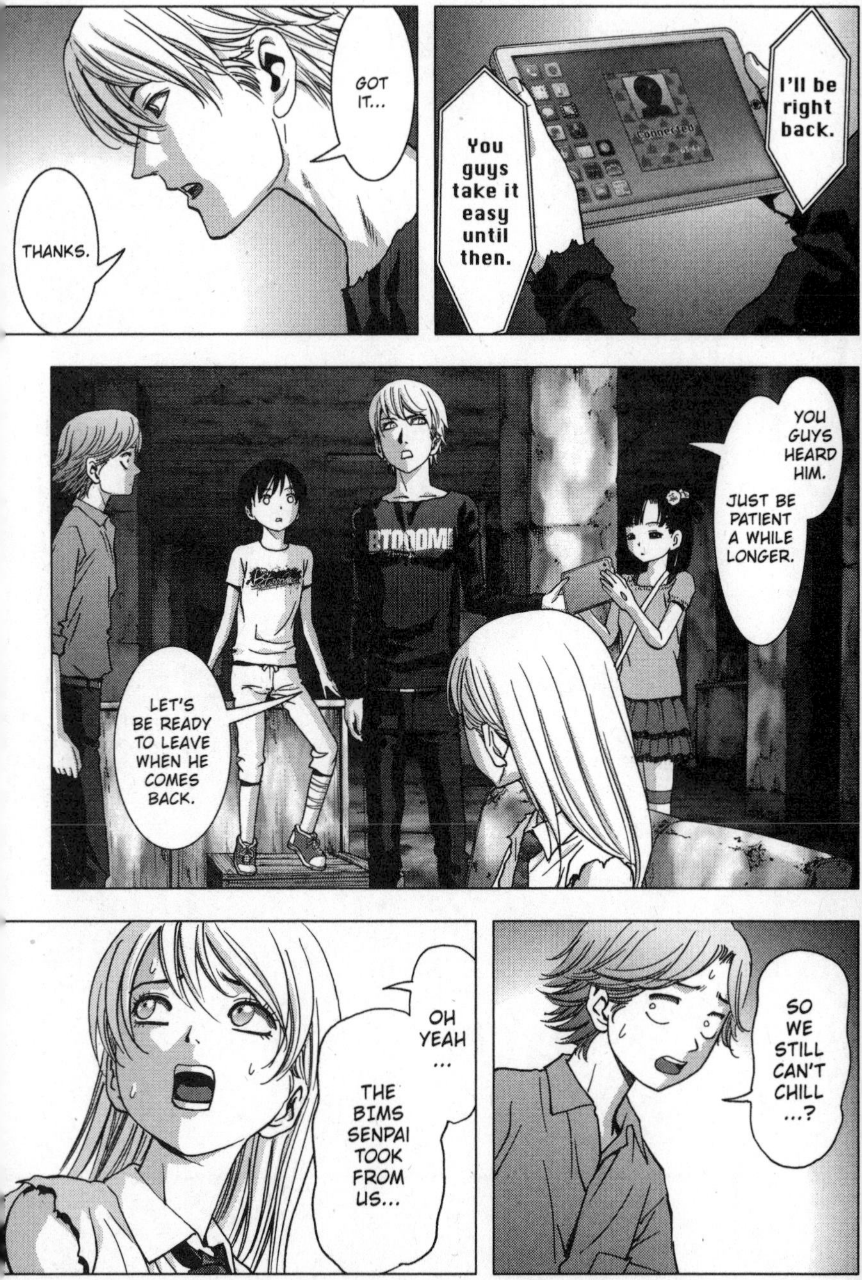
I'll be right back.
You guys take it easy until then.
GOT IT...
THANKS.
YOU GUYS HEARD HIM.
JUST BE PATIENT A WHILE LONGER.
LET'S BE READY TO LEAVE WHEN HE COMES BACK.
SO WE STILL CAN'T CHILL ...?
OH YEAH ...
THE BIMS SENPAI TOOK FROM US...

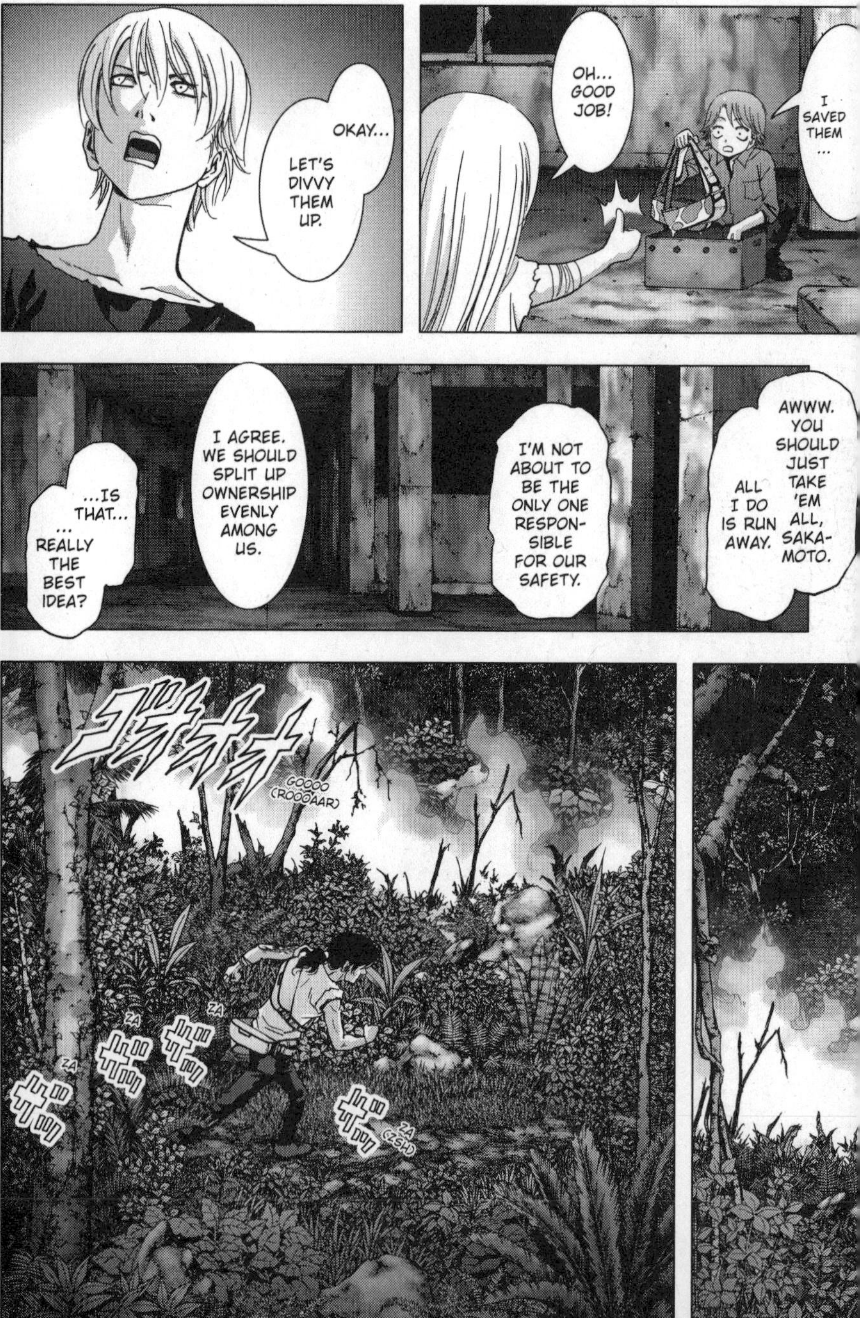
I SAVED THEM ...
OH... GOOD JOB!
OKAY...
LET'S DIVVY THEM UP.
AWWW. YOU SHOULD JUST TAKE 'EM ALL, SAKAMOTO.
ALL I DO IS RUN AWAY.
I'M NOT ABOUT TO BE THE ONLY ONE RESPONSIBLE FOR OUR SAFETY.
I AGREE. WE SHOULD SPLIT UP OWNERSHIP EVENLY AMONG US.
...IS THAT... ...REALLY THE BEST IDEA?
GOOOO (ROOOAAR)
ZA
ZA
ZA
ZA (ZSH)

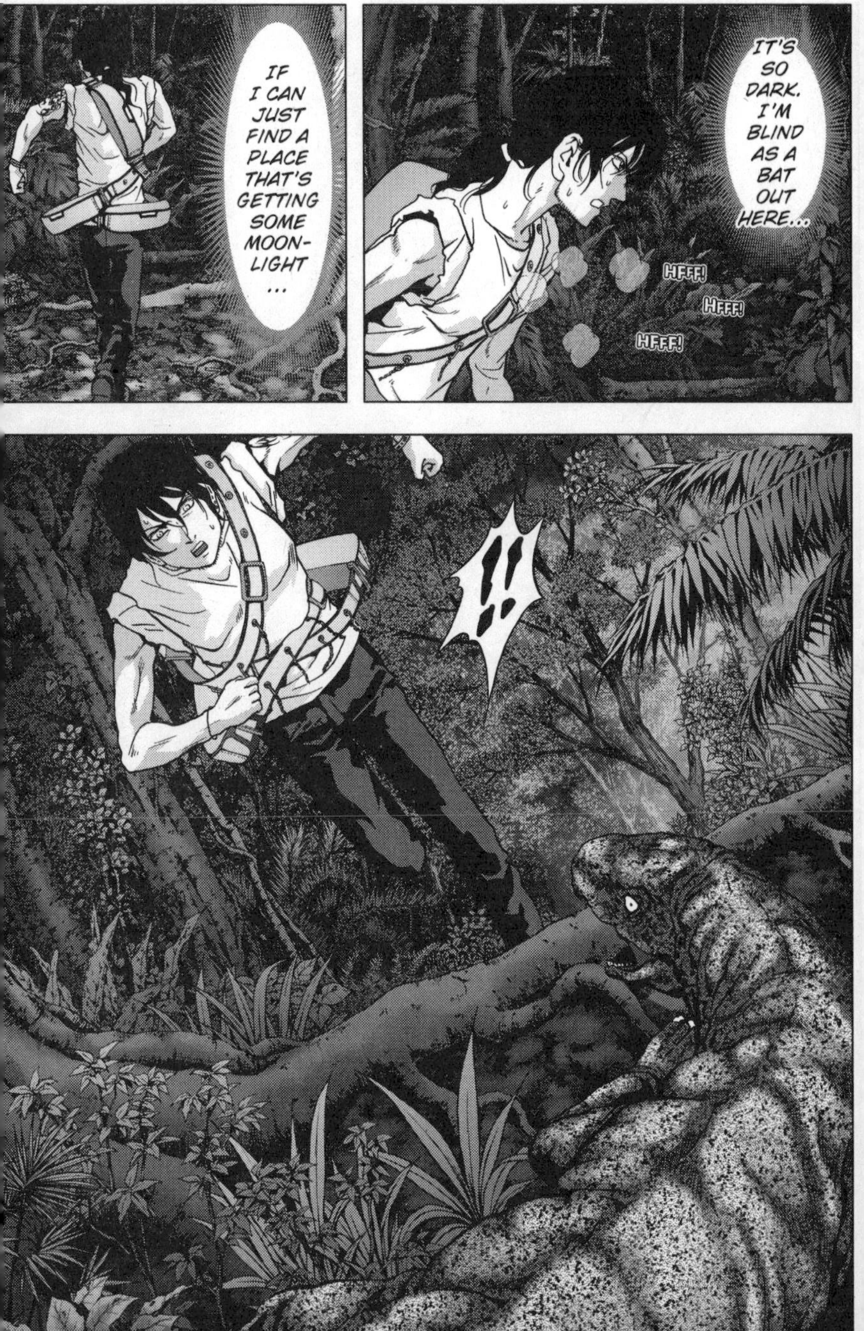
IT'S SO DARK. I'M BLIND AS A BAT OUT HERE...
HFFF!
HFFF!
HFFF!
IF I CAN JUST FIND A PLACE THAT'S GETTING SOME MOON-LIGHT ...
!!

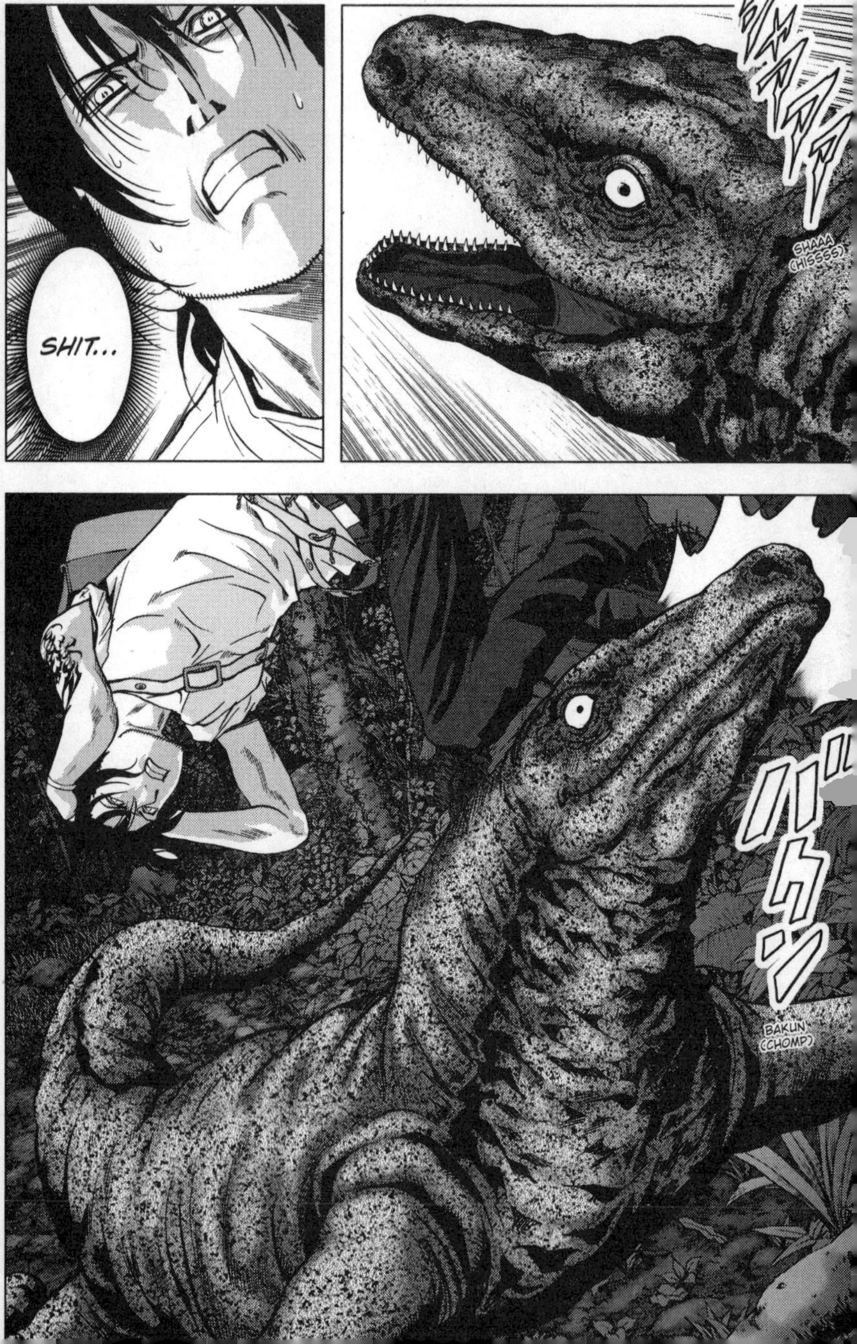
SHAAA (HISSSS)
SHIT...
BAKUN (CHOMP)

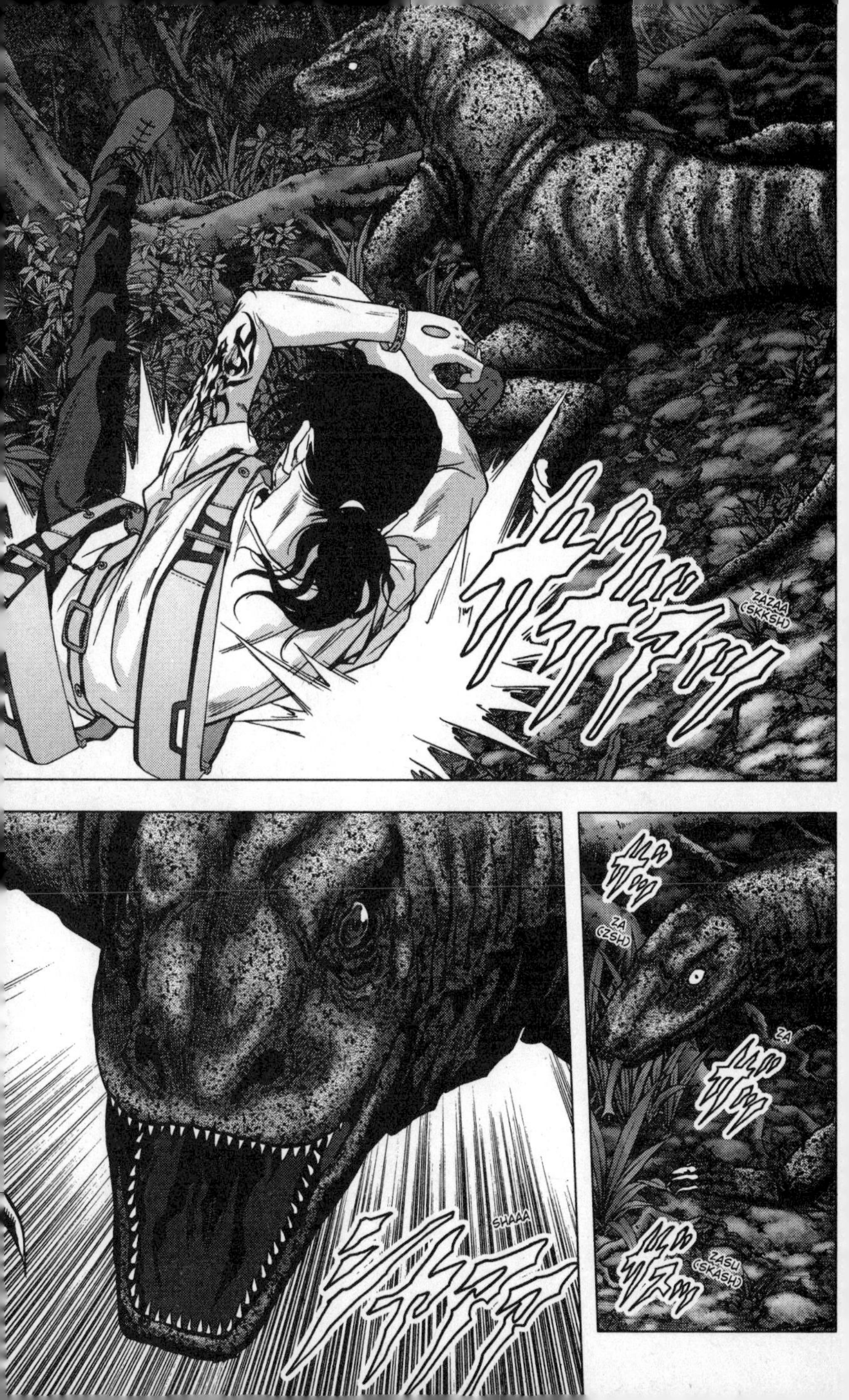
ZAZAA
(SKKSH)
ZA
(ZSH)
ZA
ZASU
(SKASH)
SHAAA

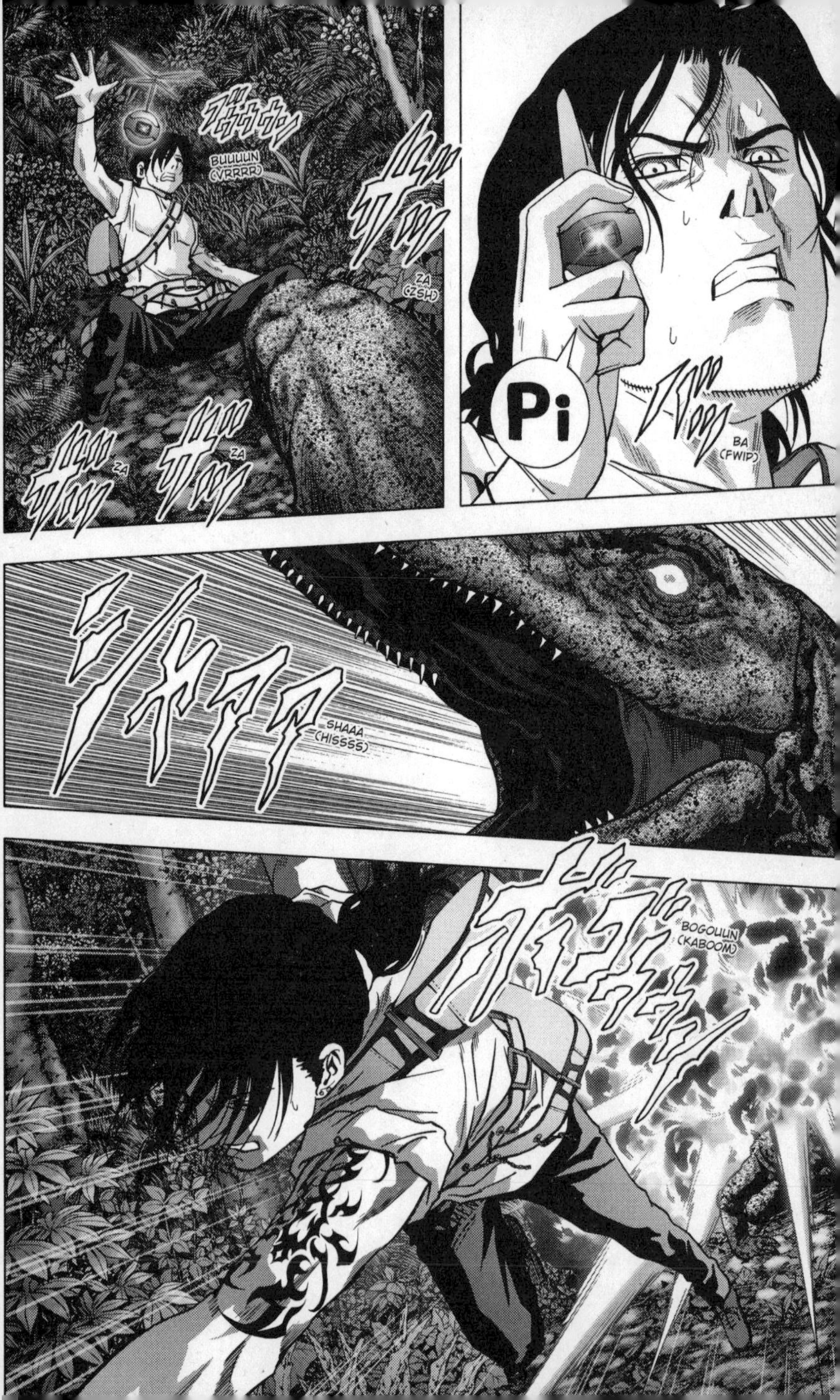
Pi
BA (FWIP)
BUUUUN (VRRRR)
ZA (ZSH)
ZA
ZA
SHAAA (HISSSS)
BOGOUUN (KABOOM)

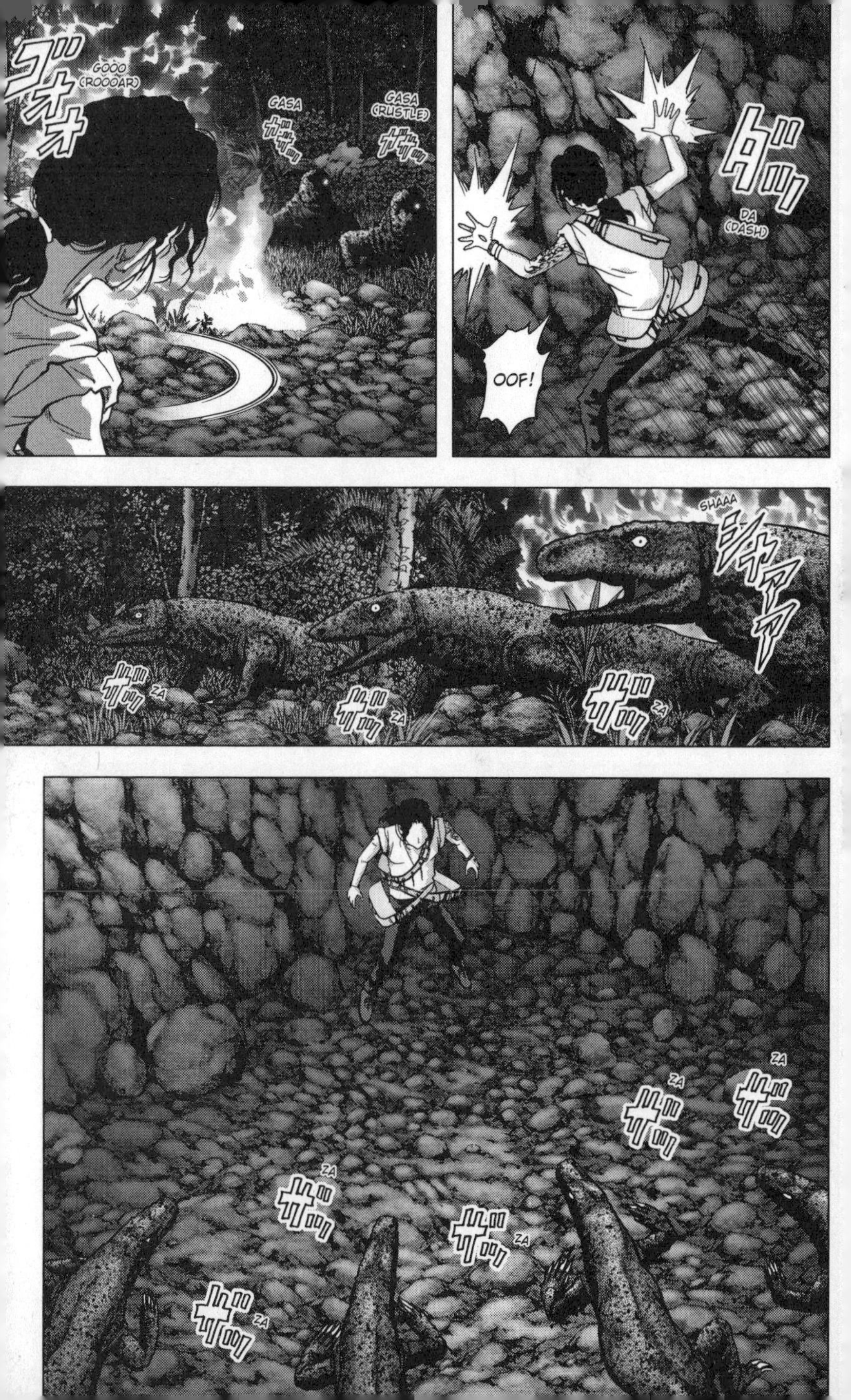

ダッ
DA (DASH)
OOF!
ガサッ
GASA (RUSTLE)
ガサッ
GASA
ゴォオ
GOOO (ROOOAR)
シャアア
SHAAA
ザッ
ZA
ザッ
ZA
ザッ
ZA
ZA
ZA
ZA
ZA
ZA

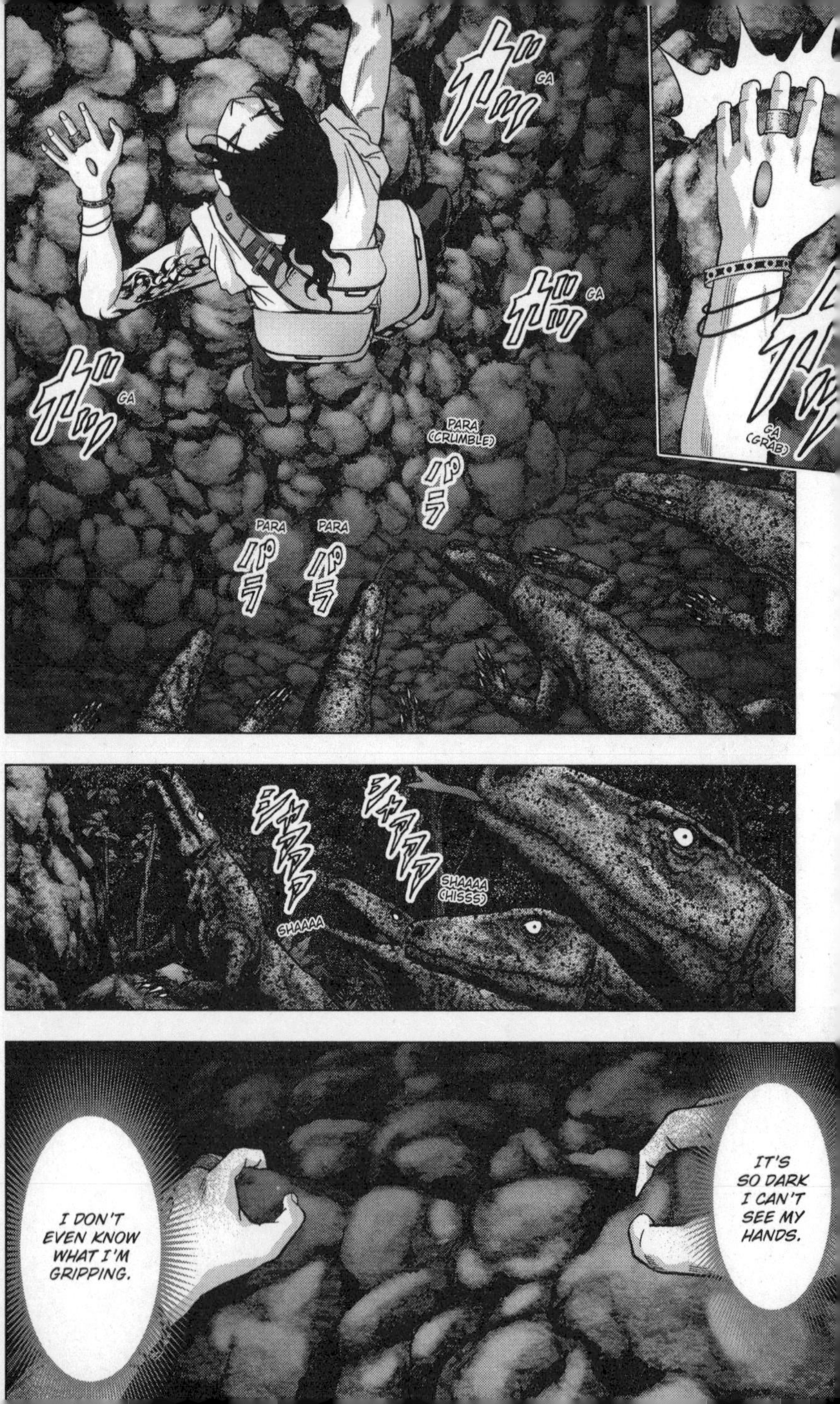
GA (GRAB)
GA
GA
PARA (CRUMBLE)
PARA
PARA
GA
SHAAAA (HISSS)
SHAAAA
IT'S SO DARK I CAN'T SEE MY HANDS.
I DON'T EVEN KNOW WHAT I'M GRIPPING.

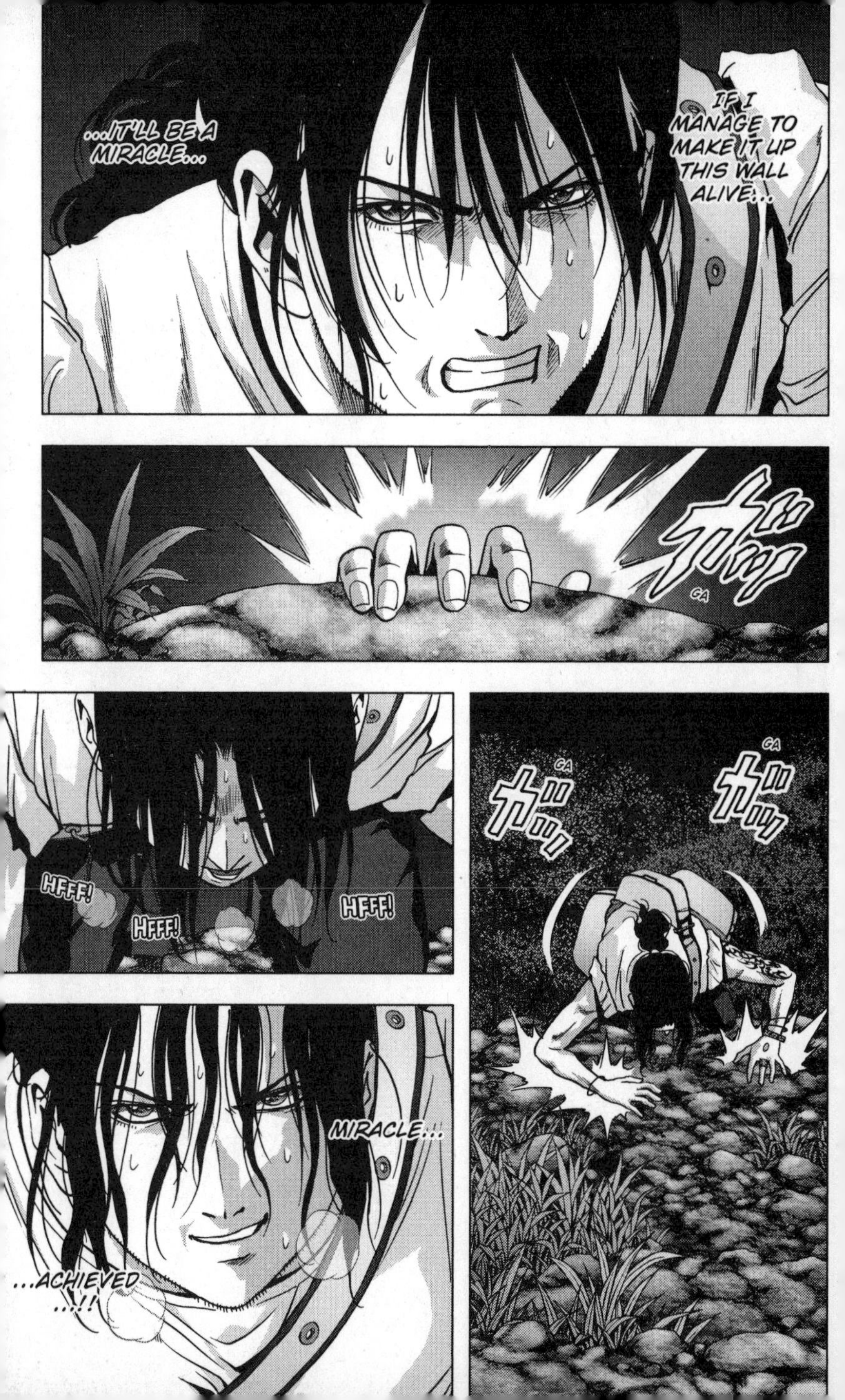
IF I MANAGE TO MAKE IT UP THIS WALL ALIVE...
...IT'LL BE A MIRACLE...
GA
GA
GA
HFFF!
HFFF!
HFFF!
MIRACLE...
...ACHIEVED ...!!

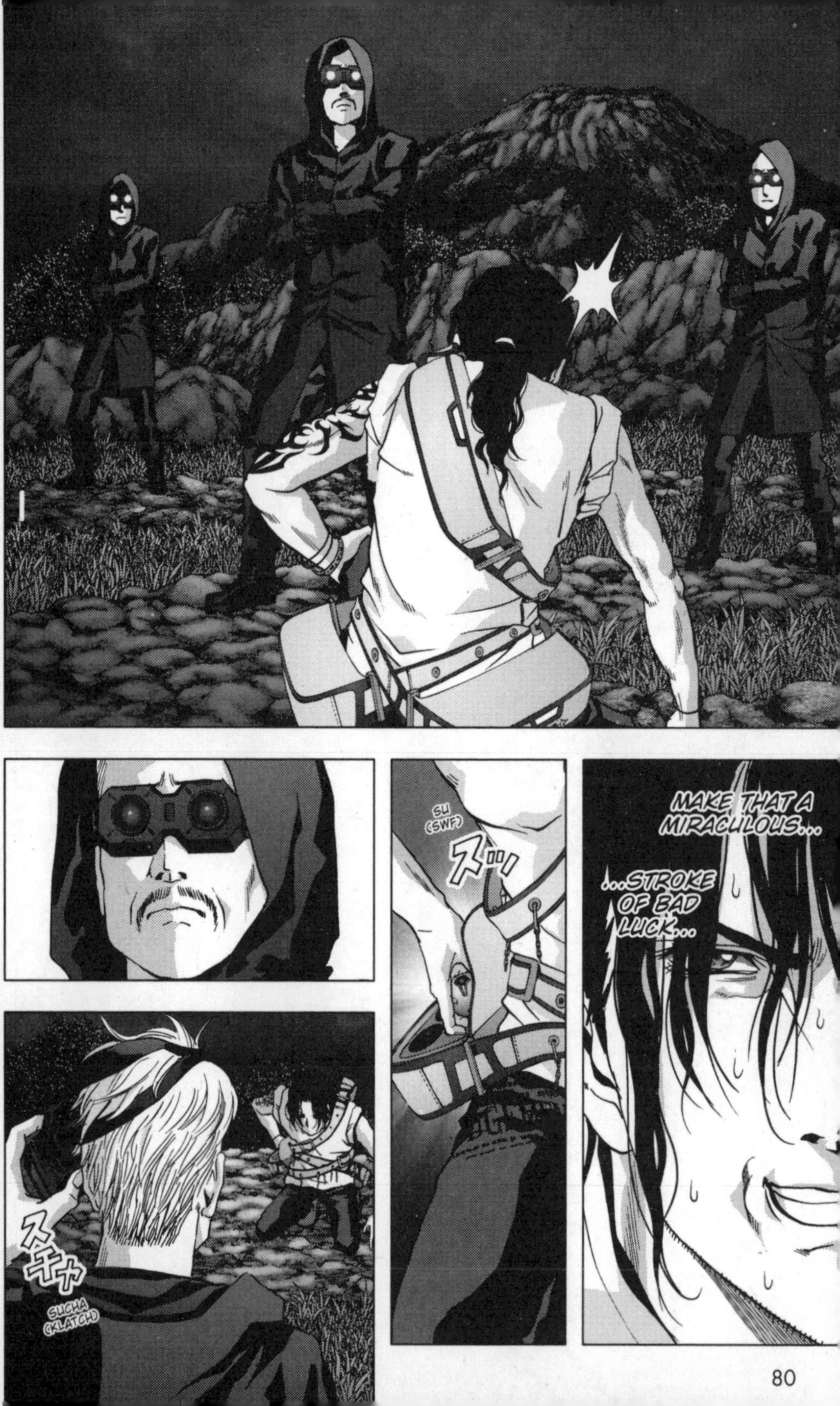
MAKE THAT A MIRACULOUS...
...STROKE OF BAD LUCK...
ズッ
SU (SWF)
スチャ
SUCHA (KLATCH)

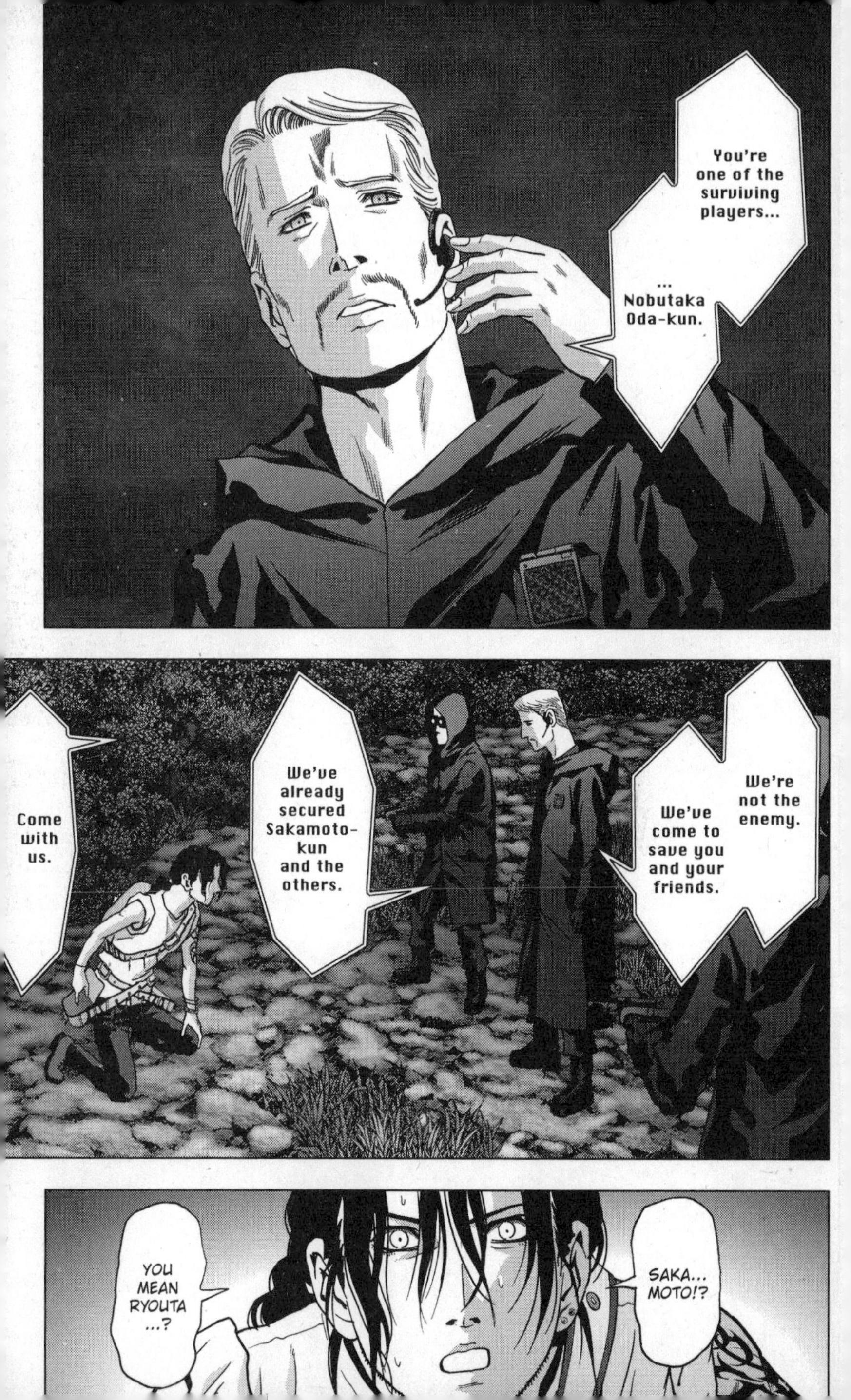
You're one of the surviving players...
... Nobutaka Oda-kun.
We're not the enemy.
We've come to save you and your friends.
We've already secured Sakamoto-kun and the others.
Come with us.
SAKA... MOTO!?
YOU MEAN RYOUTA ...?

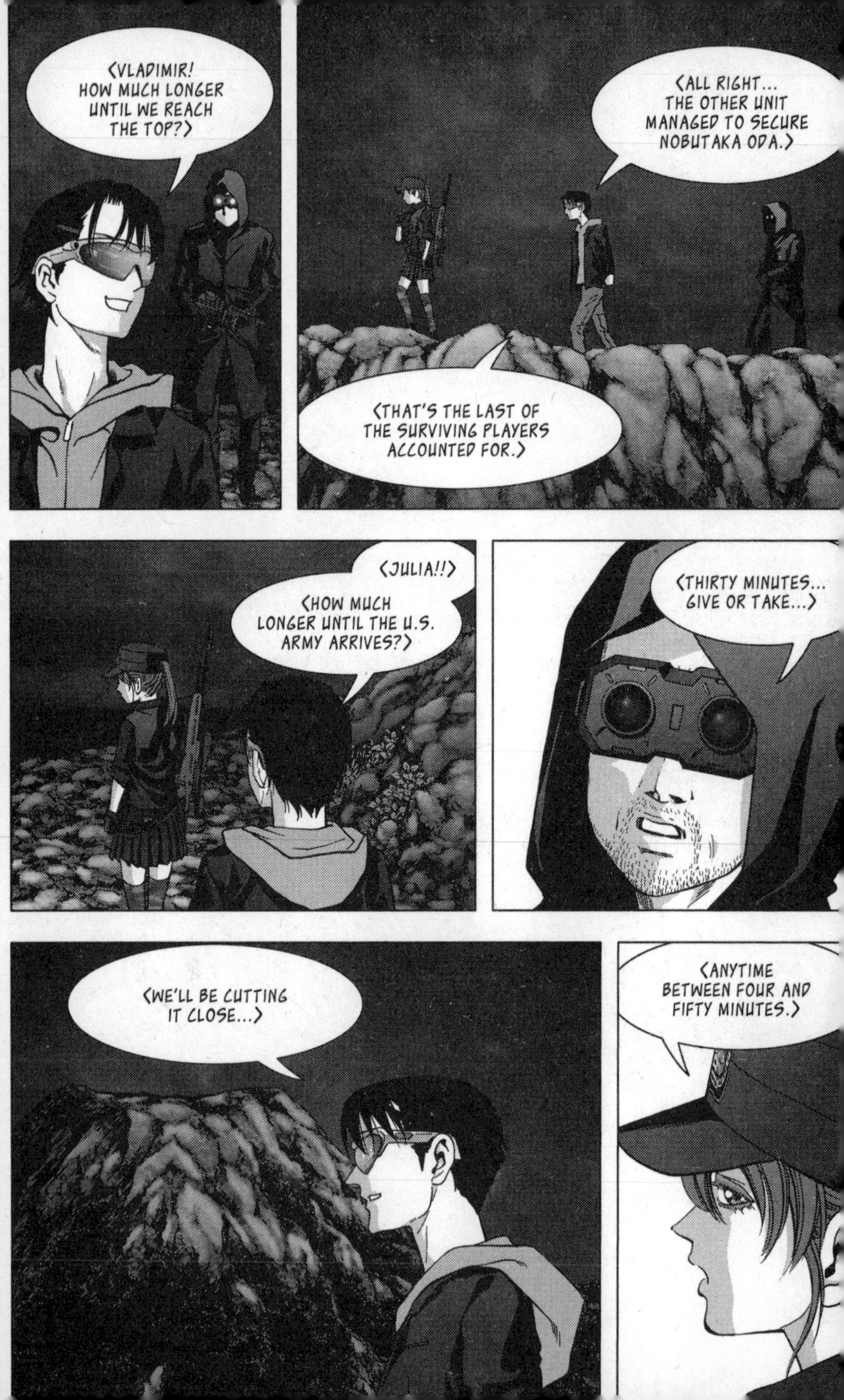

<ALL RIGHT... THE OTHER UNIT MANAGED TO SECURE NOBUTAKA ODA.>
<THAT'S THE LAST OF THE SURVIVING PLAYERS ACCOUNTED FOR.>
<VLADIMIR! HOW MUCH LONGER UNTIL WE REACH THE TOP?>
<THIRTY MINUTES... GIVE OR TAKE...>
<JULIA!!>
<HOW MUCH LONGER UNTIL THE U.S. ARMY ARRIVES?>
<ANYTIME BETWEEN FOUR AND FIFTY MINUTES.>
<WE'LL BE CUTTING IT CLOSE...>

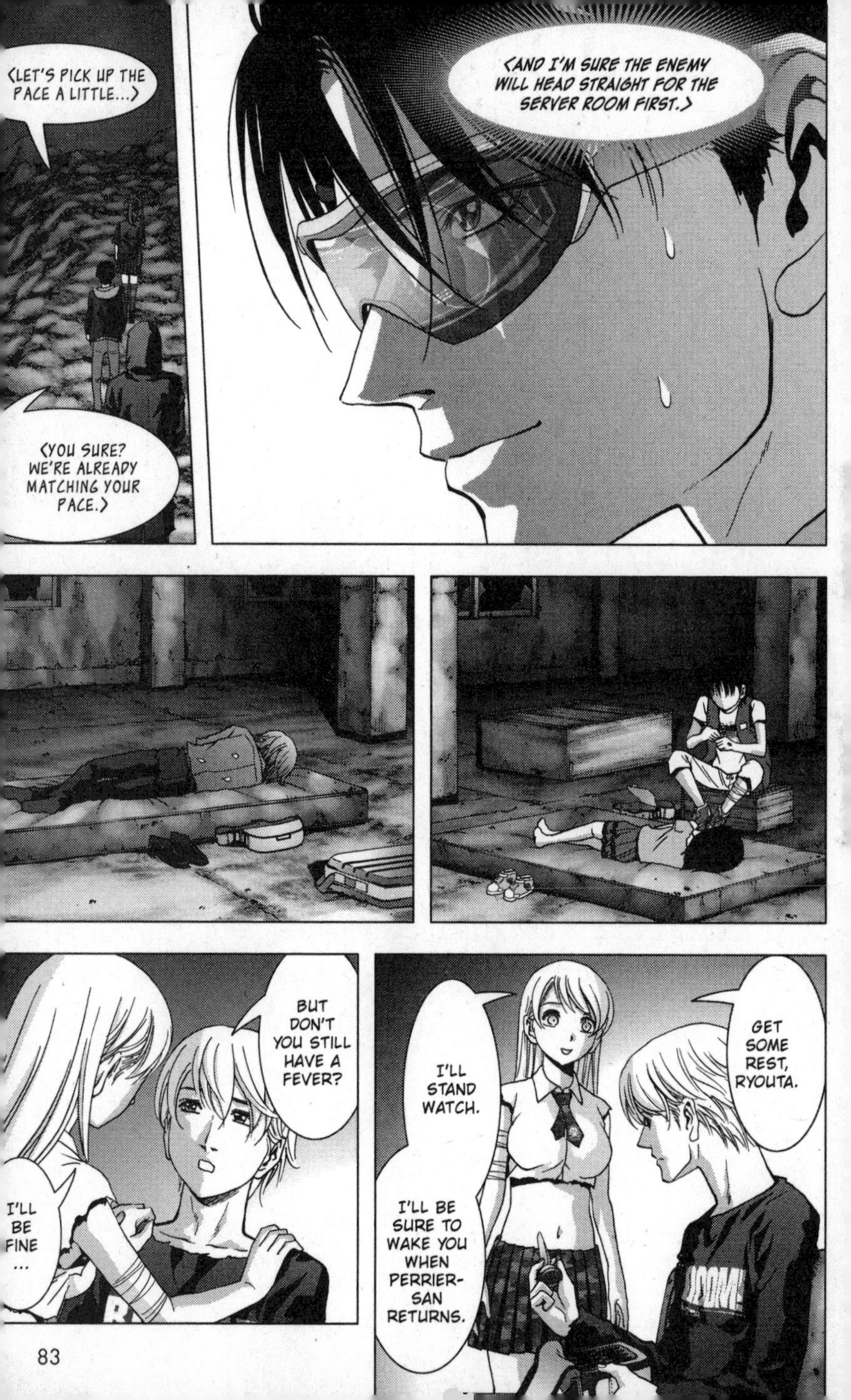

<AND I'M SURE THE ENEMY WILL HEAD STRAIGHT FOR THE SERVER ROOM FIRST.>
<LET'S PICK UP THE PACE A LITTLE...>
<YOU SURE? WE'RE ALREADY MATCHING YOUR PACE.>
GET SOME REST, RYOUTA.
I'LL STAND WATCH.
I'LL BE SURE TO WAKE YOU WHEN PERRIER-SAN RETURNS.
BUT DON'T YOU STILL HAVE A FEVER?
I'LL BE FINE ...

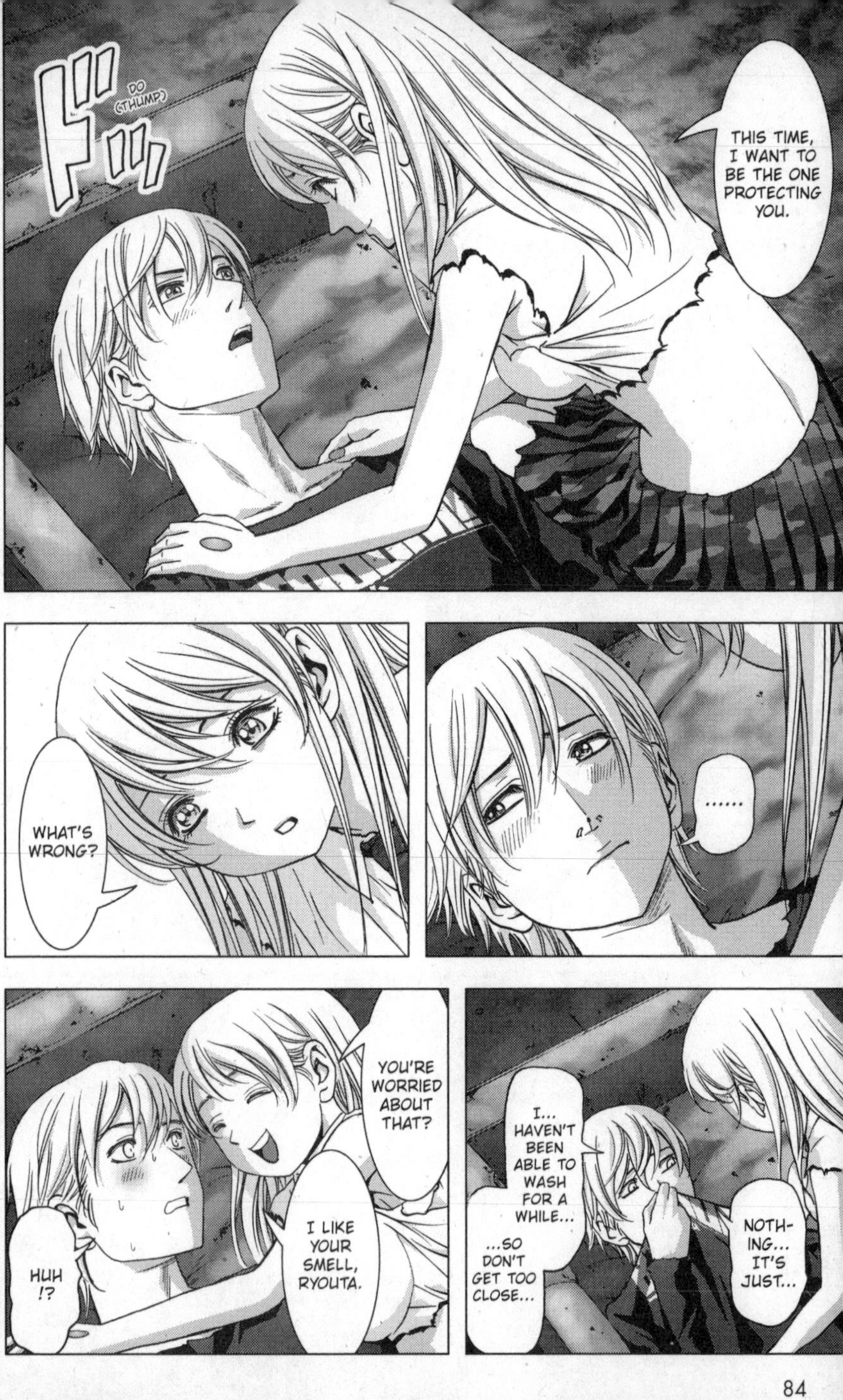
THIS TIME, I WANT TO BE THE ONE PROTECTING YOU.
ド
DO (THUMP)
......
WHAT'S WRONG?
NOTH-ING... IT'S JUST...
I... HAVEN'T BEEN ABLE TO WASH FOR A WHILE...
...SO DON'T GET TOO CLOSE...
YOU'RE WORRIED ABOUT THAT?
I LIKE YOUR SMELL, RYOUTA.
HUH !?

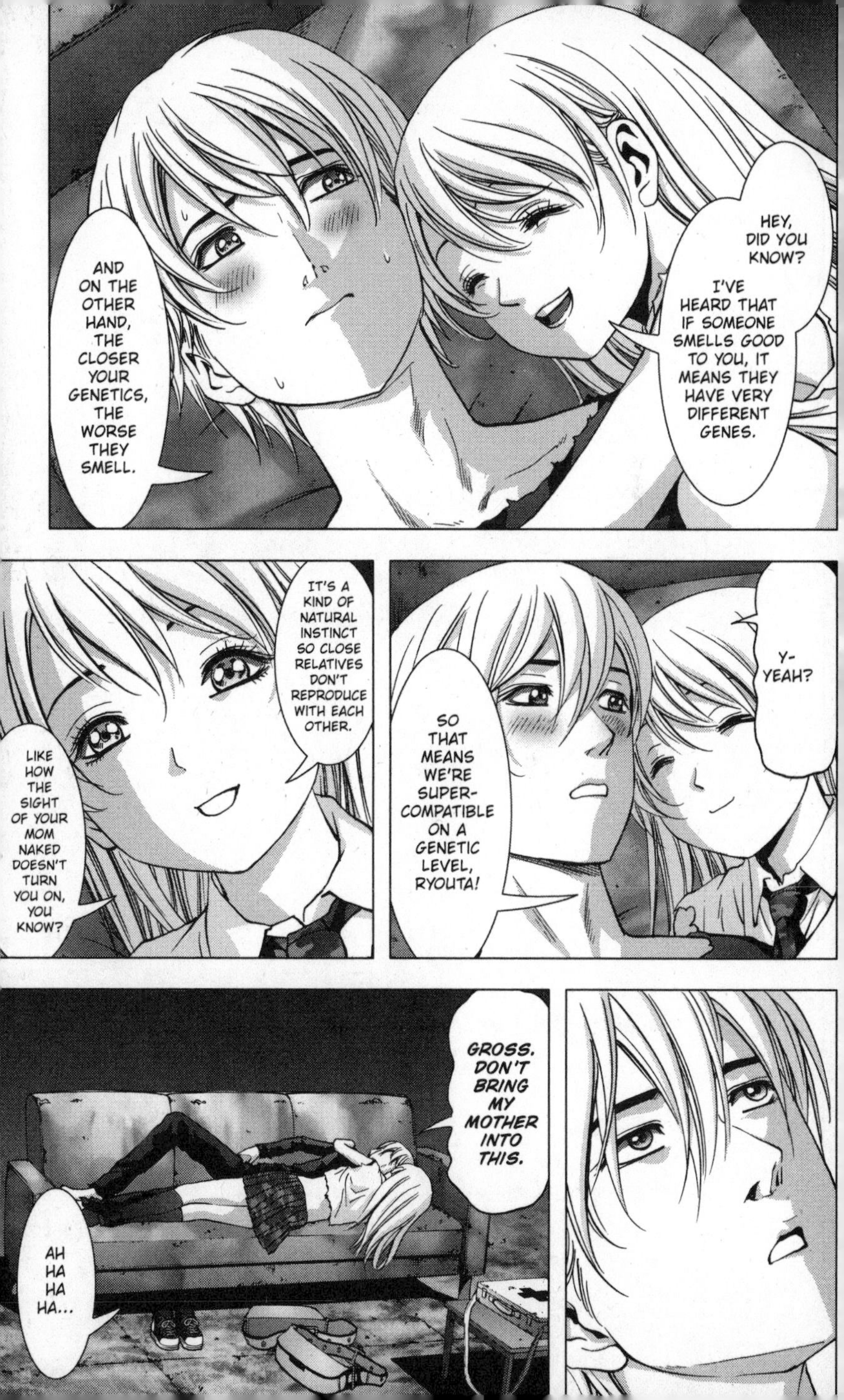
HEY, DID YOU KNOW?
I'VE HEARD THAT IF SOMEONE SMELLS GOOD TO YOU, IT MEANS THEY HAVE VERY DIFFERENT GENES.
AND ON THE OTHER HAND, THE CLOSER YOUR GENETICS, THE WORSE THEY SMELL.
Y-YEAH?
SO THAT MEANS WE'RE SUPER-COMPATIBLE ON A GENETIC LEVEL, RYOUTA!
IT'S A KIND OF NATURAL INSTINCT SO CLOSE RELATIVES DON'T REPRODUCE WITH EACH OTHER.
LIKE HOW THE SIGHT OF YOUR MOM NAKED DOESN'T TURN YOU ON, YOU KNOW?
GROSS. DON'T BRING MY MOTHER INTO THIS.
AH HA HA HA...

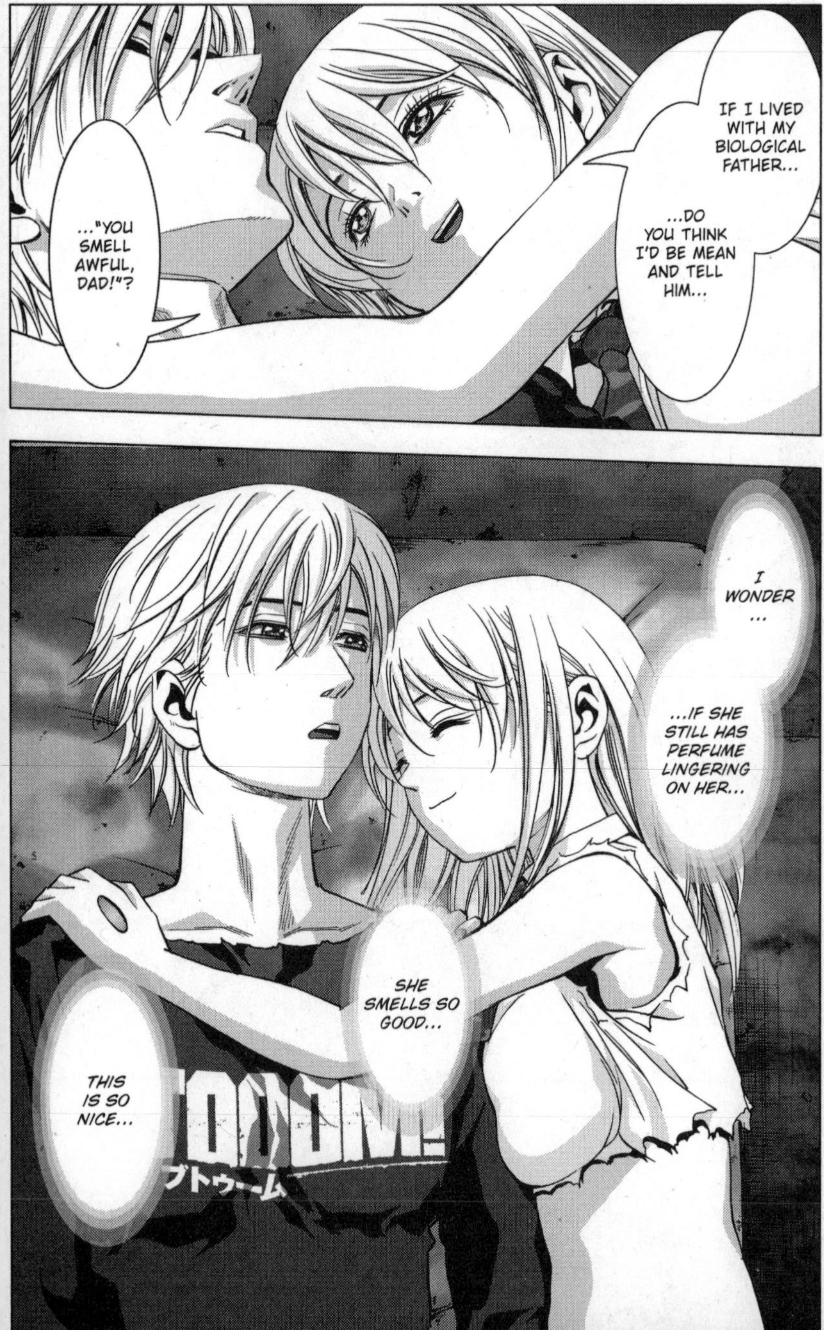
IF I LIVED WITH MY BIOLOGICAL FATHER...
...DO YOU THINK I'D BE MEAN AND TELL HIM...
..."YOU SMELL AWFUL, DAD!"?
I WONDER...
...IF SHE STILL HAS PERFUME LINGERING ON HER...
SHE SMELLS SO GOOD...
THIS IS SO NICE...

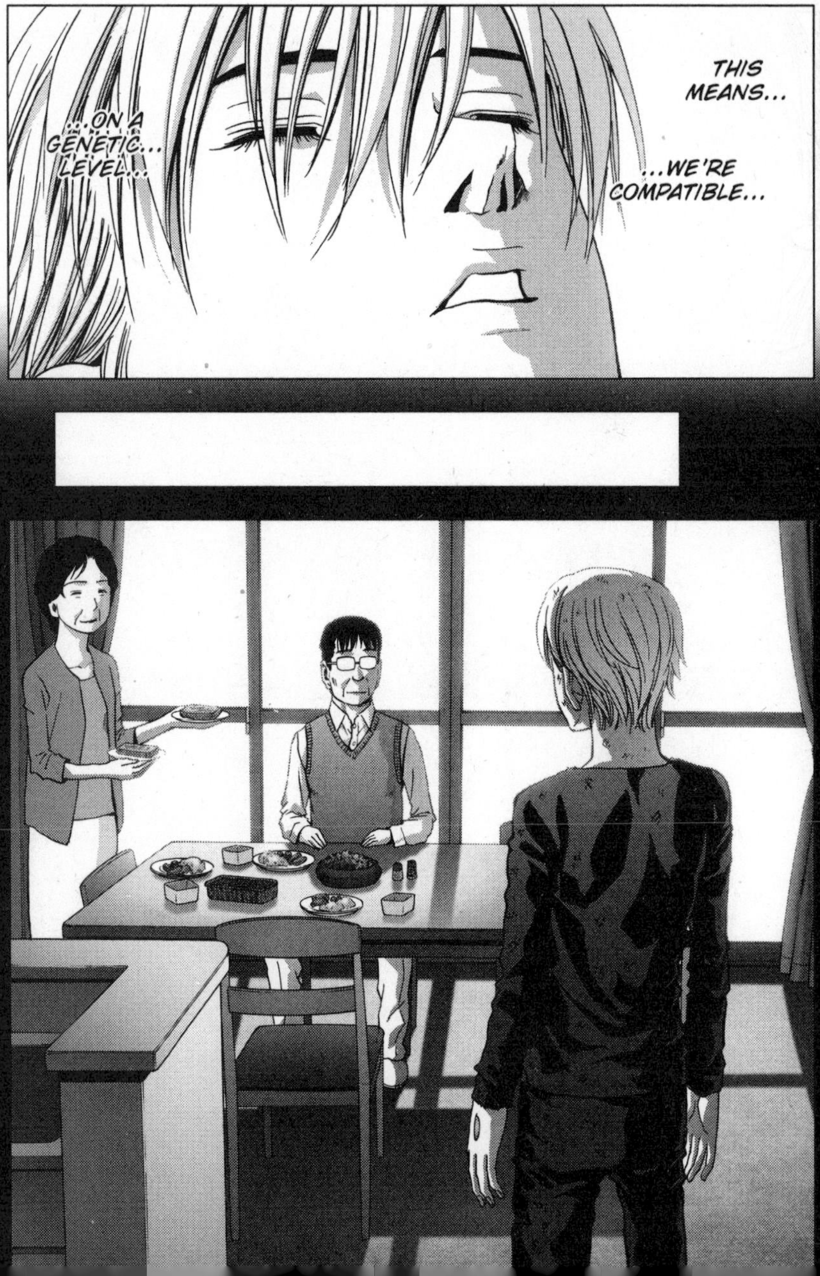
THIS MEANS...
...WE'RE COMPATIBLE...
...ON A GENETIC... LEVEL...

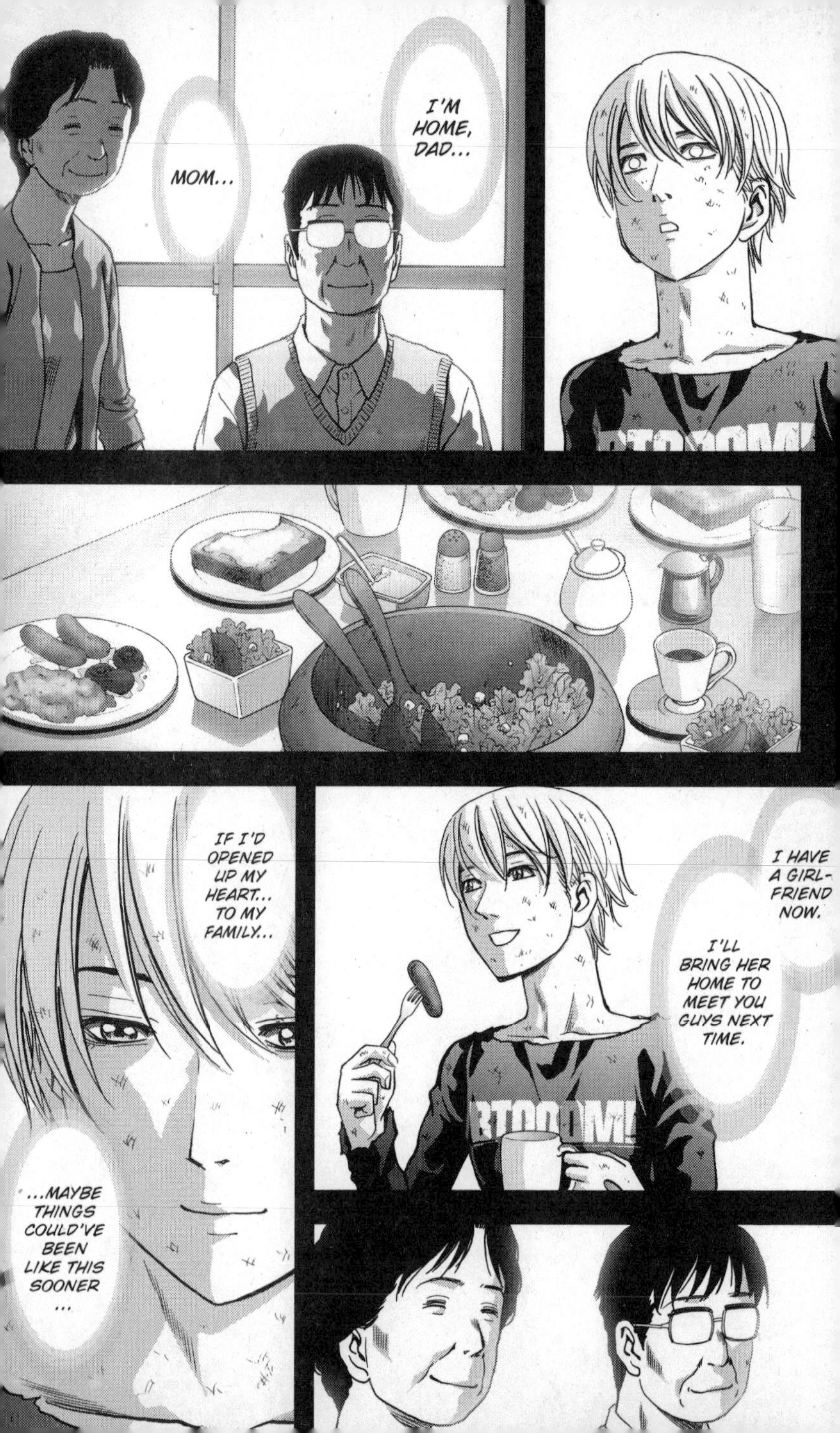
I'M HOME, DAD...
MOM...
I HAVE A GIRL-FRIEND NOW.
I'LL BRING HER HOME TO MEET YOU GUYS NEXT TIME.
IF I'D OPENED UP MY HEART... TO MY FAMILY...
...MAYBE THINGS COULD'VE BEEN LIKE THIS SOONER ...

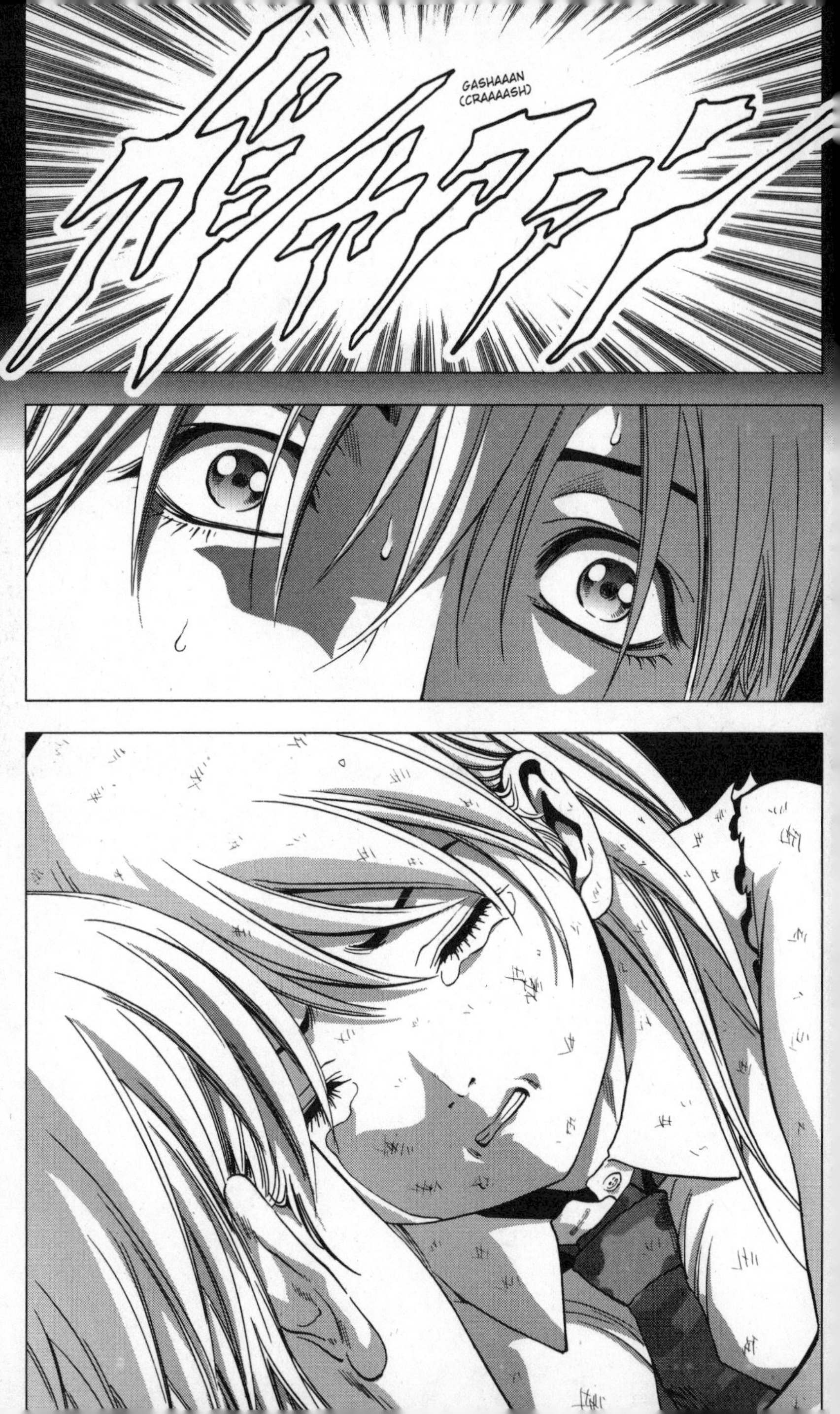
GASHAAAN
(CRAAAASH)

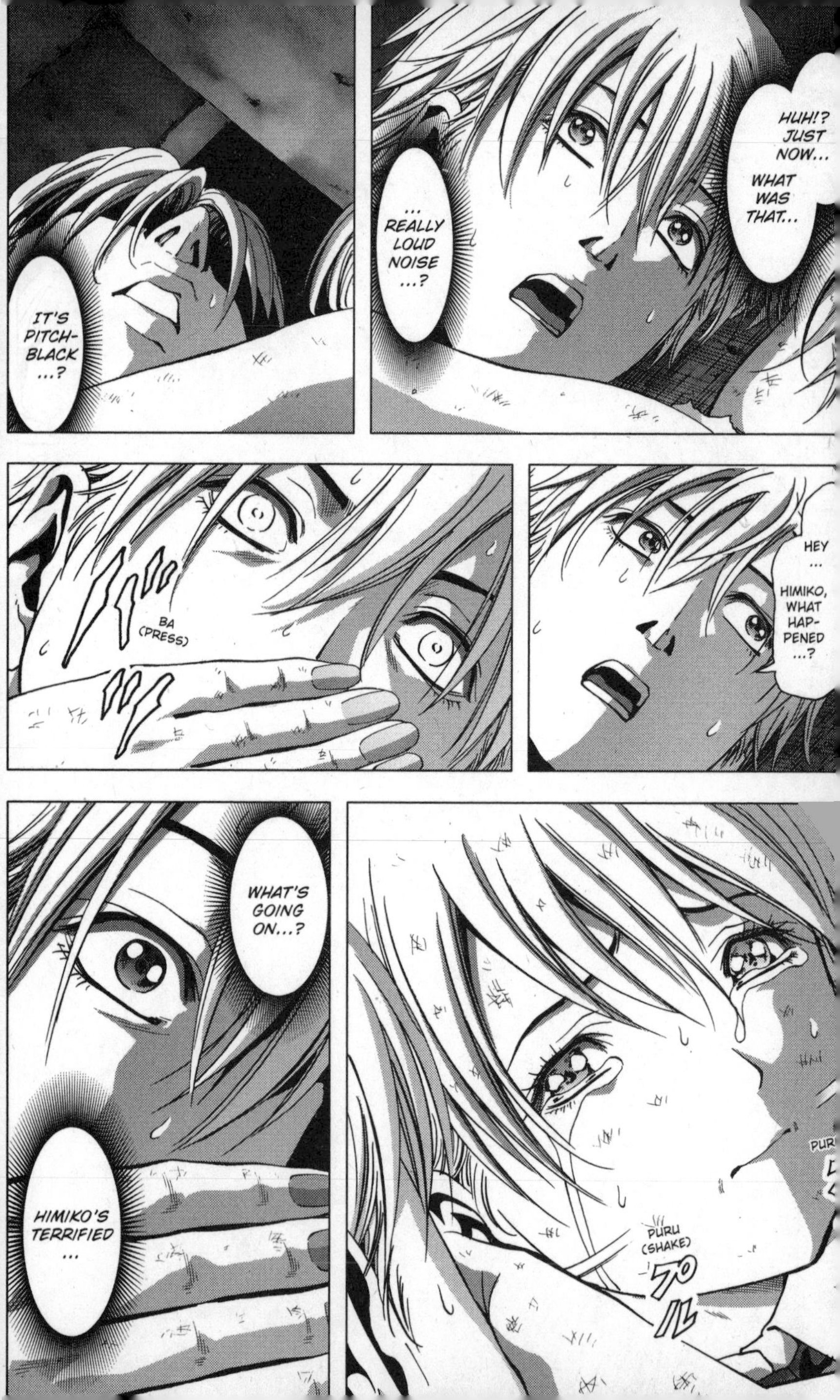
HUH!? JUST NOW... WHAT WAS THAT...
...REALLY LOUD NOISE...?
IT'S PITCH-BLACK...?
HEY... HIMIKO, WHAT HAPPENED...?
BA (PRESS)
PURU
PURU (SHAKE)
WHAT'S GOING ON...?
HIMIKO'S TERRIFIED...

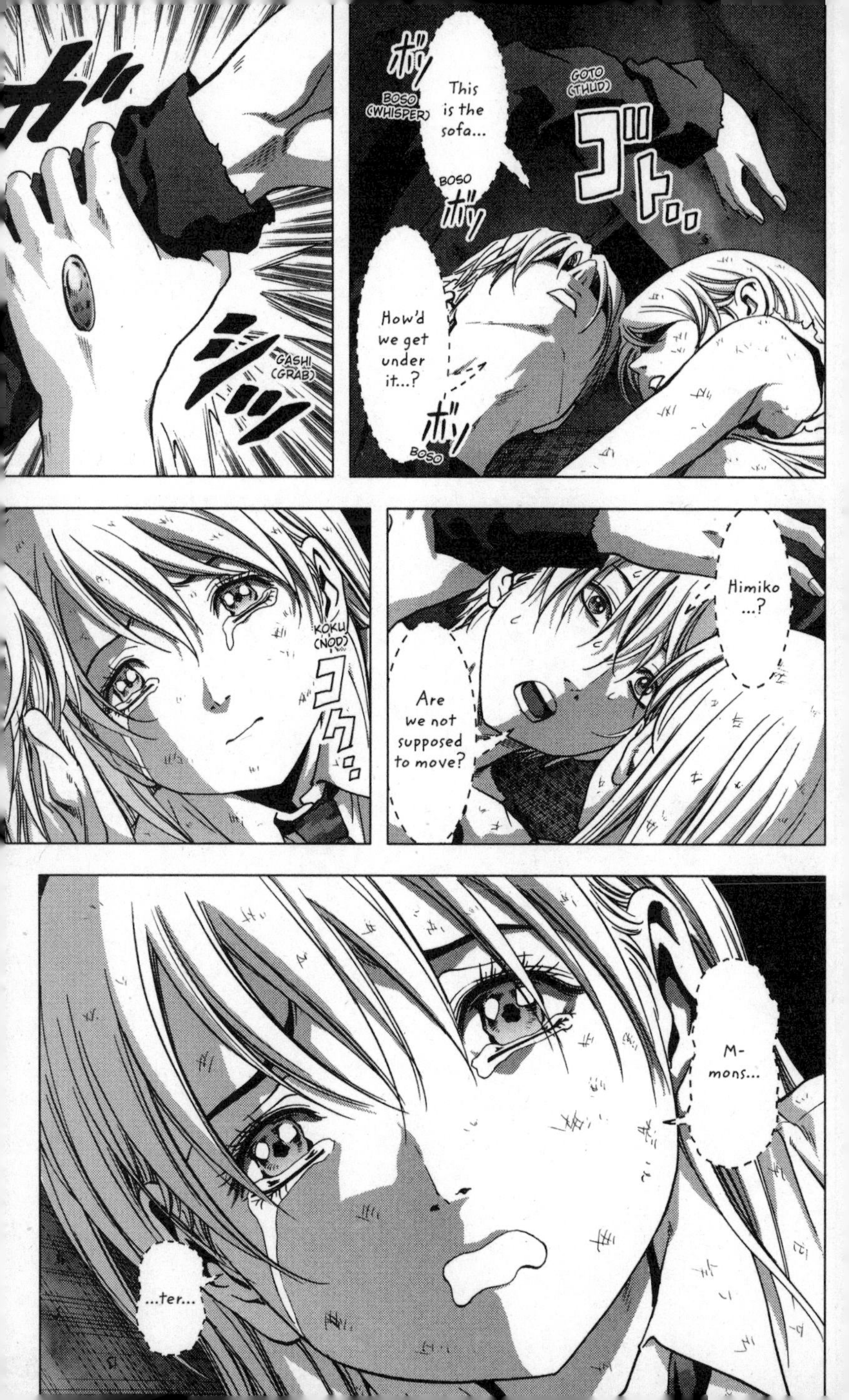
BOSO (WHISPER)
This is the sofa...
BOSO
How'd we get under it...?
BOSO
GOTO (THUD)
GASHI (GRAB)
Himiko ...?
Are we not supposed to move?
KOKU (NOD)
M-mons...
...ter...

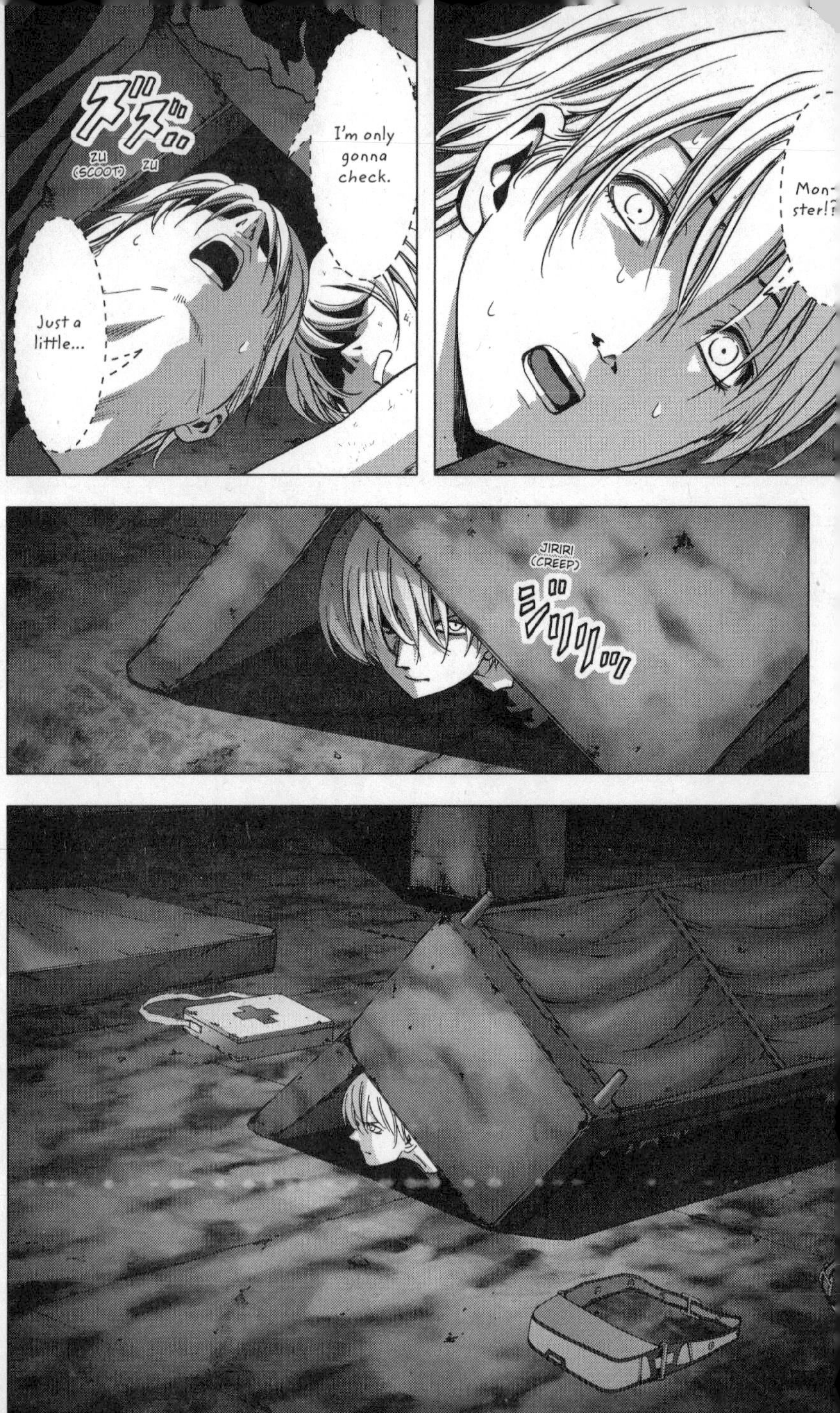
Mon-
ster!?
I'm only gonna check.
ZU (SCOOT) ZU
Just a little...
JIRIRI (CREEP)

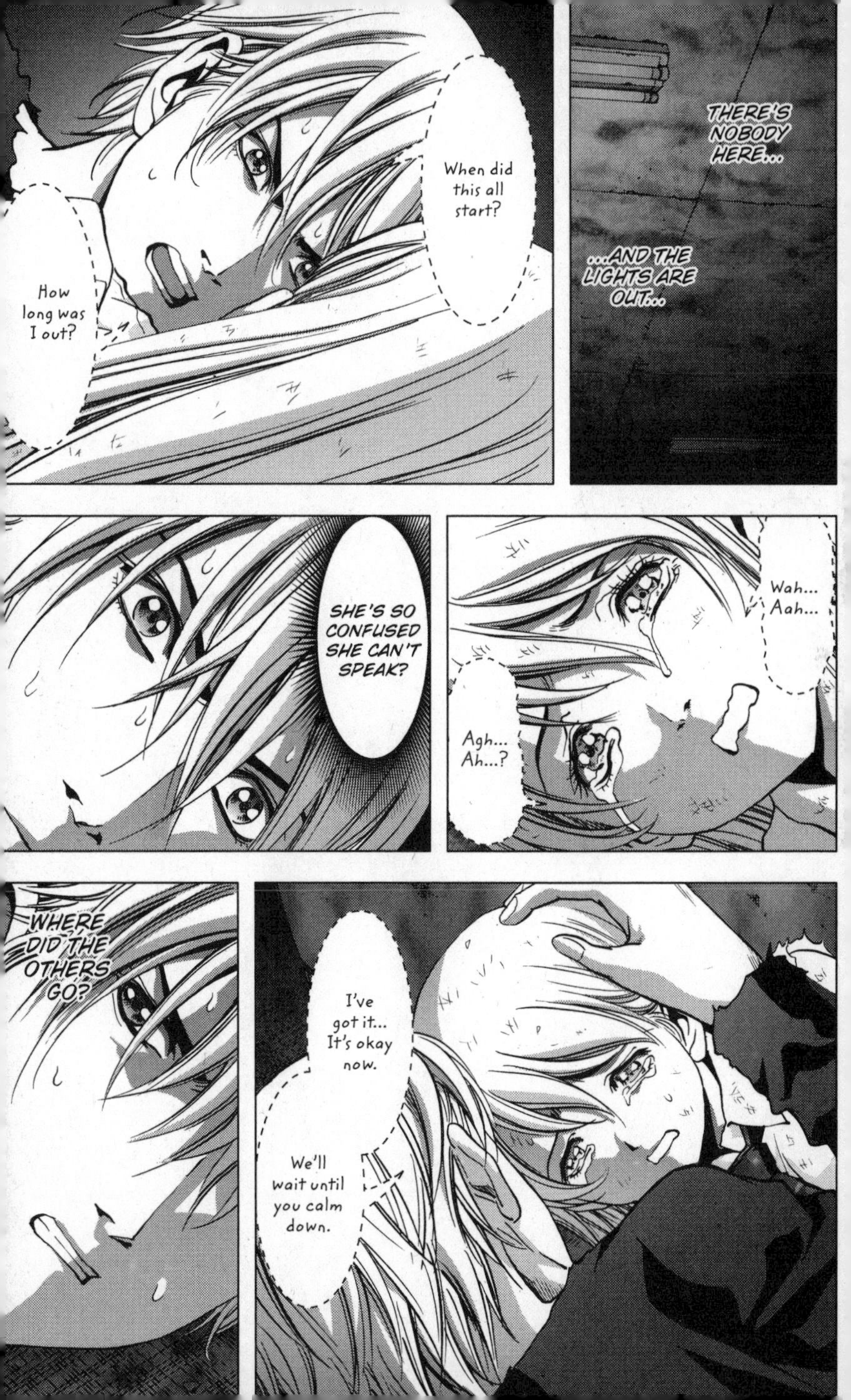
THERE'S NOBODY HERE...
...AND THE LIGHTS ARE OUT...
When did this all start?
How long was I out?
Wah... Aah...
Agh... Ah...?
SHE'S SO CONFUSED SHE CAN'T SPEAK?
I've got it... It's okay now.
We'll wait until you calm down.
WHERE DID THE OTHERS GO?

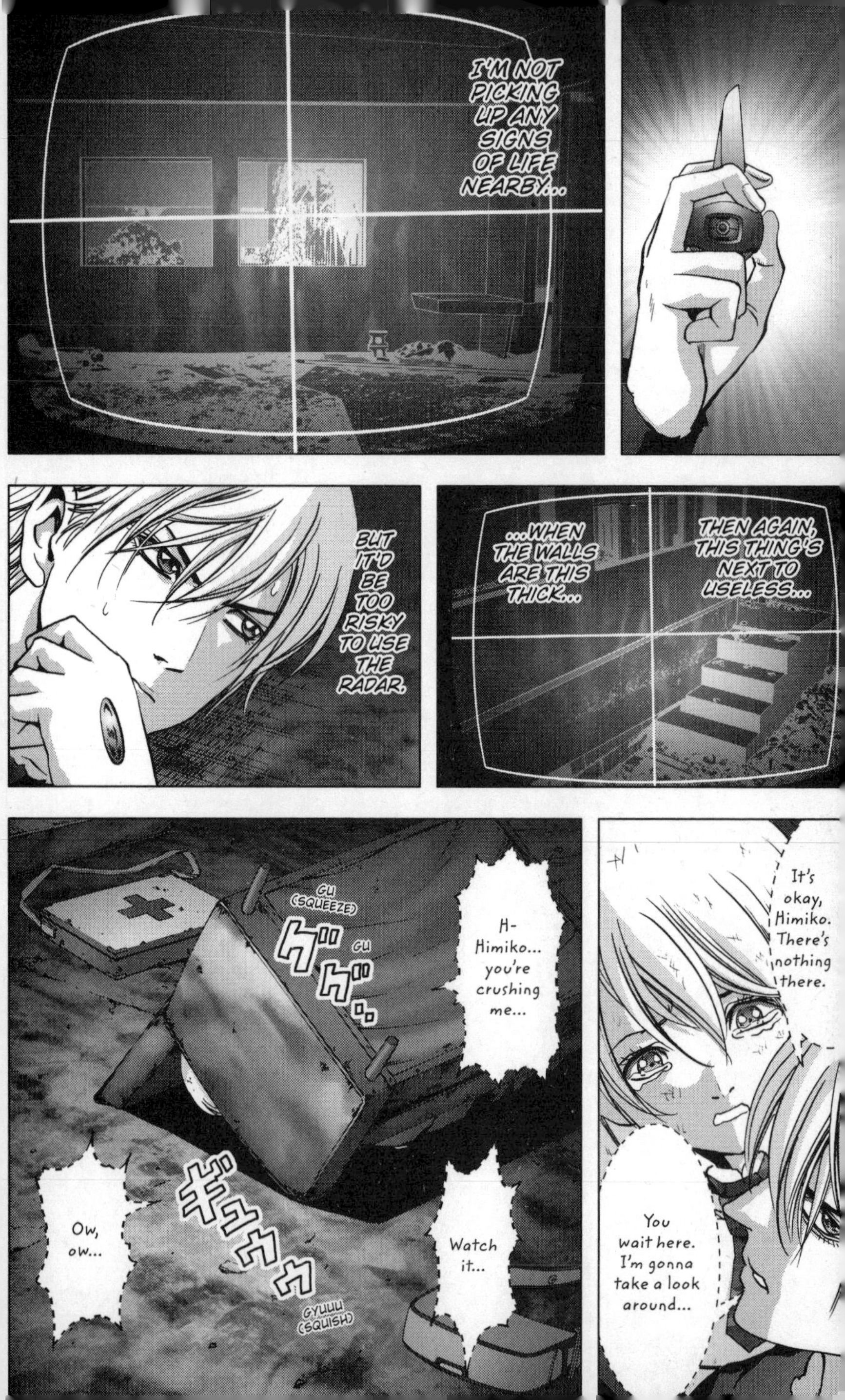

I'M NOT PICKING UP ANY SIGNS OF LIFE NEARBY...
THEN AGAIN, THIS THING'S NEXT TO USELESS...
...WHEN THE WALLS ARE THIS THICK...
BUT IT'D BE TOO RISKY TO USE THE RADAR.
It's okay, Himiko. There's nothing there.
You wait here. I'm gonna take a look around...
H-Himiko... you're crushing me...
GU (SQUEEZE)
GU
Watch it...
GYUUU (SQUISH)
Ow, ow...

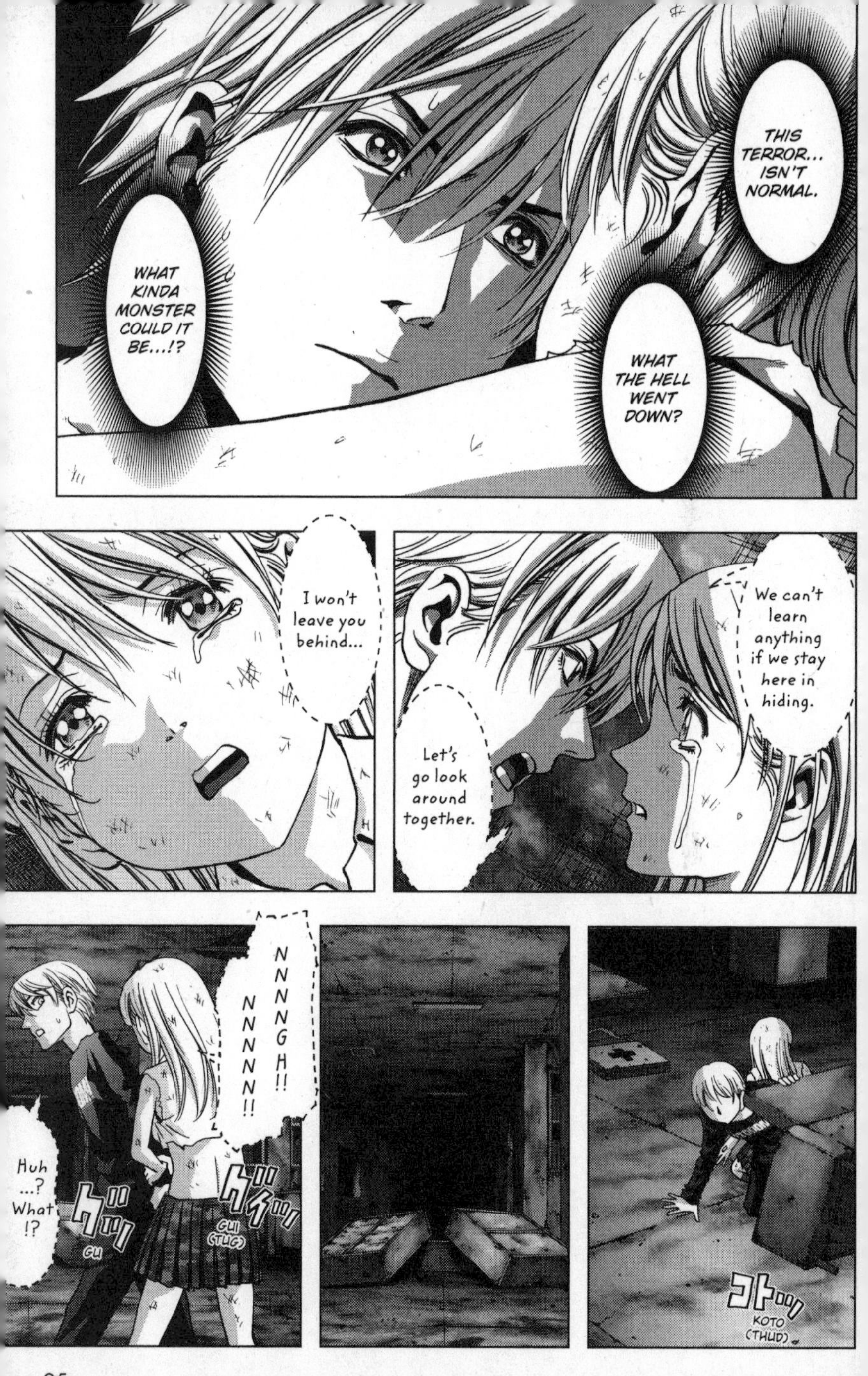
THIS TERROR... ISN'T NORMAL.
WHAT THE HELL WENT DOWN?
WHAT KINDA MONSTER COULD IT BE...!?
We can't learn anything if we stay here in hiding.
Let's go look around together.
I won't leave you behind...
KOTO (THUD)
NNNNGH!! NNNNN!!
GUI (TUG)
GU
Huh ...? What !?

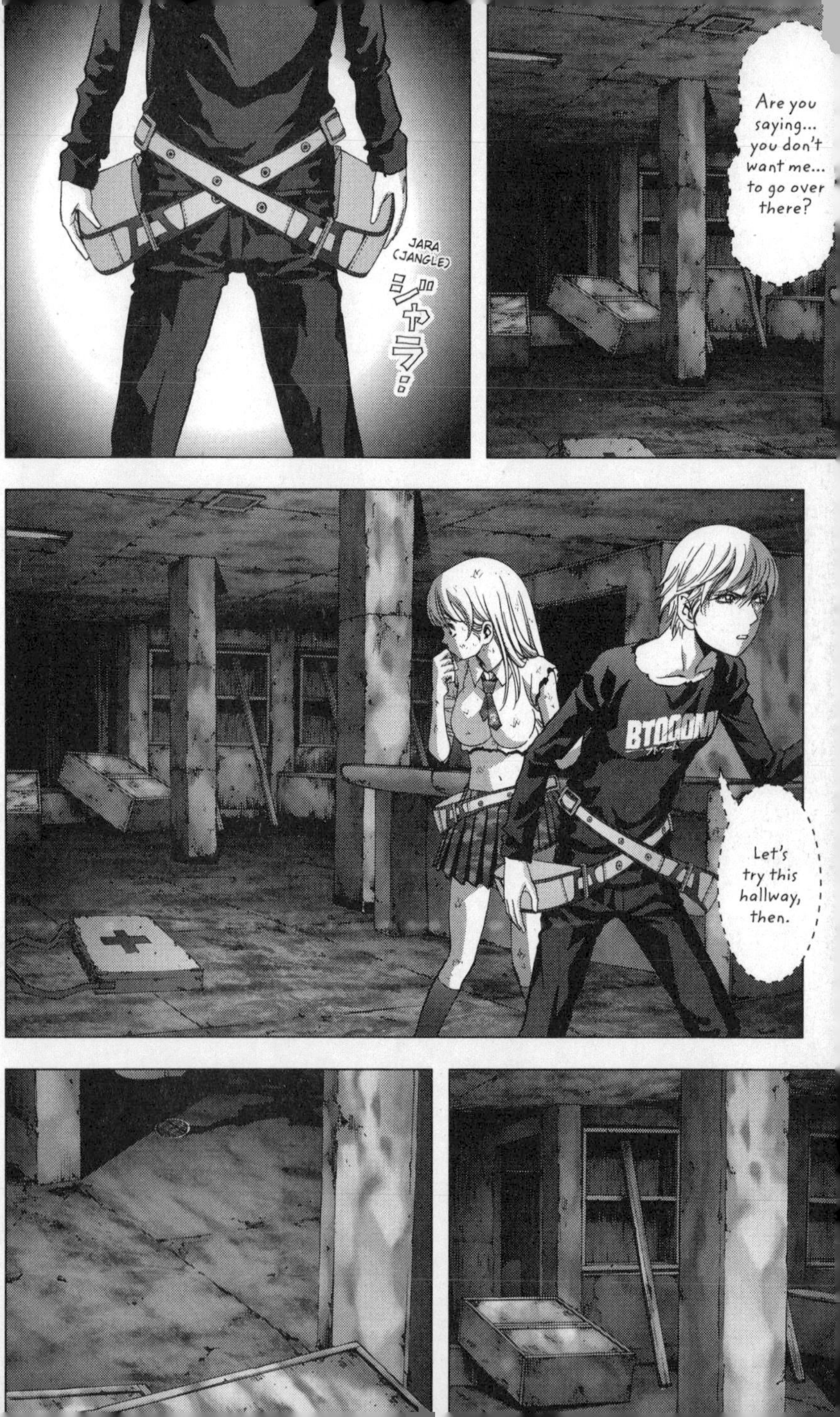
Are you saying... you don't want me... to go over there?
JARA (JANGLE)
ジャラ・
BTOOOM
Let's try this hallway, then.

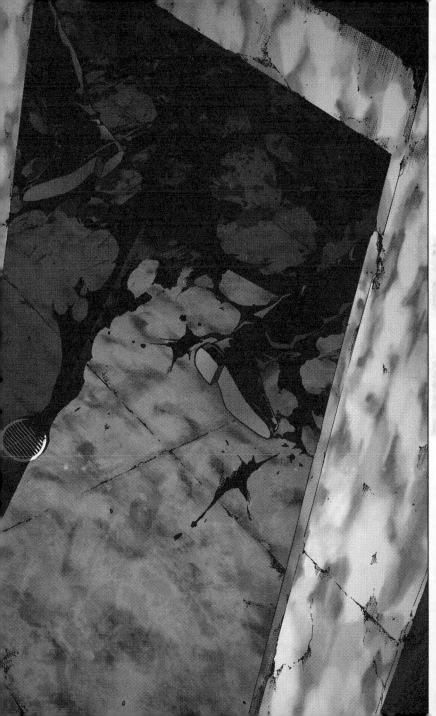

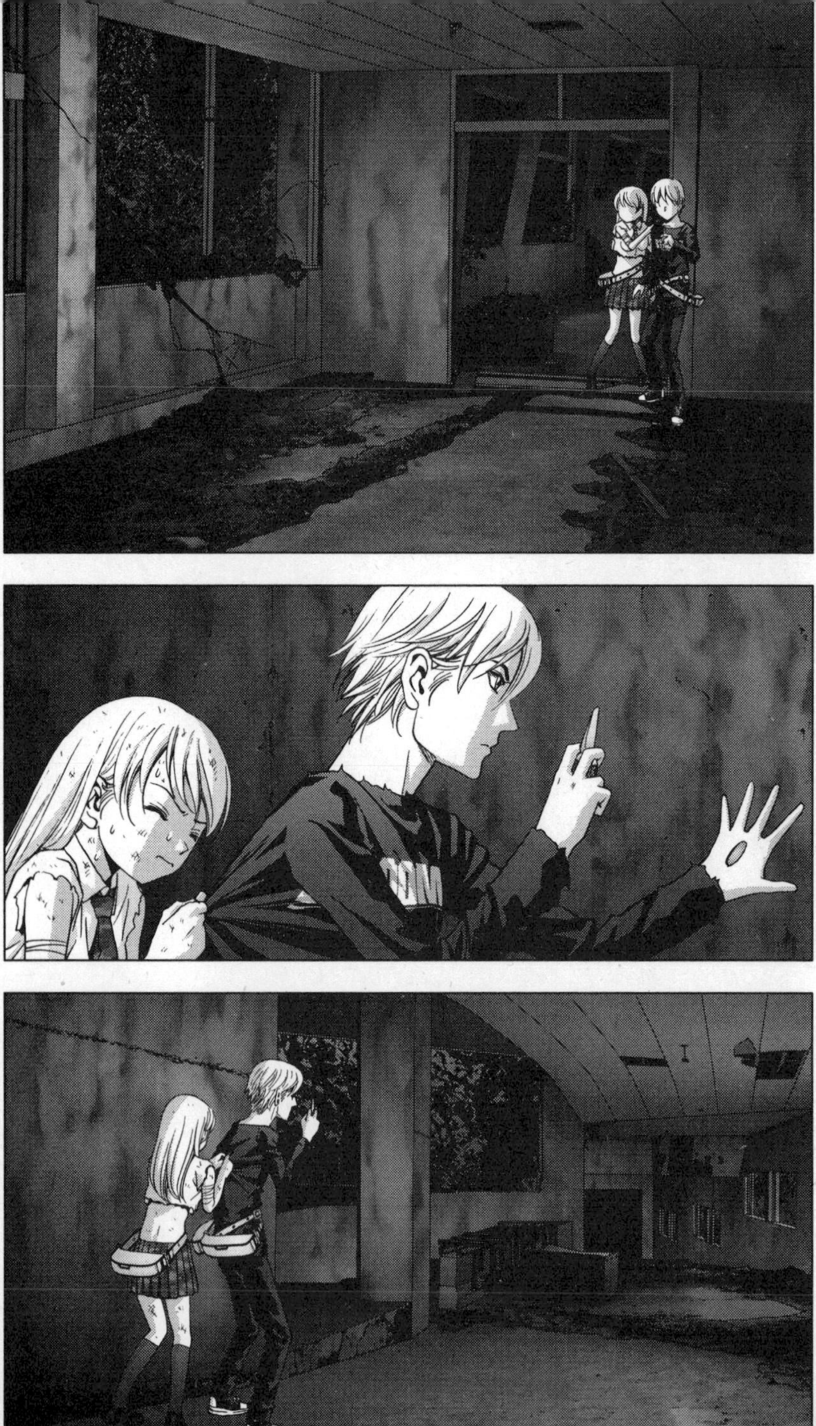

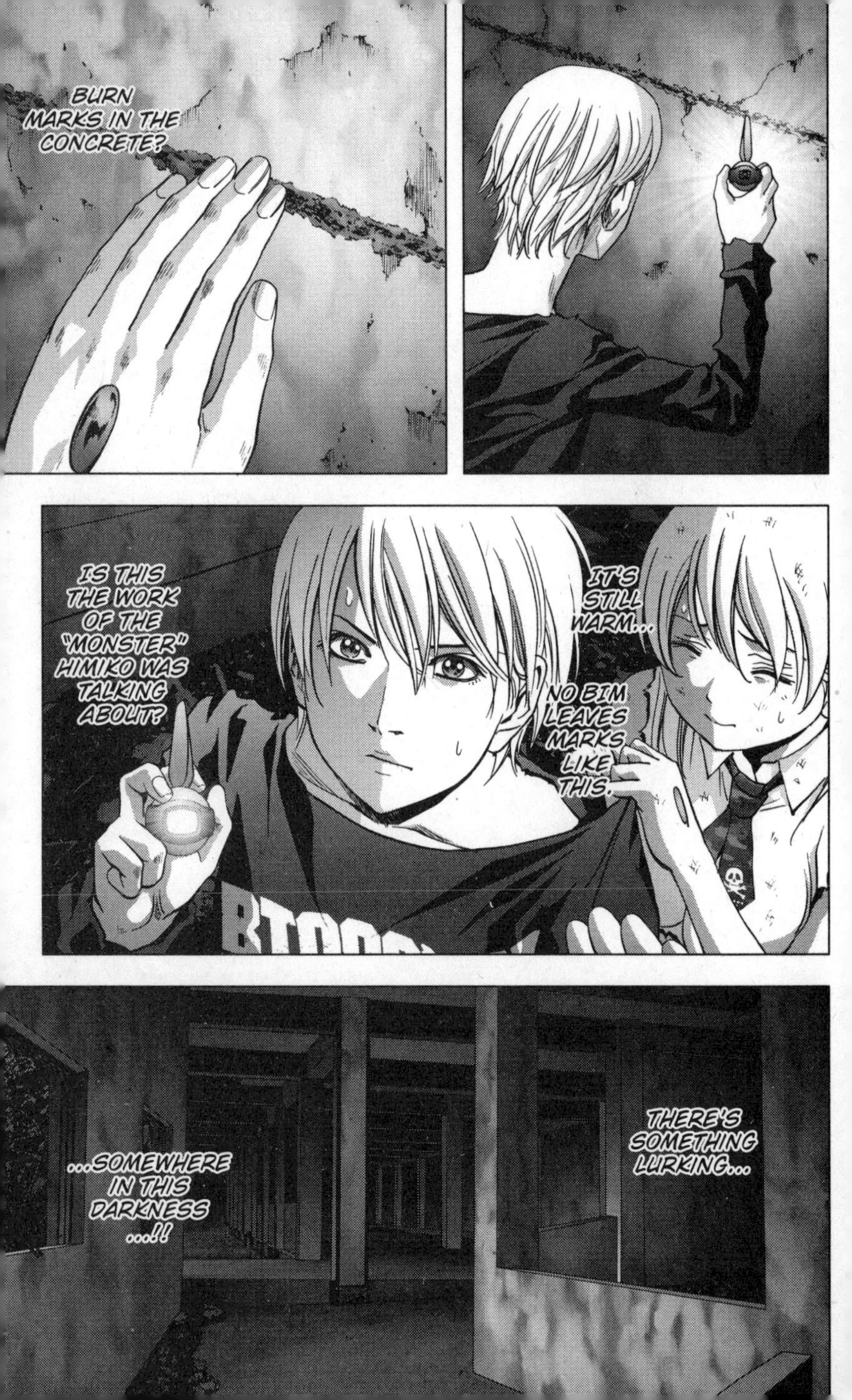
BURN MARKS IN THE CONCRETE?
IT'S STILL WARM...
NO BIM LEAVES MARKS LIKE THIS.
IS THIS THE WORK OF THE "MONSTER" HIMIKO WAS TALKING ABOUT?
THERE'S SOMETHING LURKING...
...SOMEWHERE IN THIS DARKNESS ...!!

HUH
...?

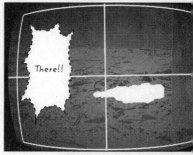

There!!

Hey!
Are
you
okay
...!?

Kira!!

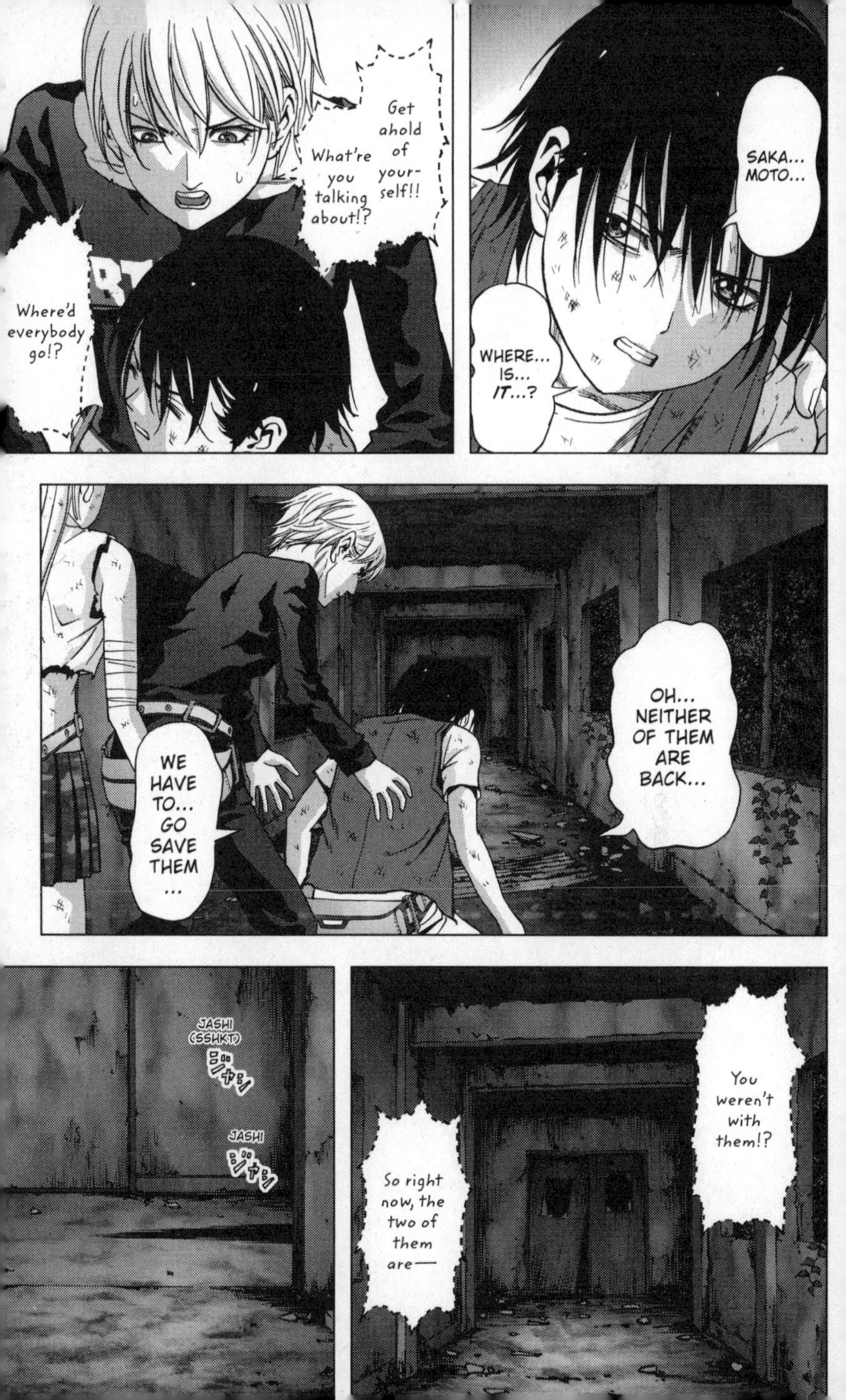
SAKA... MOTO...
WHERE... IS... IT...?
Get ahold of your-self!!
What're you talking about!?
Where'd everybody go!?
OH... NEITHER OF THEM ARE BACK...
WE HAVE TO... GO SAVE THEM ...
You weren't with them!?
So right now, the two of them are—
JASHI (SSHKT)
ジャシ
JASHI
ジャシ

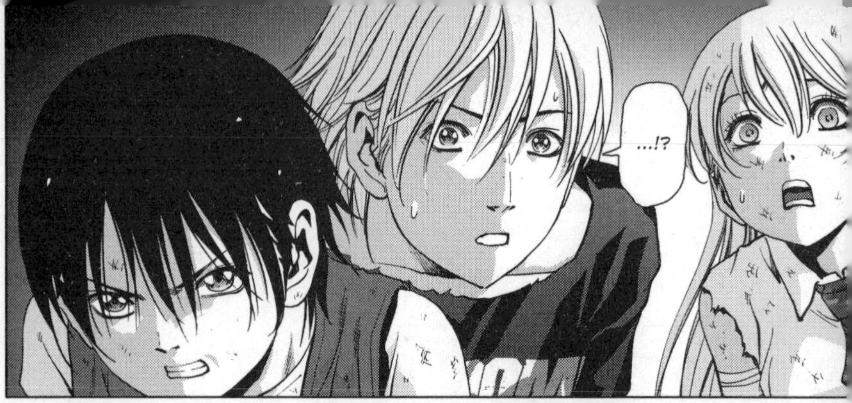
...!?

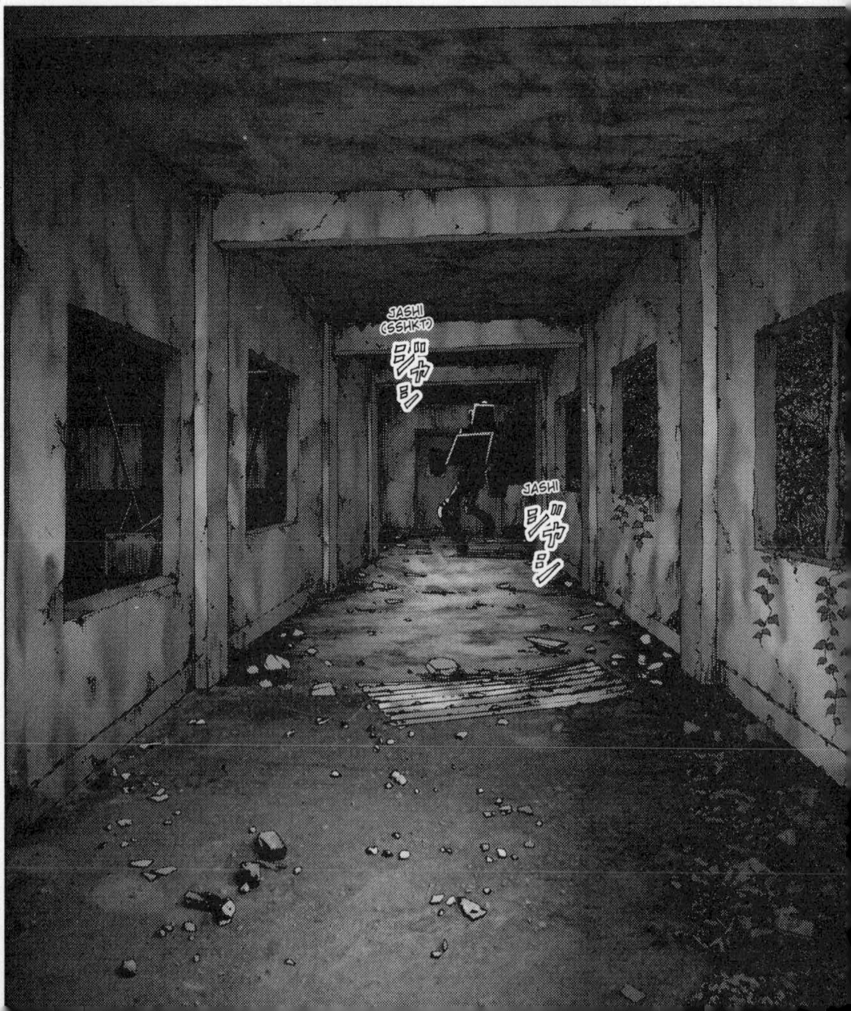
JASHI (SSHKT)
ジャリ
JASHI
ジャリ

N-5963
4:07
TARGETING
014987314689763106
X 16.87946113
Y 145.84625244
BTOOOM!-108
108
DRONE UNIT

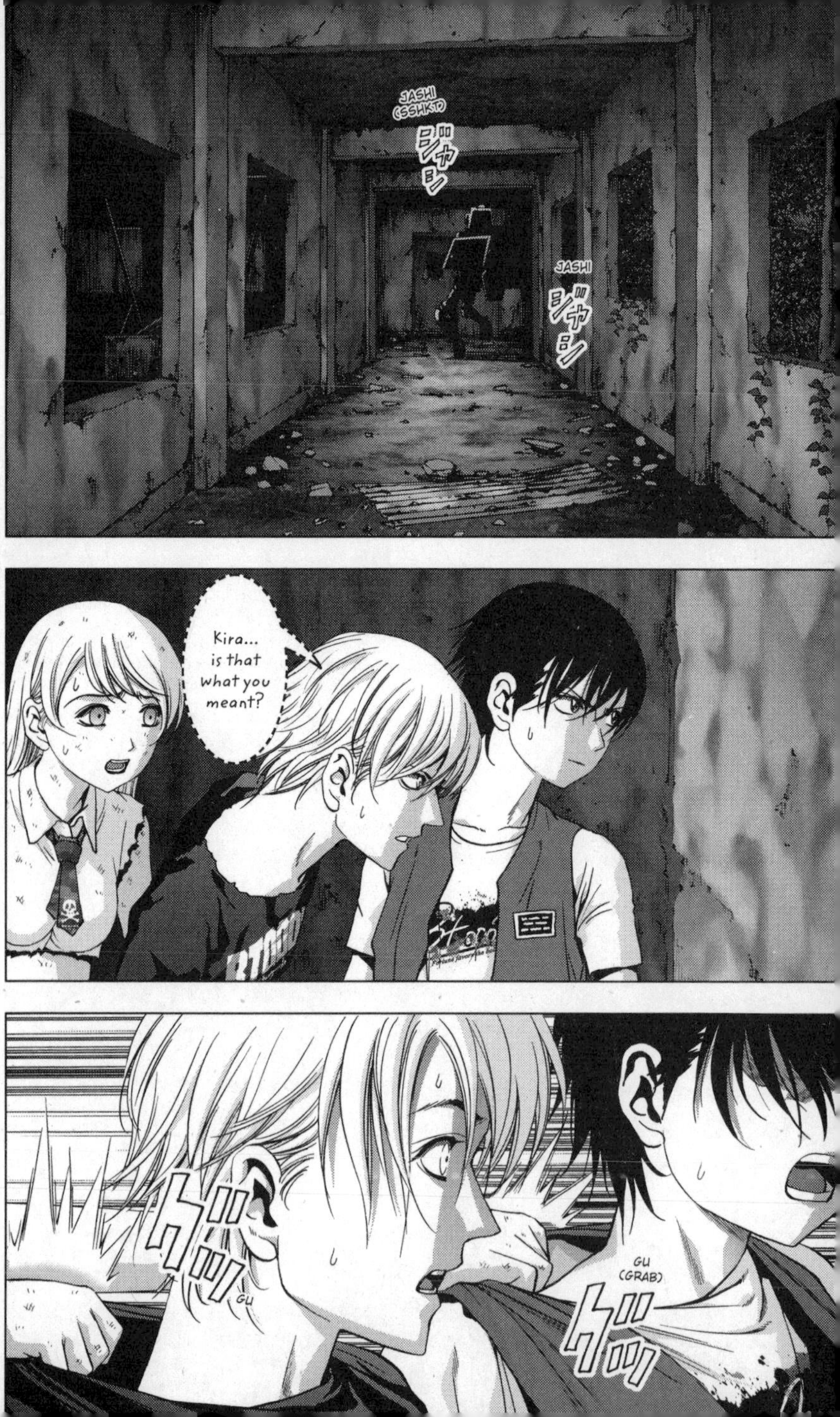
JASHI (SSHKT)
ジャシ
JASHI
ジャシ
Kira... is that what you meant?
GU (GRAB)
グッ
GU
グッ

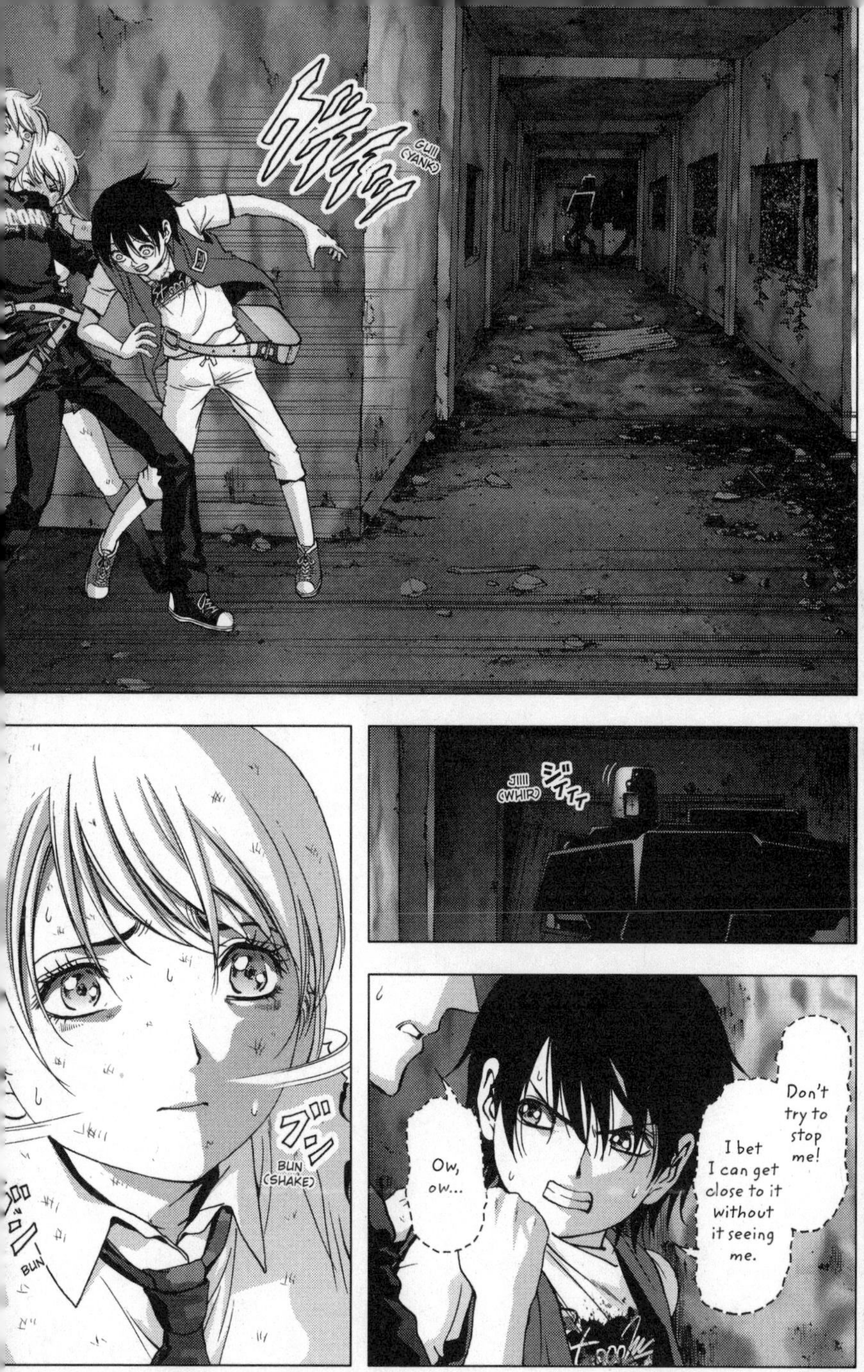
GUII (YANK)
JIIII (WHIR)
Don't try to stop me!
I bet I can get close to it without it seeing me.
Ow, ow...
BUN (SHAKE)
BUN

JASHI (SSHKT)
JASHI
JASHI
JA
JA
JA
JA (KLANK)
JA
JA
JA
JA
JA
JA
JA

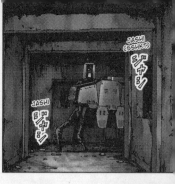

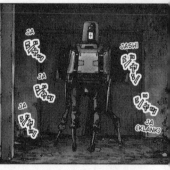

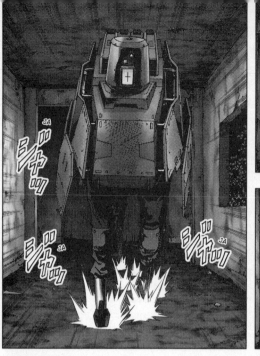

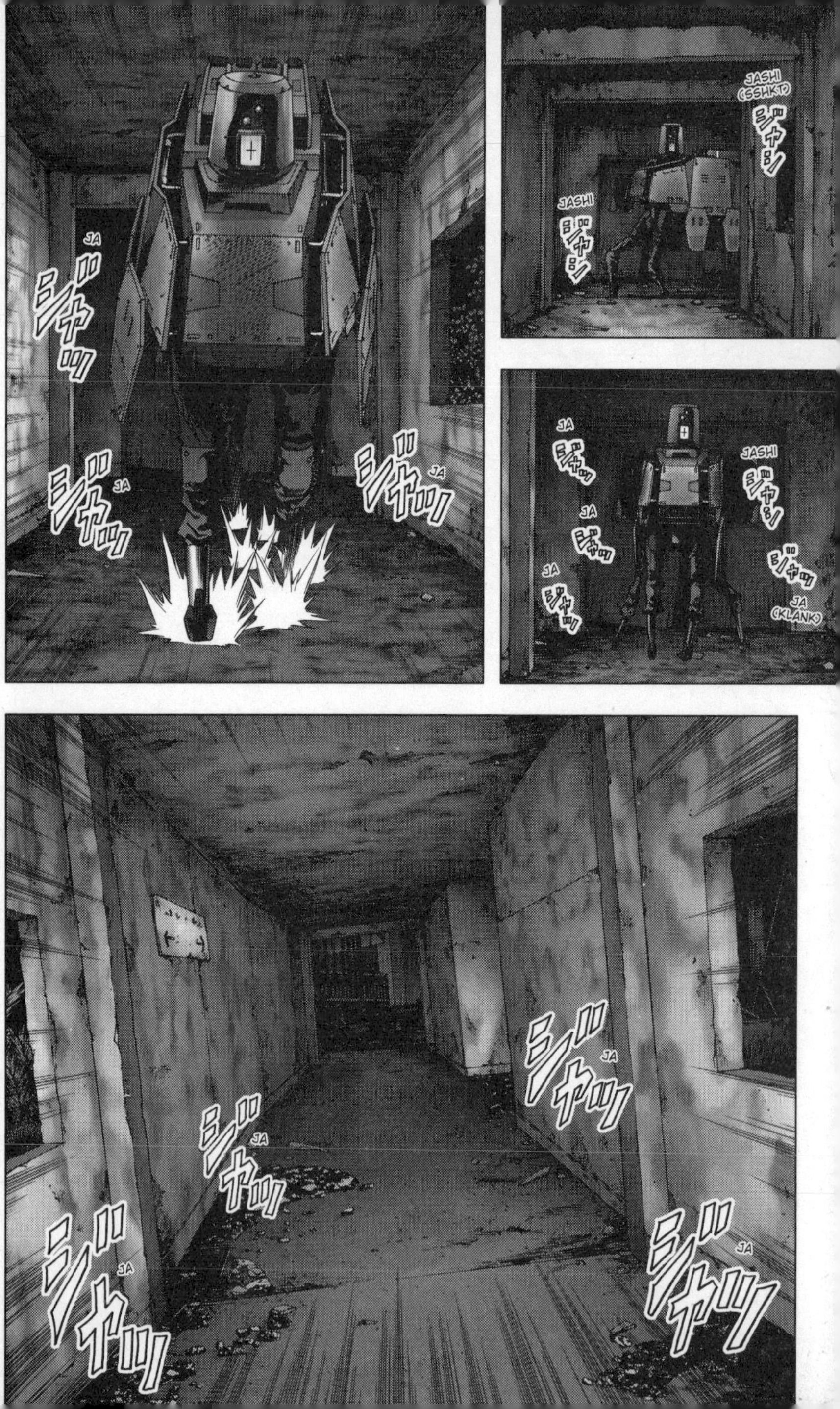

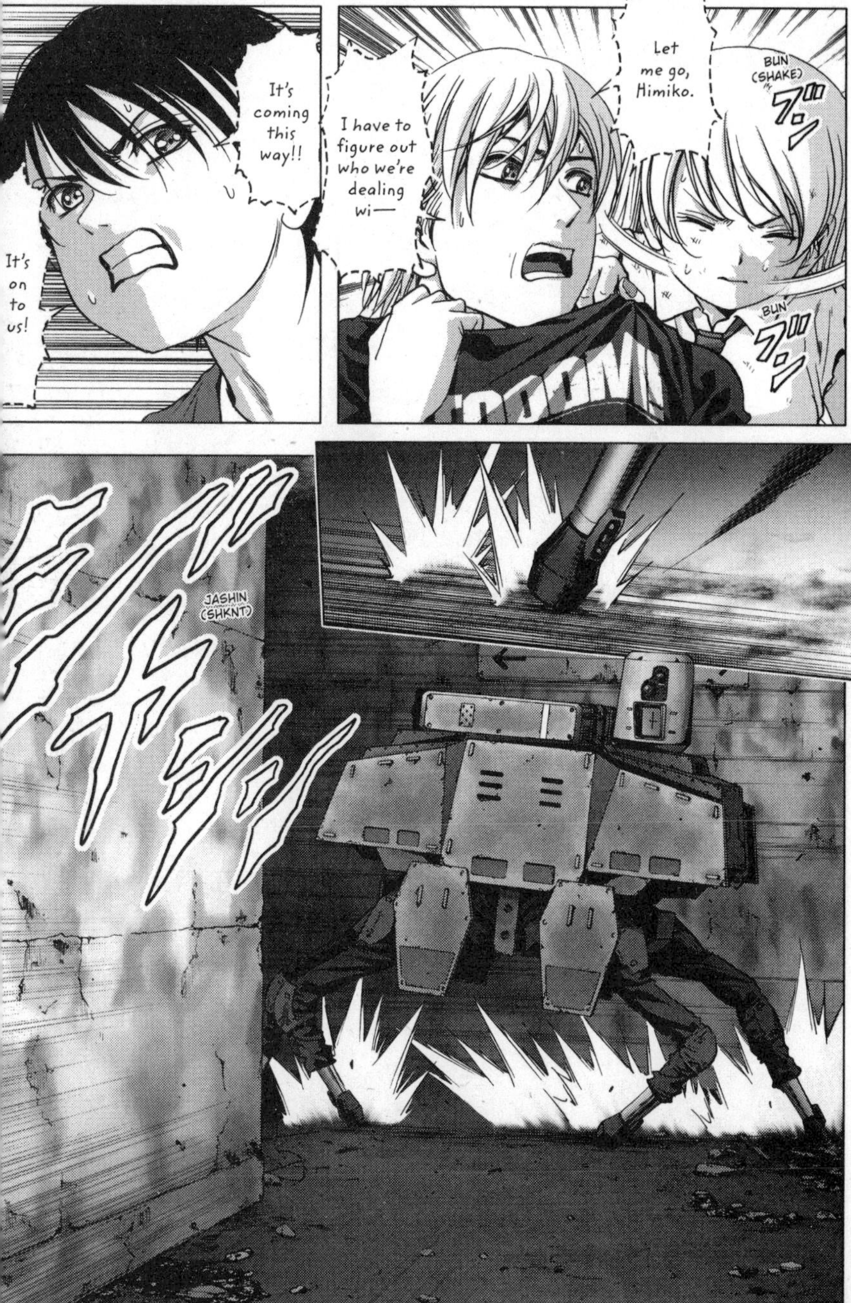

Let me go, Himiko.
BUN (SHAKE)
BUN
I have to figure out who we're dealing wi—
It's coming this way!!
It's on to us!
JASHIN (SHKNT)

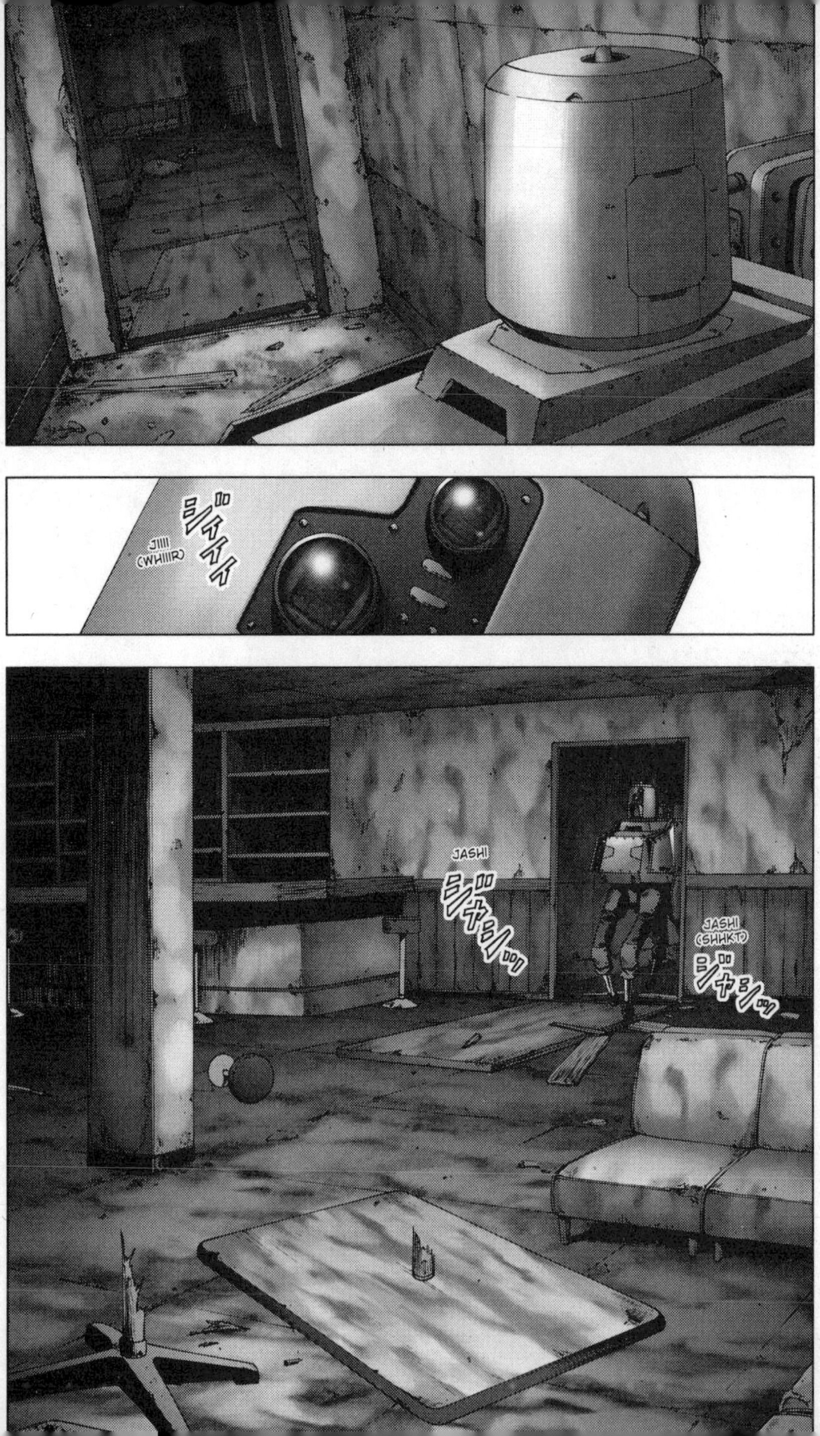
JIIII (WHIIIR)
ジャシッ
JASHI
ジャシッ
JASHI (SHHKT)

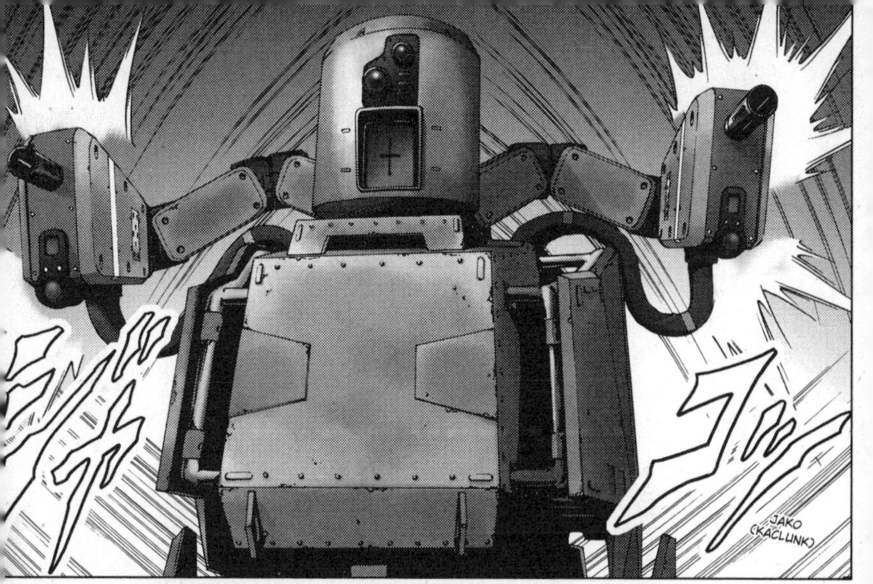
JAKO
(KACLUNK)

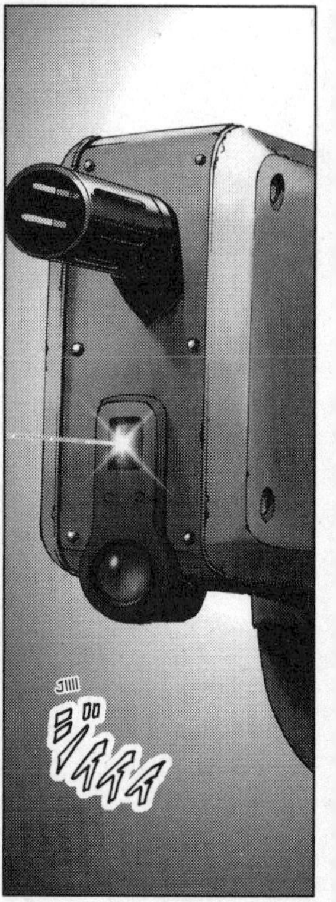
JIIII

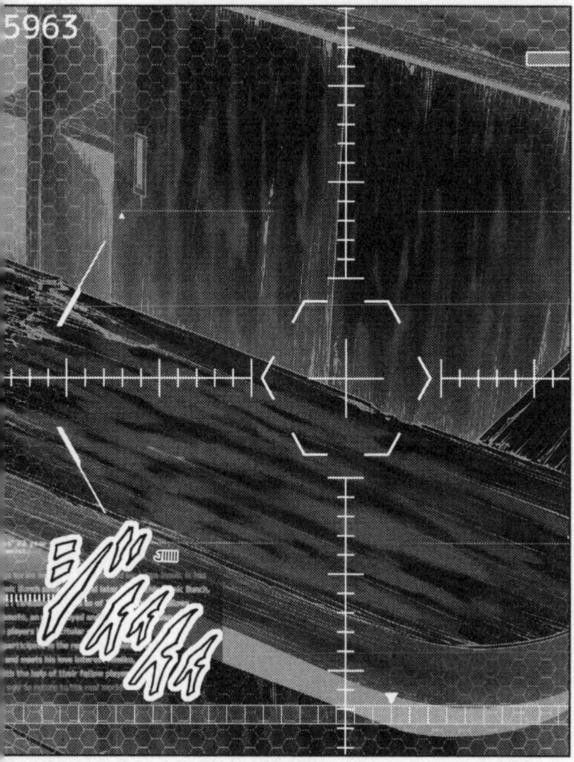
5963
JIIII

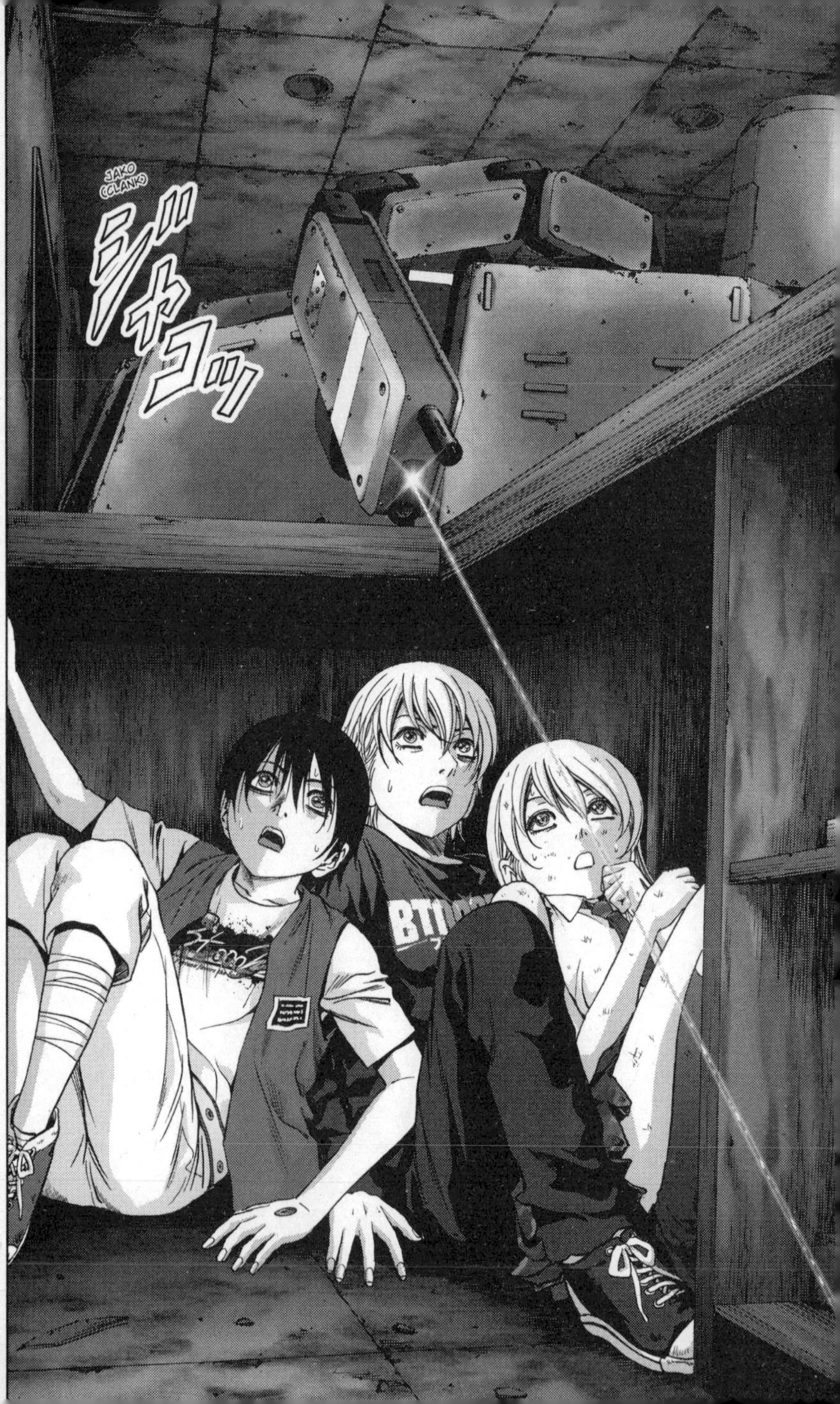
JAKO (CLANK)

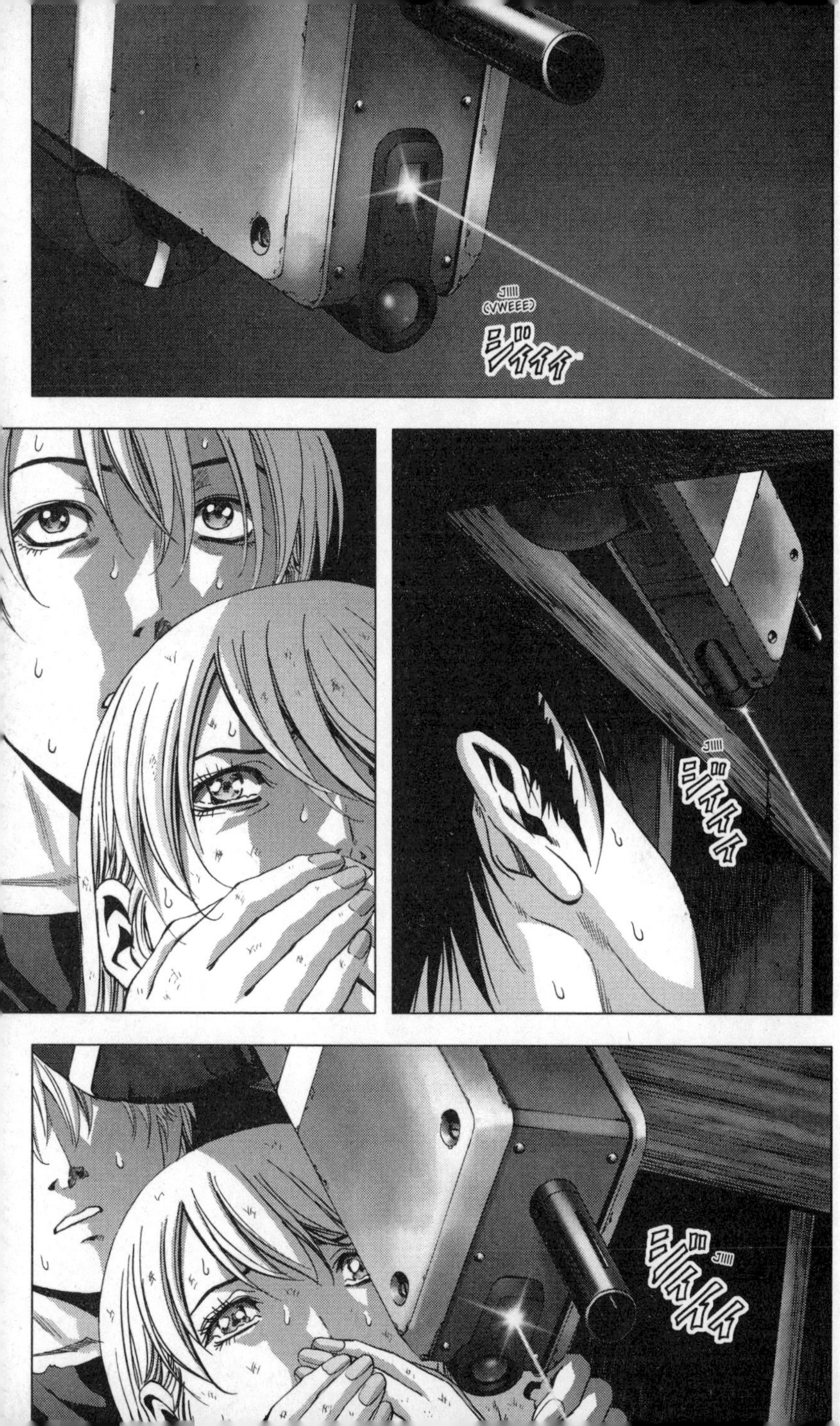
JIIII
(VWEEE)
ジィィィ
JIIII
ジィィィ
JIIII
ジィィィィ

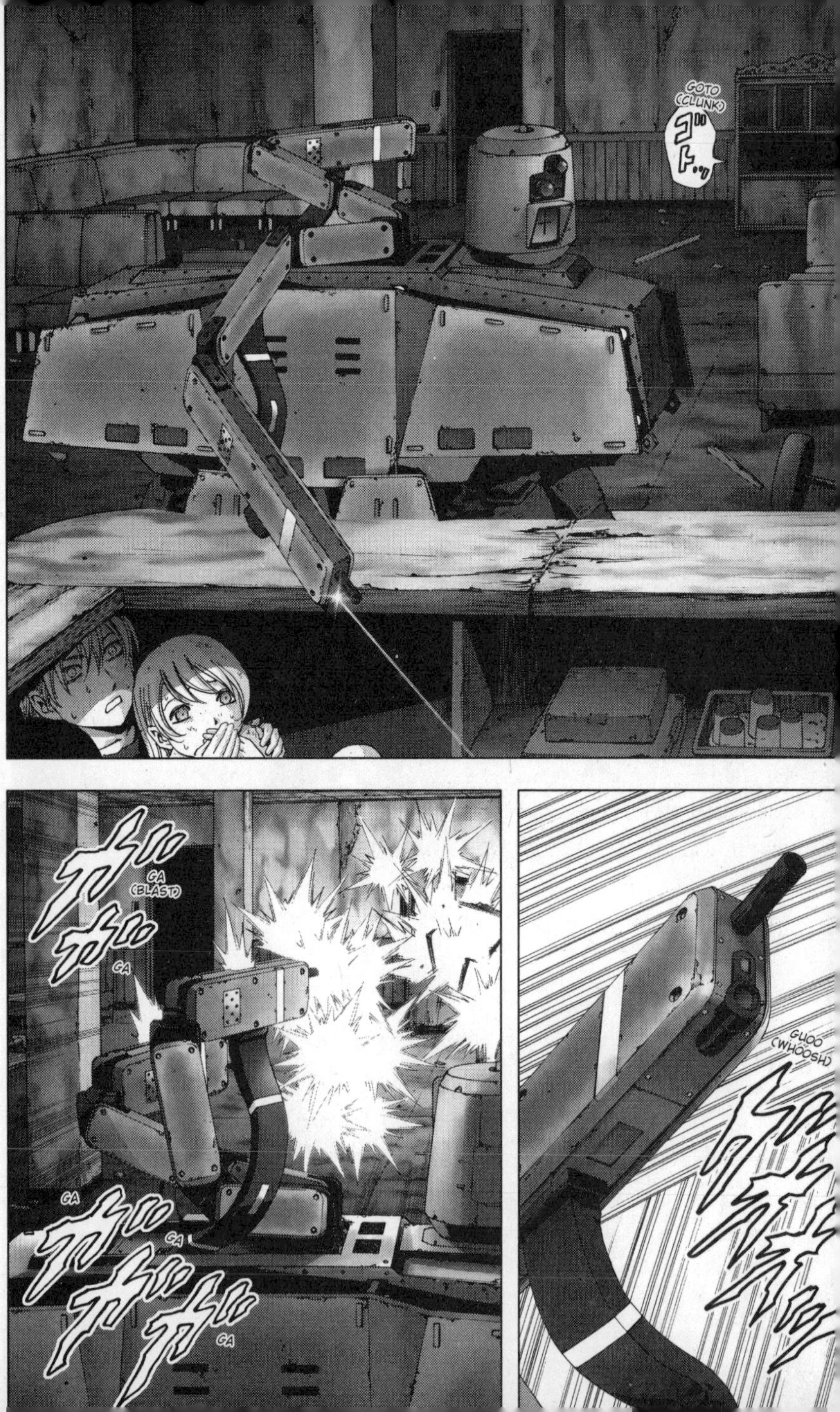
GOTO
(CLUNK)
GUOO
(WHOOSH)
GA
(BLAST)
GA
GA
GA
GA

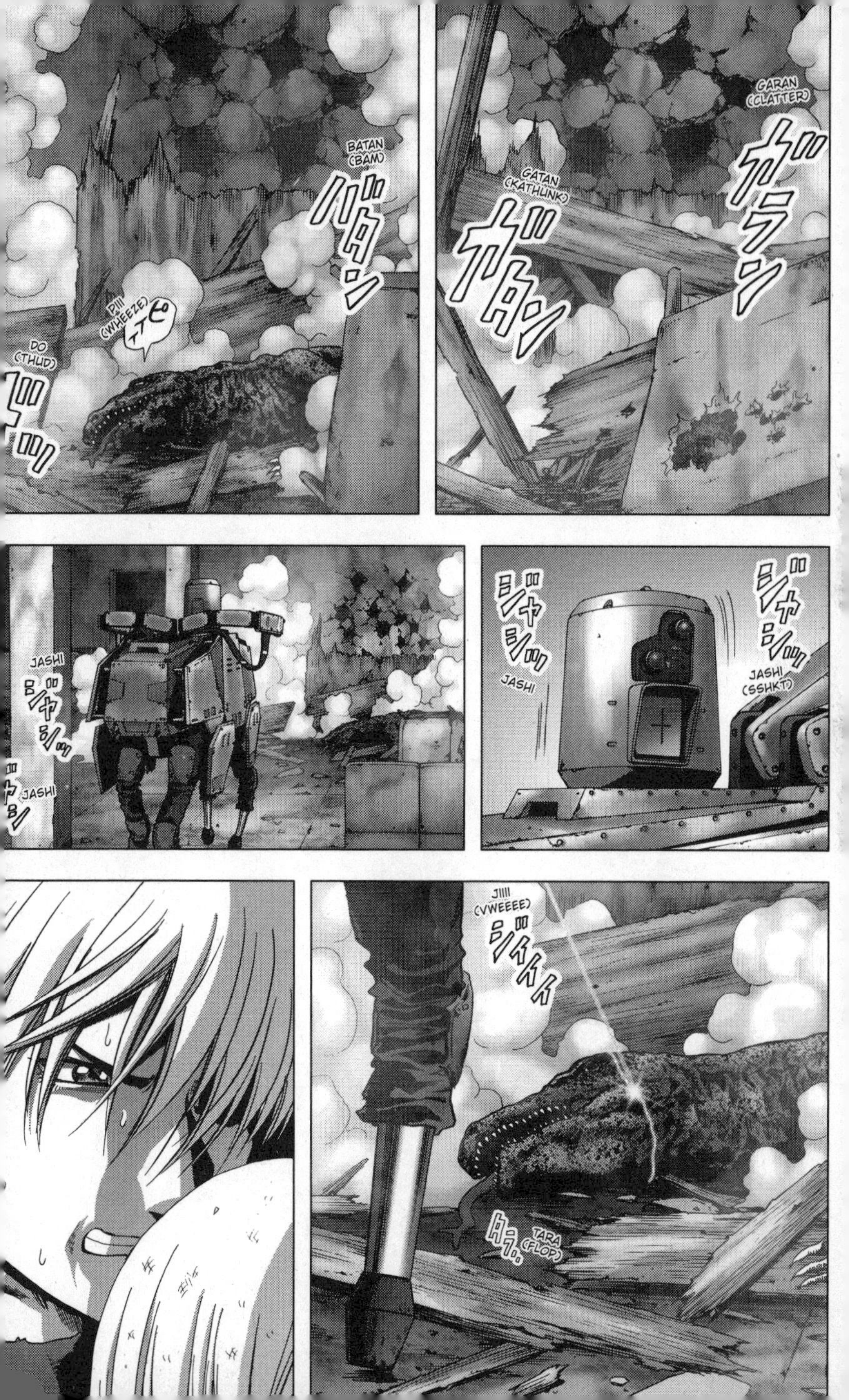
GARAN (CLATTER)
GATAN (KATHUNK)
BATAN (BAM)
PIII (WHEEZE)
DO (THUD)
JASHI (SSHKT)
JASHI
JASHI
JASHI
JIIII (VWEEEE)
TARA (FLOP)

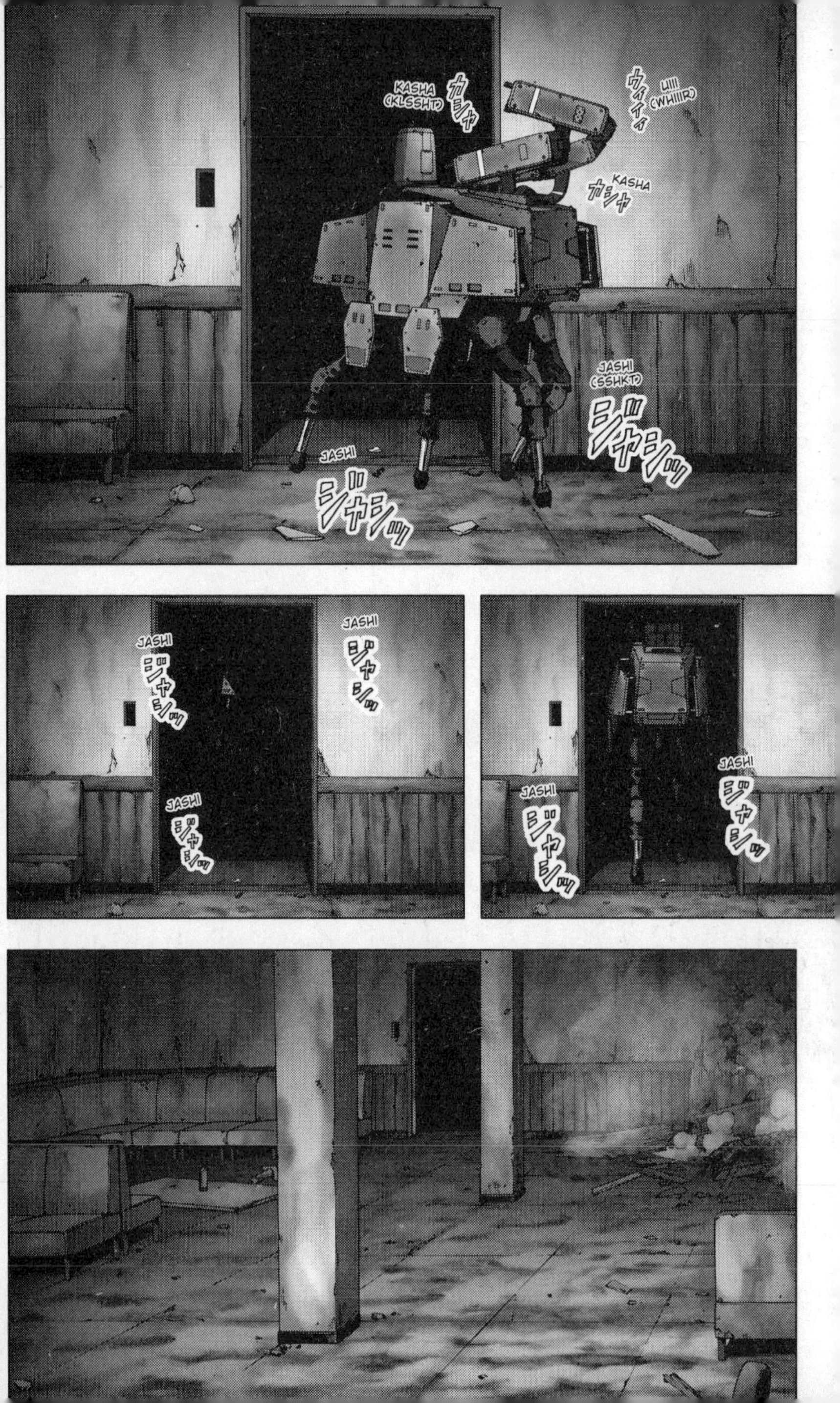

ウィィィ
UIII (WHIIIR)
カシャ
KASHA
カシャ
KASHA (KLSSHT)
ジャシッ
JASHI (SSHKT)
ジャシッ
JASHI
ジャシッ
JASHI
ジャシッ
JASHI
ジャシッ
JASHI
ジャシッ
JASHI
ジャシッ
JASHI

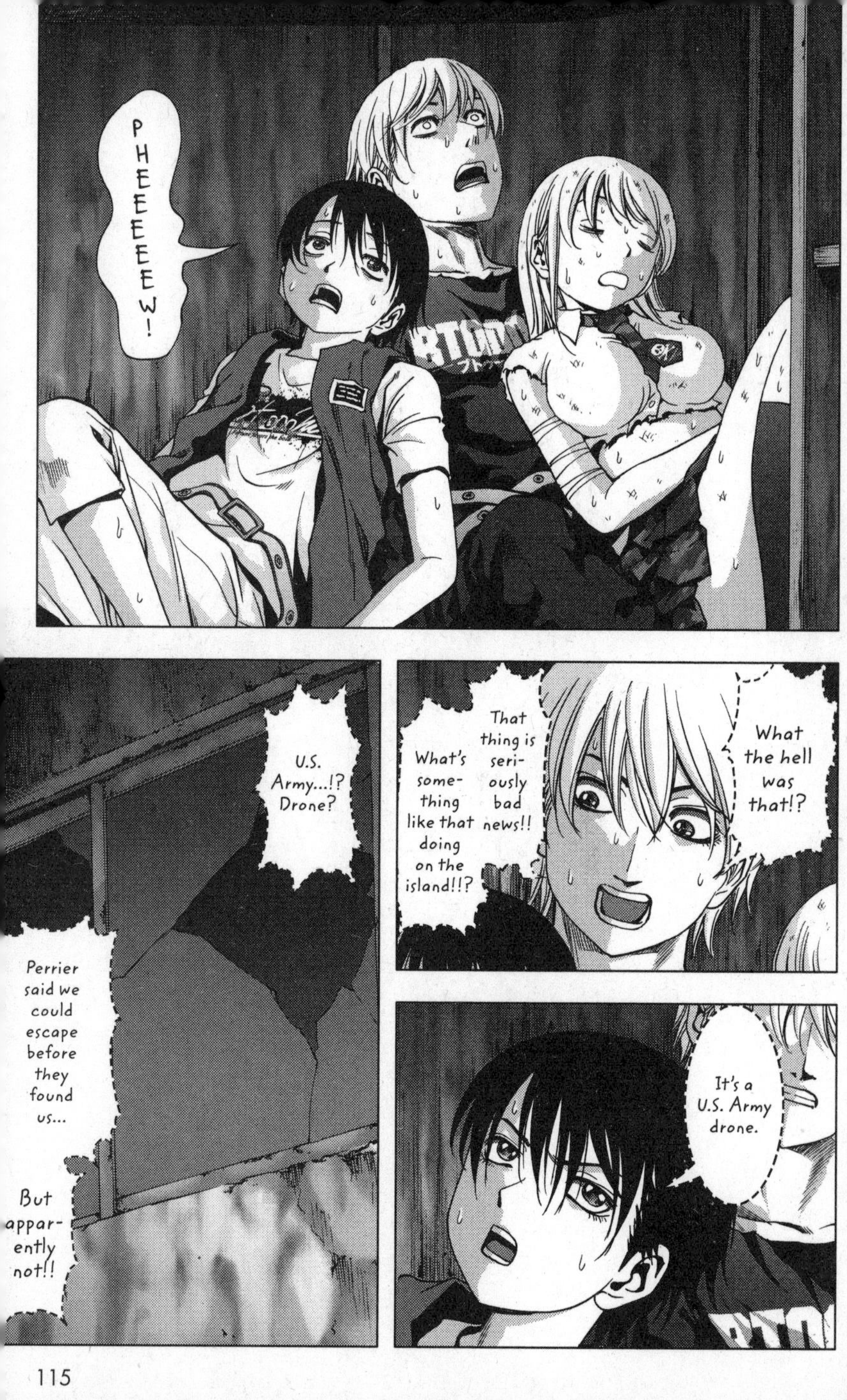
PHEEEEEW!
What the hell was that!?
That thing is seriously bad news!!
What's something like that doing on the island!!?
It's a U.S. Army drone.
U.S. Army...!? Drone?
Perrier said we could escape before they found us...
But apparently not!!

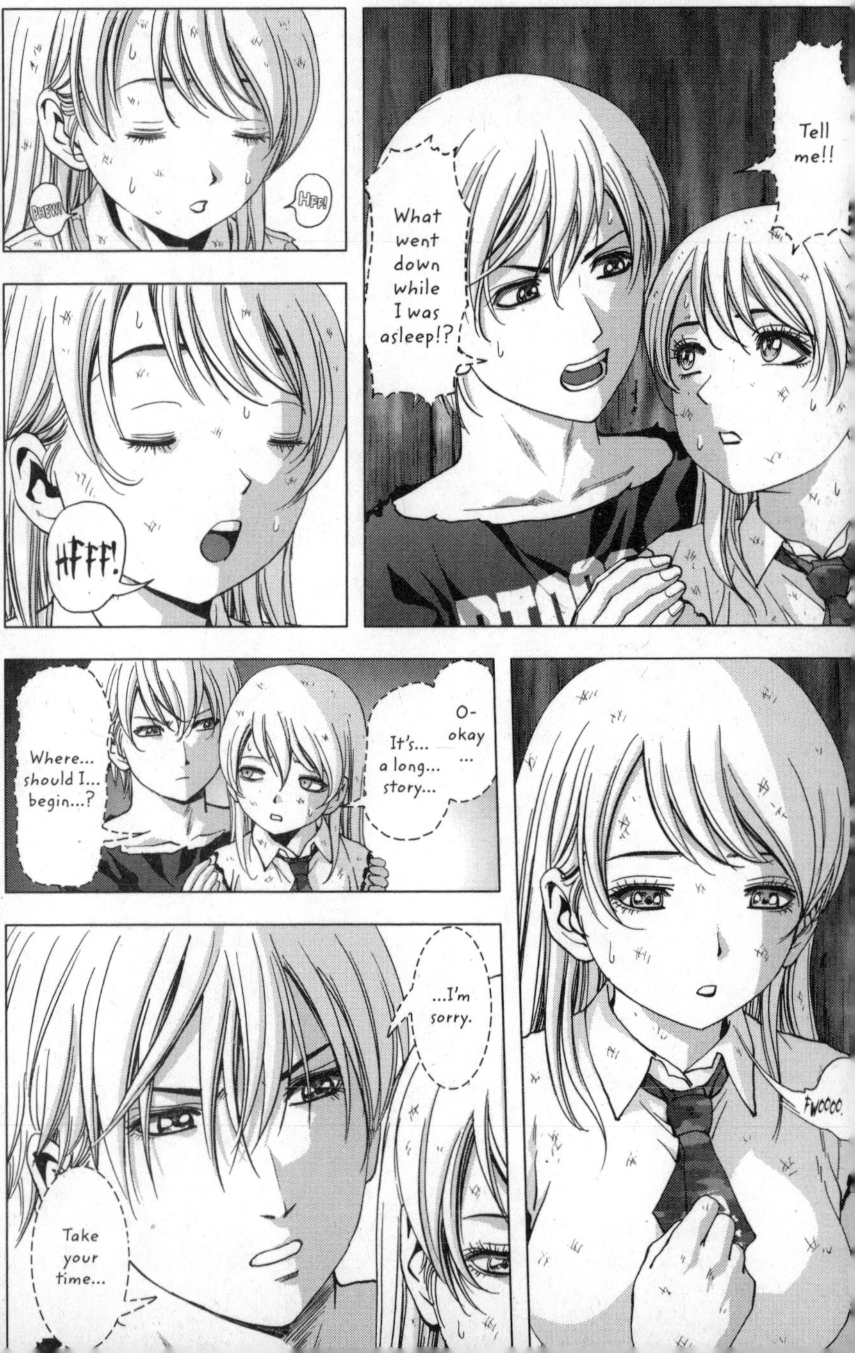
Tell me!!
What went down while I was asleep!?
HFF!
PHEW!
HFFF!
FWOOOO.
O-okay...
It's... a long... story...
Where... should I... begin...?
...I'm sorry.
Take your time...

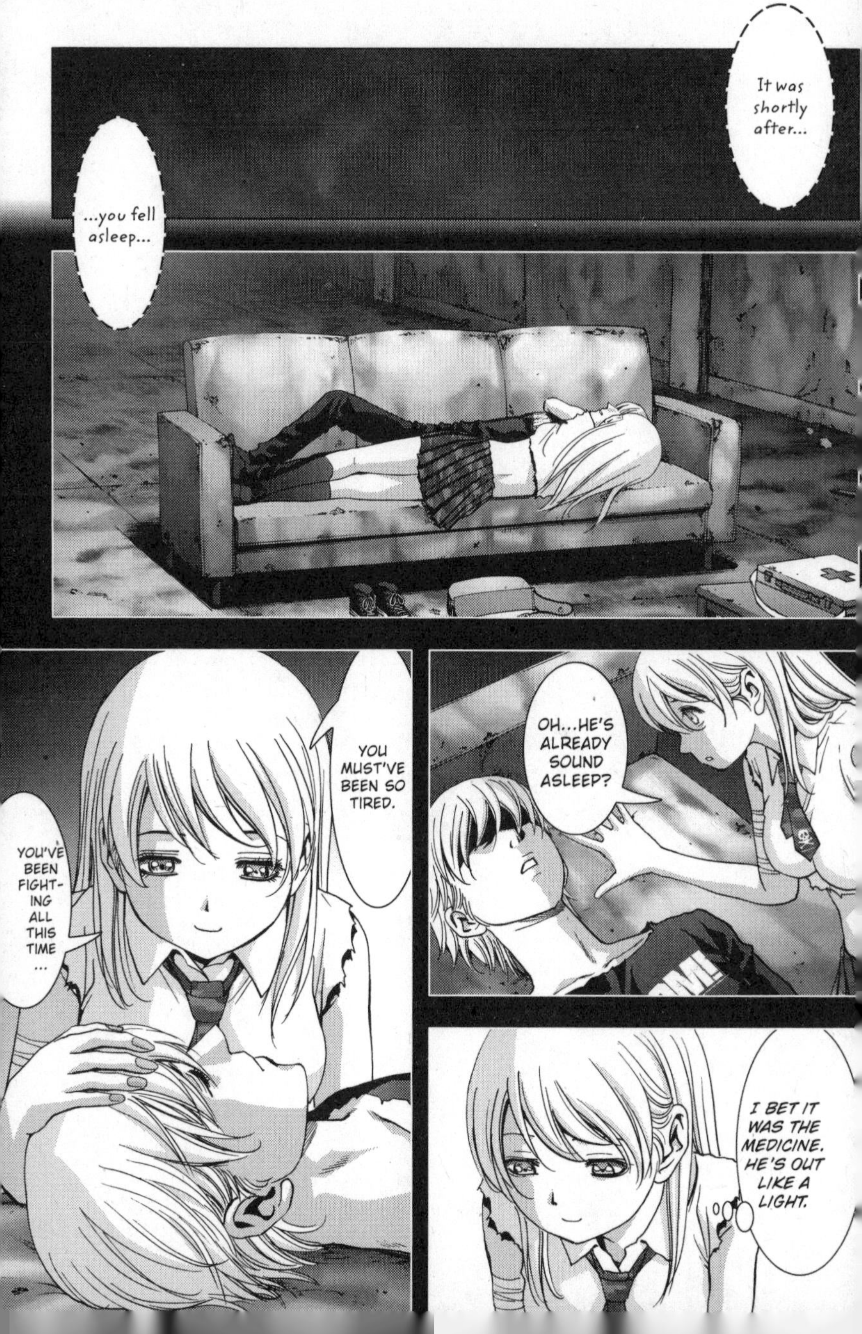

It was shortly after...
...you fell asleep...
OH...HE'S ALREADY SOUND ASLEEP?
I BET IT WAS THE MEDICINE. HE'S OUT LIKE A LIGHT.
YOU MUST'VE BEEN SO TIRED.
YOU'VE BEEN FIGHTING ALL THIS TIME...

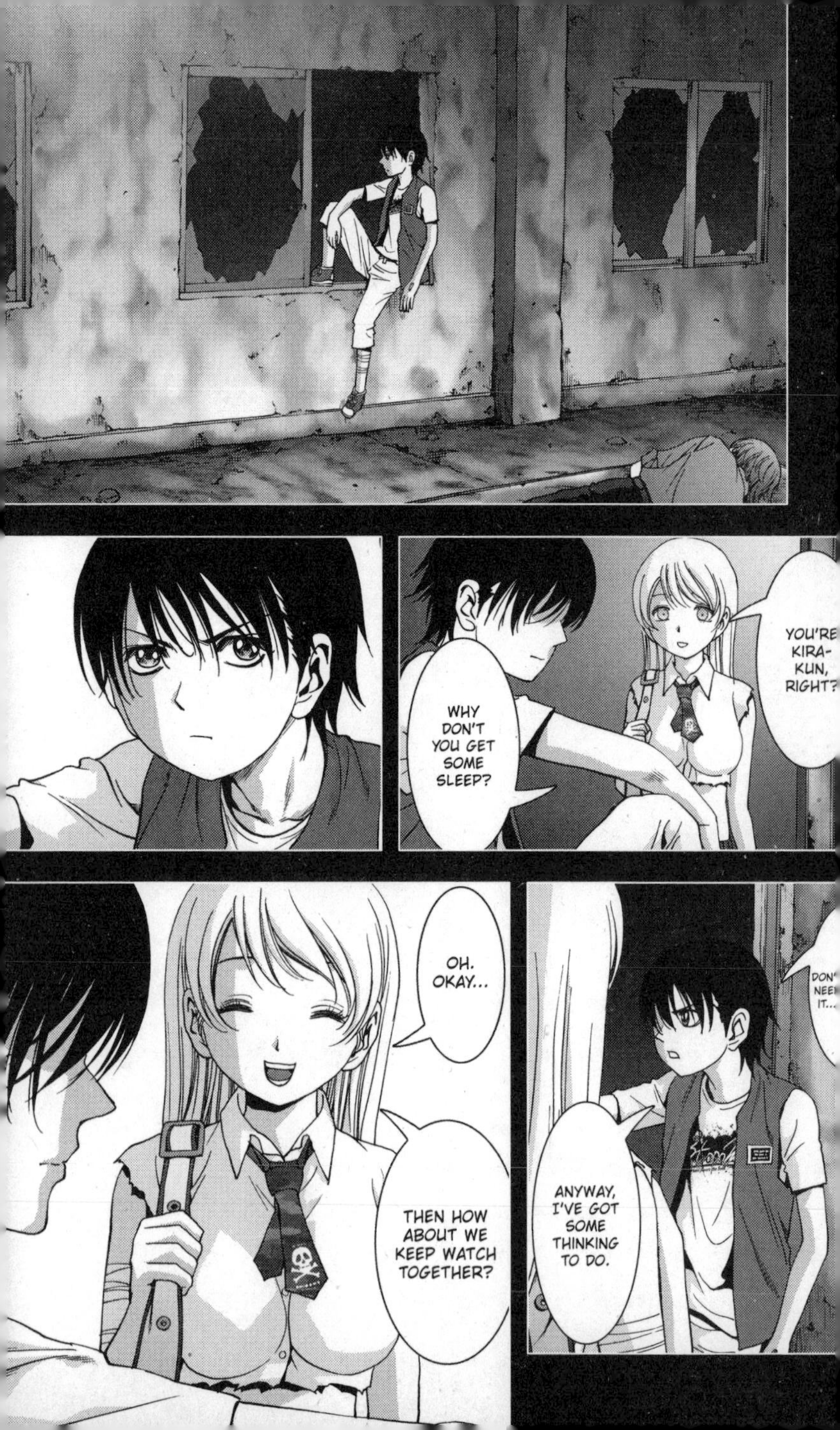
YOU'RE KIRA-KUN, RIGHT?
WHY DON'T YOU GET SOME SLEEP?
ANYWAY, I'VE GOT SOME THINKING TO DO.
OH. OKAY...
THEN HOW ABOUT WE KEEP WATCH TOGETHER?

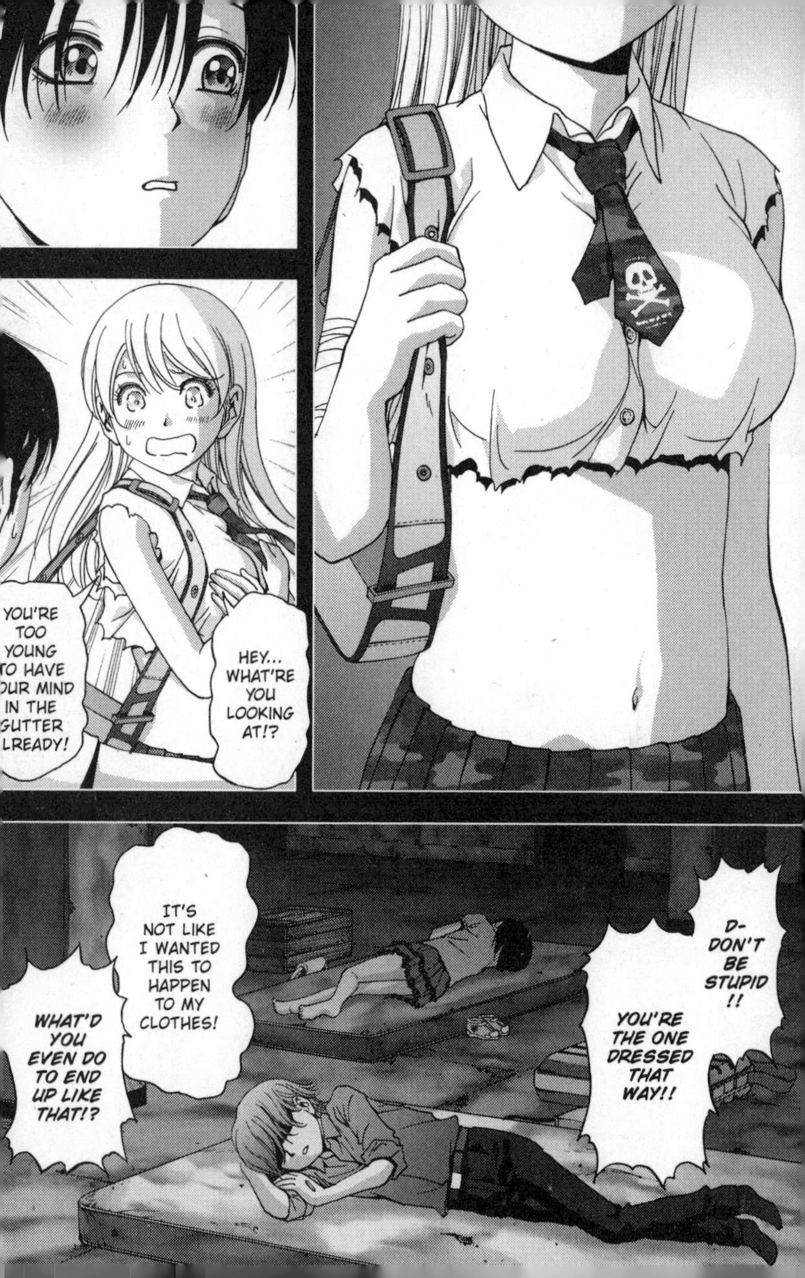
HEY... WHAT'RE YOU LOOKING AT!?
YOU'RE TOO YOUNG TO HAVE OUR MIND IN THE GUTTER LREADY!
D-DON'T BE STUPID!!
YOU'RE THE ONE DRESSED THAT WAY!!
IT'S NOT LIKE I WANTED THIS TO HAPPEN TO MY CLOTHES!
WHAT'D YOU EVEN DO TO END UP LIKE THAT!?

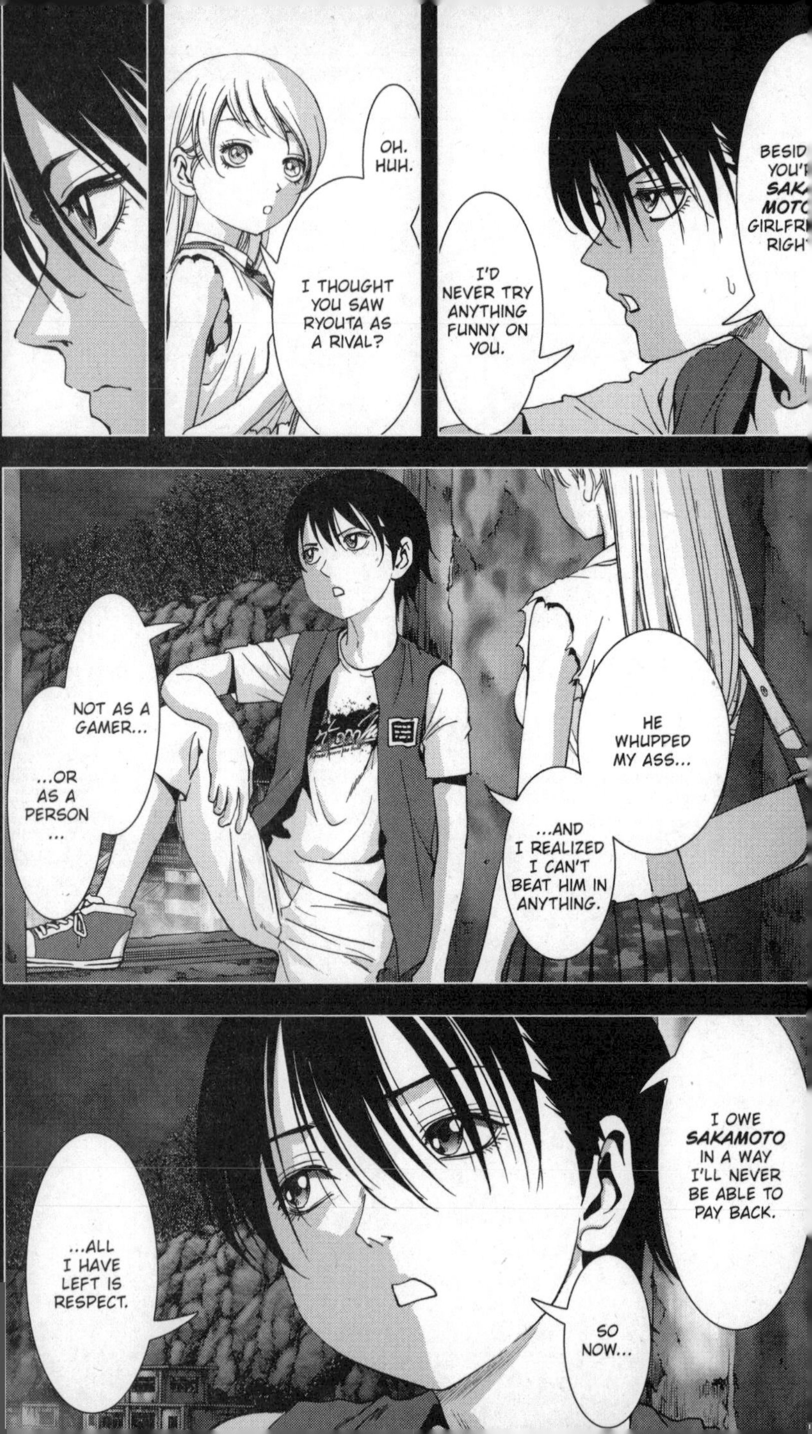
BESID YOU'I SAKA MOTO GIRLFR RIGHT
I'D NEVER TRY ANYTHING FUNNY ON YOU.
OH. HUH.
I THOUGHT YOU SAW RYOUTA AS A RIVAL?
HE WHUPPED MY ASS...
...AND I REALIZED I CAN'T BEAT HIM IN ANYTHING.
NOT AS A GAMER...
...OR AS A PERSON...
I OWE SAKAMOTO IN A WAY I'LL NEVER BE ABLE TO PAY BACK.
SO NOW...
...ALL I HAVE LEFT IS RESPECT.

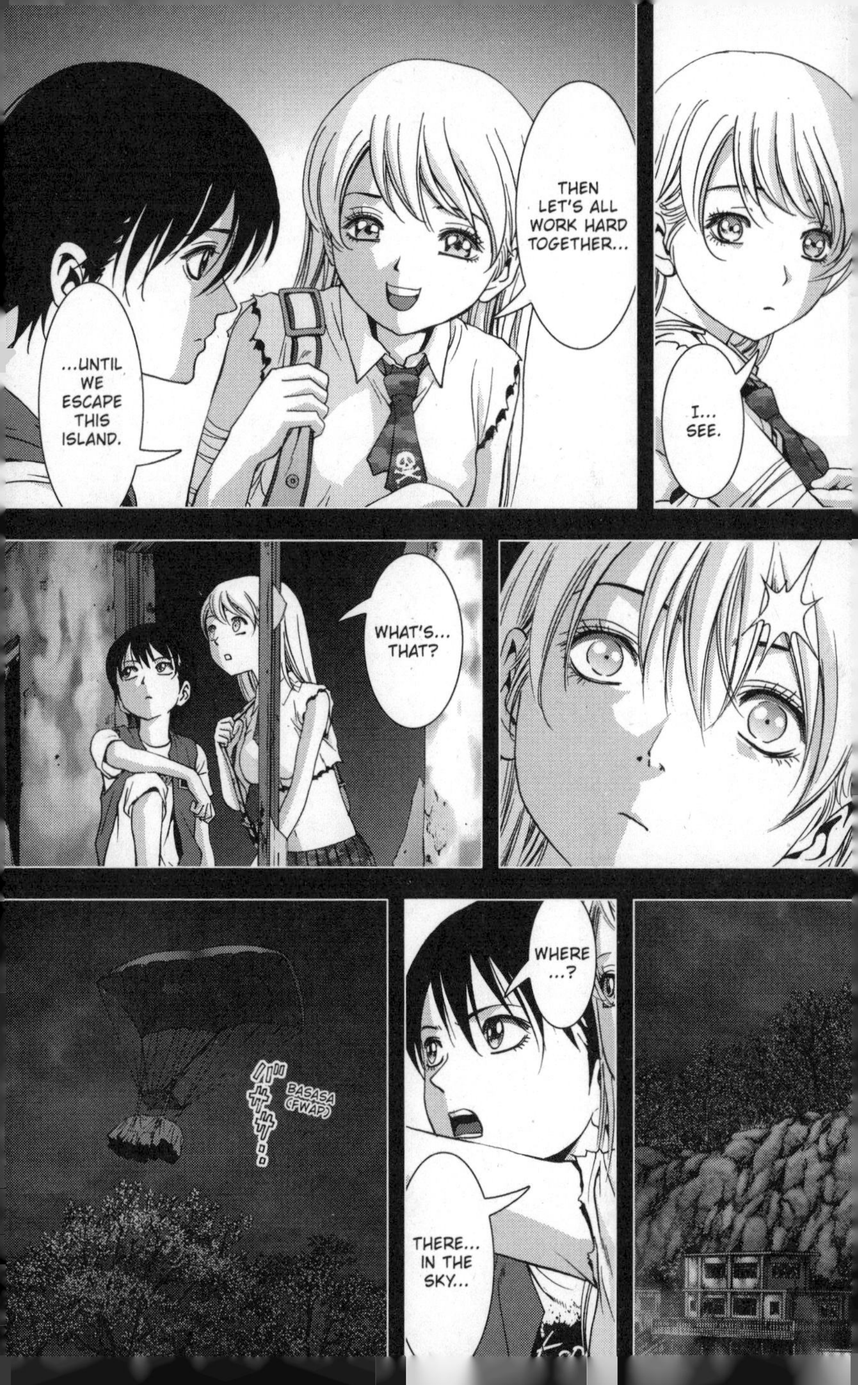
I... SEE.
THEN LET'S ALL WORK HARD TOGETHER...
...UNTIL WE ESCAPE THIS ISLAND.
WHAT'S... THAT?
WHERE ...?
THERE... IN THE SKY...
BASASA (FWAP)

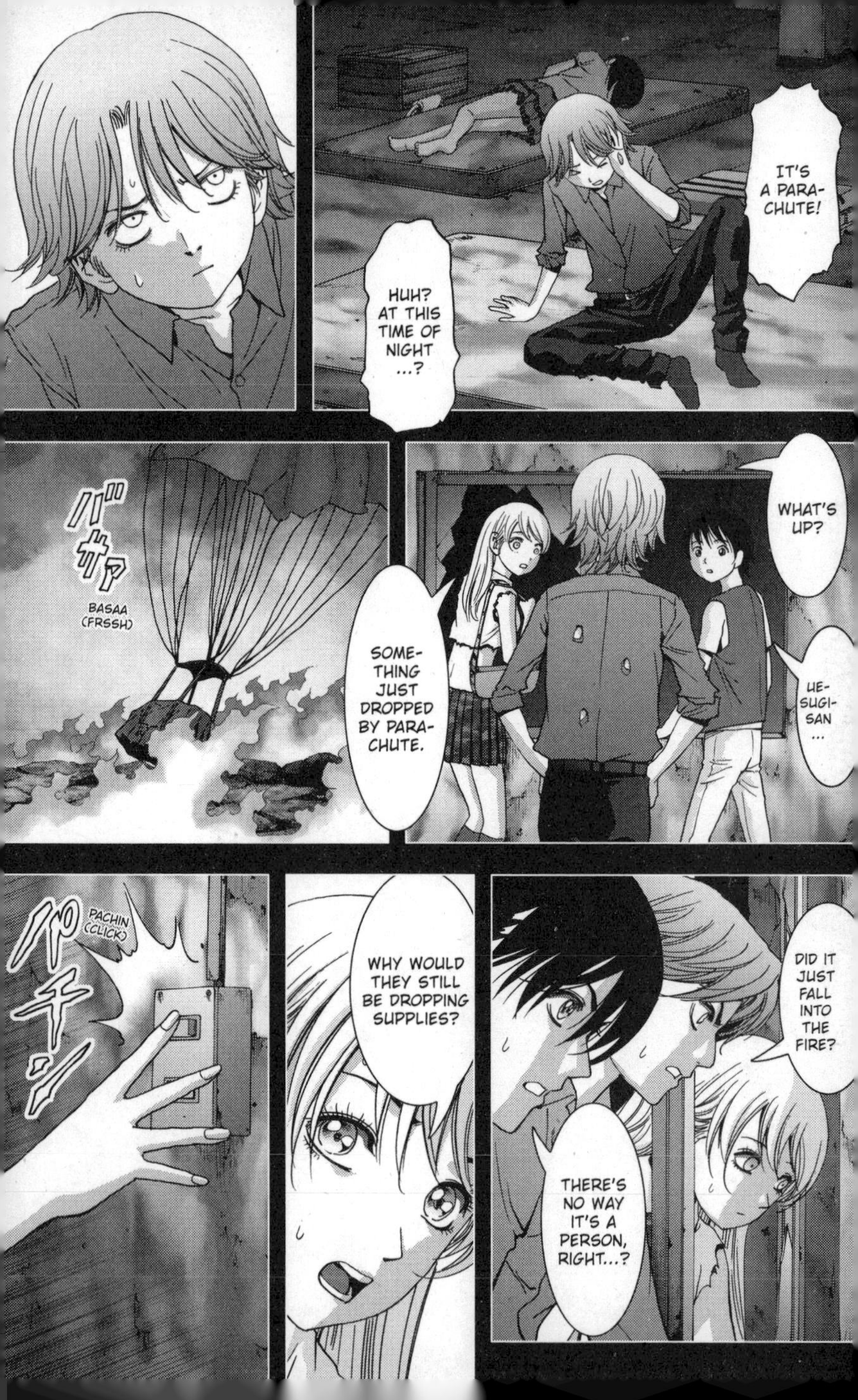
IT'S A PARA-CHUTE!
HUH? AT THIS TIME OF NIGHT ...?
WHAT'S UP?
UE-SUGI-SAN ...
SOME-THING JUST DROPPED BY PARA-CHUTE.
バサァ
BASAA (FRSSH)
DID IT JUST FALL INTO THE FIRE?
THERE'S NO WAY IT'S A PERSON, RIGHT...?
WHY WOULD THEY STILL BE DROPPING SUPPLIES?
パチン
PACHIN (CLICK)

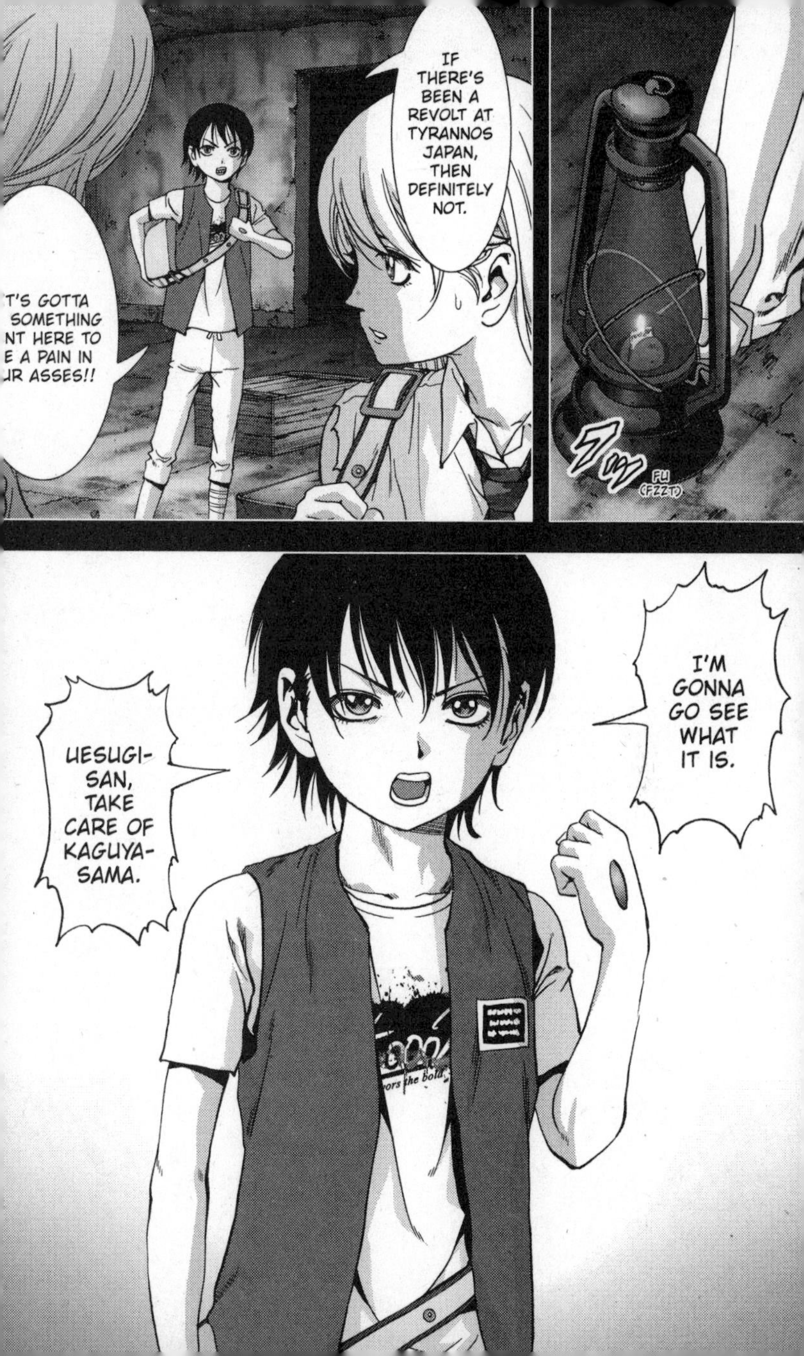
FU (FZZT)
IF THERE'S BEEN A REVOLT AT TYRANNOS JAPAN, THEN DEFINITELY NOT.
T'S GOTTA SOMETHING NT HERE TO E A PAIN IN UR ASSES!!
I'M GONNA GO SEE WHAT IT IS.
UESUGI-SAN, TAKE CARE OF KAGUYA-SAMA.

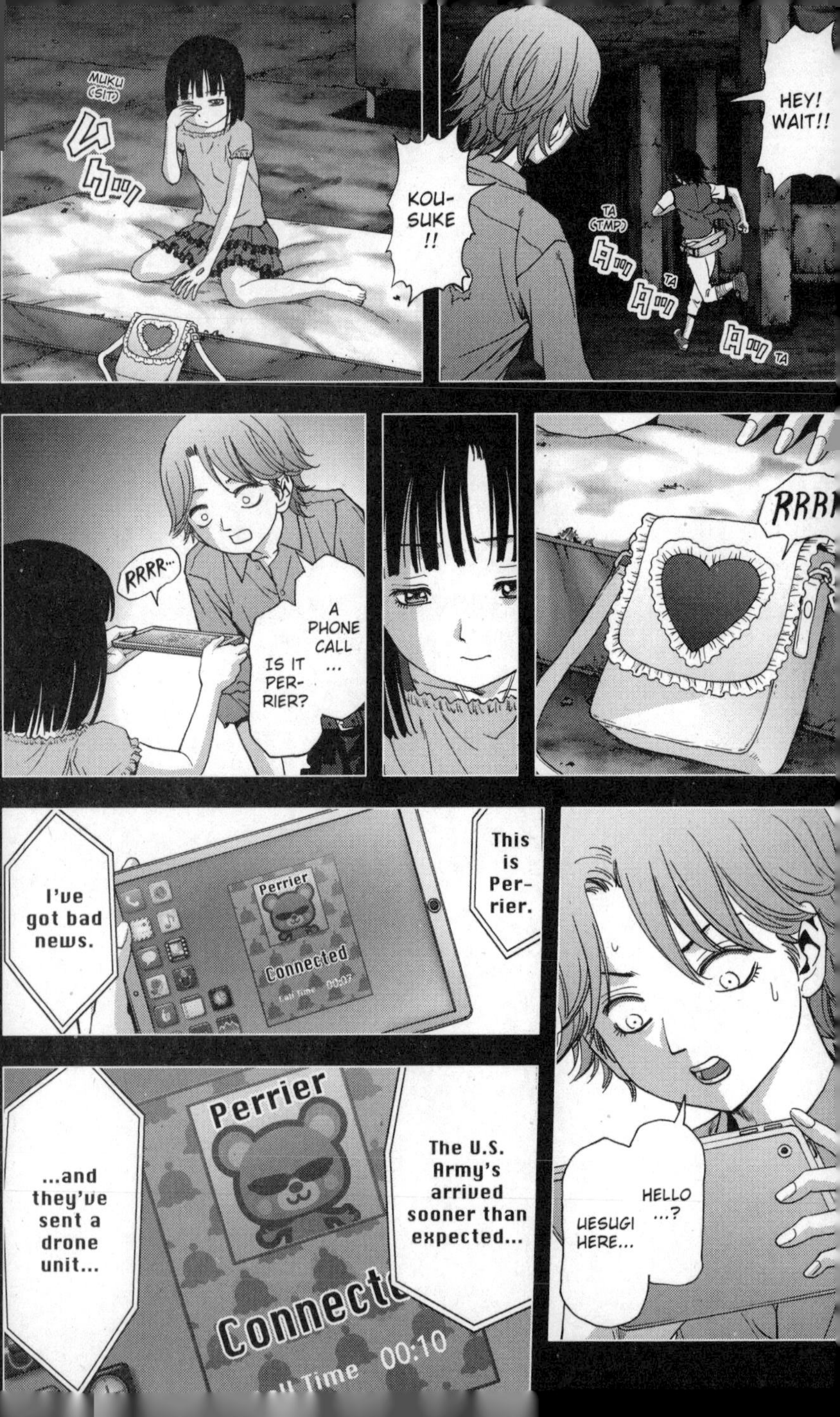
HEY! WAIT!!
KOU-SUKE!!
TA (TMP)
TA
TA
MUKU (SIT)
RRRR
A PHONE CALL ...
IS IT PER-RIER?
RRRR...
HELLO ...?
UESUGI HERE...
This is Per-rier.
Perrier
Connected
00:07
I've got bad news.
The U.S. Army's arrived sooner than expected...
Perrier
00:10
...and they've sent a drone unit...

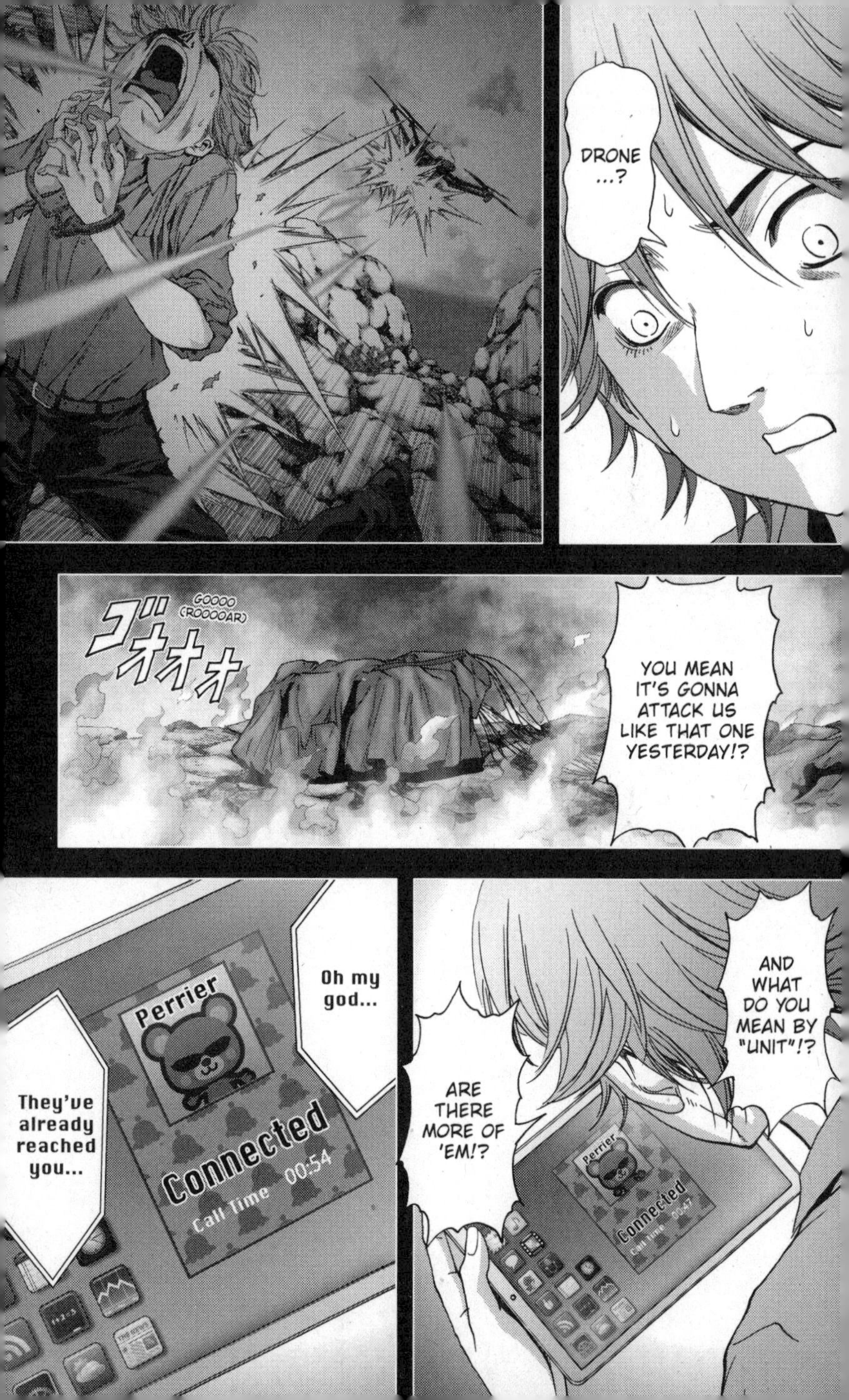
DRONE ...?
YOU MEAN IT'S GONNA ATTACK US LIKE THAT ONE YESTERDAY!?
ゴオオオ
GOOOO (ROOOOAR)
AND WHAT DO YOU MEAN BY "UNIT"!?
ARE THERE MORE OF 'EM!?
Perrier
Connected
Call Time 00:47
Oh my god...
Perrier
Connected
Call Time 00:54
They've already reached you...

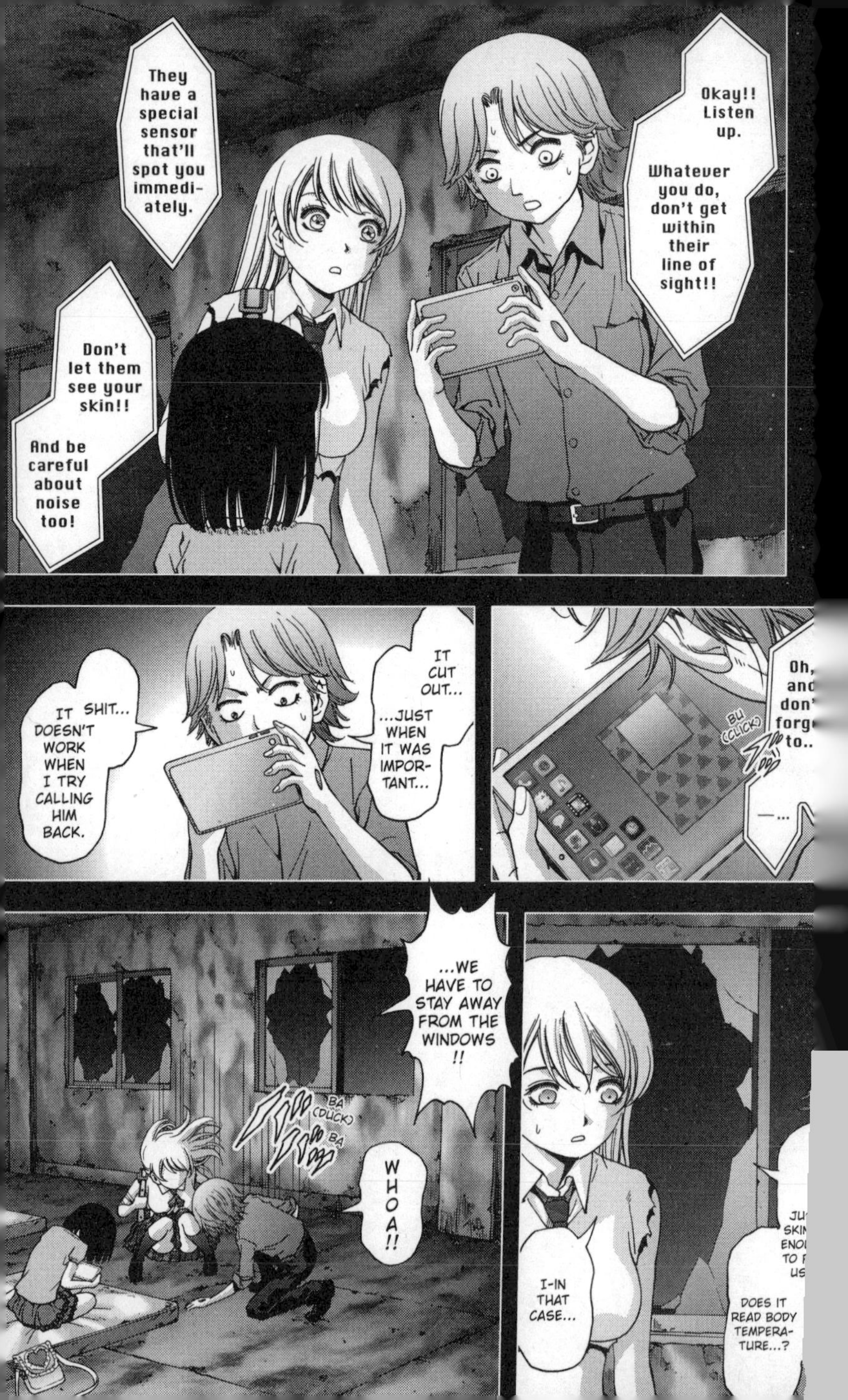

Okay!! Listen up.
Whatever you do, don't get within their line of sight!!
They have a special sensor that'll spot you immediately.
Don't let them see your skin!!
And be careful about noise too!
Oh, and don' forg to..
BU (CLICK)
—...
IT CUT OUT...
...JUST WHEN IT WAS IMPORTANT...
SHIT...
IT DOESN'T WORK WHEN I TRY CALLING HIM BACK.
DOES IT READ BODY TEMPERATURE...?
I-IN THAT CASE...
...WE HAVE TO STAY AWAY FROM THE WINDOWS!!
BA (DUCK) BA
WHOA!!

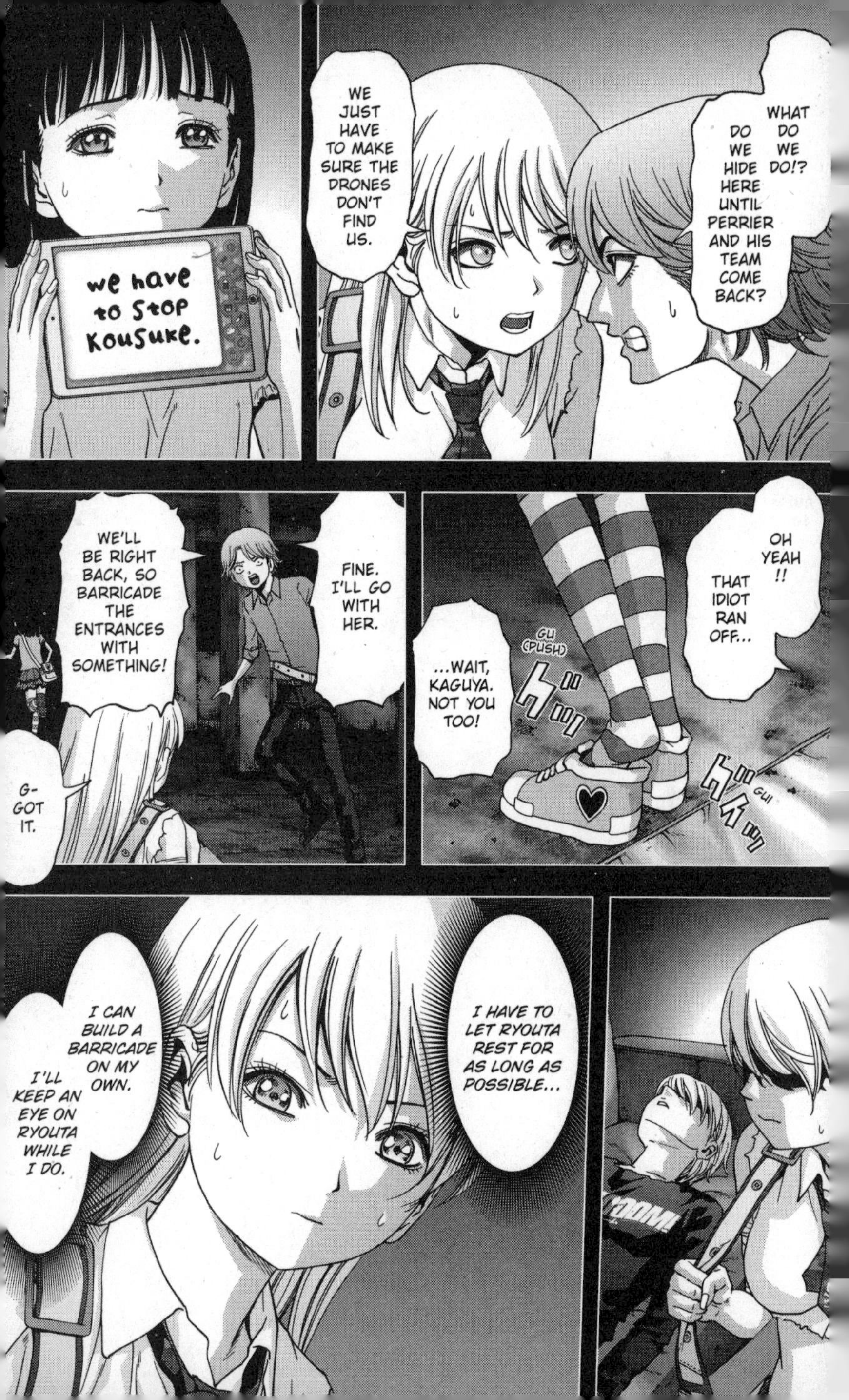
WHAT DO WE DO!?
DO WE HIDE HERE UNTIL PERRIER AND HIS TEAM COME BACK?
WE JUST HAVE TO MAKE SURE THE DRONES DON'T FIND US.
we have to stop Kousuke.
OH YEAH!!
THAT IDIOT RAN OFF...
GU (PUSH)
...WAIT, KAGUYA. NOT YOU TOO!
GUI
FINE. I'LL GO WITH HER.
WE'LL BE RIGHT BACK, SO BARRICADE THE ENTRANCES WITH SOMETHING!
G-GOT IT.
I HAVE TO LET RYOUTA REST FOR AS LONG AS POSSIBLE...
I CAN BUILD A BARRICADE ON MY OWN.
I'LL KEEP AN EYE ON RYOUTA WHILE I DO.

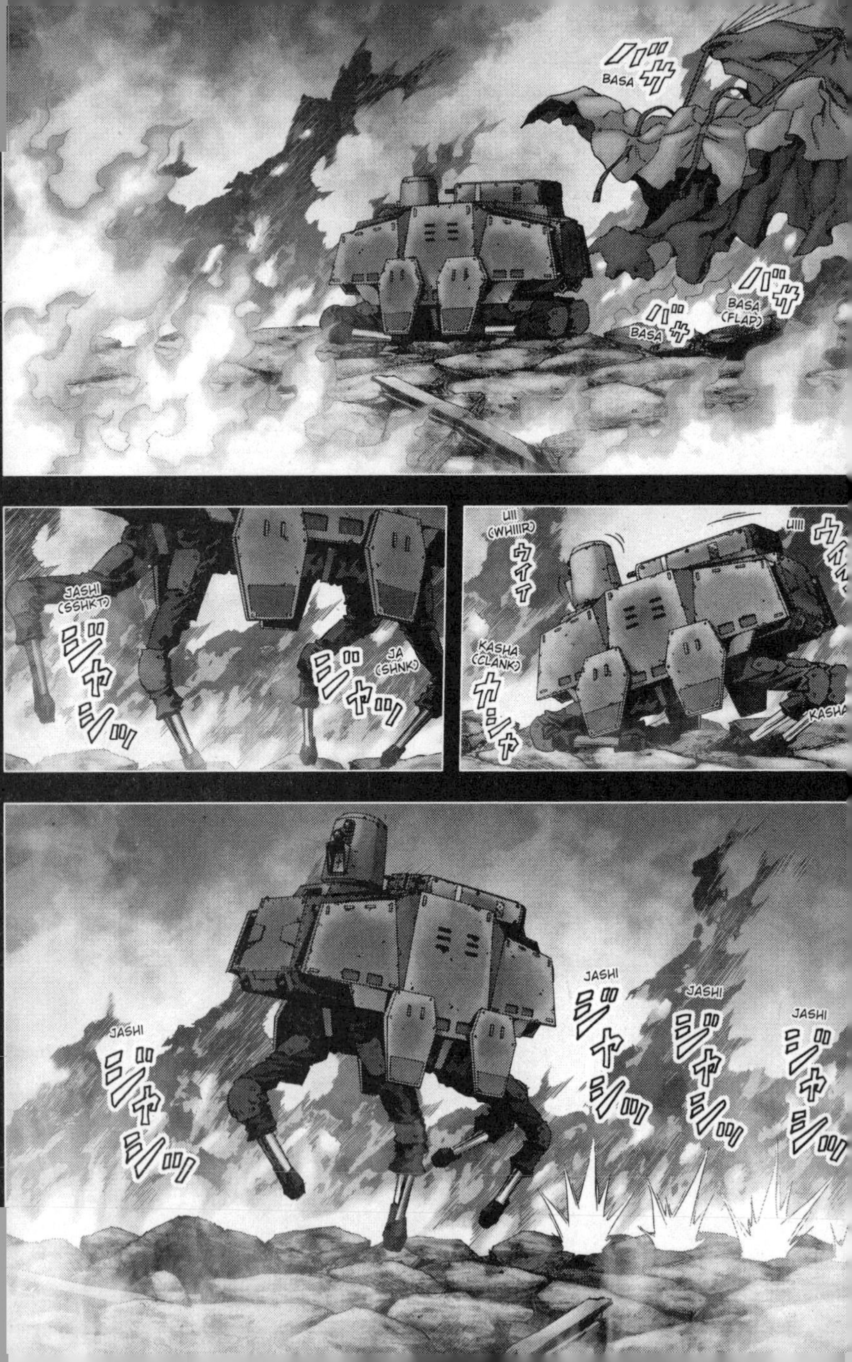
BASA
BASA (FLAP)
BASA
UIII
UII (WHIIIR)
KASHA (CLANK)
KASHA
JA (SHNK)
JASHI (SSHKT)
JASHI
JASHI
JASHI
JASHI

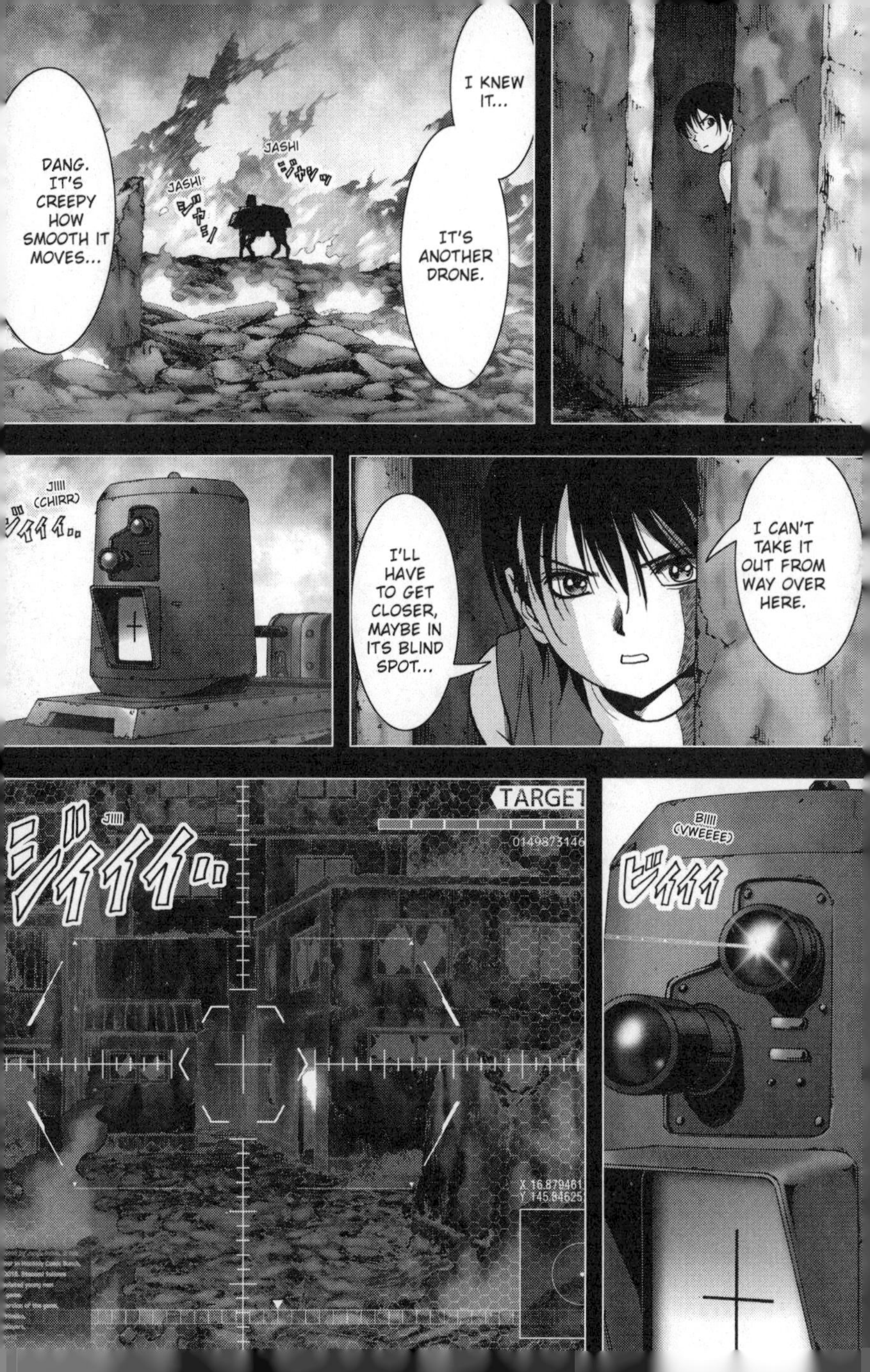
I KNEW IT...
IT'S ANOTHER DRONE.
JASHI
JASHI
DANG. IT'S CREEPY HOW SMOOTH IT MOVES...
I CAN'T TAKE IT OUT FROM WAY OVER HERE.
I'LL HAVE TO GET CLOSER, MAYBE IN ITS BLIND SPOT...
JIIII (CHIRR)
ジィィィ。。
BIIII (VWEEEE)
ビィィィ
TARGET
0149873146
JIIII
ジィィィ。。
X 16.879461
Y 145.84625

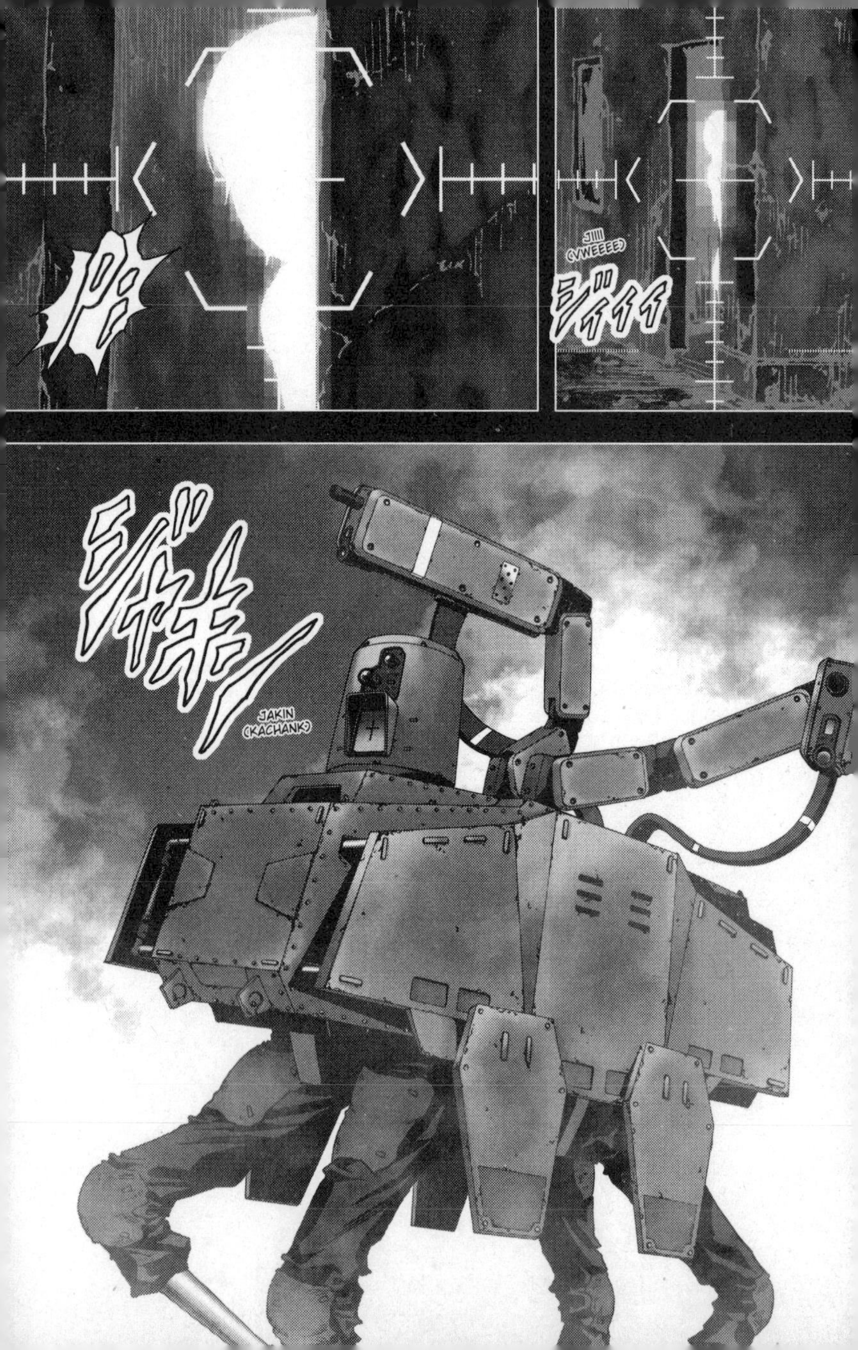
ジィィィ
JIII (VWEEEE)
ジャキン
JAKIN (KACHANK)

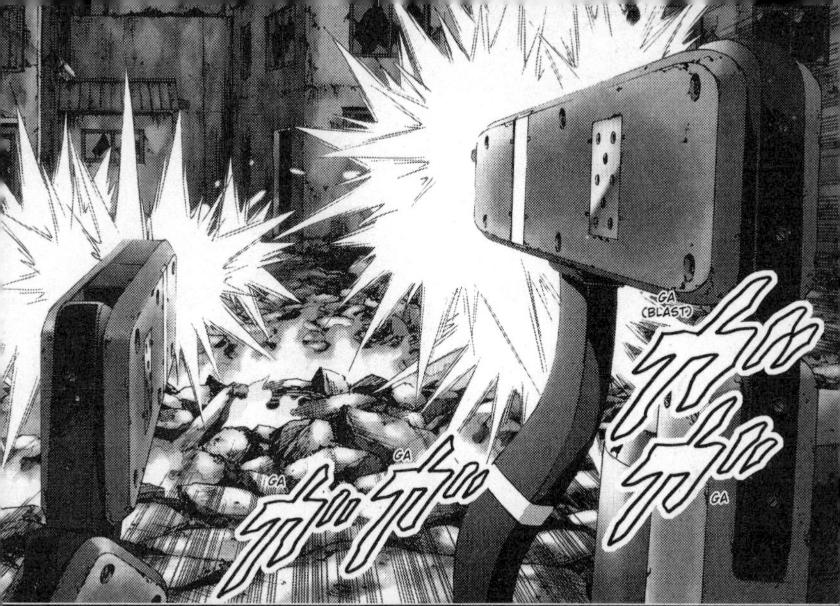
GA
(BLAST)
GA
GA
GA

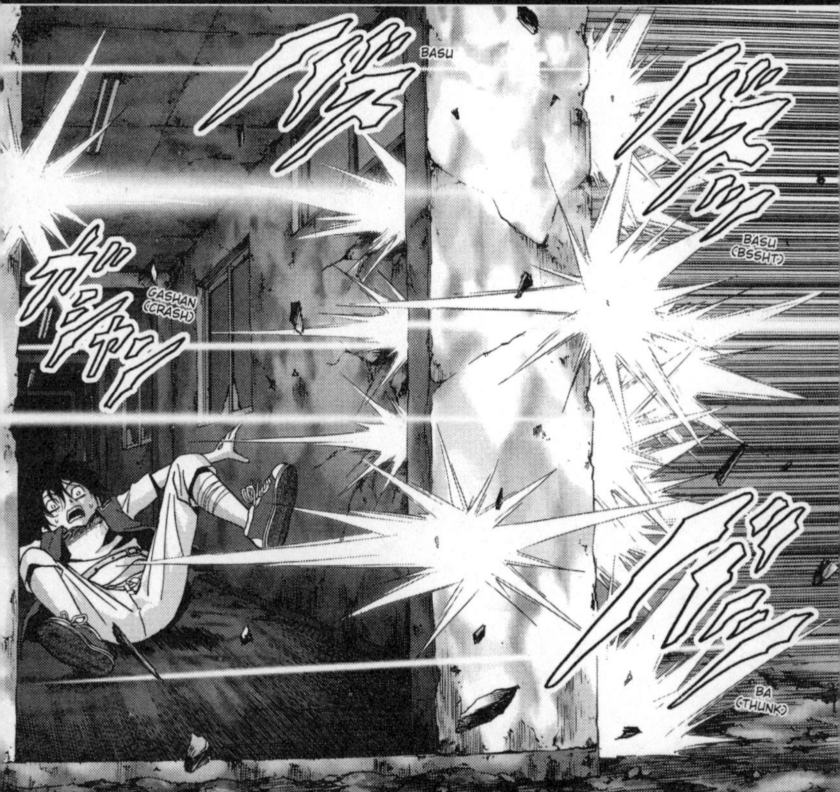
BASU
BASU
(BSSHT)
GASHAN
(CRASH)
BA
(THUNK)

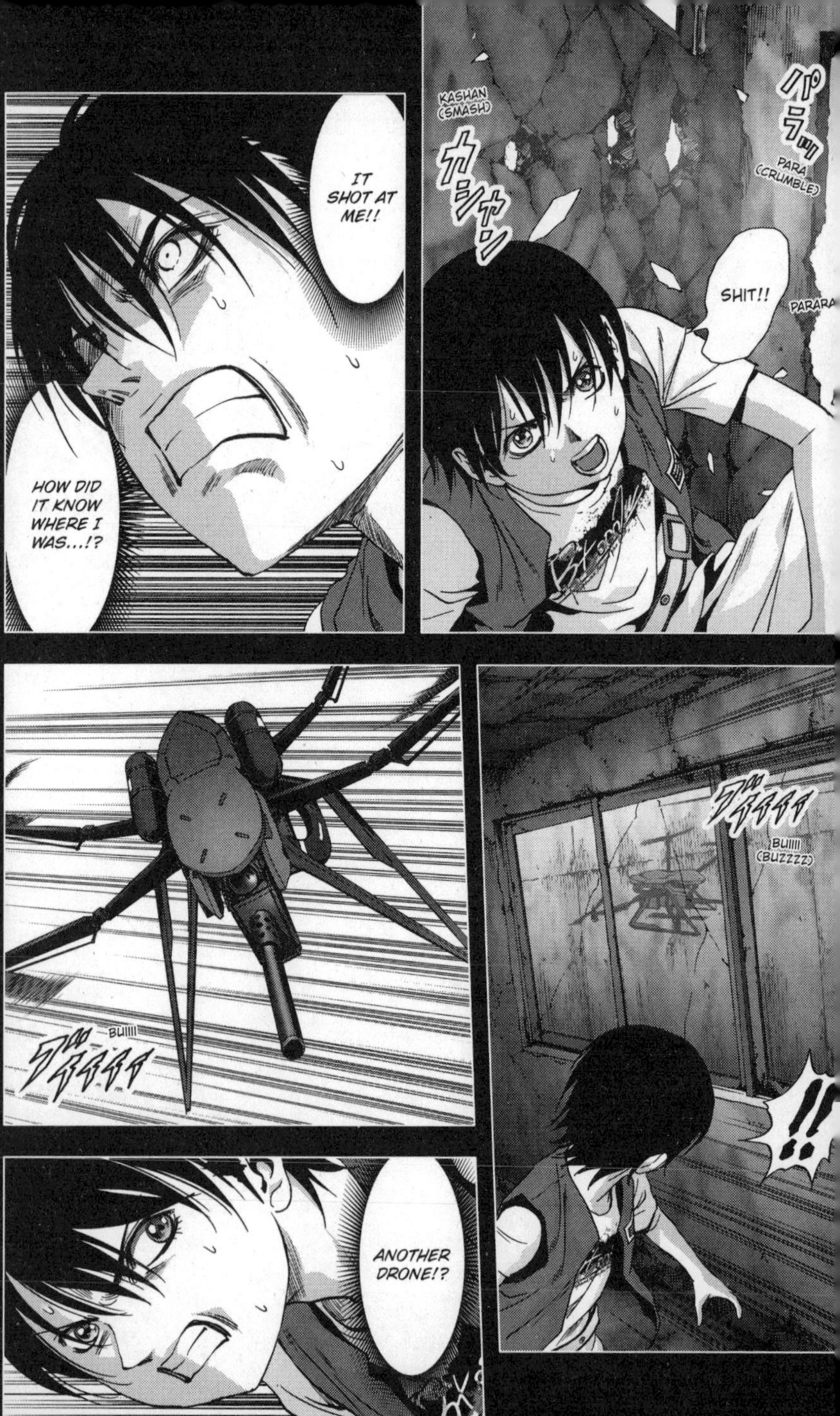
パラッ
PARA (CRUMBLE)
カシャン
KASHAN (SMASH)
SHIT!!
PARARA
IT SHOT AT ME!!
HOW DID IT KNOW WHERE I WAS...!?
ブィィィィ
BUIIII (BUZZZZ)
!!
ブィィィィ
BUIIII
ANOTHER DRONE!?

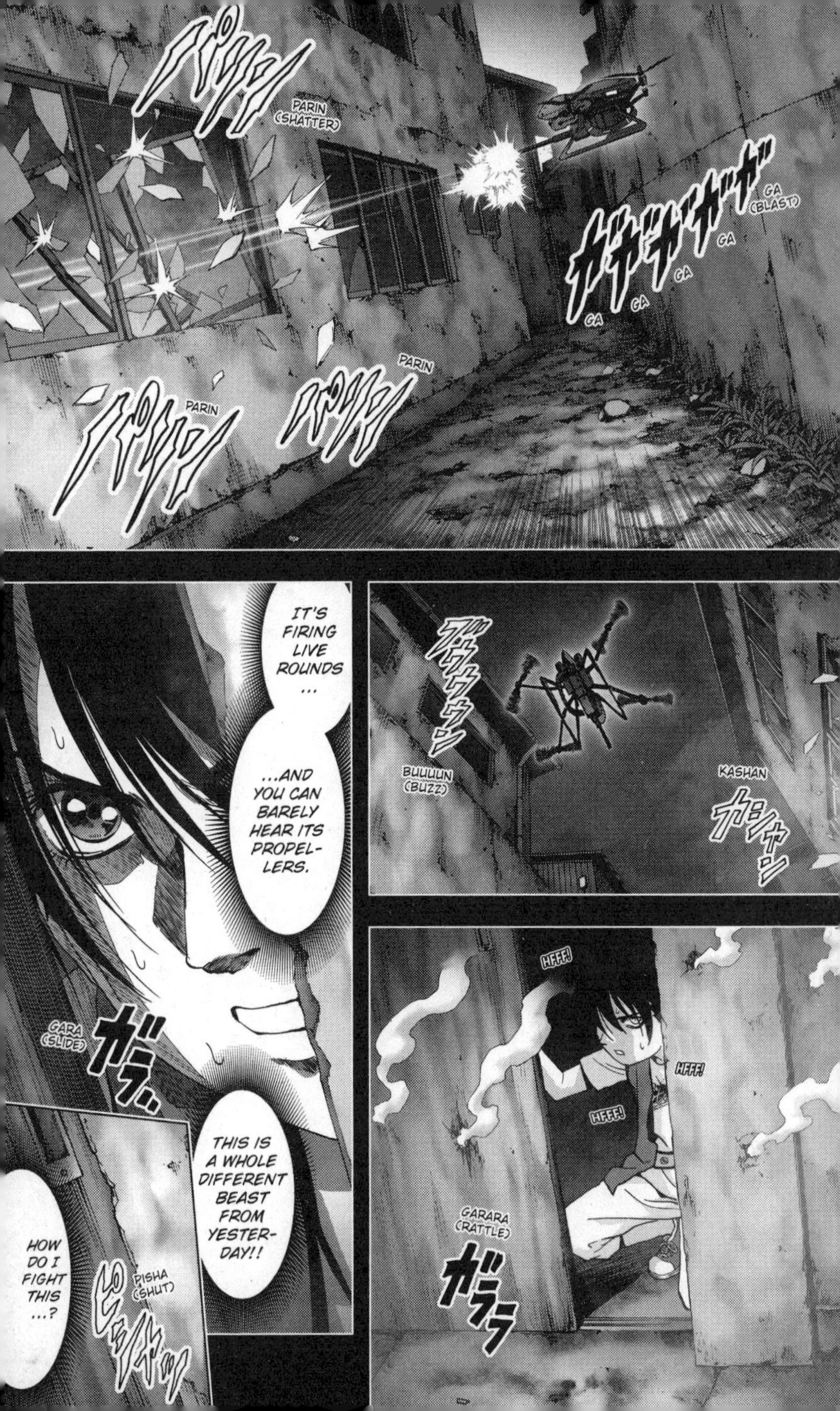
GA (BLAST)
GA
GA
GA
GA
PARIN (SHATTER)
PARIN
PARIN
KASHAN
BUUUUN (BUZZ)
HFFF!
HFFF!
HFFF!
GARARA (RATTLE)
IT'S FIRING LIVE ROUNDS...
...AND YOU CAN BARELY HEAR ITS PROPELLERS.
GARA (SLIDE)
THIS IS A WHOLE DIFFERENT BEAST FROM YESTERDAY!!
PISHA (SHUT)
HOW DO I FIGHT THIS...?

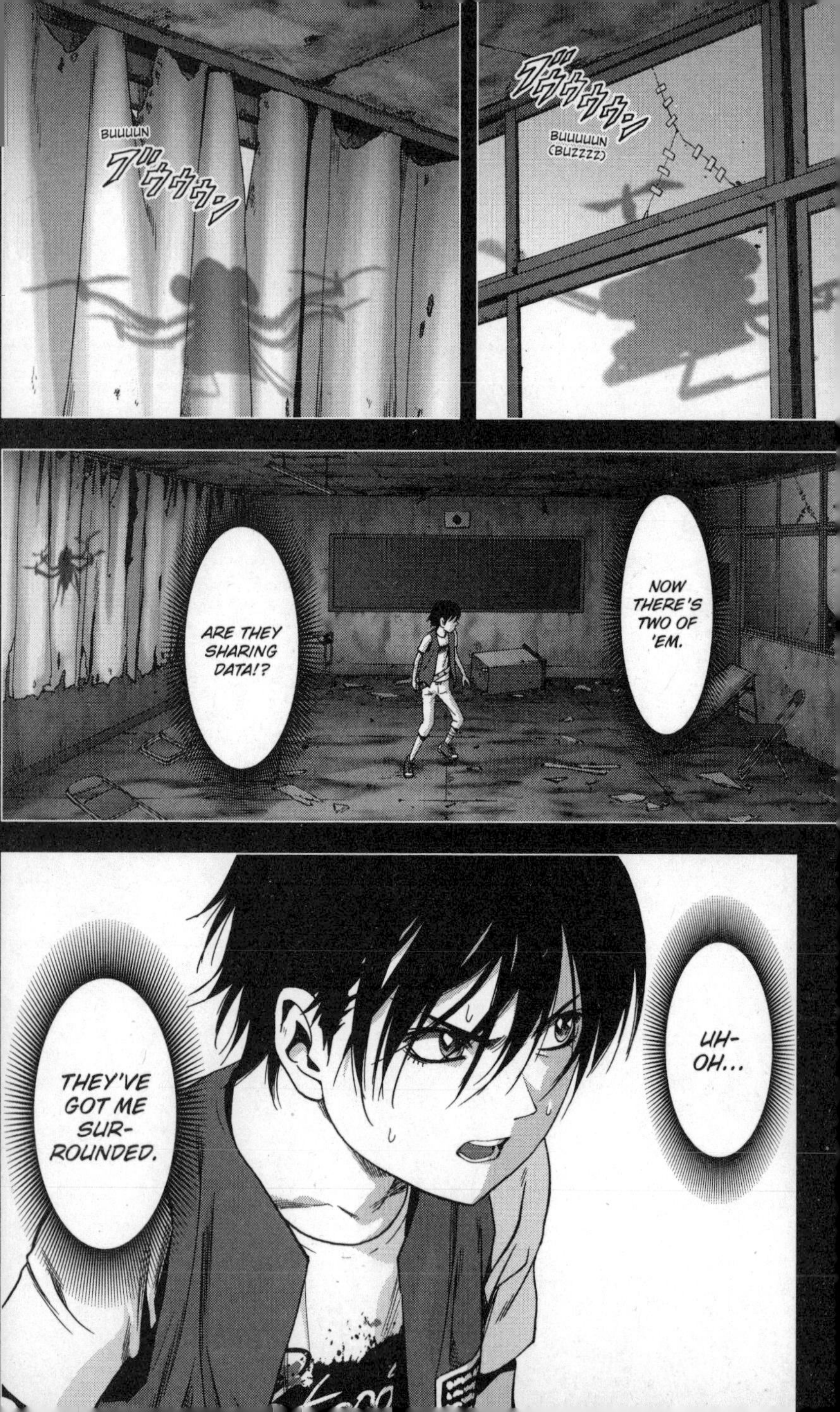
BUUUUUN (BUZZZZ)
BUUUUN
NOW THERE'S TWO OF 'EM.
ARE THEY SHARING DATA!?
UH-OH...
THEY'VE GOT ME SUR-ROUNDED.

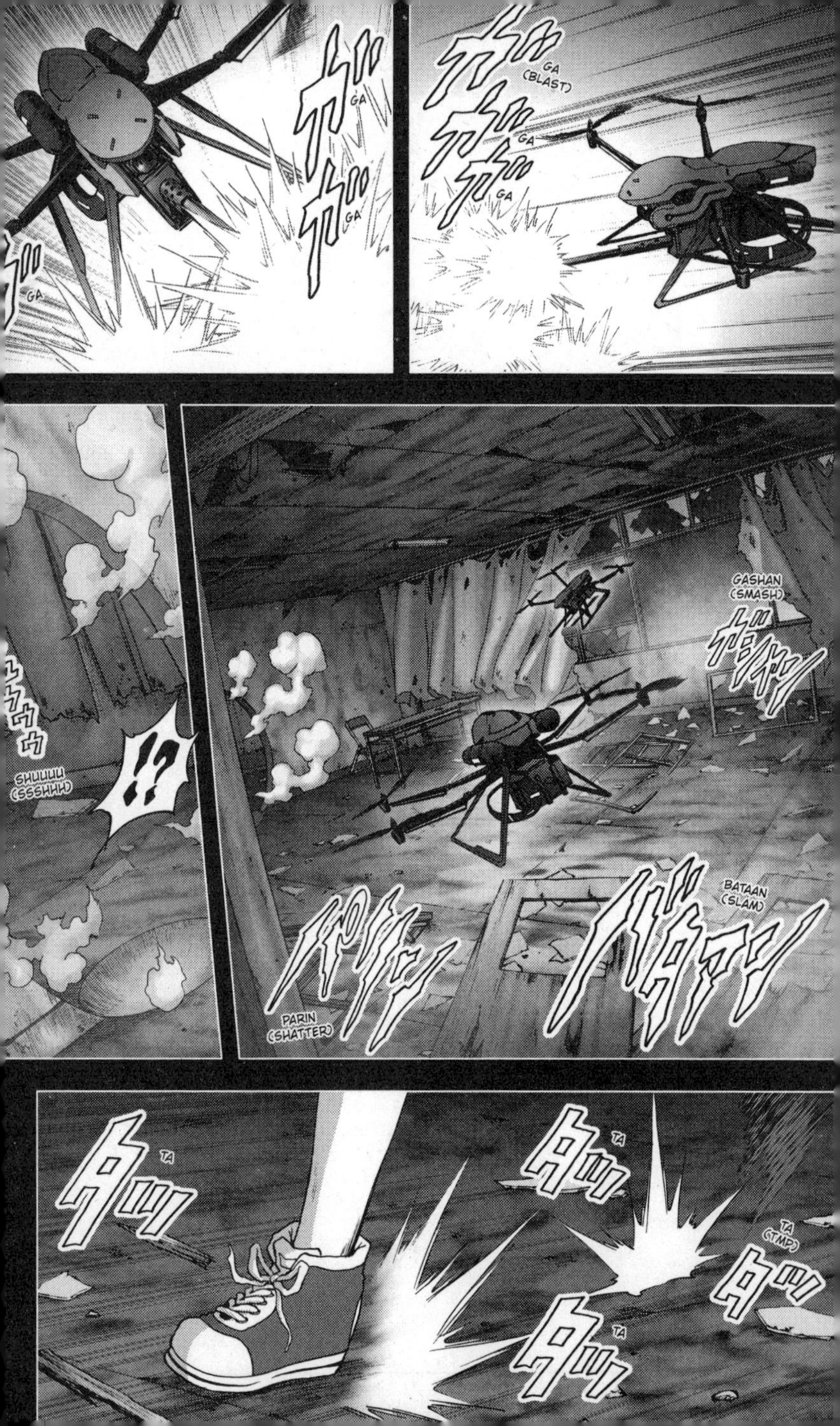

GA (BLAST)
GA
GA
GA
GA
GA
GASHAN (SMASH)
BATAAN (SLAM)
PARIN (SHATTER)
SHUUUU (SSSHHH)
!?
TA
TA (TMP)
TA
TA

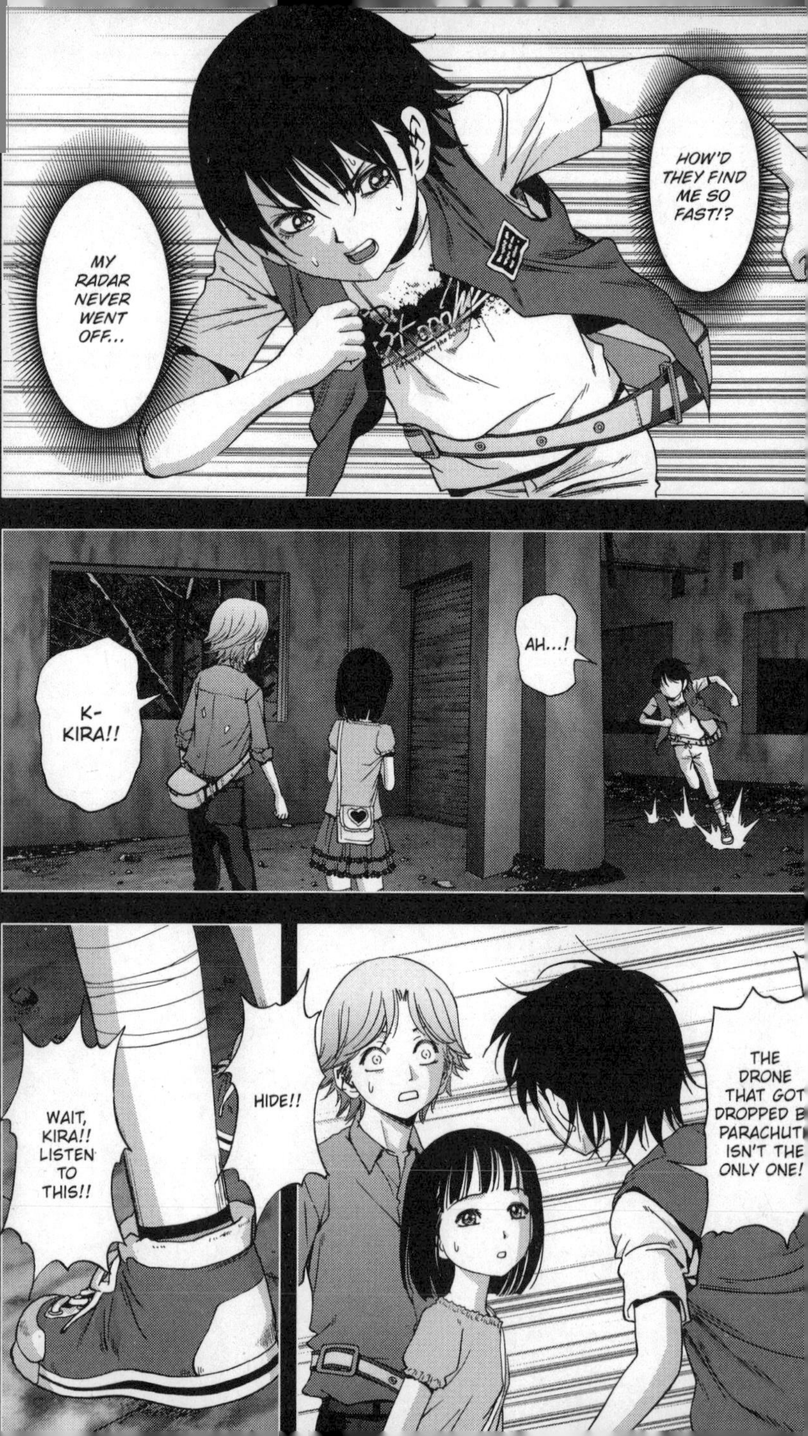
HOW'D THEY FIND ME SO FAST!?
MY RADAR NEVER WENT OFF...
AH...!
K-KIRA!!
THE DRONE THAT GOT DROPPED B PARACHUT ISN'T THE ONLY ONE!
HIDE!!
WAIT, KIRA!! LISTEN TO THIS!!

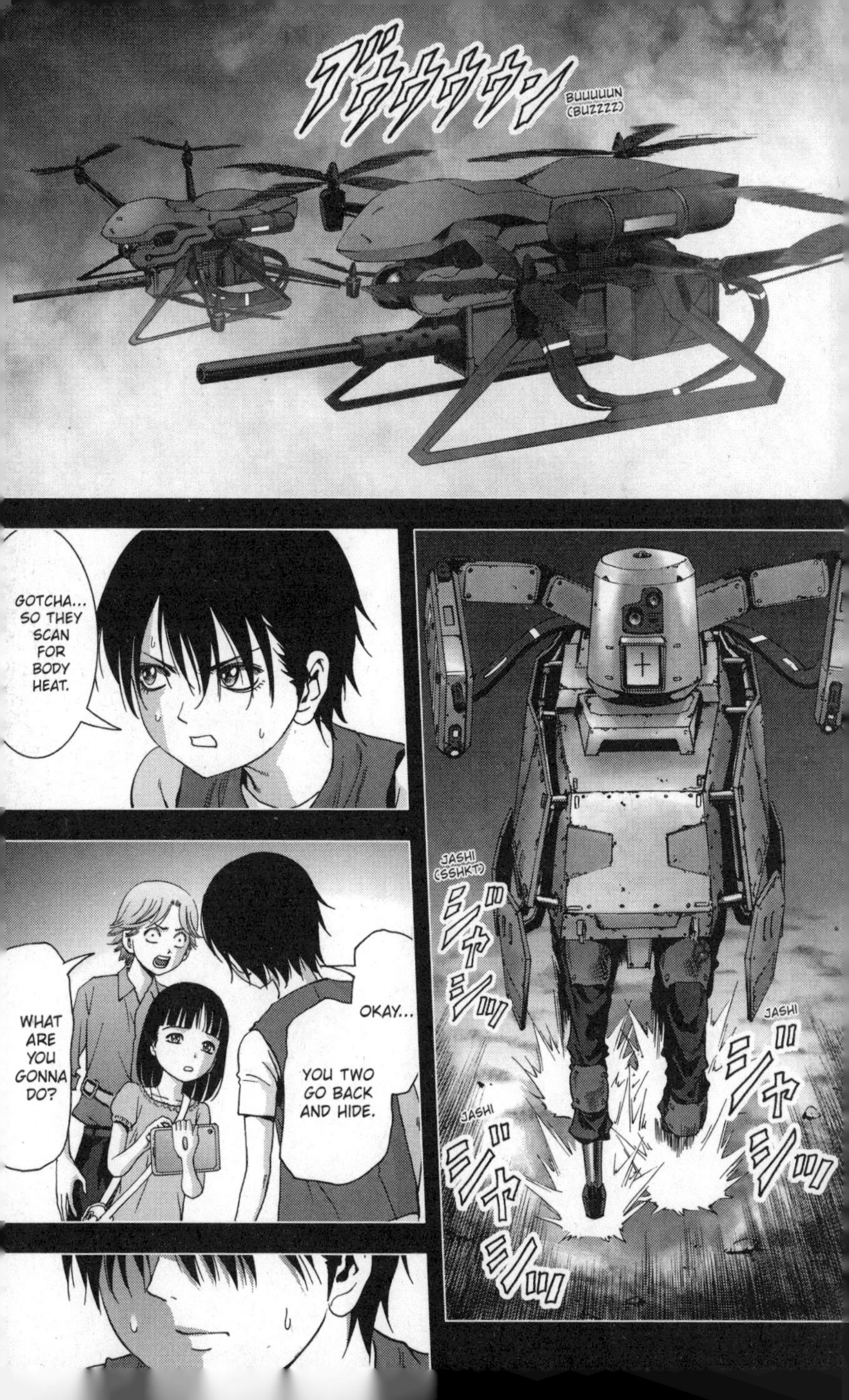
BUUUUUN (BUZZZZ)
JASHI (SSHKT)
JASHI
JASHI
GOTCHA... SO THEY SCAN FOR BODY HEAT.
OKAY...
YOU TWO GO BACK AND HIDE.
WHAT ARE YOU GONNA DO?

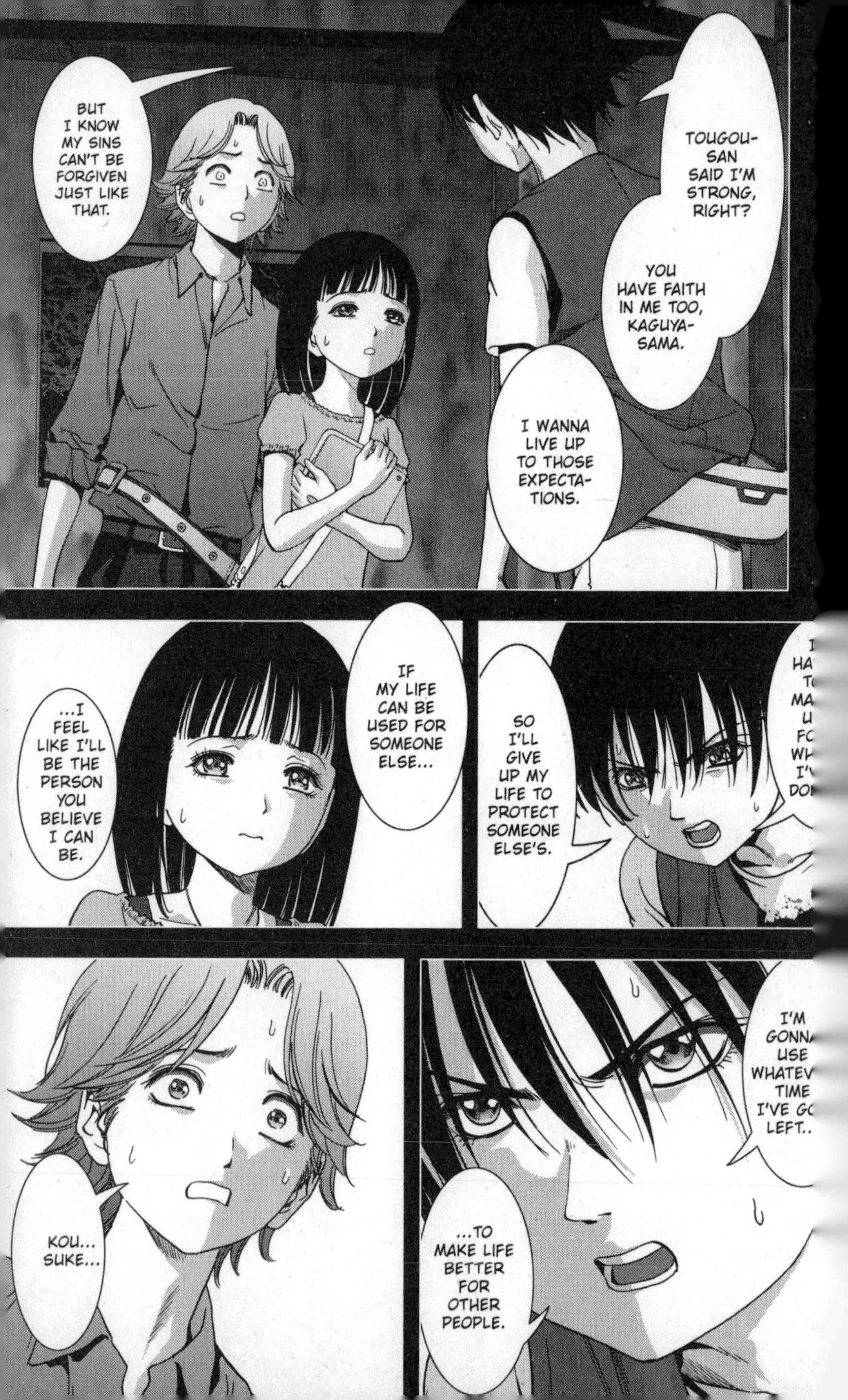
TOUGOU-SAN SAID I'M STRONG, RIGHT?
YOU HAVE FAITH IN ME TOO, KAGUYA-SAMA.
I WANNA LIVE UP TO THOSE EXPECTATIONS.
BUT I KNOW MY SINS CAN'T BE FORGIVEN JUST LIKE THAT.
SO I'LL GIVE UP MY LIFE TO PROTECT SOMEONE ELSE'S.
IF MY LIFE CAN BE USED FOR SOMEONE ELSE...
...I FEEL LIKE I'LL BE THE PERSON YOU BELIEVE I CAN BE.
I'M GONNA USE WHATEV TIME I'VE GO LEFT..
...TO MAKE LIFE BETTER FOR OTHER PEOPLE.
KOU... SUKE...

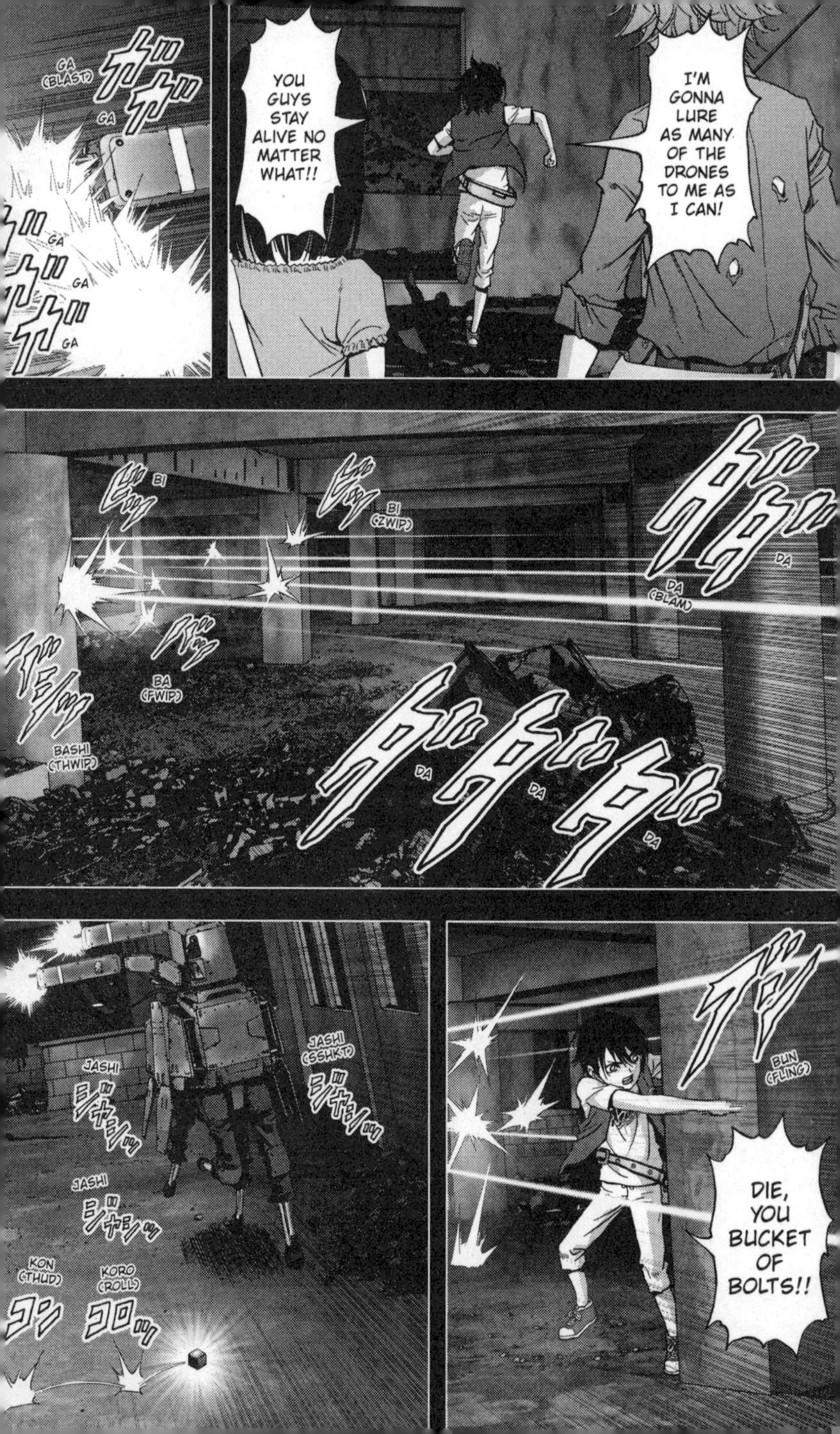
I'M GONNA LURE AS MANY OF THE DRONES TO ME AS I CAN!
YOU GUYS STAY ALIVE NO MATTER WHAT!!
GA (BLAST)
GA
GA
GA
GA
DA
DA (BLAM)
BI (ZWIP)
BI
BA (FWIP)
DA
DA
DA
BASHI (THWIP)
BUN (FLING)
DIE, YOU BUCKET OF BOLTS!!
JASHI (SSHKT)
JASHI
JASHI
KORO (ROLL)
KON (THUD)

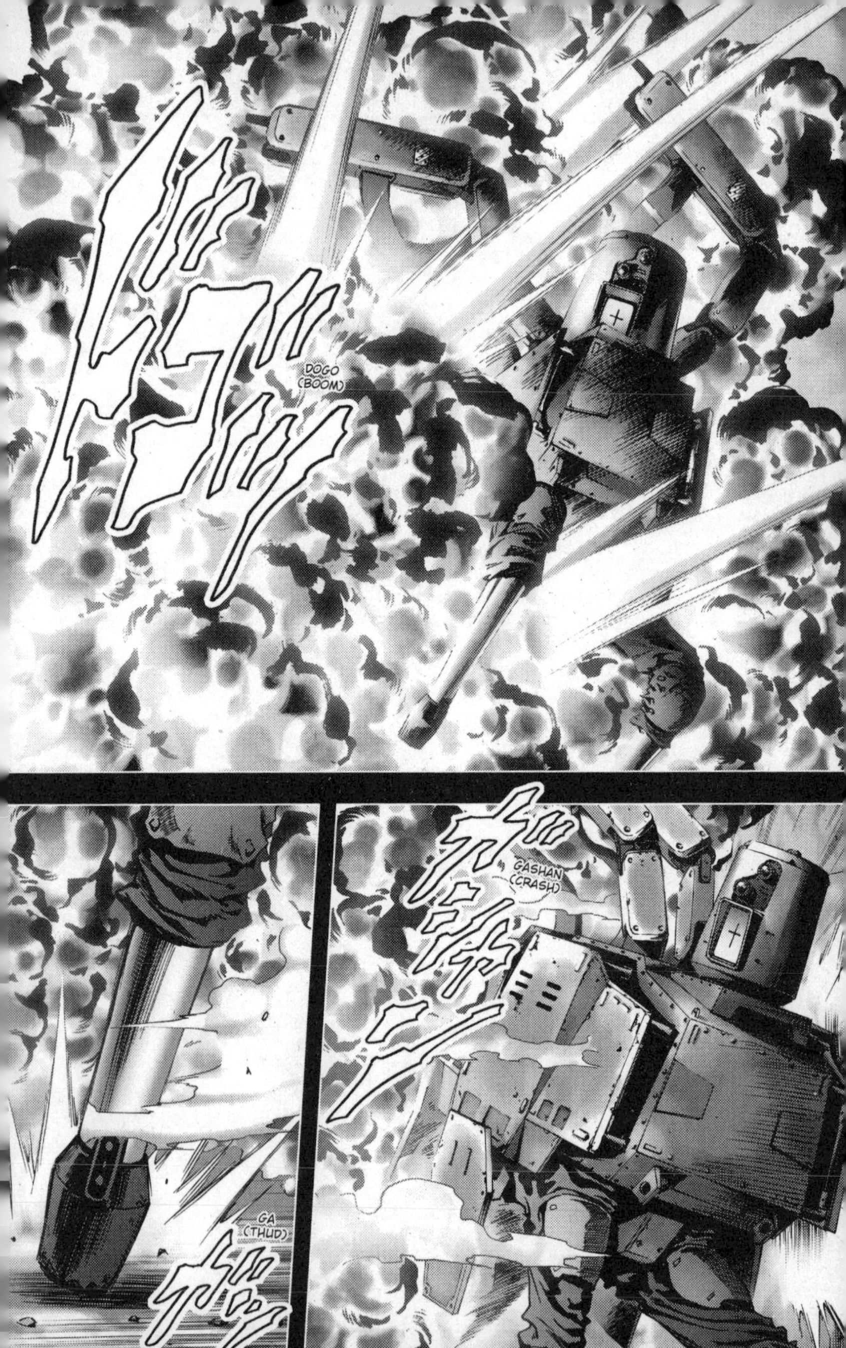
DOGO (BOOM)
GASHAN (CRASH)
GA (THUD)

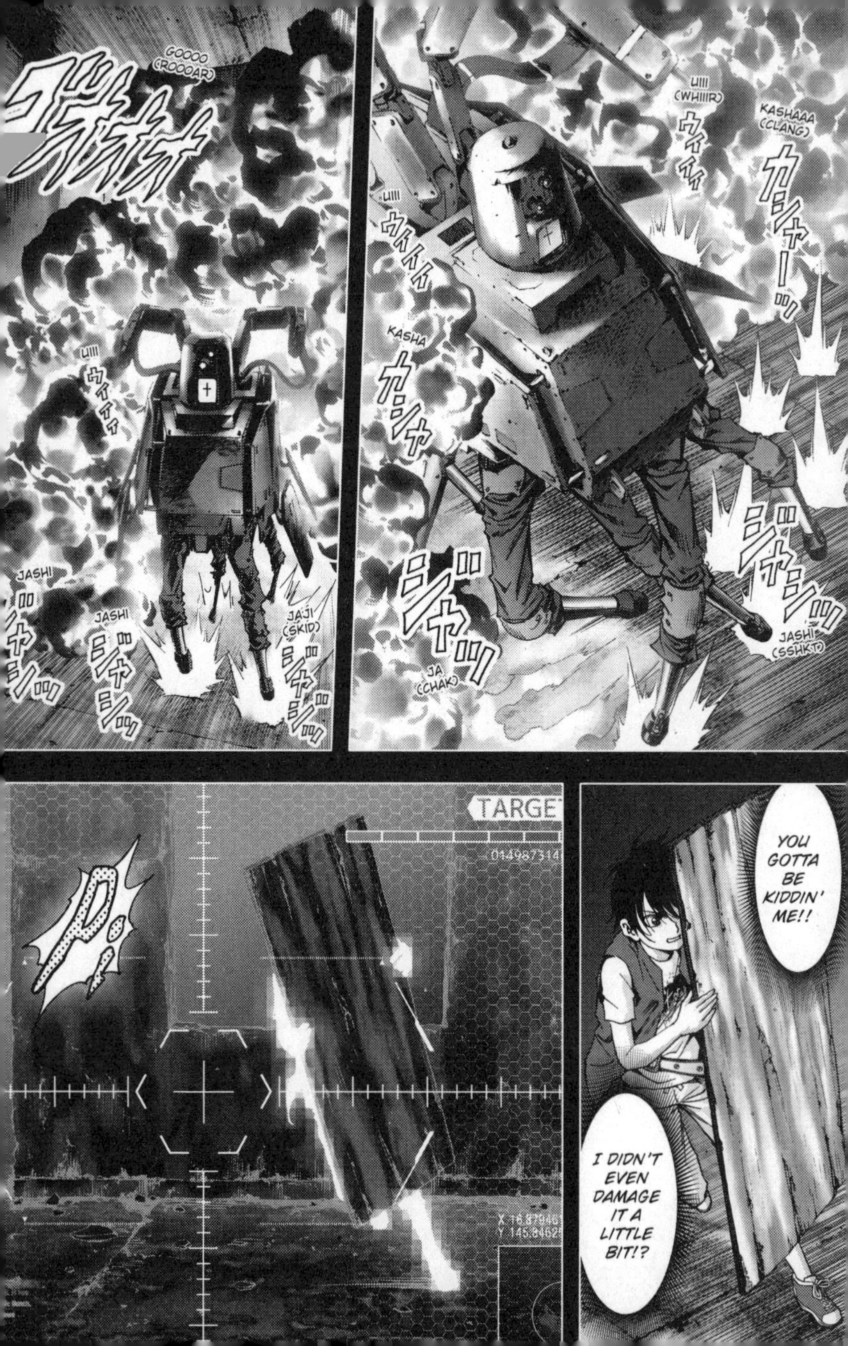
UIII (WHIIIR)
KASHAAA (CLANG)
UIII
KASHA
JASHI (SSHKT)
JA (CHAK)
GOOOO (ROOOAR)
UIII
JAJI (SKID)
JASHI
JASHI
YOU GOTTA BE KIDDIN' ME!!
I DIDN'T EVEN DAMAGE IT A LITTLE BIT!?
TARGE

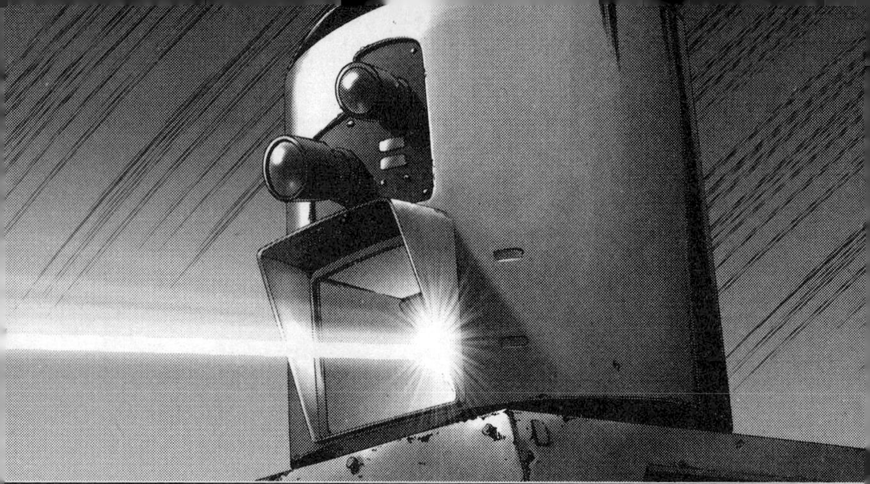

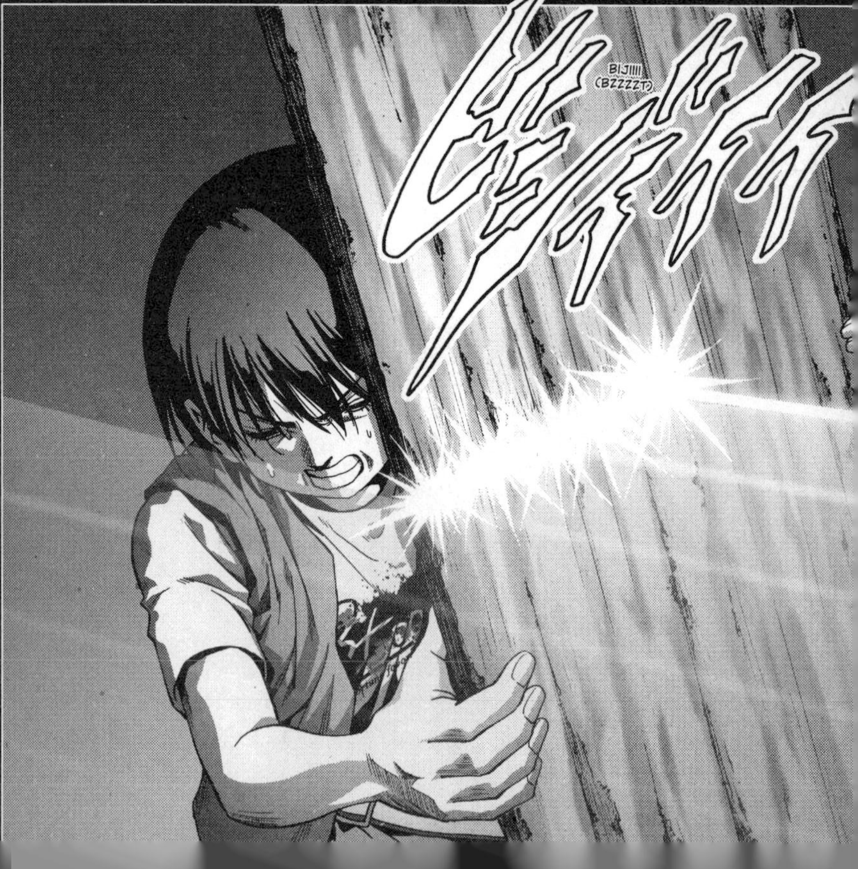
BIJIIII
(BZZZZT)

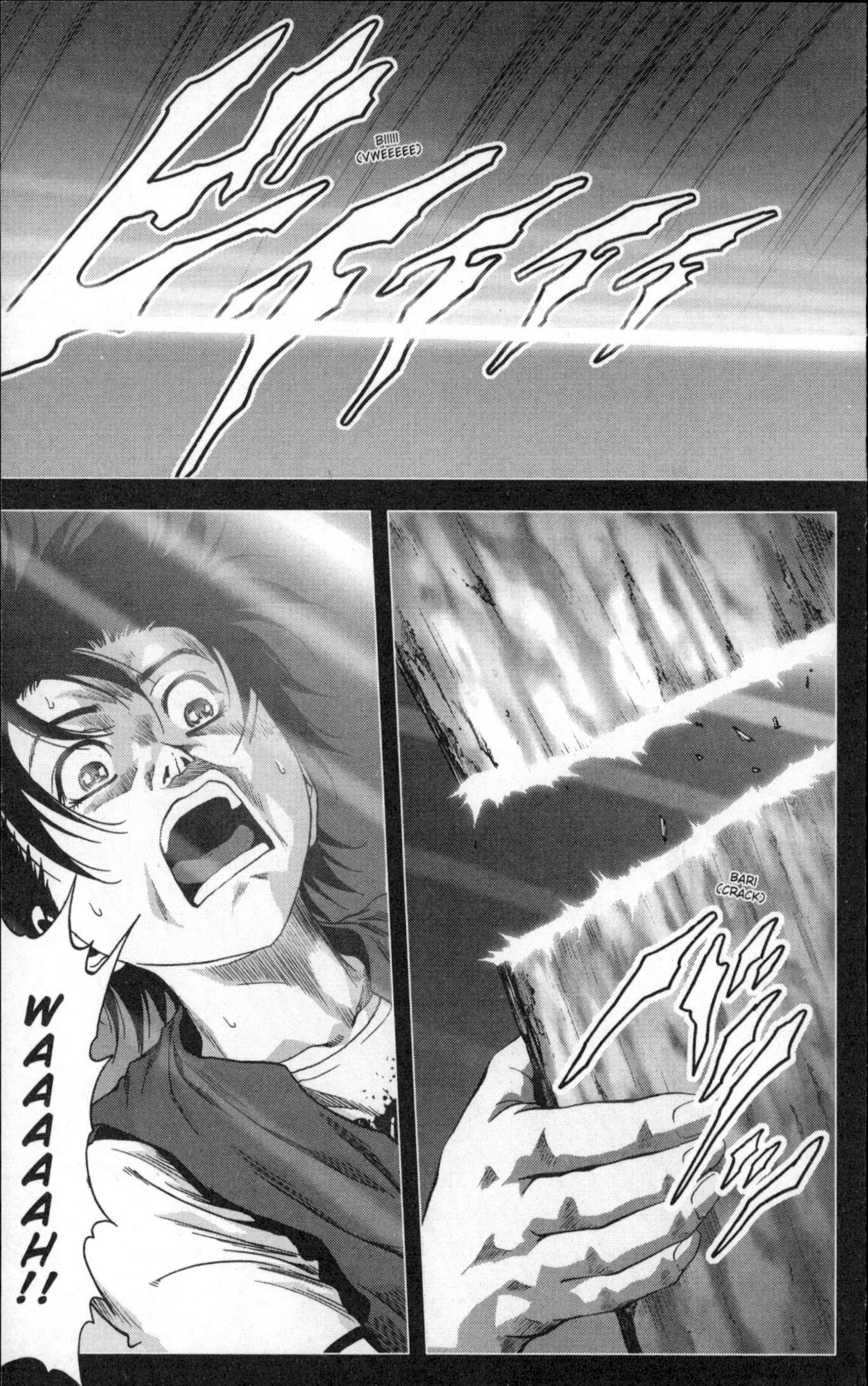
BIIIII
(VWEEEEE)
BARI
(CRACK)
WAAAAAAAAH!!

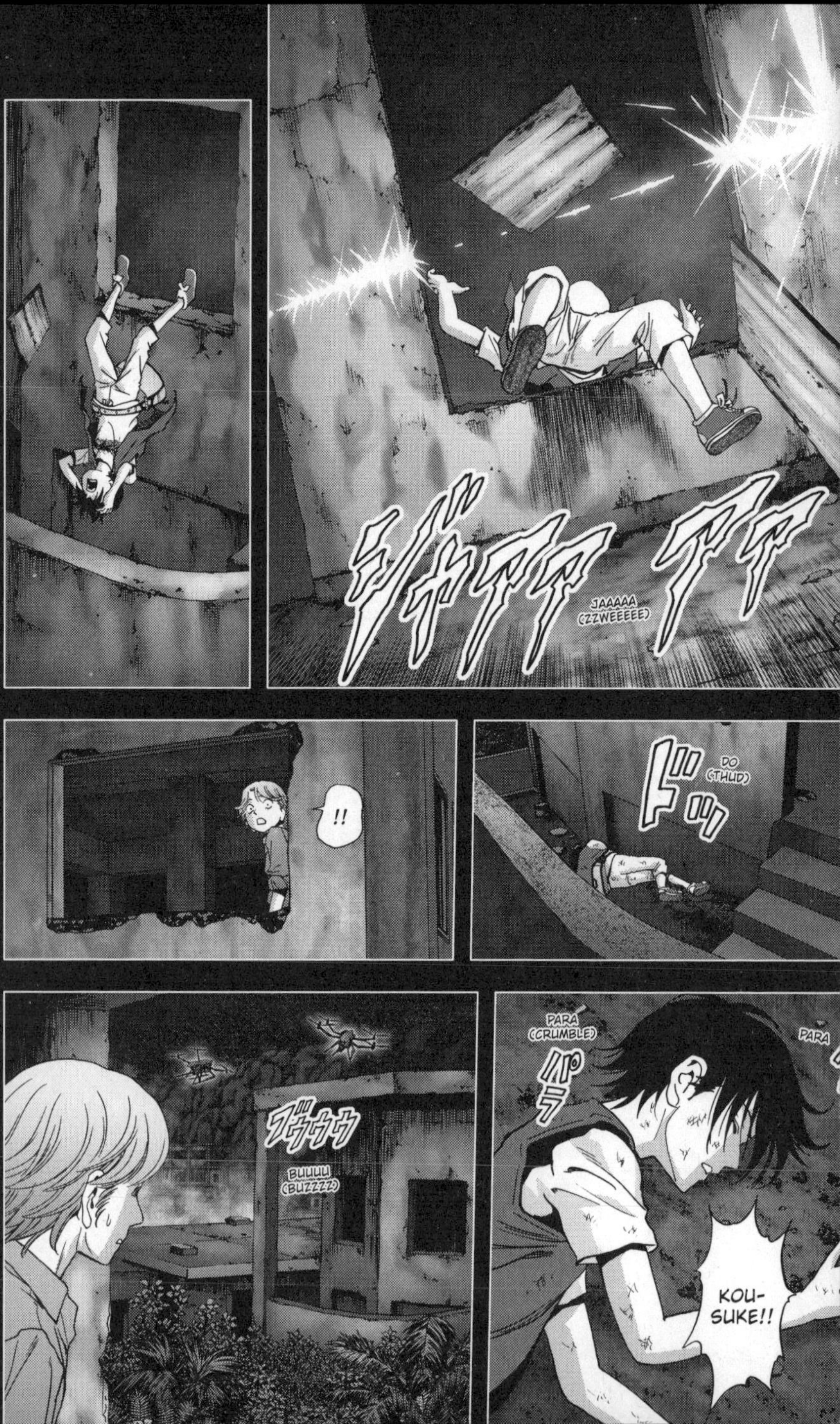

JAAAAA (ZZWEEEEE)
DO (THUD)
!!
PARA
PARA (CRUMBLE)
KOU-SUKE!!
BUUUU (BUZZZZ)

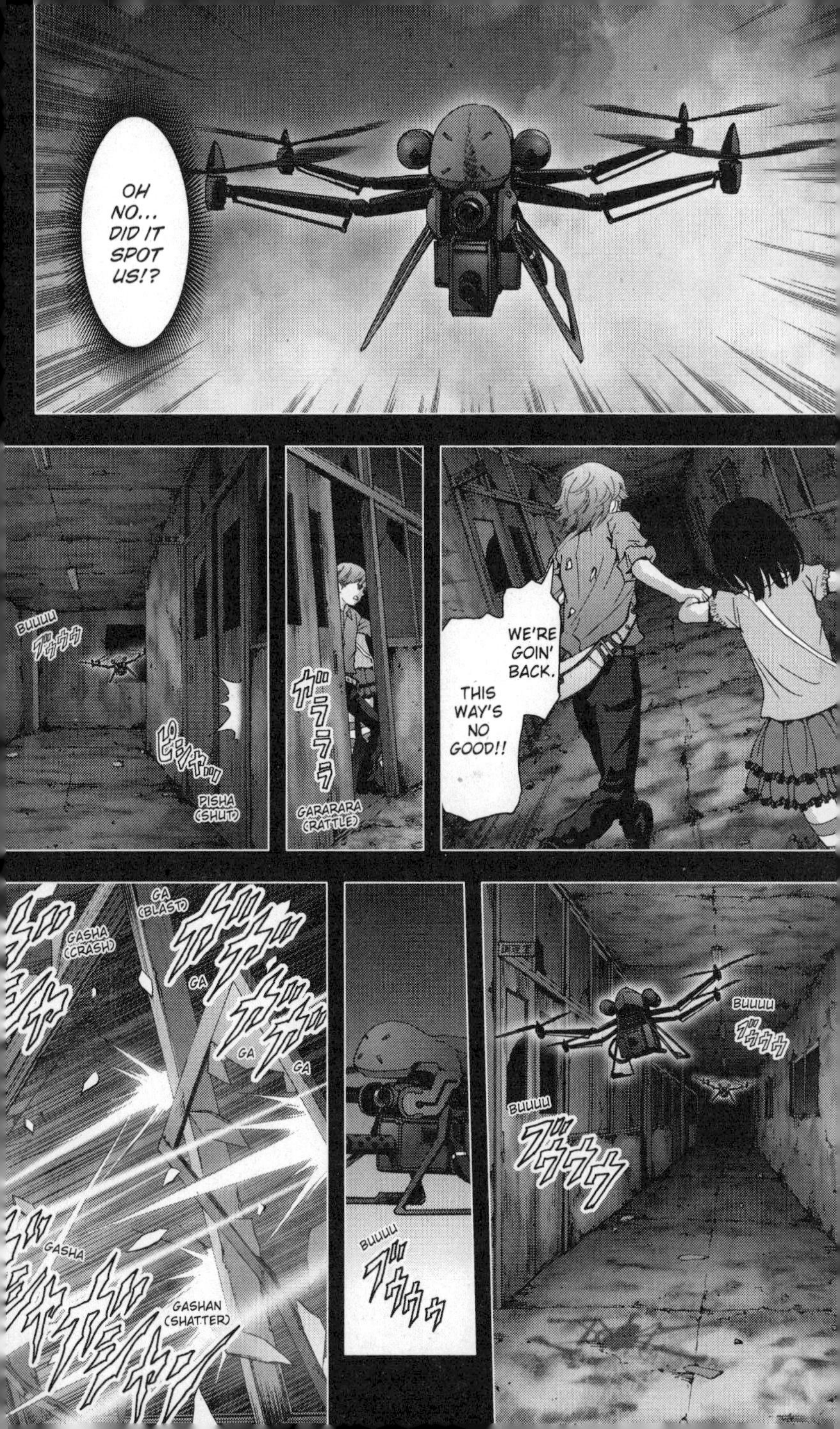
OH NO... DID IT SPOT US!?
WE'RE GOIN' BACK.
THIS WAY'S NO GOOD!!
GARARARA (RATTLE)
BUUUU
PISHA (SHUT)
BUUUU
BUUUU
BUUUU
GA (BLAST)
GASHA (CRASH)
GA
GA
GA
GASHA
GASHAN (SHATTER)

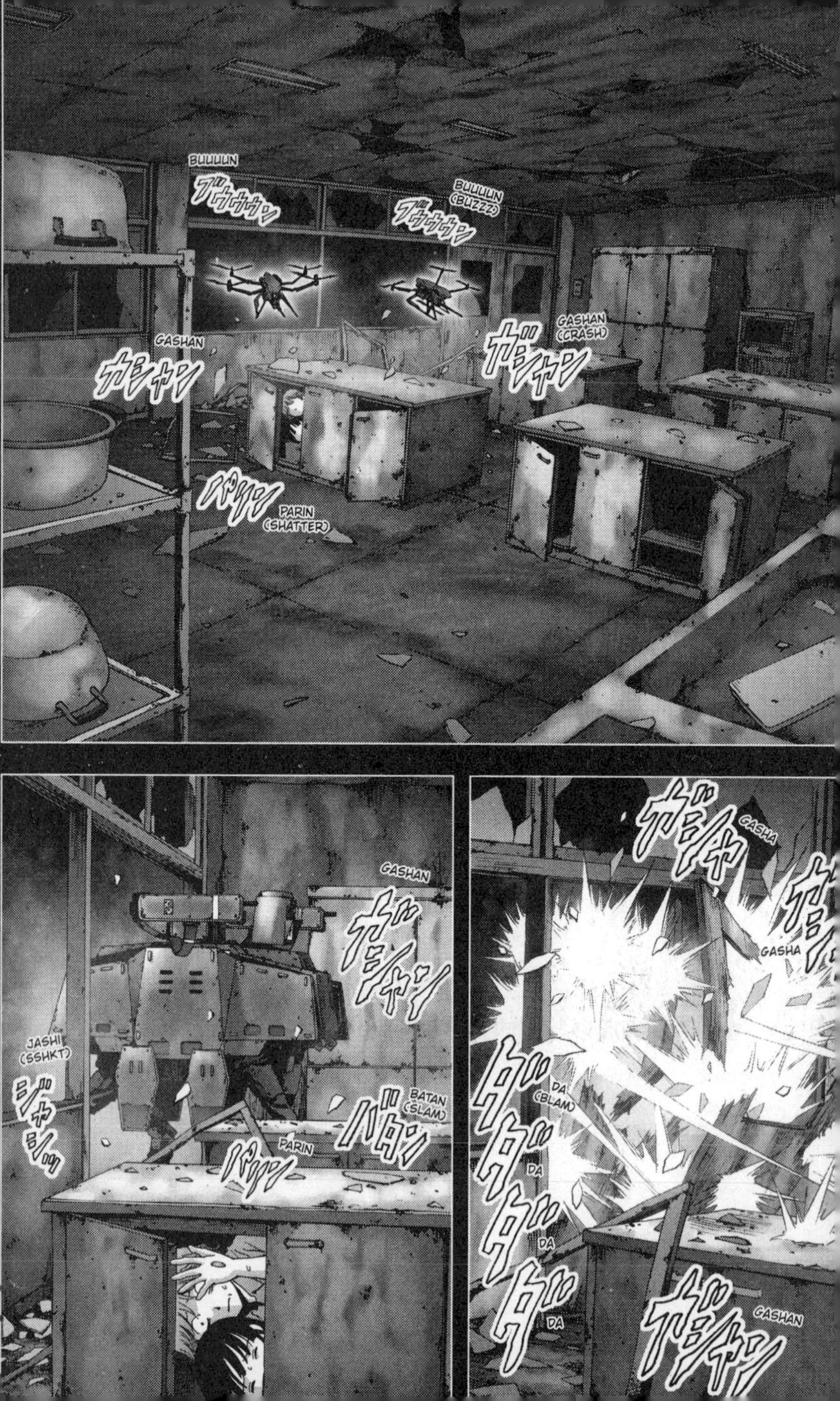
BUUUUN
(BUZZZ)
GASHAN
(CRASH)
BUUUUN
GASHAN
PARIN
(SHATTER)
GASHA
GASHA
DA
(BLAM)
DA
DA
DA
GASHAN
GASHAN
BATAN
(SLAM)
PARIN
JASHI
(SSHKT)

PATA
(SHUT)
パタ‥

SUUU
(SLIDE)
スウゥ

HOW DID I END UP IN THIS MESS!!?

WEREN'T THEY JUST SAYING THE GAME WAS OVER AND WE COULD GO HOME...?

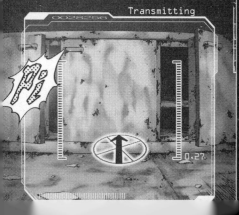

Transmitting
0028256

0.27

BUUUU
ブゥウゥ

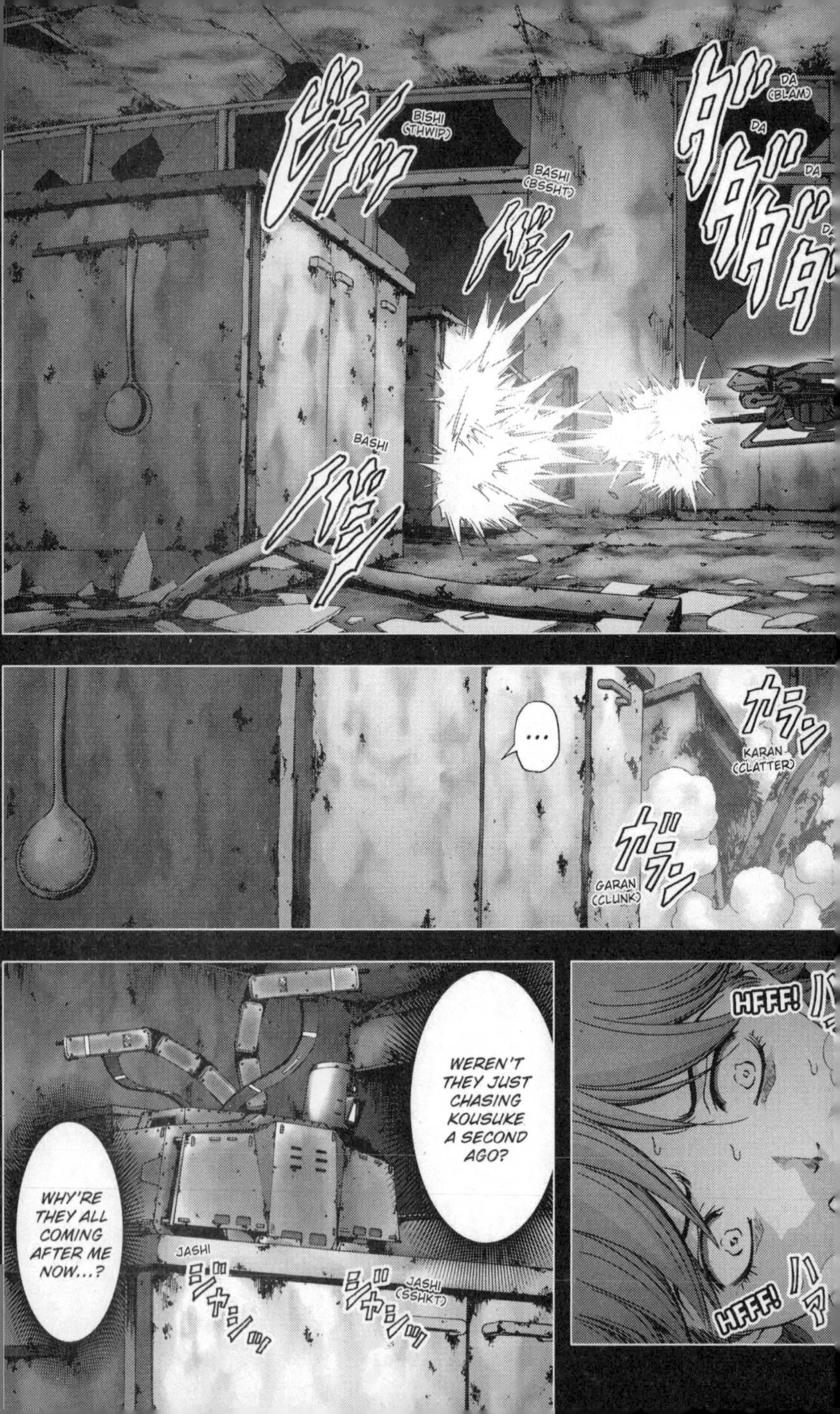
DA (BLAM)
DA
DA
DA
BISHI (THWIP)
BASHI (BSSHT)
BASHI
KARAN (CLATTER)
GARAN (CLUNK)
...
HFFF!
HFFF!
WEREN'T THEY JUST CHASING KOUSUKE A SECOND AGO?
JASHI (SSHKT)
JASHI
WHY'RE THEY ALL COMING AFTER ME NOW...?

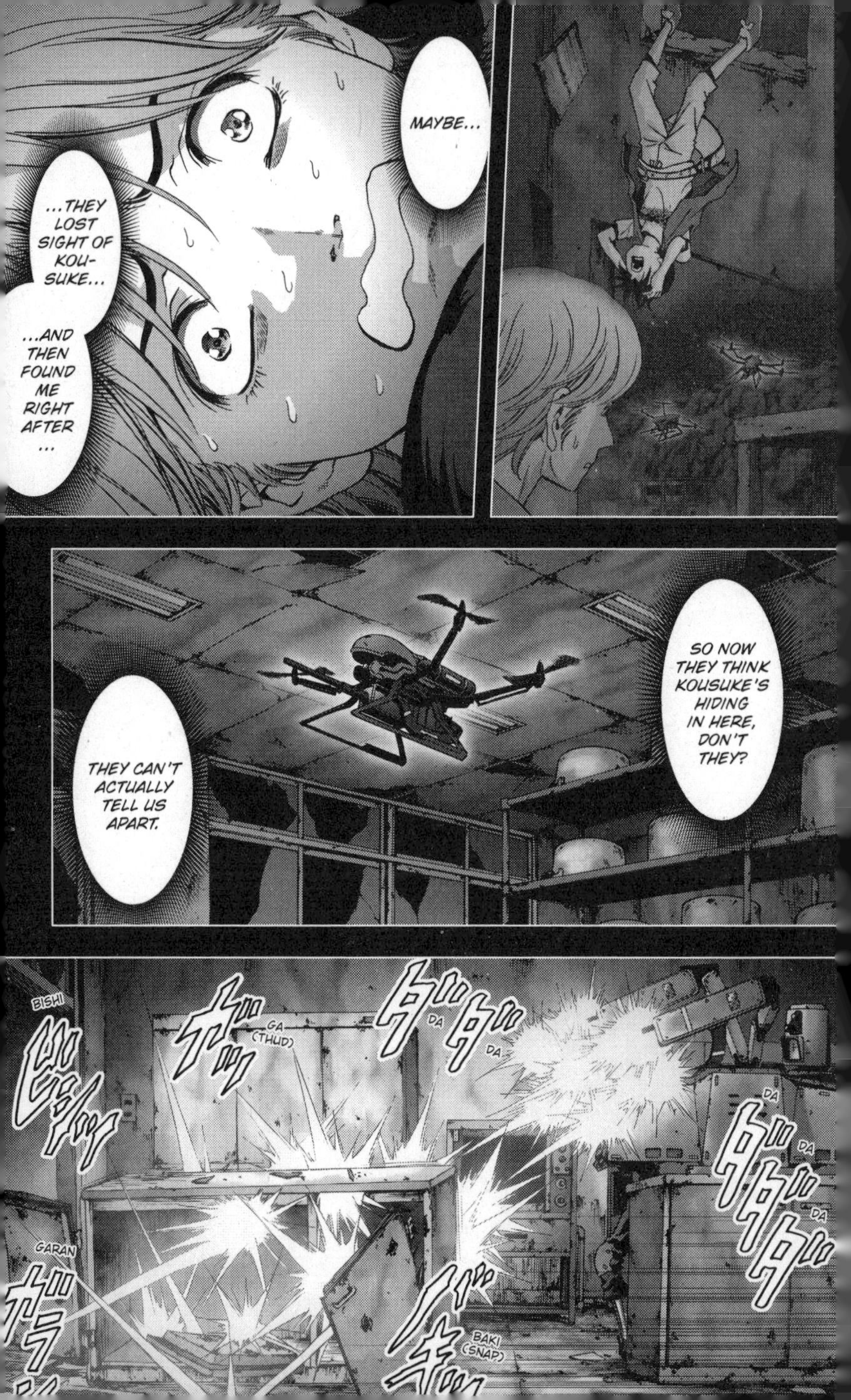
MAYBE...
...THEY LOST SIGHT OF KOU-SUKE...
...AND THEN FOUND ME RIGHT AFTER...
SO NOW THEY THINK KOUSUKE'S HIDING IN HERE, DON'T THEY?
THEY CAN'T ACTUALLY TELL US APART.
DA DA DA
DA DA
GA (THUD)
BISHI
BAKI (SNAP)
GARAN

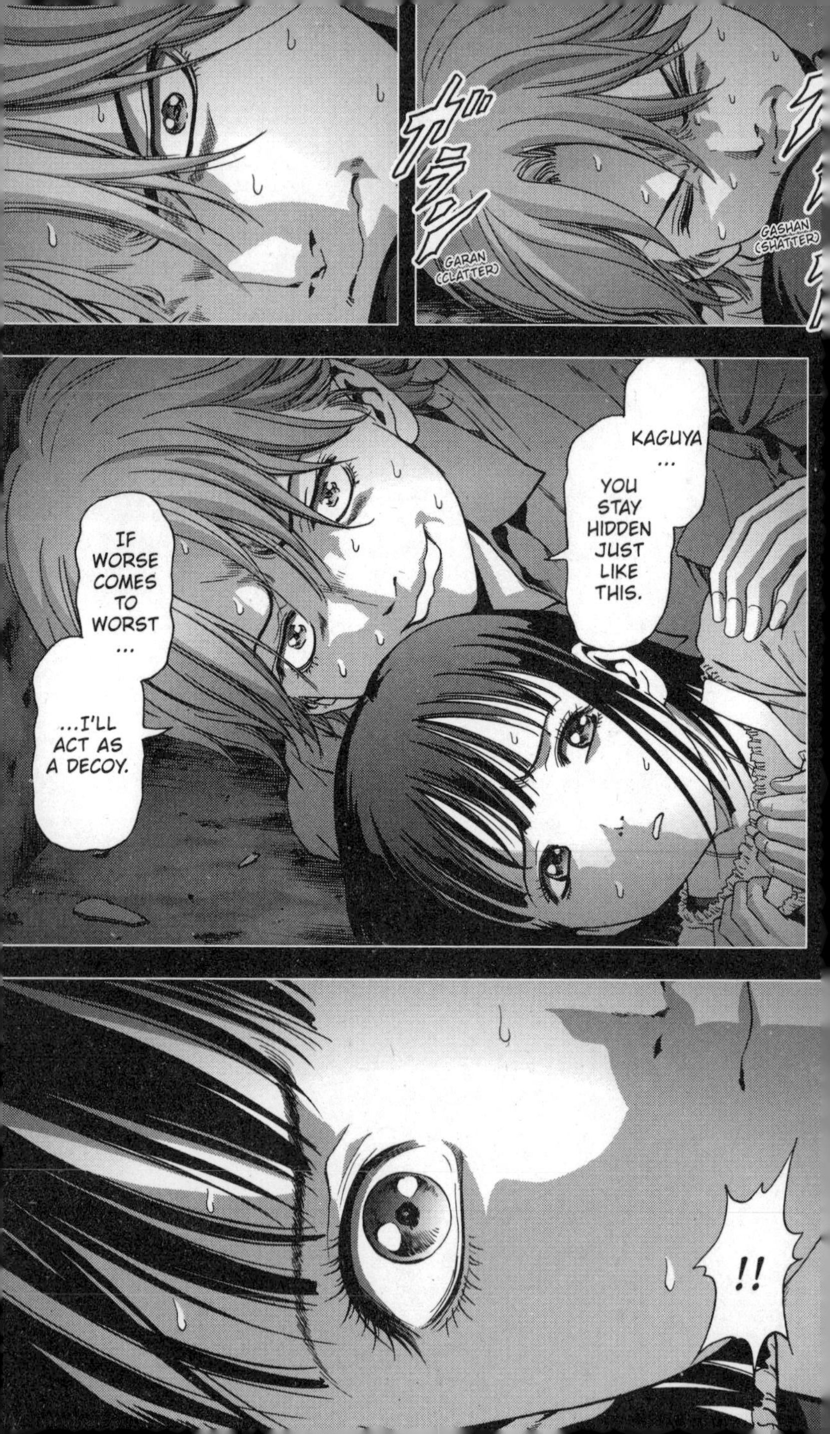
GASHAN (SHATTER)
GARAN (CLATTER)
KAGUYA... YOU STAY HIDDEN JUST LIKE THIS.
IF WORSE COMES TO WORST...
...I'LL ACT AS A DECOY.
!!

109 Brutal Murder

BTOOOM!-109

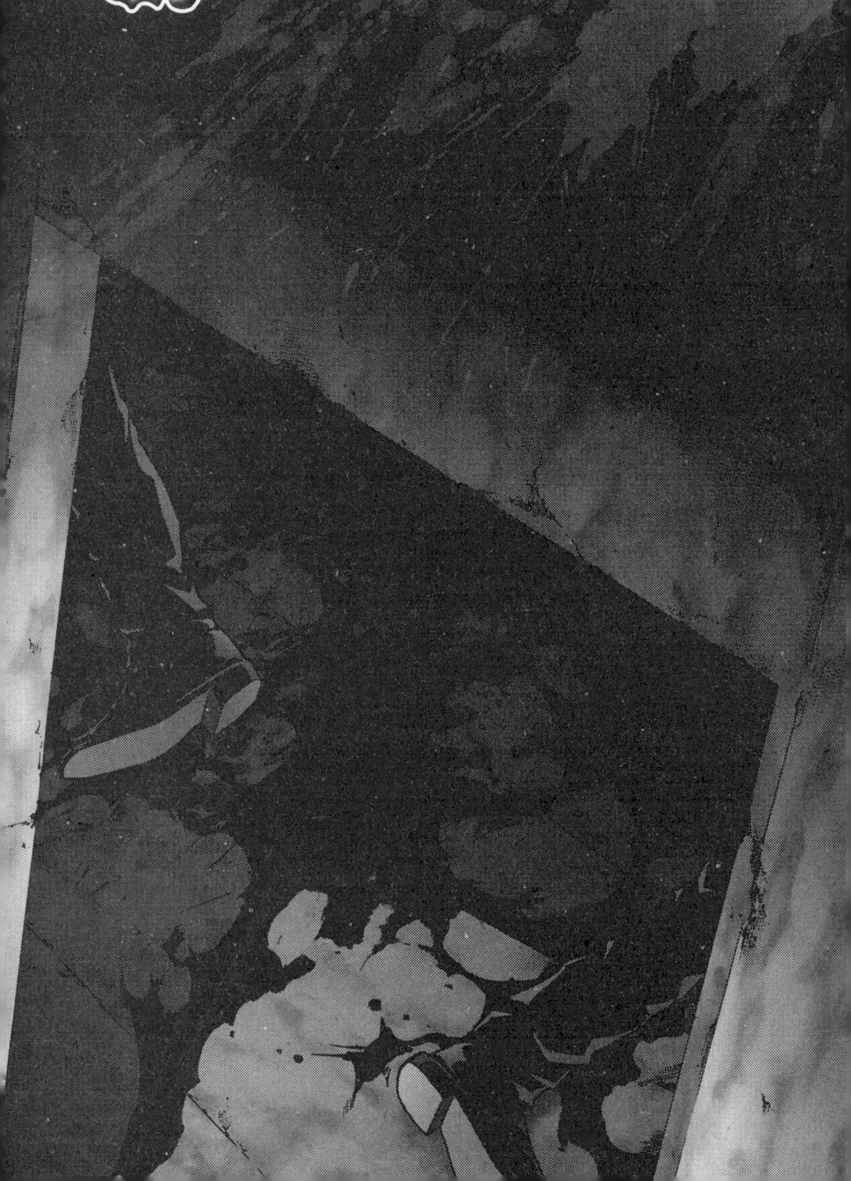

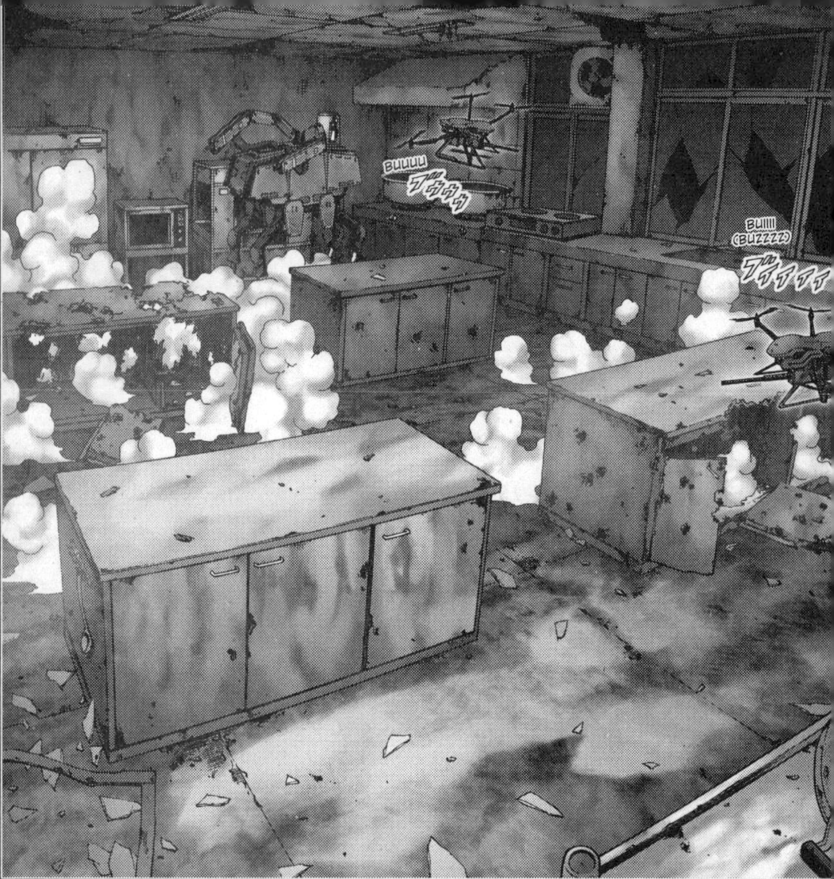
BUIIII
(BUZZZZ)
ブィィィィ
BUUUU
ブゥゥゥ
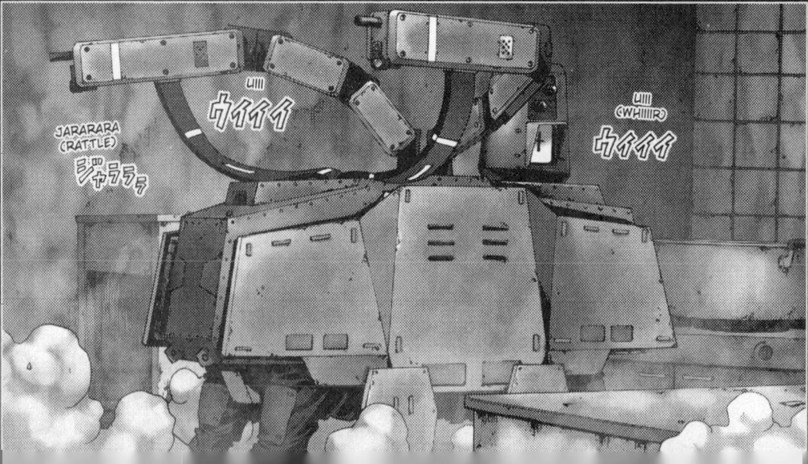
UIII
(WHIIIIR)
ウイイイ
UIII
ウイイイ
JARARARA
(RATTLE)
ジャラララ

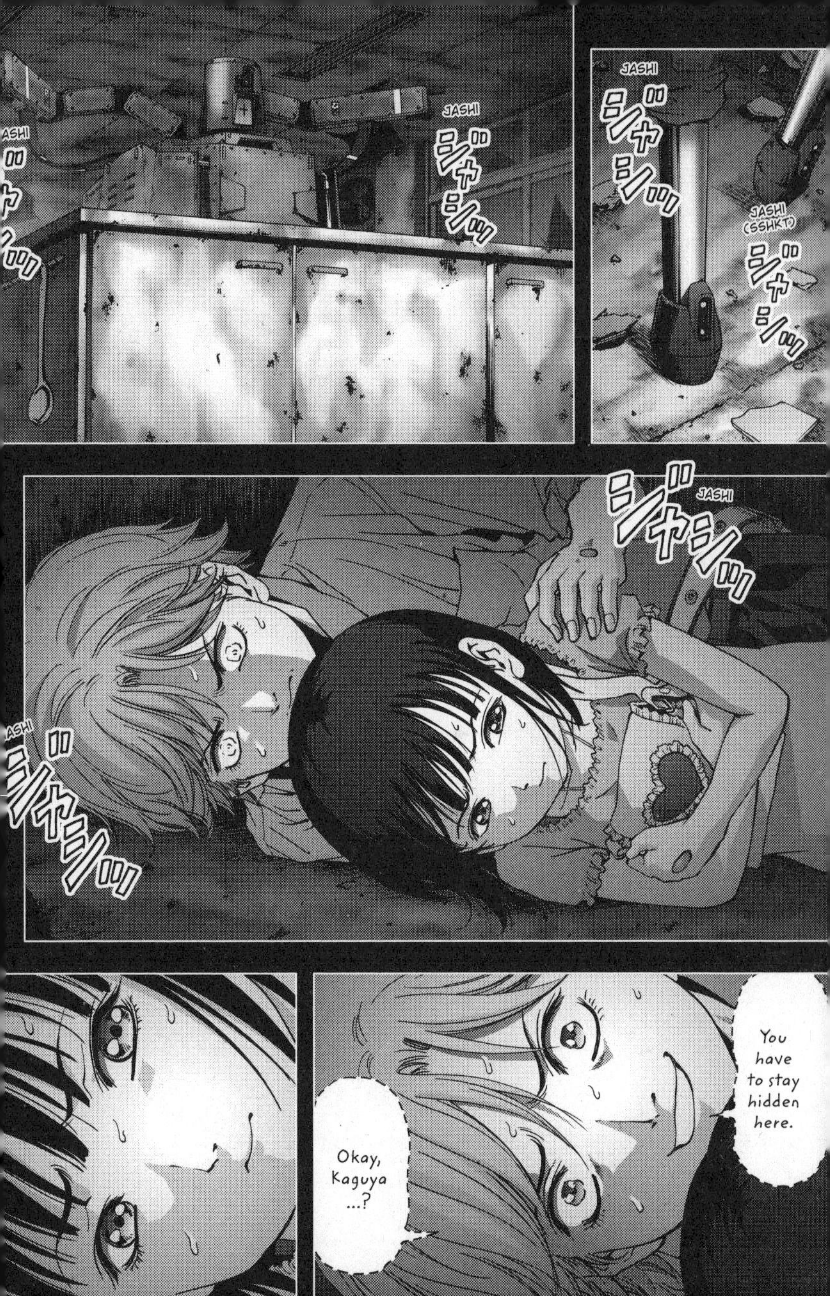
JASHI
JASHI (SSHKT)
JASHI
JASHI
JASHI
JASHI
You have to stay hidden here.
Okay, Kaguya ...?

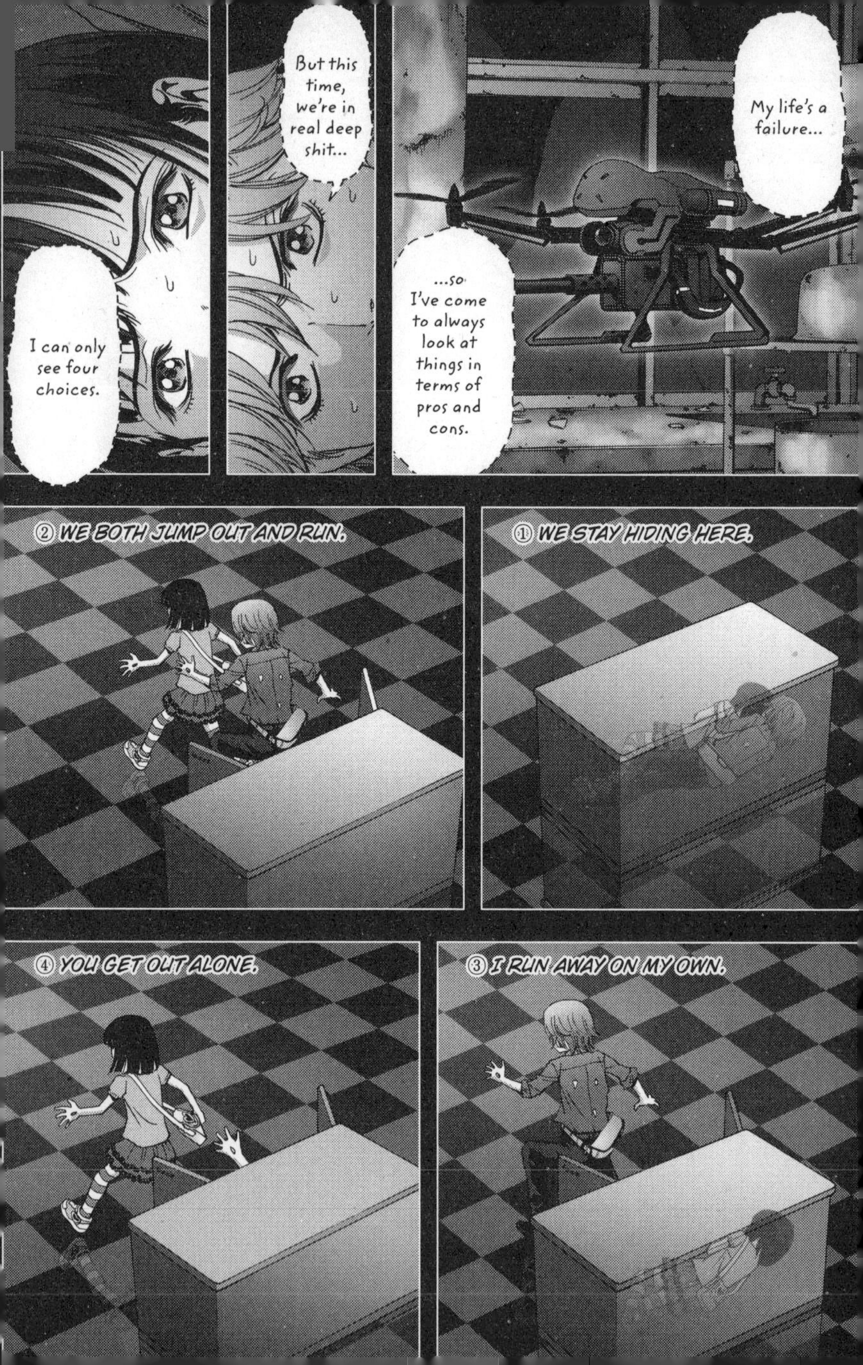
My life's a failure...
...so I've come to always look at things in terms of pros and cons.
But this time, we're in real deep shit...
I can only see four choices.
① WE STAY HIDING HERE.
② WE BOTH JUMP OUT AND RUN.
③ I RUN AWAY ON MY OWN.
④ YOU GET OUT ALONE.

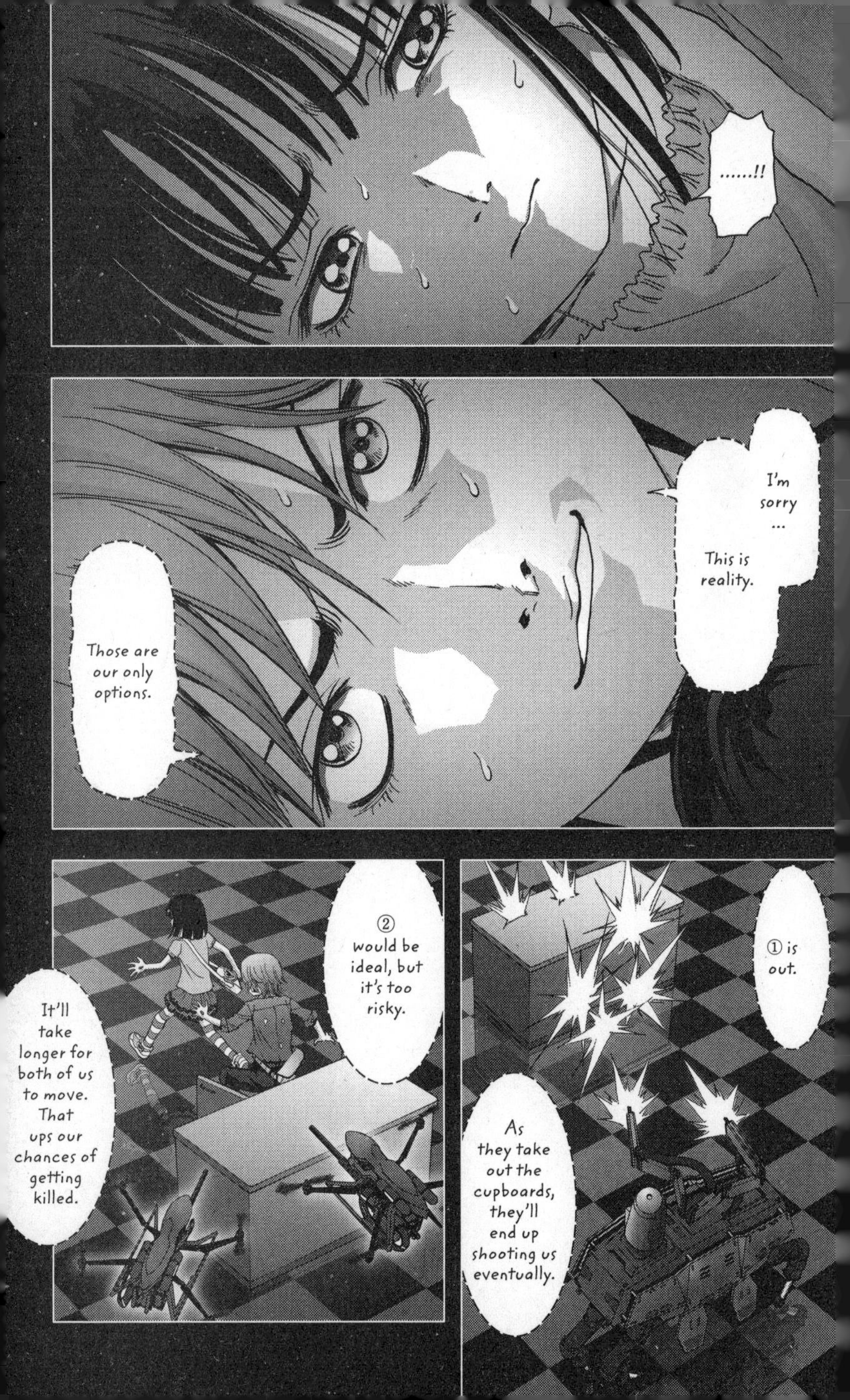
......!!
I'm sorry ... This is reality.
Those are our only options.
① is out.
As they take out the cupboards, they'll end up shooting us eventually.
② would be ideal, but it's too risky.
It'll take longer for both of us to move. That ups our chances of getting killed.

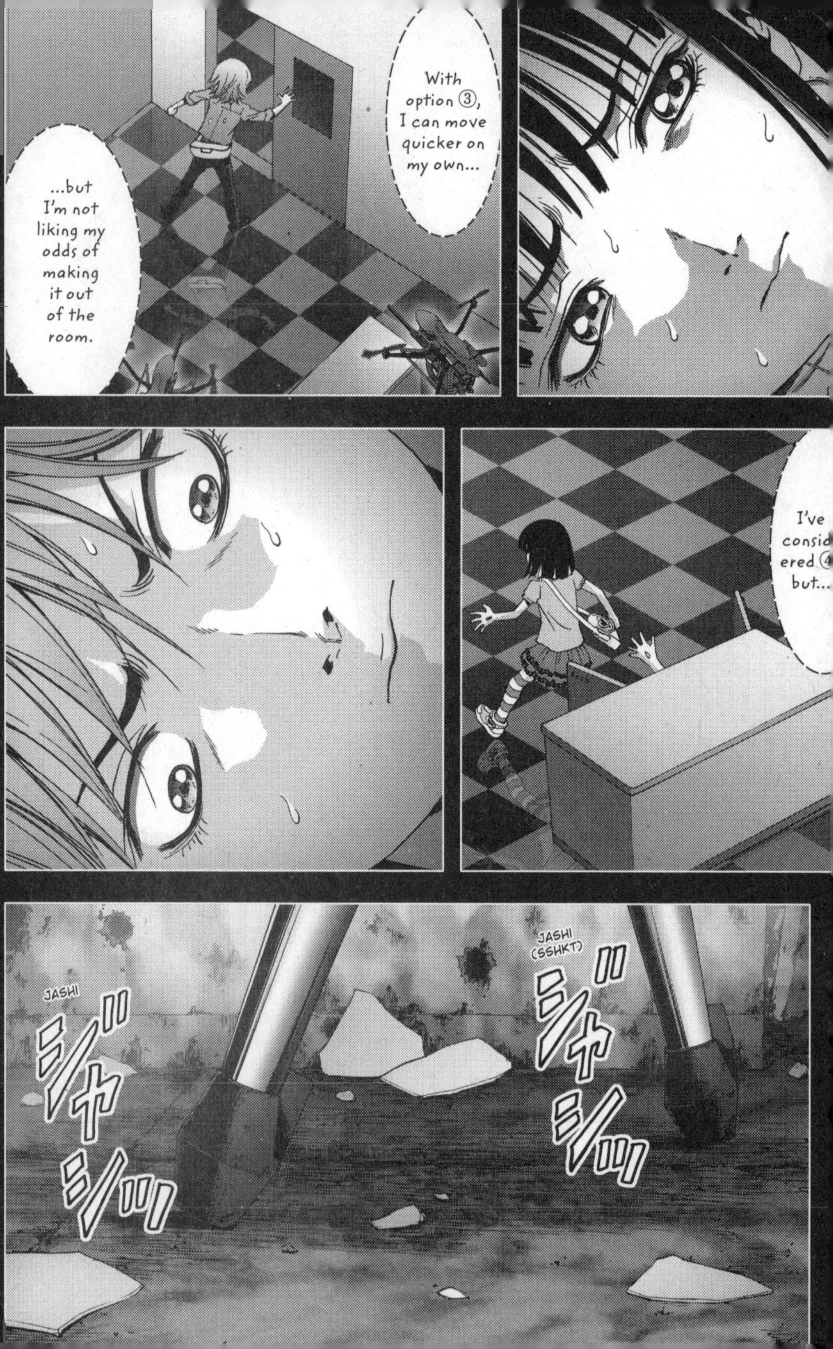

With option ③, I can move quicker on my own...
...but I'm not liking my odds of making it out of the room.
I've consid ered ④ but...
JASHI (SSHKT)
JASHI

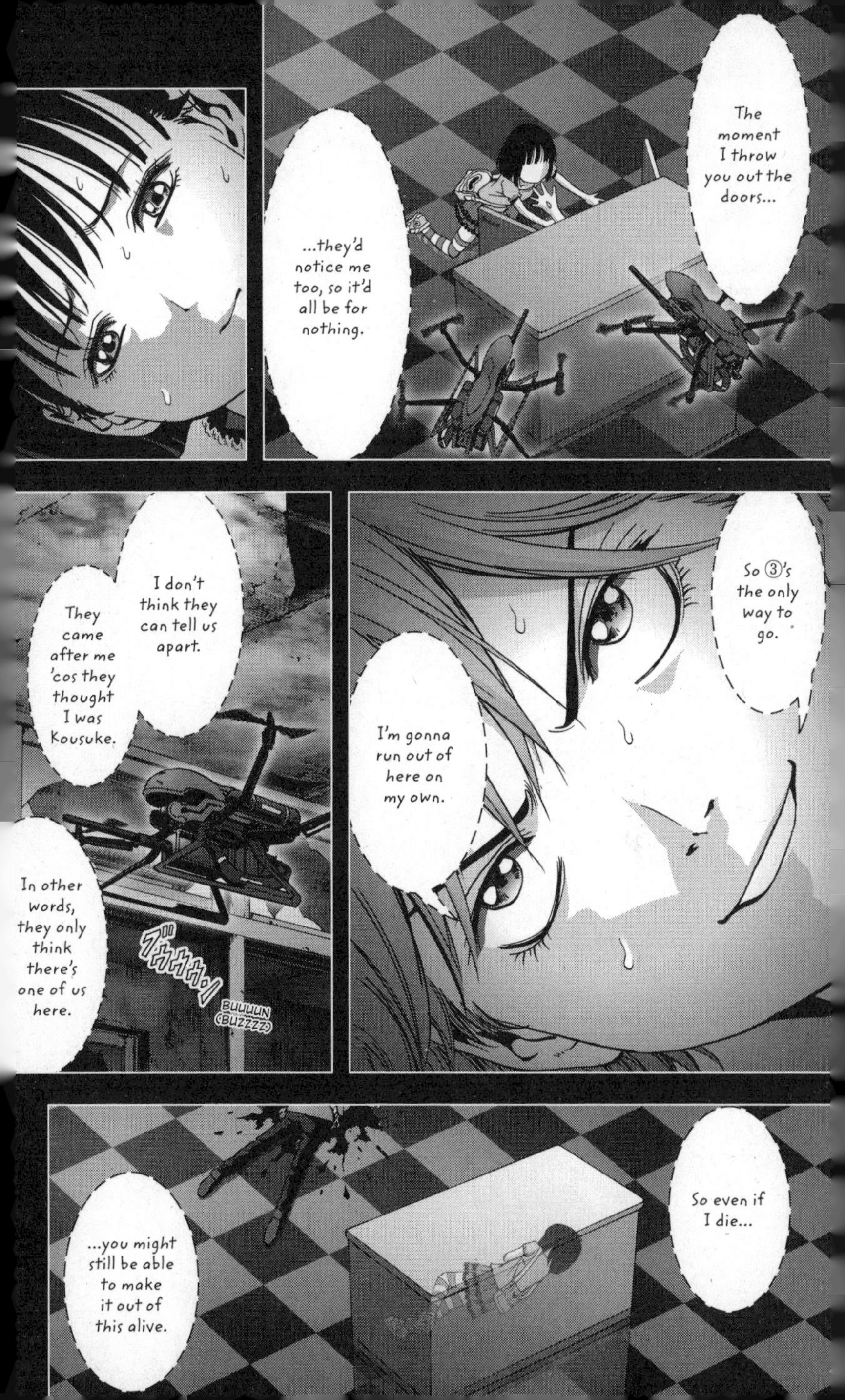
The moment I throw you out the doors...
...they'd notice me too, so it'd all be for nothing.
So ③'s the only way to go.
I'm gonna run out of here on my own.
I don't think they can tell us apart.
They came after me 'cos they thought I was Kousuke.
In other words, they only think there's one of us here.
BUUUUN (BUZZZZ)
So even if I die...
...you might still be able to make it out of this alive.

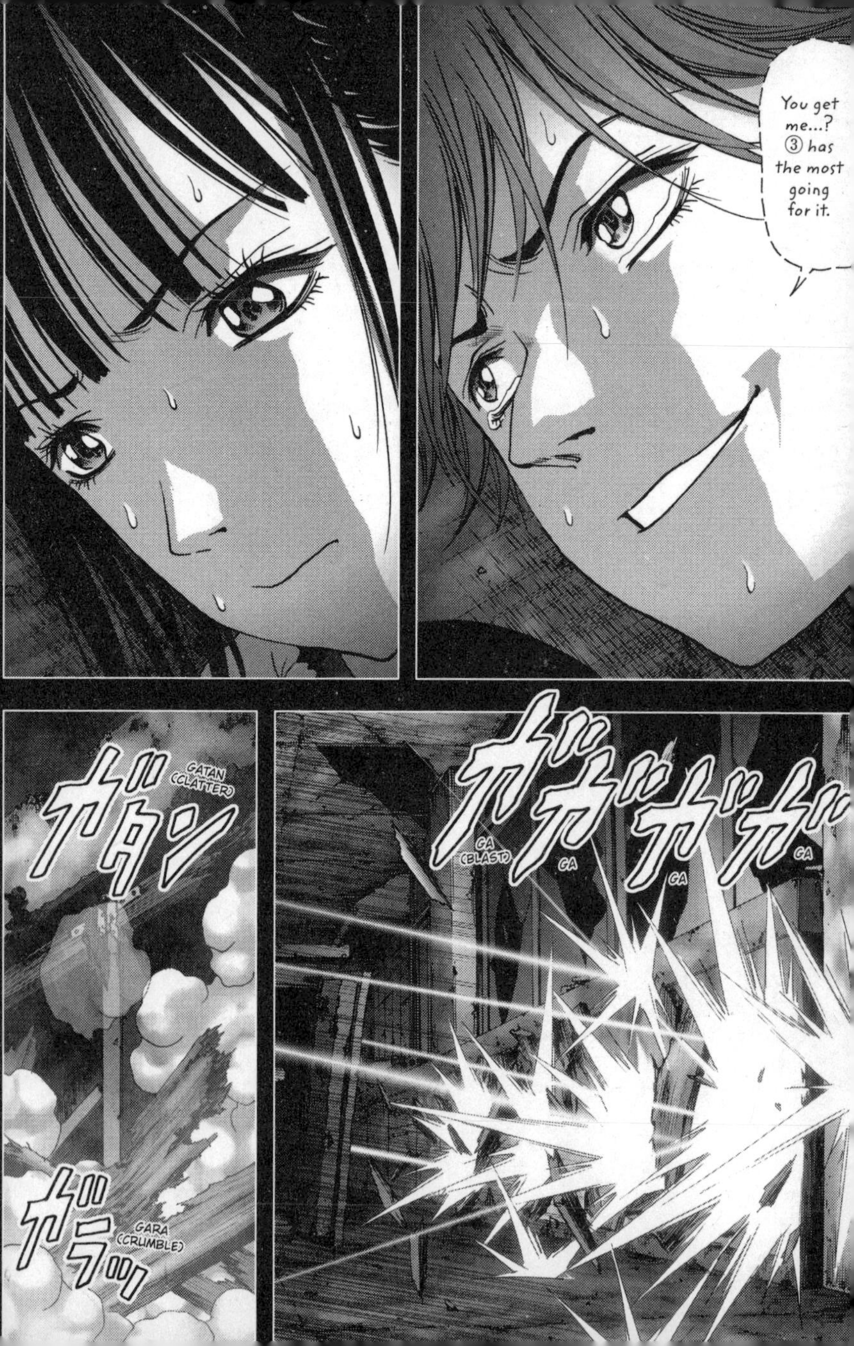
You get me...? ③ has the most going for it.
ガガガガ
GA (BLAST) GA GA GA
ガタン
GATAN (CLATTER)
ガラッ
GARA (CRUMBLE)

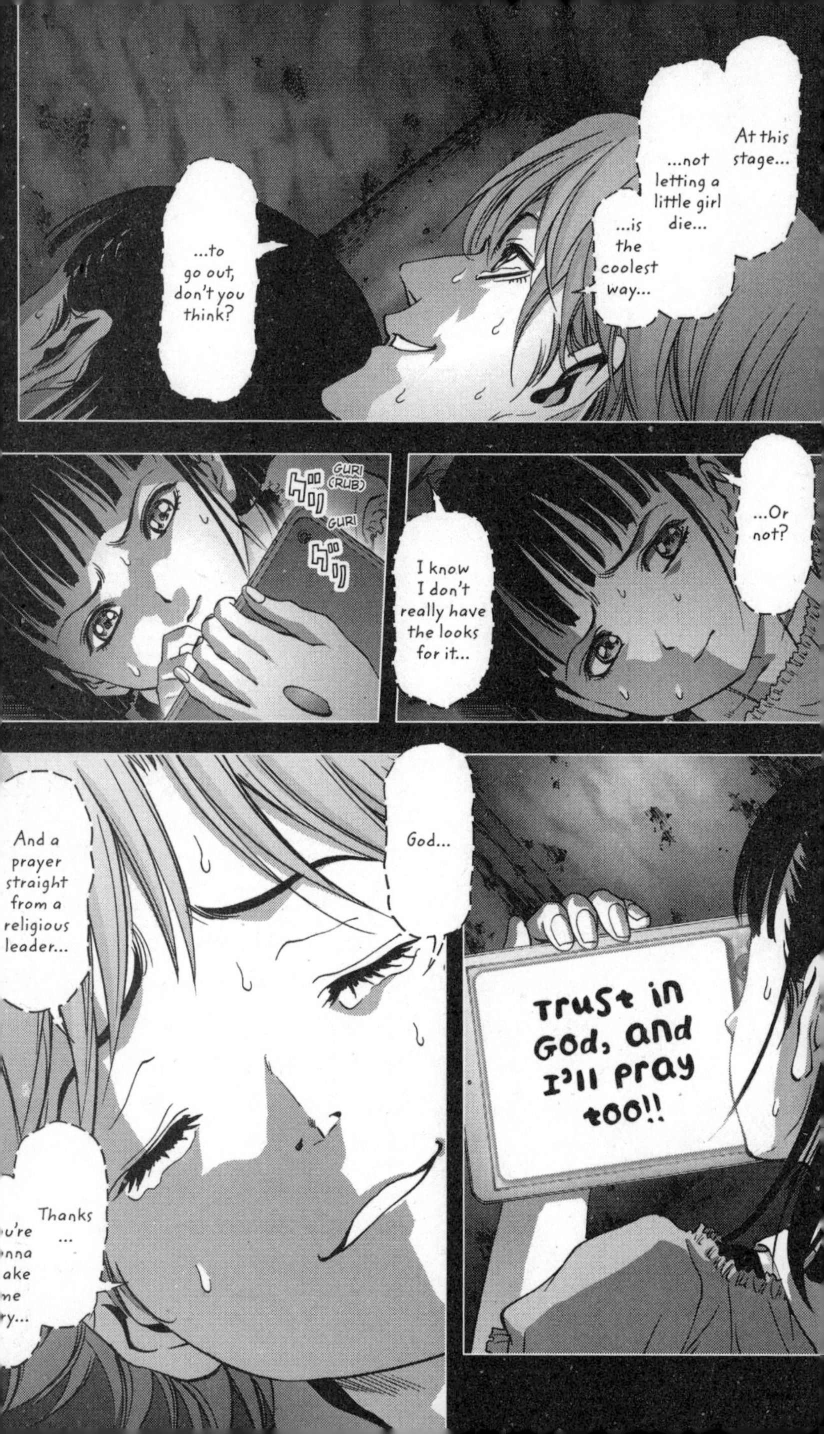
At this stage...
...not letting a little girl die...
...is the coolest way...
...to go out, don't you think?
...Or not?
I know I don't really have the looks for it...
GURI (RUB)
GURI
Trust in God, and I'll pray too!!
God...
And a prayer straight from a religious leader...
Thanks...

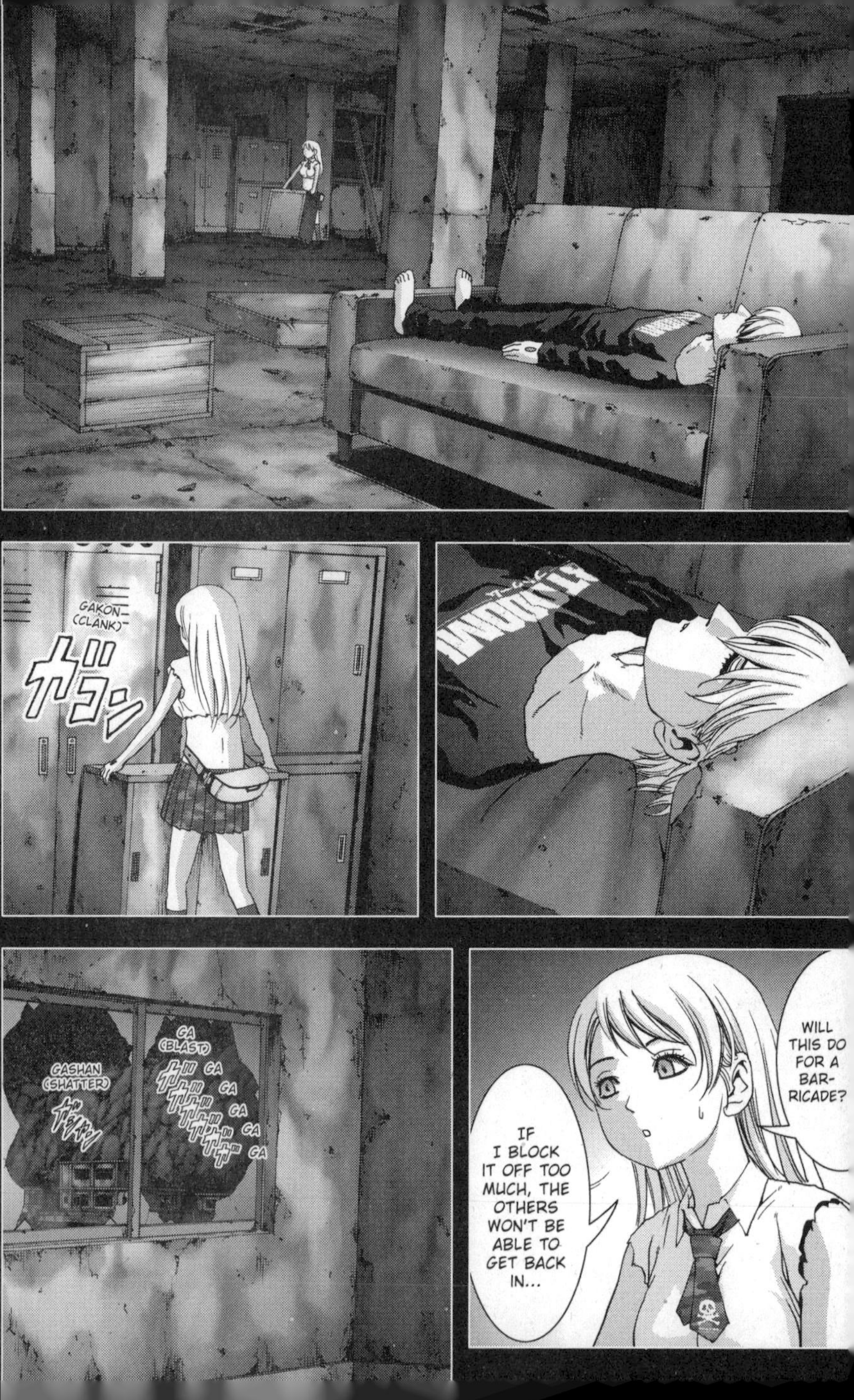
GAKON (CLANK)
ガゴン
WILL THIS DO FOR A BAR-RICADE?
IF I BLOCK IT OFF TOO MUCH, THE OTHERS WON'T BE ABLE TO GET BACK IN...
GA (BLAST)
GA GA GA GA GA
GASHAN (SHATTER)

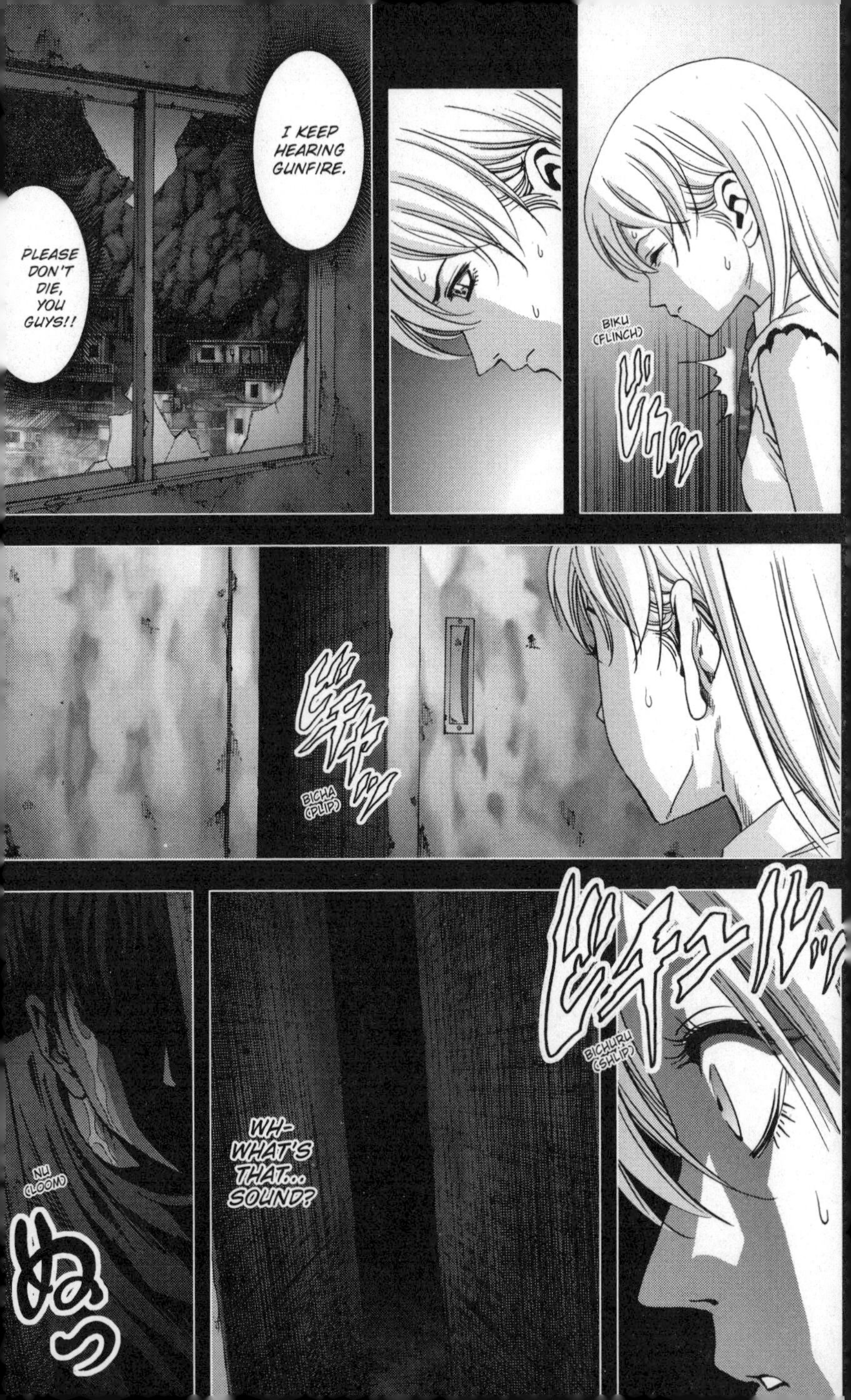
BIKU (FLINCH)
ビクッ
I KEEP HEARING GUNFIRE.
PLEASE DON'T DIE, YOU GUYS!!
ビチャッ
BICHA (PLIP)
ビチュル…
BICHURU (SHLIP)
WH-WHAT'S THAT... SOUND?
NU (LOOM)
ぬっ

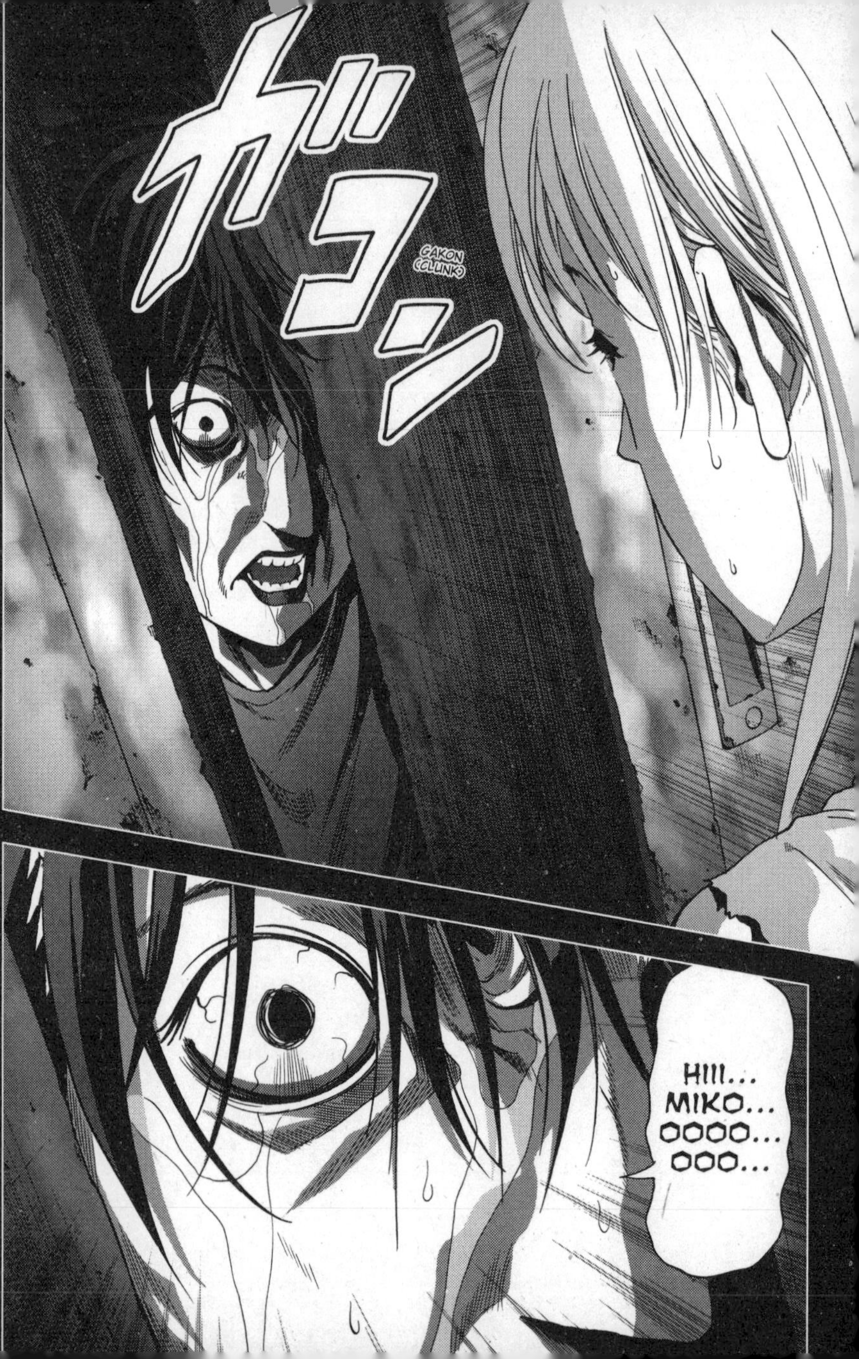
ガコン
GAKON (CLUNK)
HIII... MIKO... OOOO... OOO...

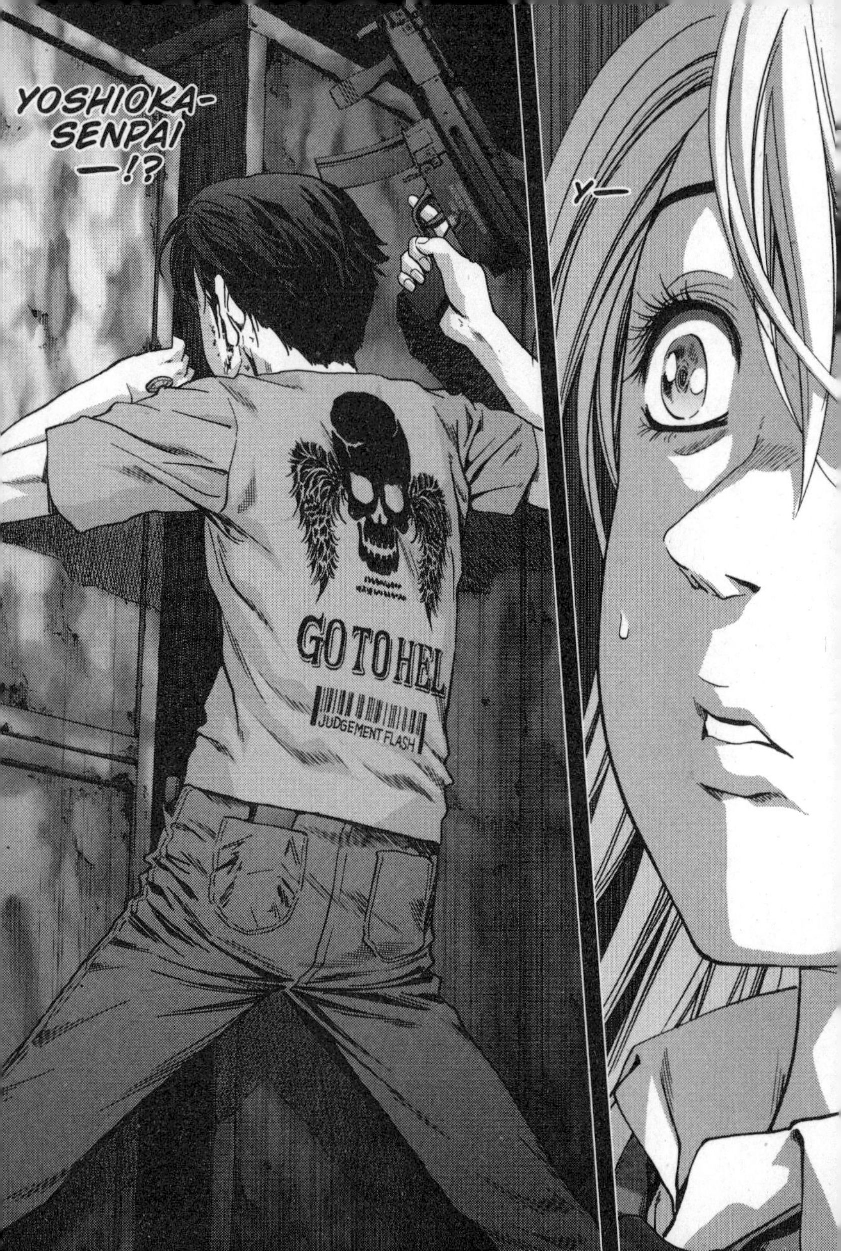
Y—
YOSHIOKA-SENPAI—!?
GO TO HEL
JUDGEMENT FLASH

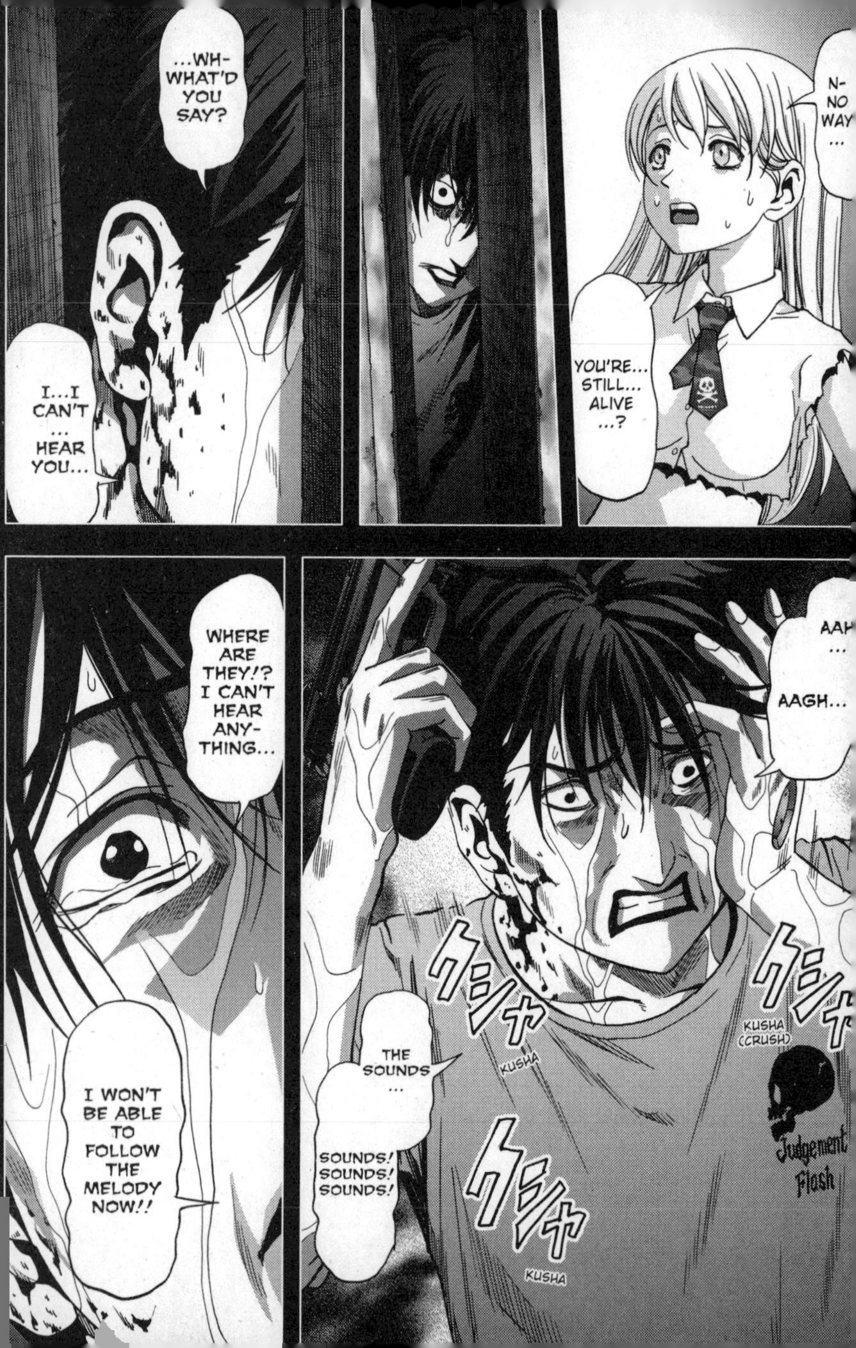
N-NO WAY...
YOU'RE... STILL... ALIVE...?
...WH-WHAT'D YOU SAY?
I...I CAN'T ... HEAR YOU...
AAH... AAGH...
クシャ
KUSHA (CRUSH)
クシャ
KUSHA
THE SOUNDS...
SOUNDS! SOUNDS! SOUNDS!
クシャ
KUSHA
Judgement Flash
WHERE ARE THEY!? I CAN'T HEAR ANYTHING...
I WON'T BE ABLE TO FOLLOW THE MELODY NOW!!

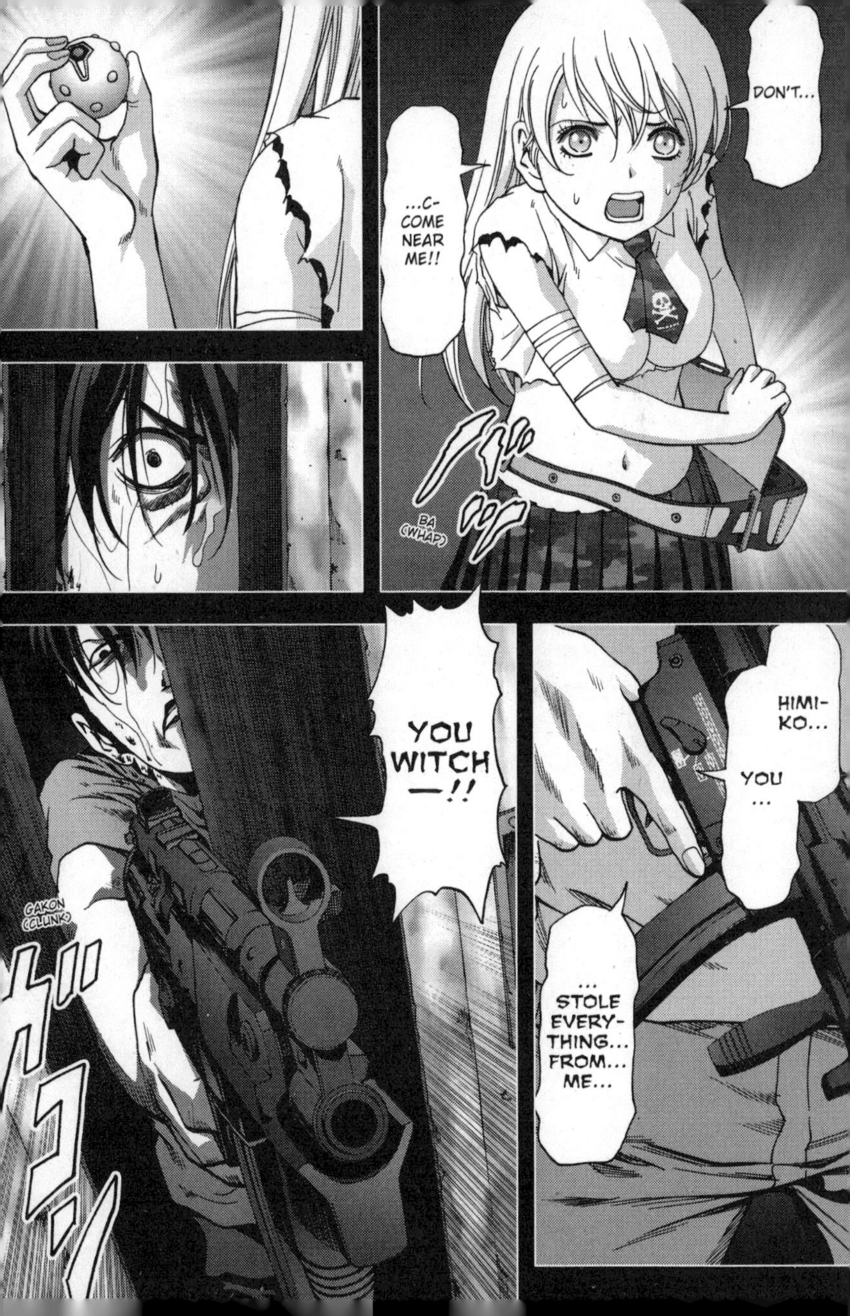
DON'T...
...C-COME NEAR ME!!
BA (WHAP)
HIMI-KO... YOU ...
...STOLE EVERY-THING... FROM... ME...
YOU WITCH—!!
GAKON (CLLINK)

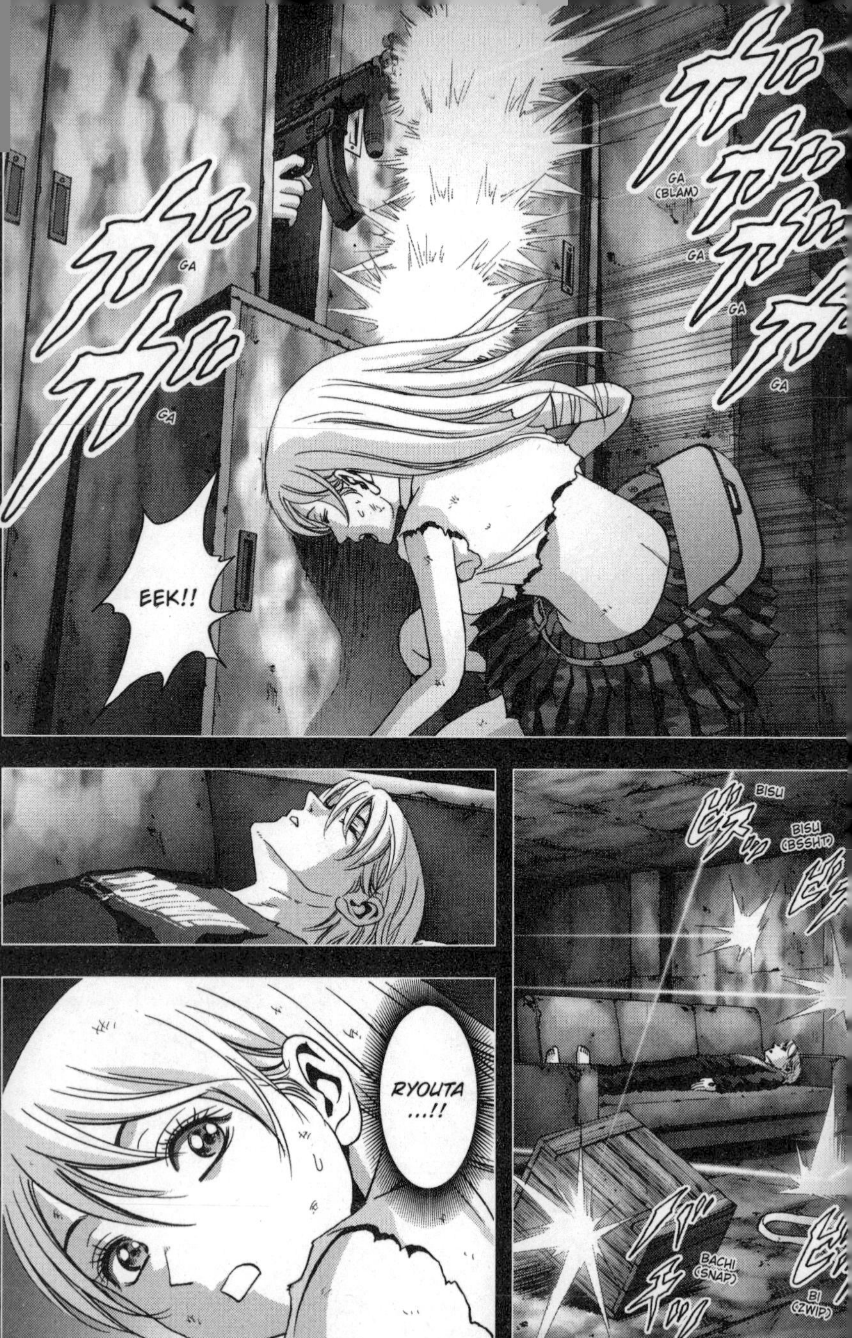
GA (BLAM)
GA
GA
GA
GA
GA
EEK!!
BISU
BISU (BSSHT)
BI (ZWIP)
BACHI (SNAP)
RYOUTA ...!!

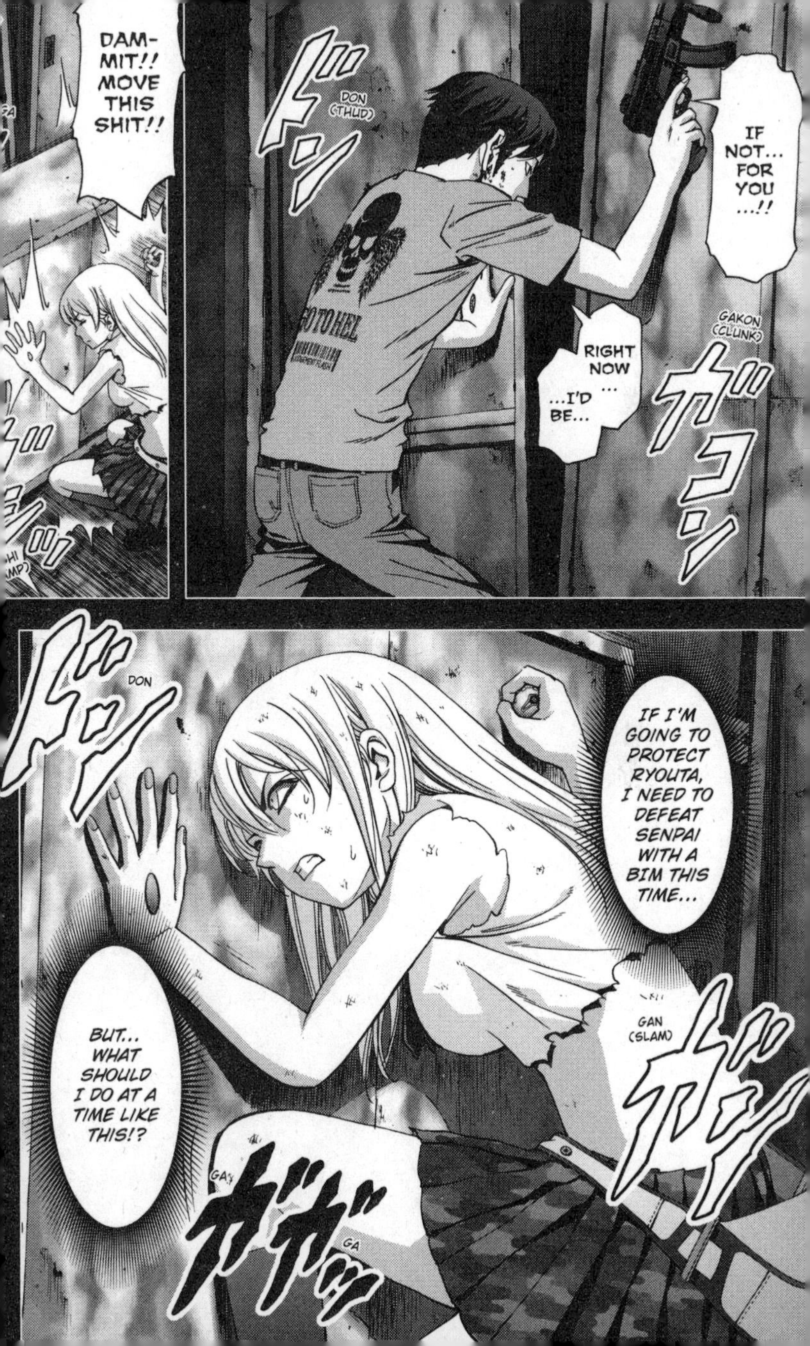
IF NOT... FOR YOU...!!
DON (THUD)
GAKON (CLUNK)
RIGHT NOW... ...I'D BE...
DAM-MIT!! MOVE THIS SHIT!!
IF I'M GOING TO PROTECT RYOUTA, I NEED TO DEFEAT SENPAI WITH A BIM THIS TIME...
DON
GAN (SLAM)
BUT... WHAT SHOULD I DO AT A TIME LIKE THIS!?
GA
GA

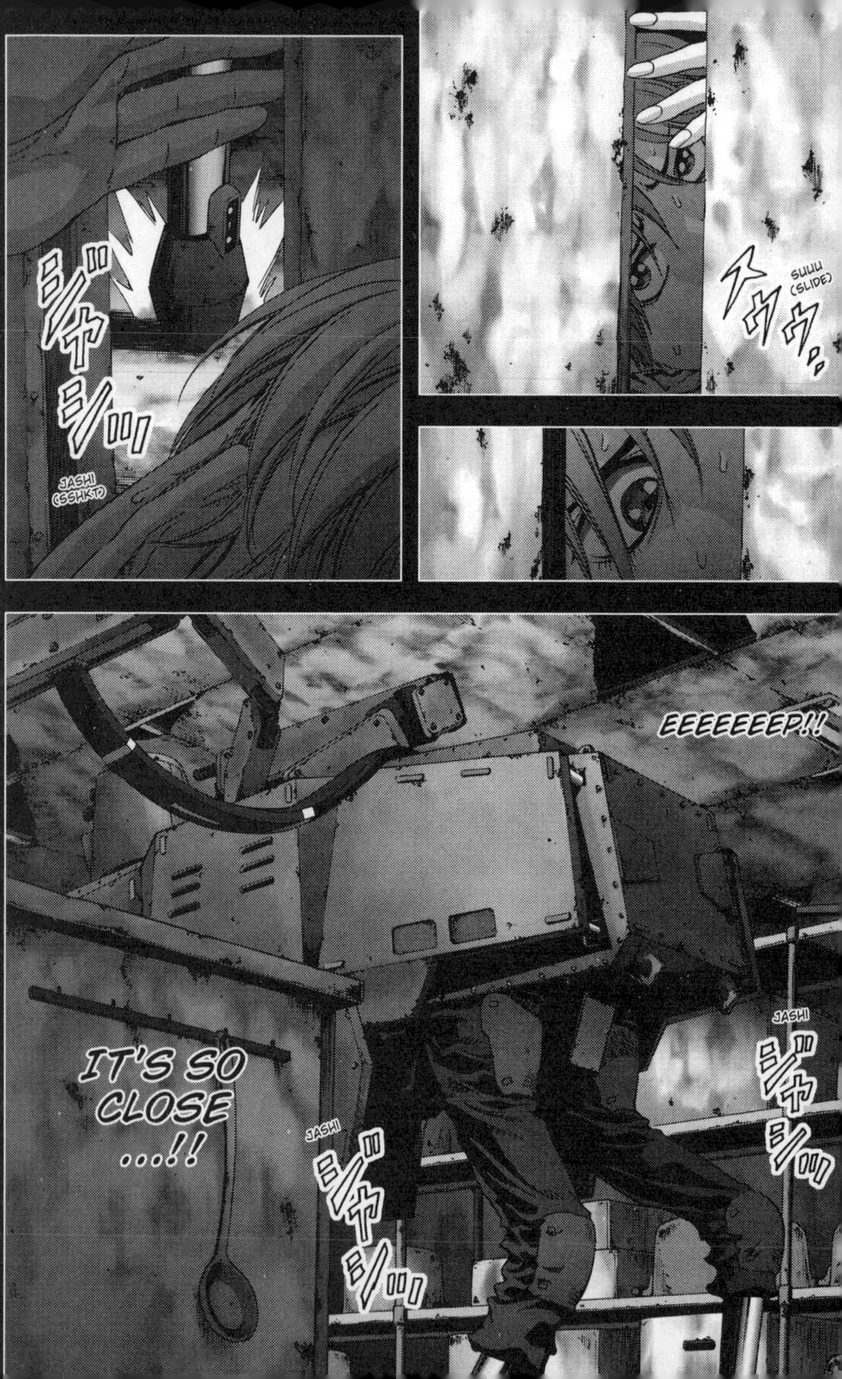
SUUU (SLIDE)
JASHI (SSHKT)
EEEEEEEP!!
JASHI
IT'S SO CLOSE ...!!
JASHI

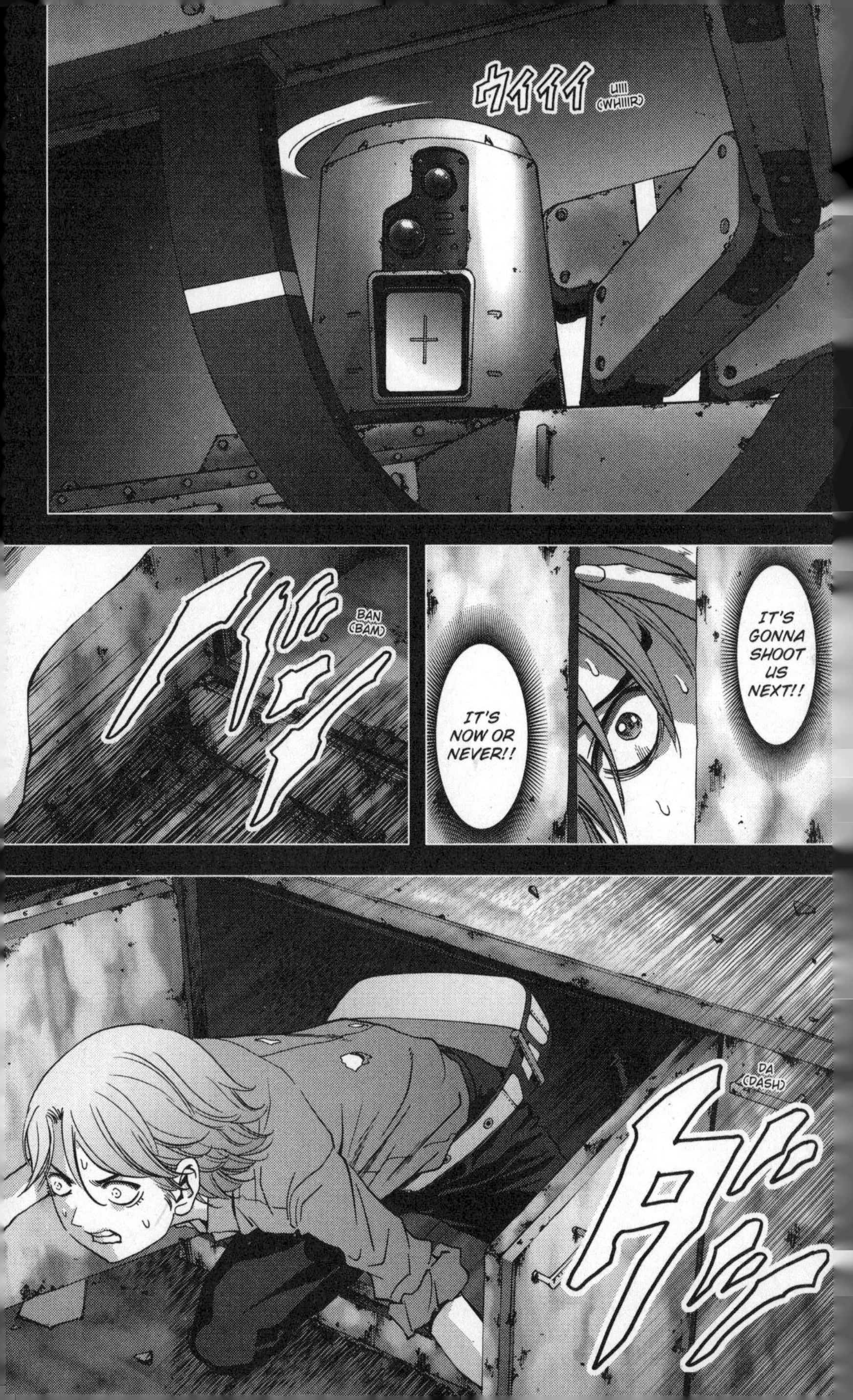
ウイイイ
UIII (WHIIIR)
IT'S GONNA SHOOT US NEXT!!
IT'S NOW OR NEVER!!
BAN (BAM)
DA (DASH)

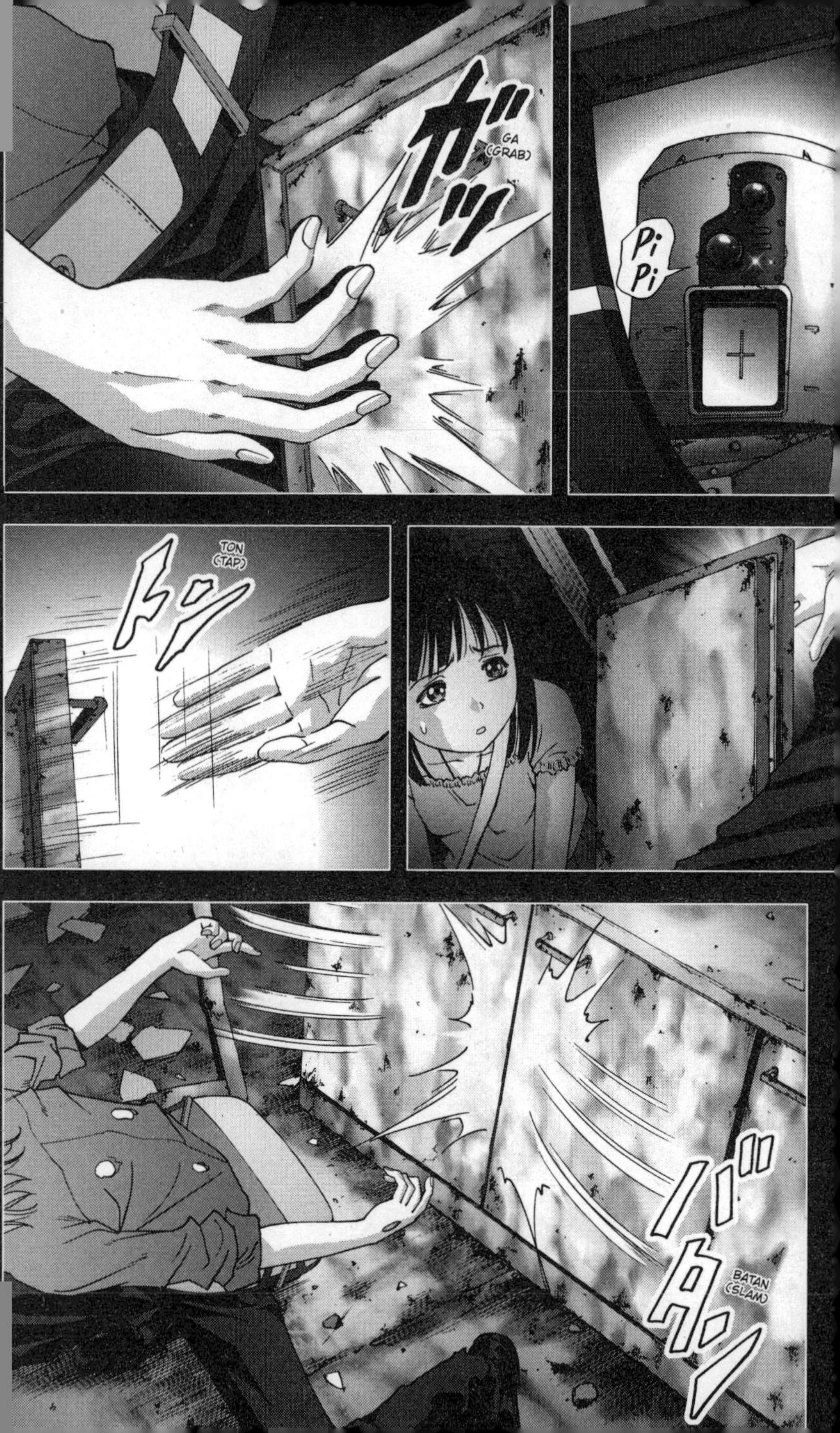
Pi
Pi
ガッ
GA (GRAB)
トン
TON (TAP)
バタン
BATAN (SLAM)

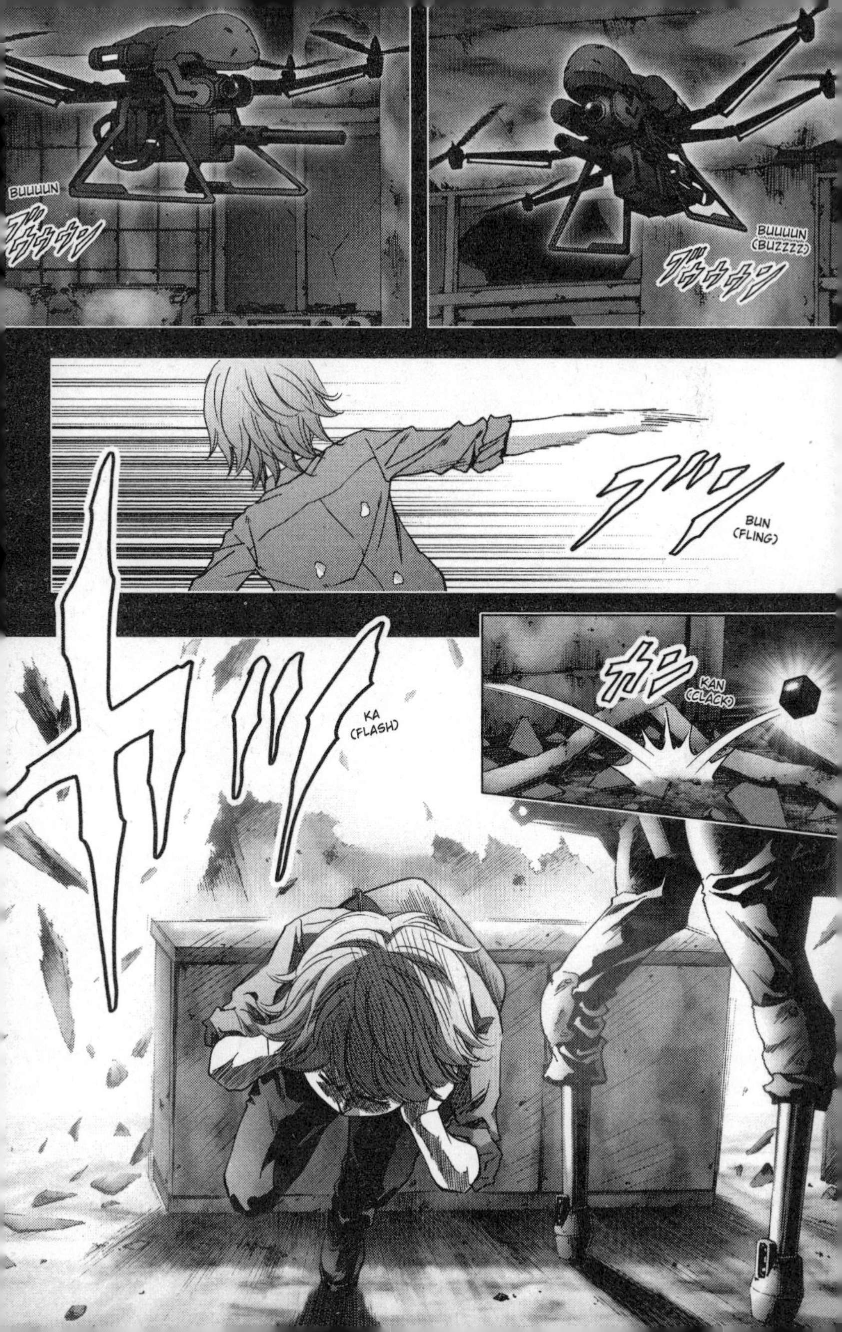

BUUUUN (BUZZZZ)
BUUUUN
BUN (FLING)
KAN (CLACK)
KA (FLASH)

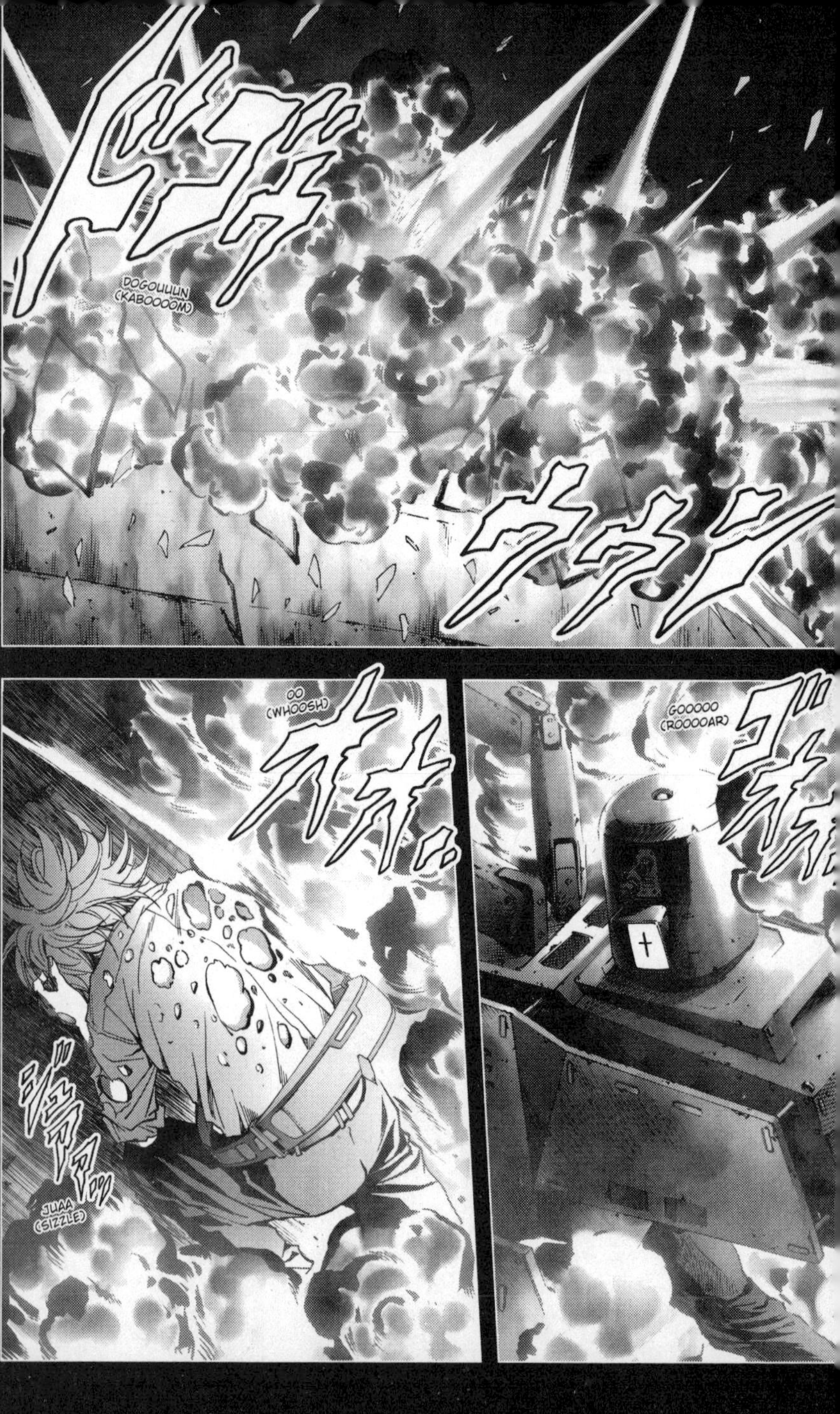
DOGOUUUN
(KABOOOOM)
GOOOOO
(ROOOOAR)
OO
(WHOOSH)
JUAA
(SIZZLE)

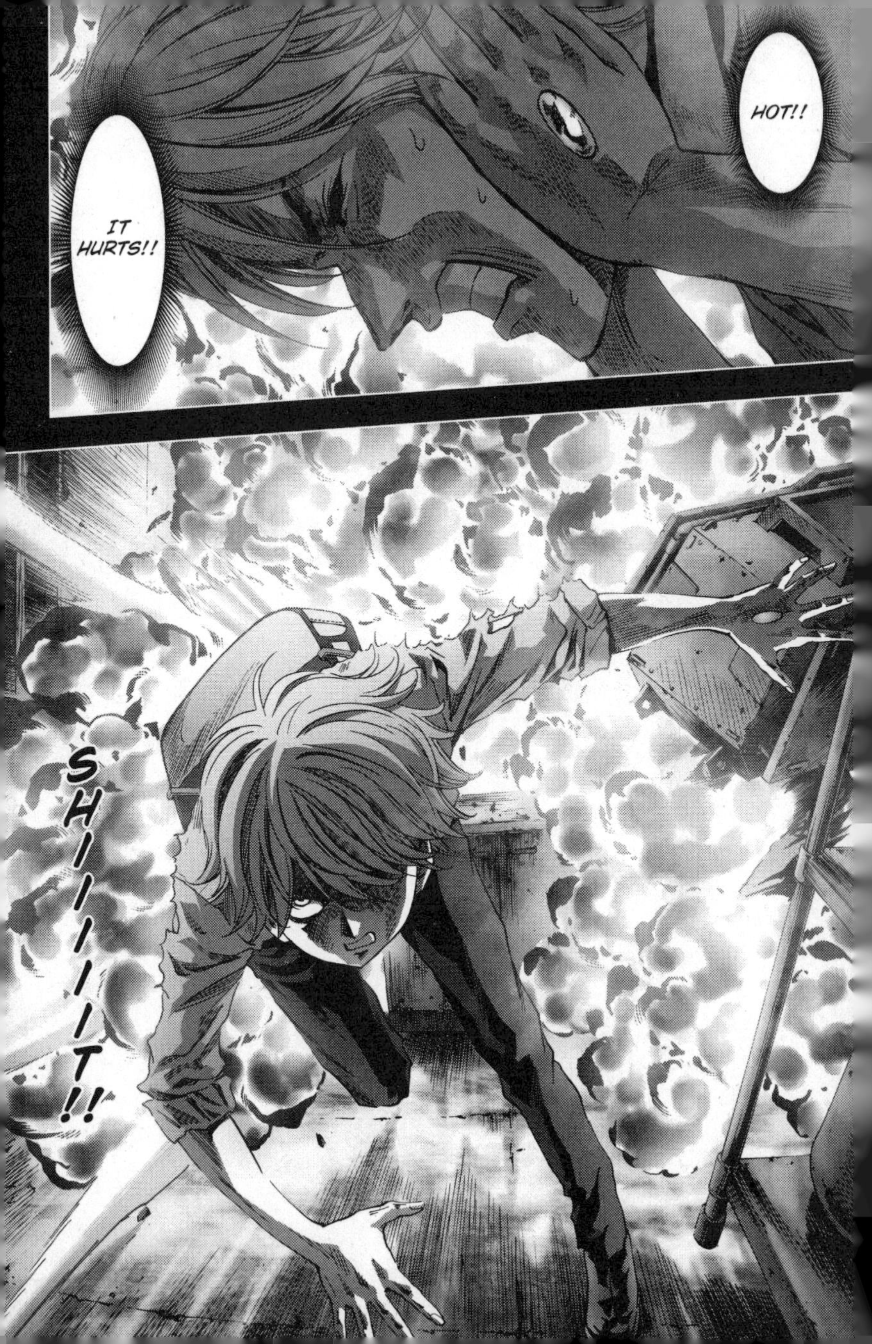
HOT!!
IT HURTS!!
SHIIIIT!!

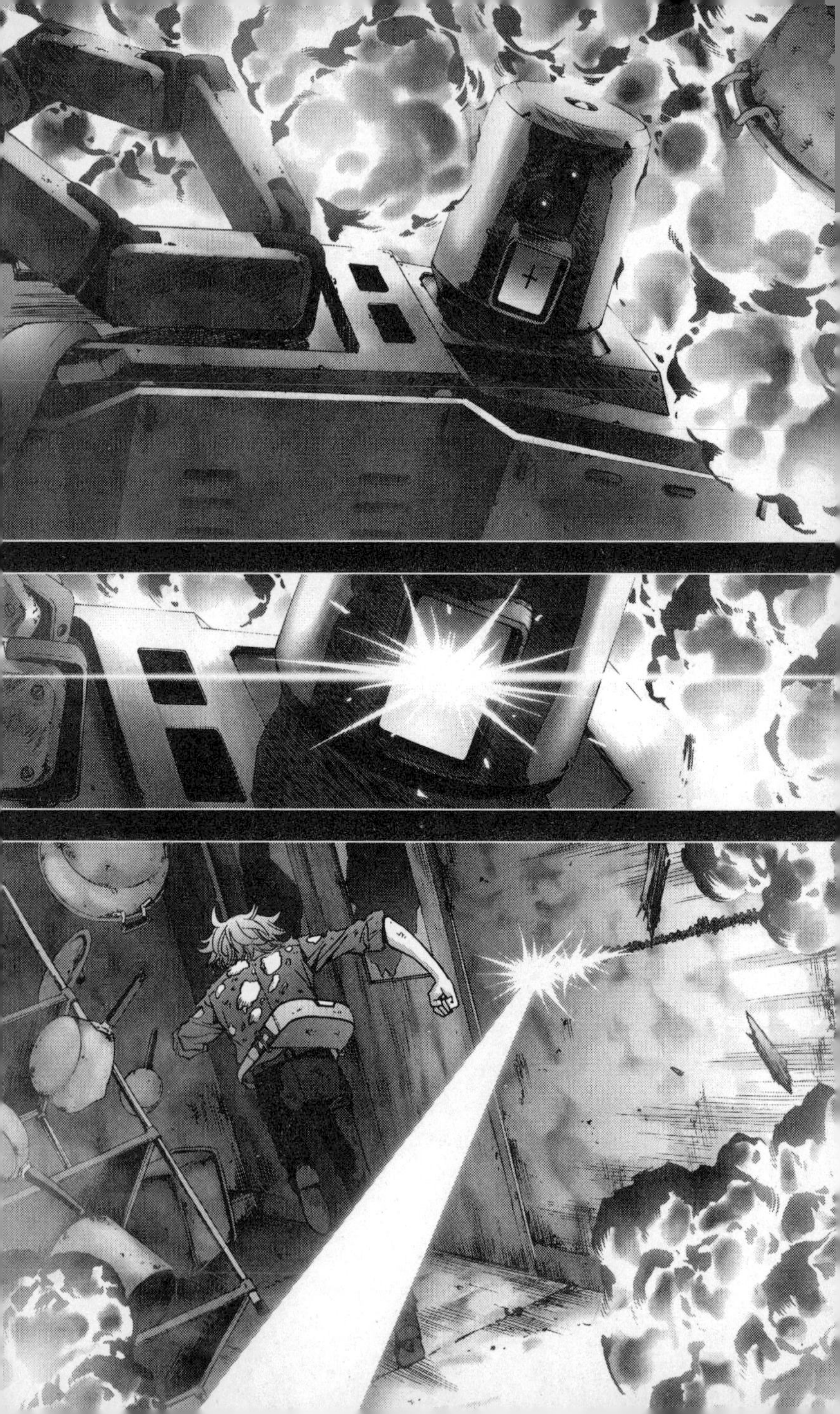

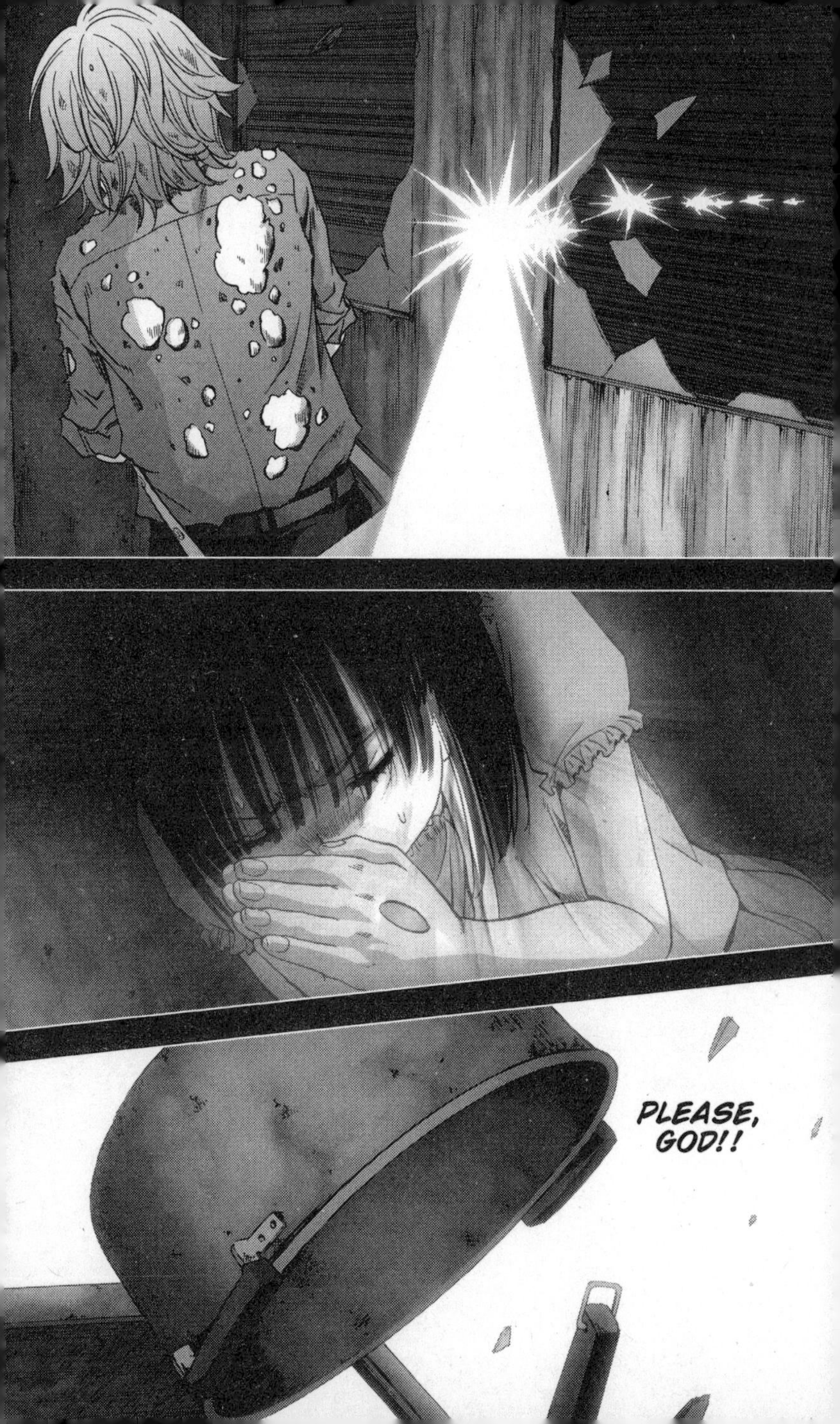
PLEASE, GOD!!

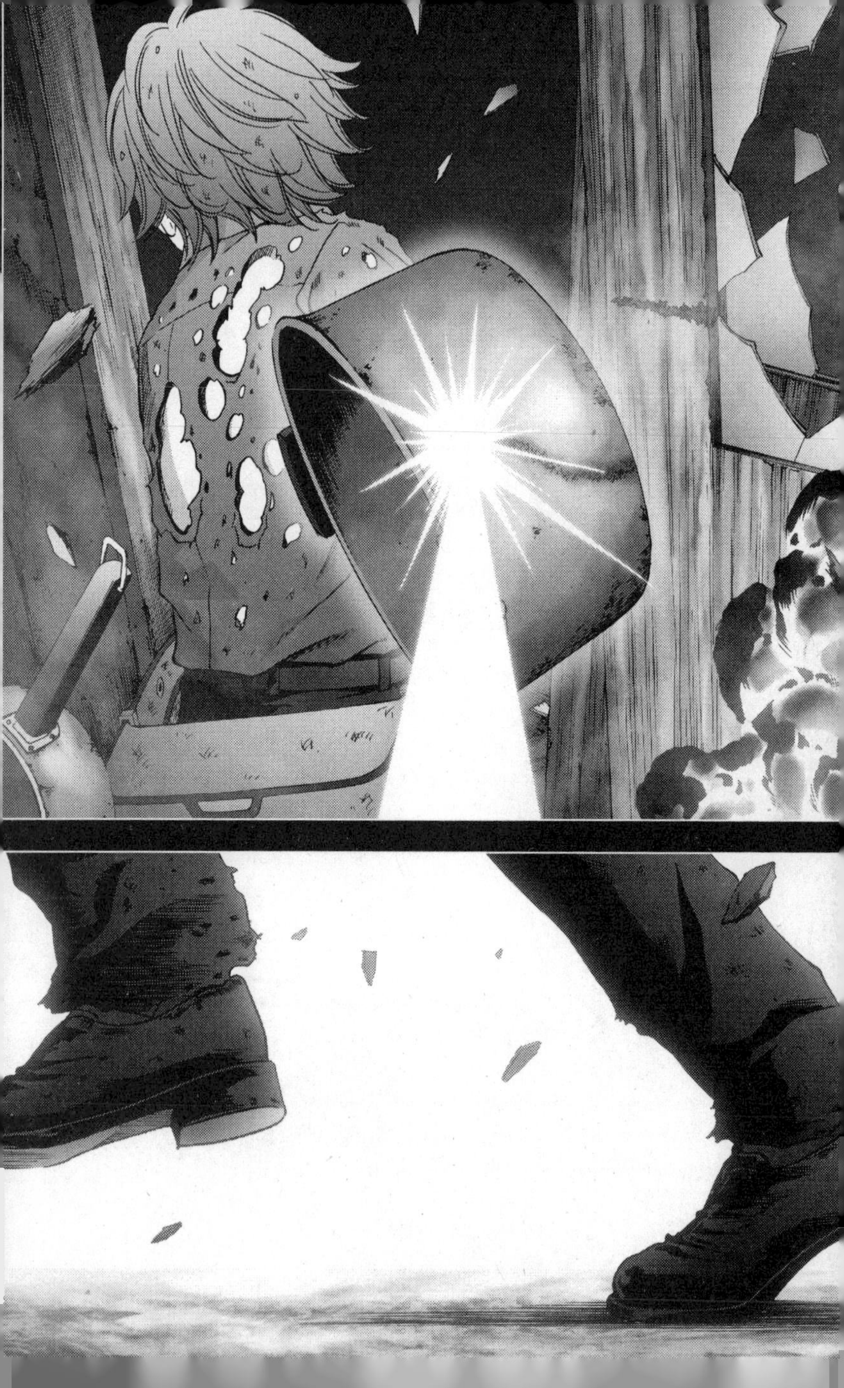

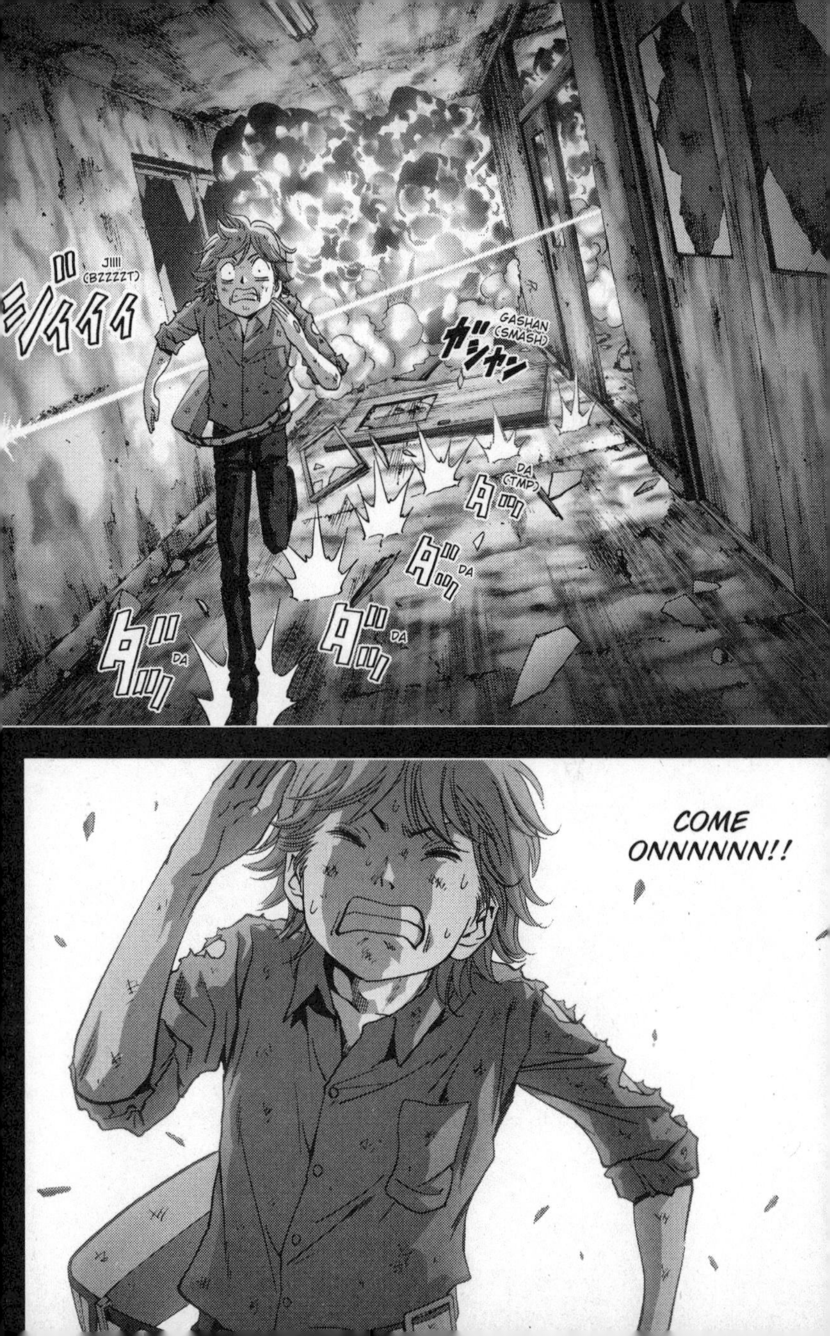
ガシャン
GASHAN (SMASH)
ジィィィィ
JIIII (BZZZZT)
ダッ
DA (TMP)
ダッ
DA
ダッ
DA
ダッ
DA
COME ONNNNNN!!

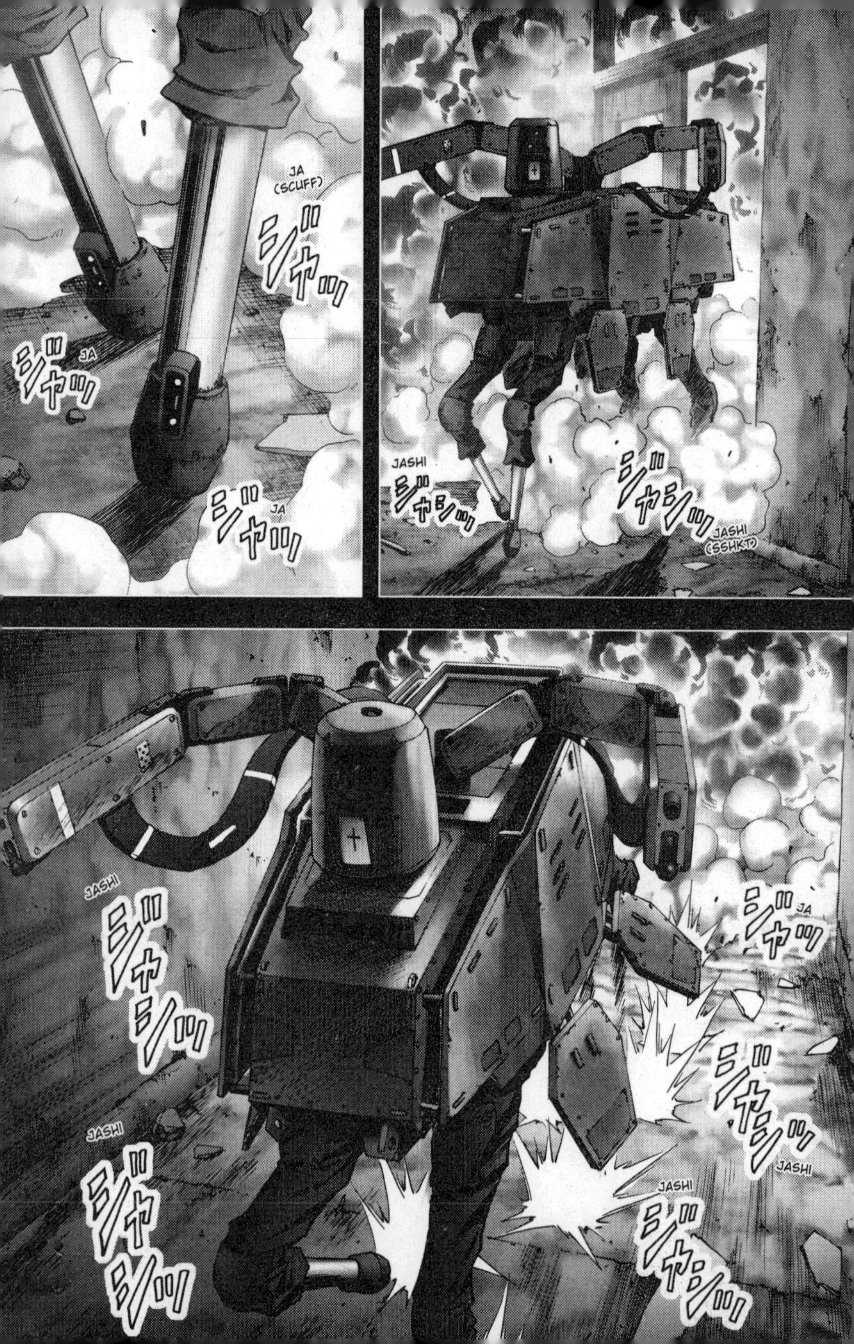
ジャシッ
JASHI (SSHKT)
ジャシッ
JASHI
ジャッ
JA (SCUFF)
ジャッ
JA
ジャッ
JA
ジャッ
JA
ジャシッ
JASHI
ジャシッ
JASHI
ジャシッ
JASHI
ジャシッ
JASHI

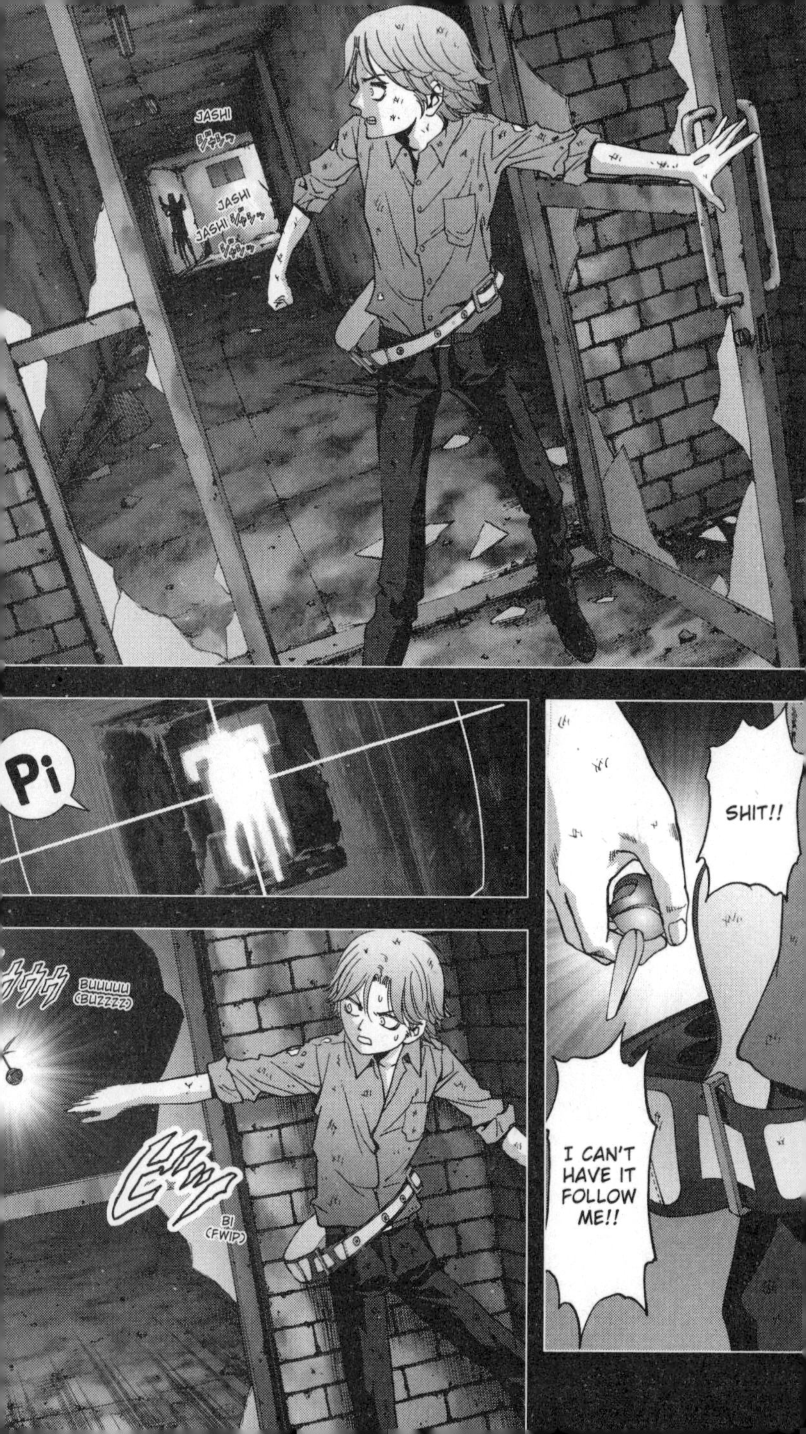
JASHI
JASHI
JASHI
SHIT!!
I CAN'T HAVE IT FOLLOW ME!!
Pi
BUUUUU (BUZZZZ)
BI (FWIP)

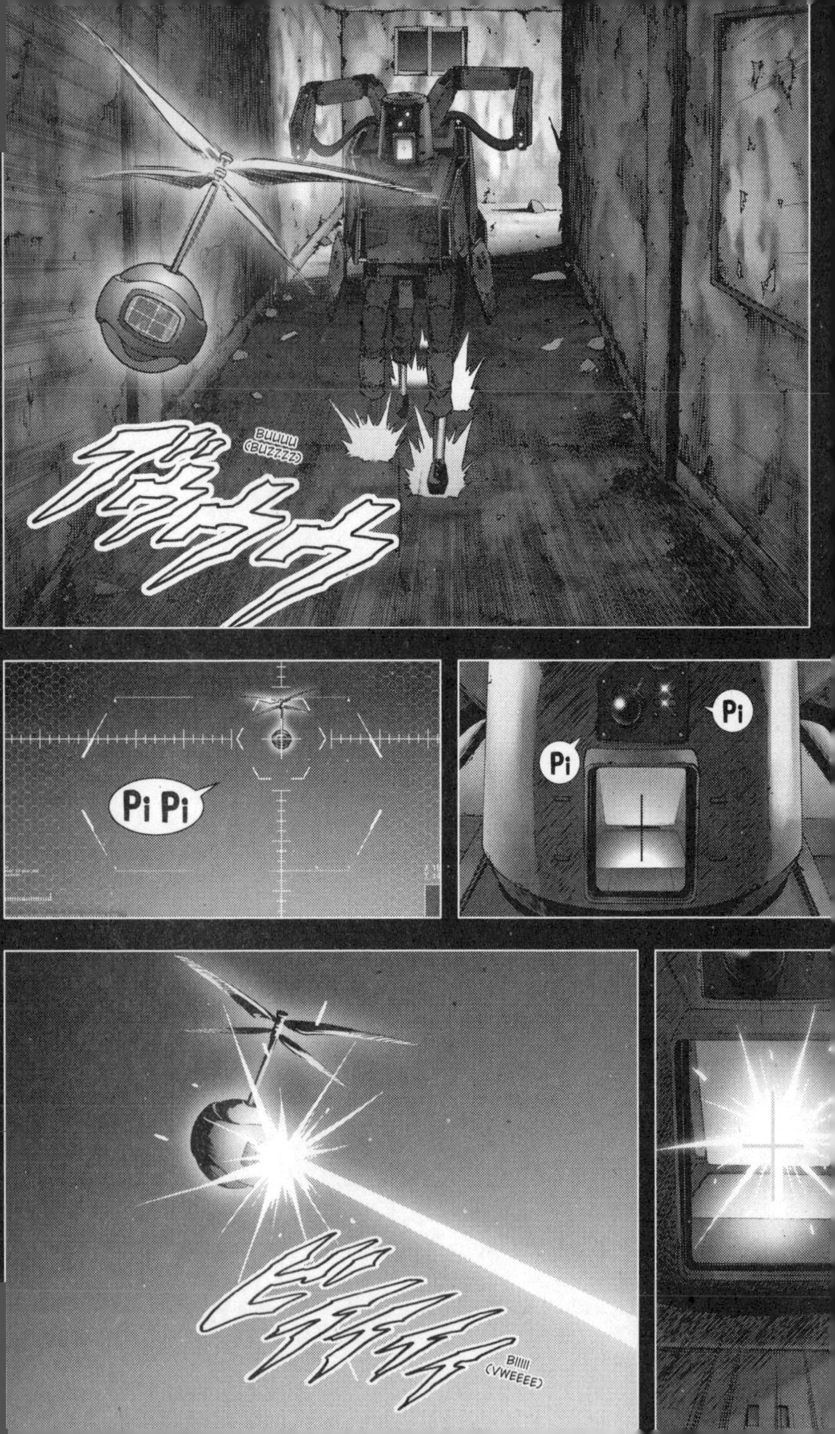
BUUUU
(BUZZZZ)
Pi
Pi
Pi Pi
BIIII
(VWEEEE)

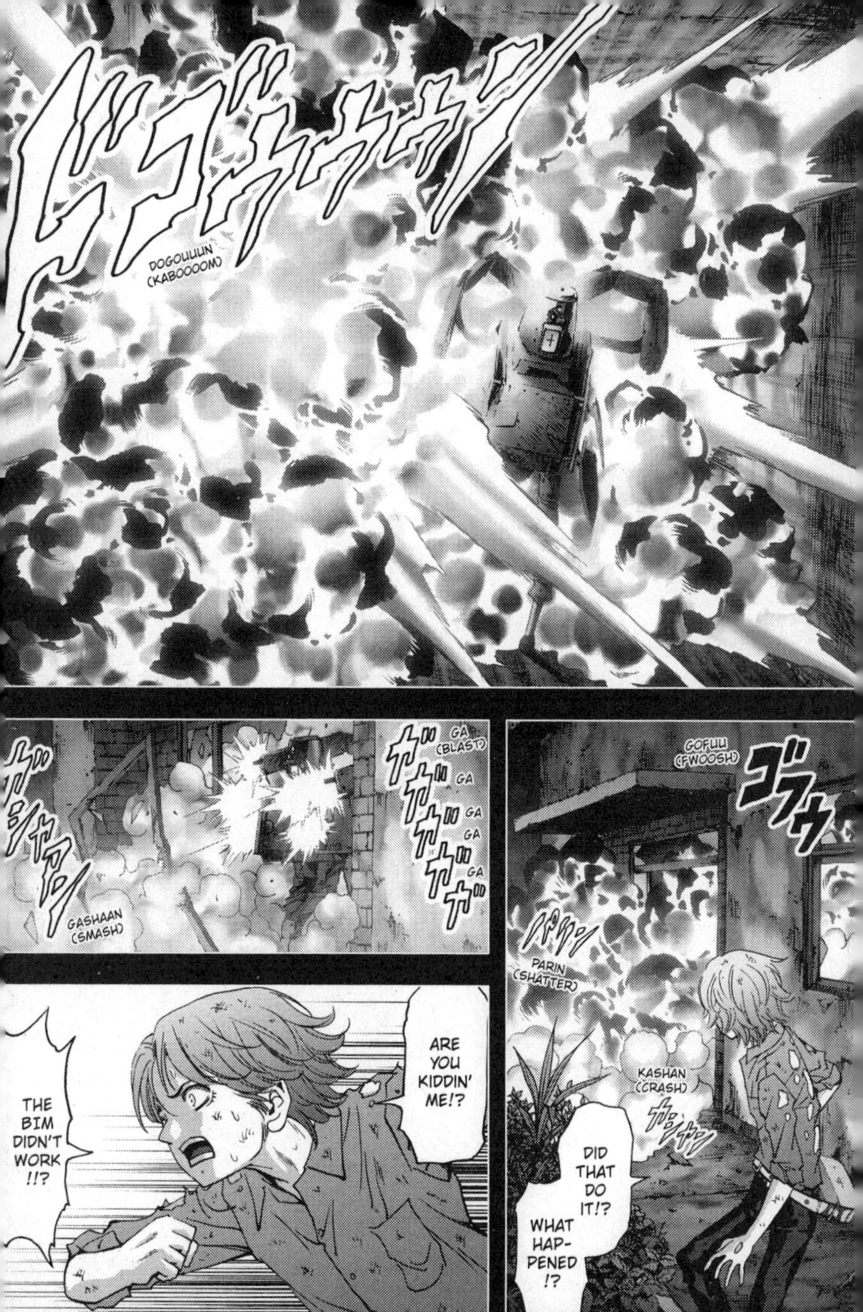
DOGOUUUN (KABOOOOM)
GOFUU (FWOOSH)
PARIN (SHATTER)
KASHAN (CRASH)
DID THAT DO IT!?
WHAT HAP-PENED !?
GA (BLAST)
GA
GA
GA
GA
GASHAAN (SMASH)
ARE YOU KIDDIN' ME!?
THE BIM DIDN'T WORK !!?

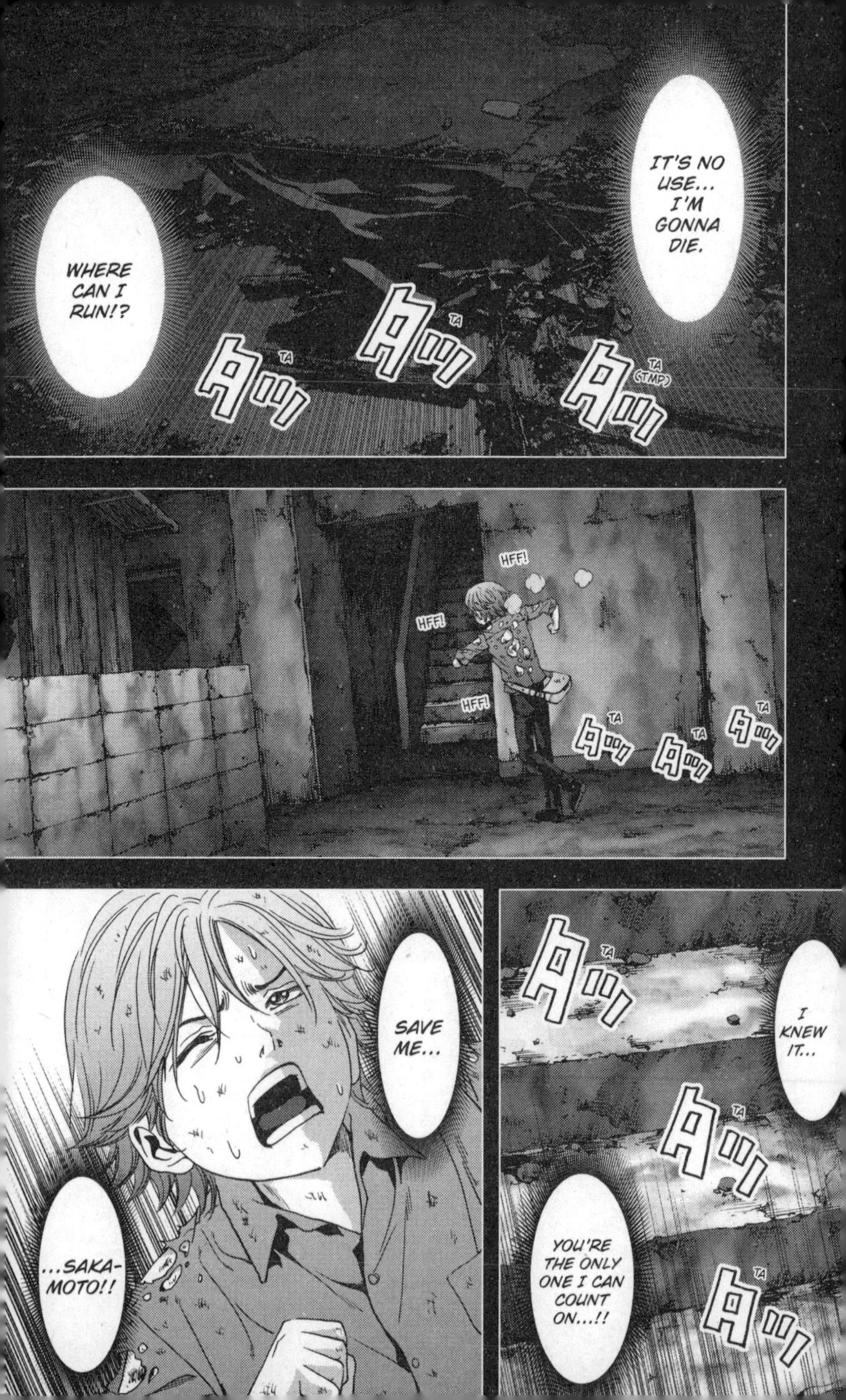
IT'S NO USE... I'M GONNA DIE.
TA (TMP)
TA
TA
WHERE CAN I RUN!?
TA
TA
TA
HFF!
HFF!
HFF!
I KNEW IT...
TA
TA
YOU'RE THE ONLY ONE I CAN COUNT ON...!!
TA
SAVE ME...
...SAKA-MOTO!!

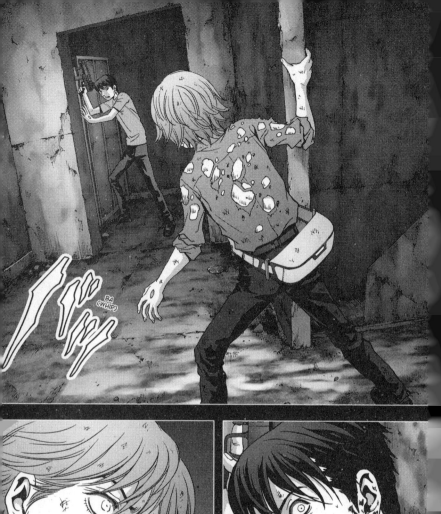

BA
(WHIP)

HFF!

HFF!

HFF!

...A BARRI- CADE?

Y-YO-SHIO-KA...?

YOU'RE ALIVE...!?

YOU... BETRAYED ME TOO, DIDN'T YOU?

UE-SUGI...

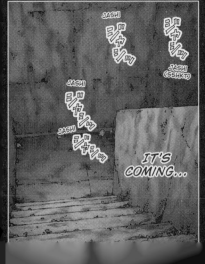

JASHI

JASHI

JASHI (CSSHKT)

JASHI

JASHI

IT'S COMING...

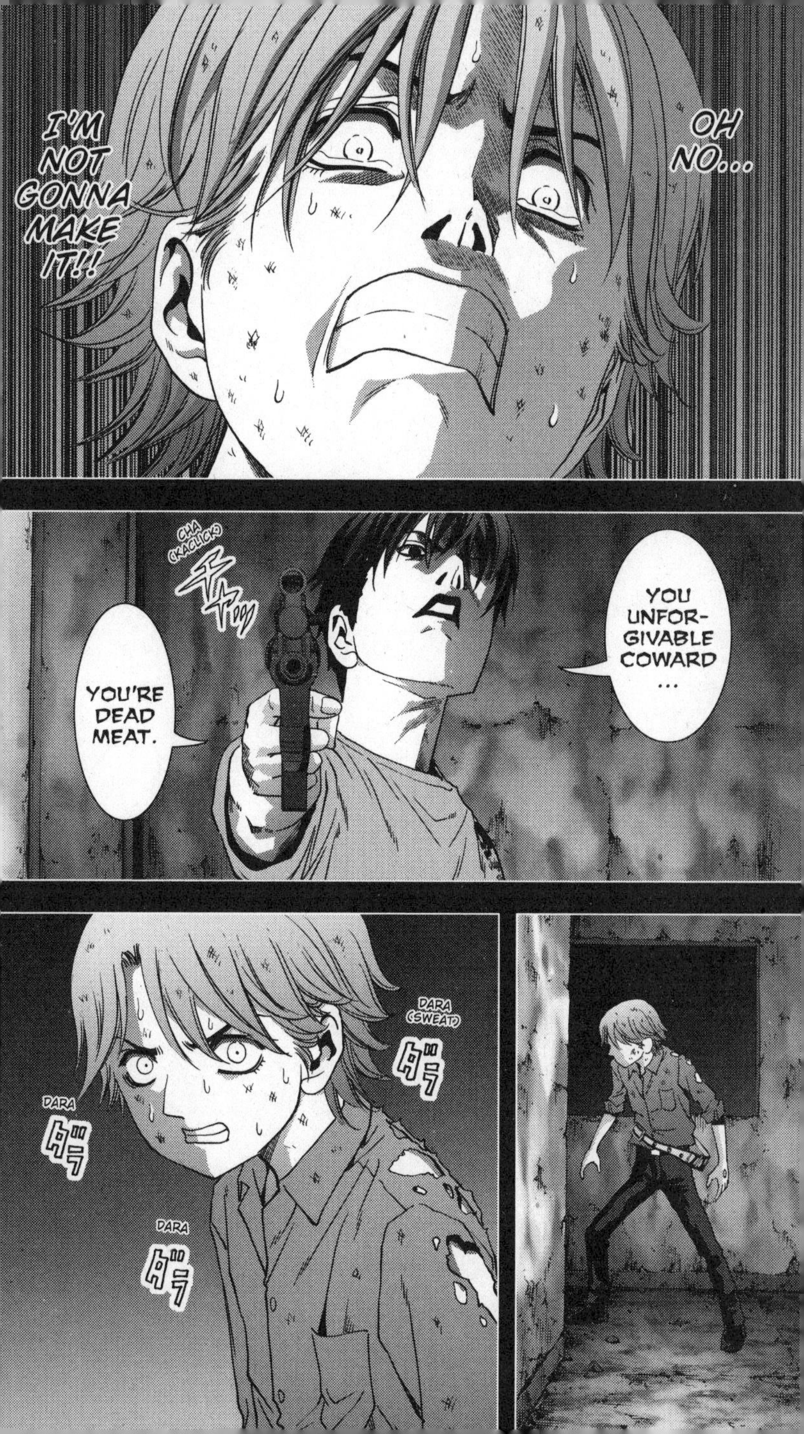
OH NO...
I'M NOT GONNA MAKE IT!!
YOU UNFORGIVABLE COWARD ...
CHA (KACLICK)
YOU'RE DEAD MEAT.
DARA (SWEAT)
DARA
DARA

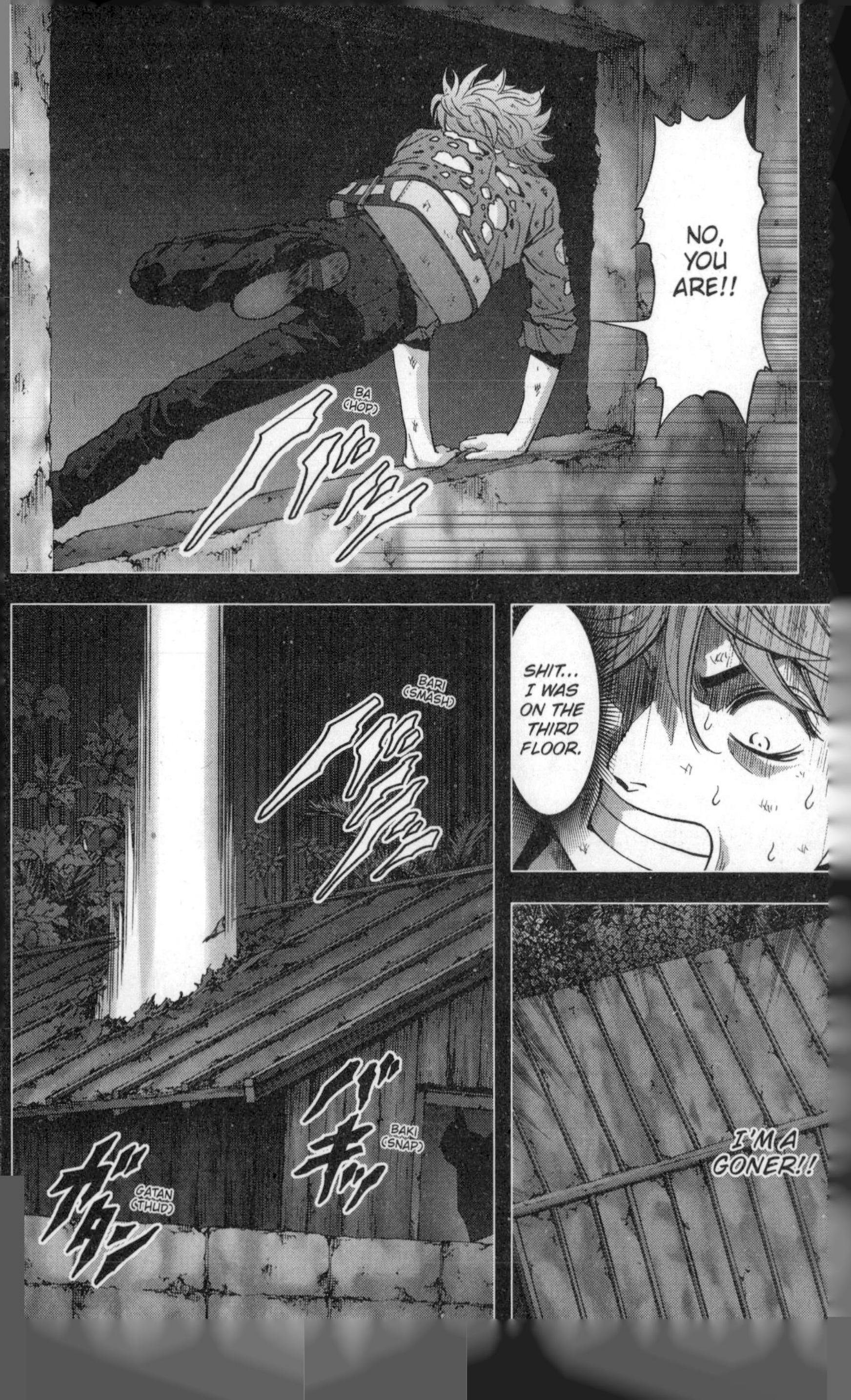
NO, YOU ARE!!
BA (HOP)
SHIT... I WAS ON THE THIRD FLOOR.
I'M A GONER!!
BARI (SMASH)
BAKI (SNAP)
GATAN (THUD)

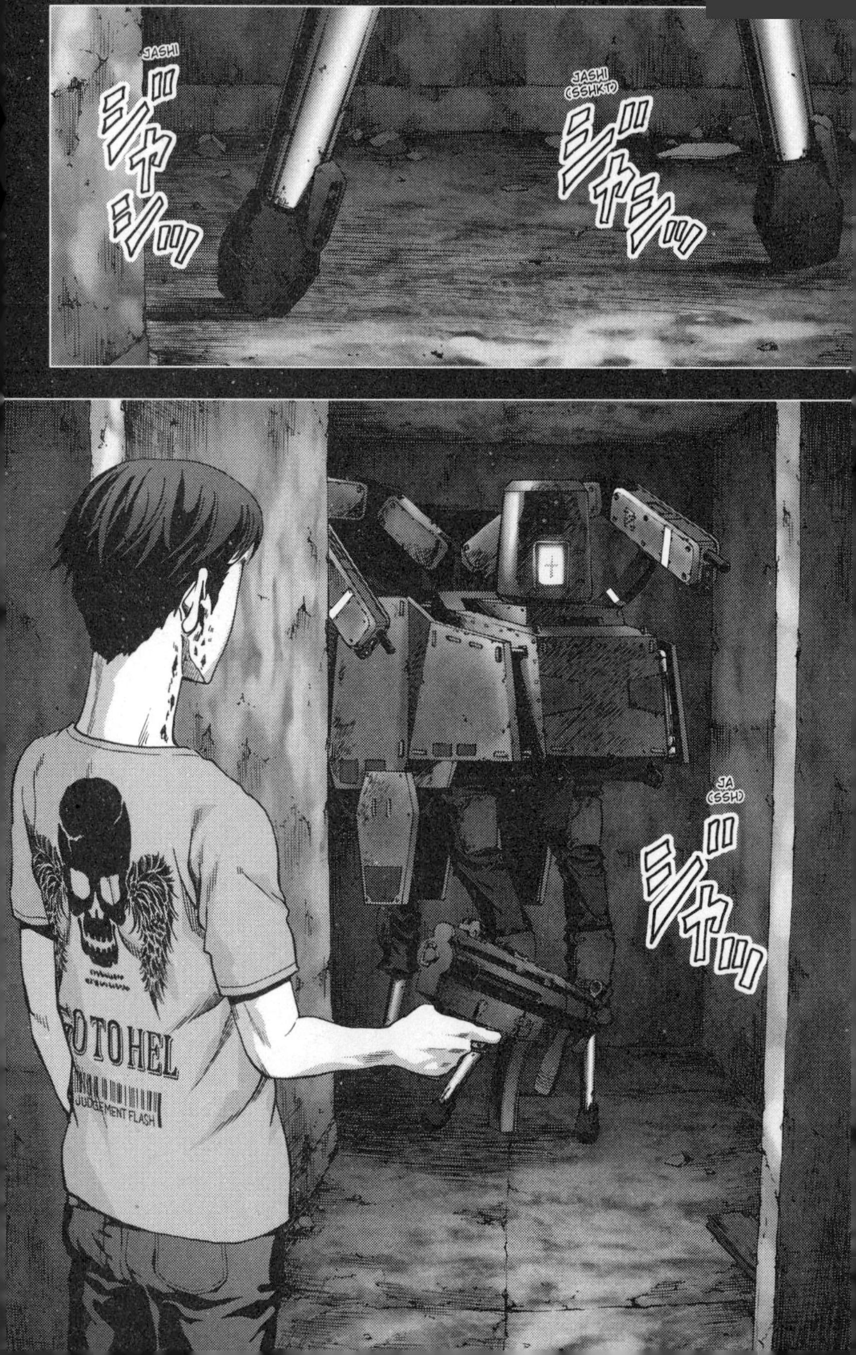
JASHI (SSHKT)
JASHI
JA (SSH)
JUDGEMENT FLASH

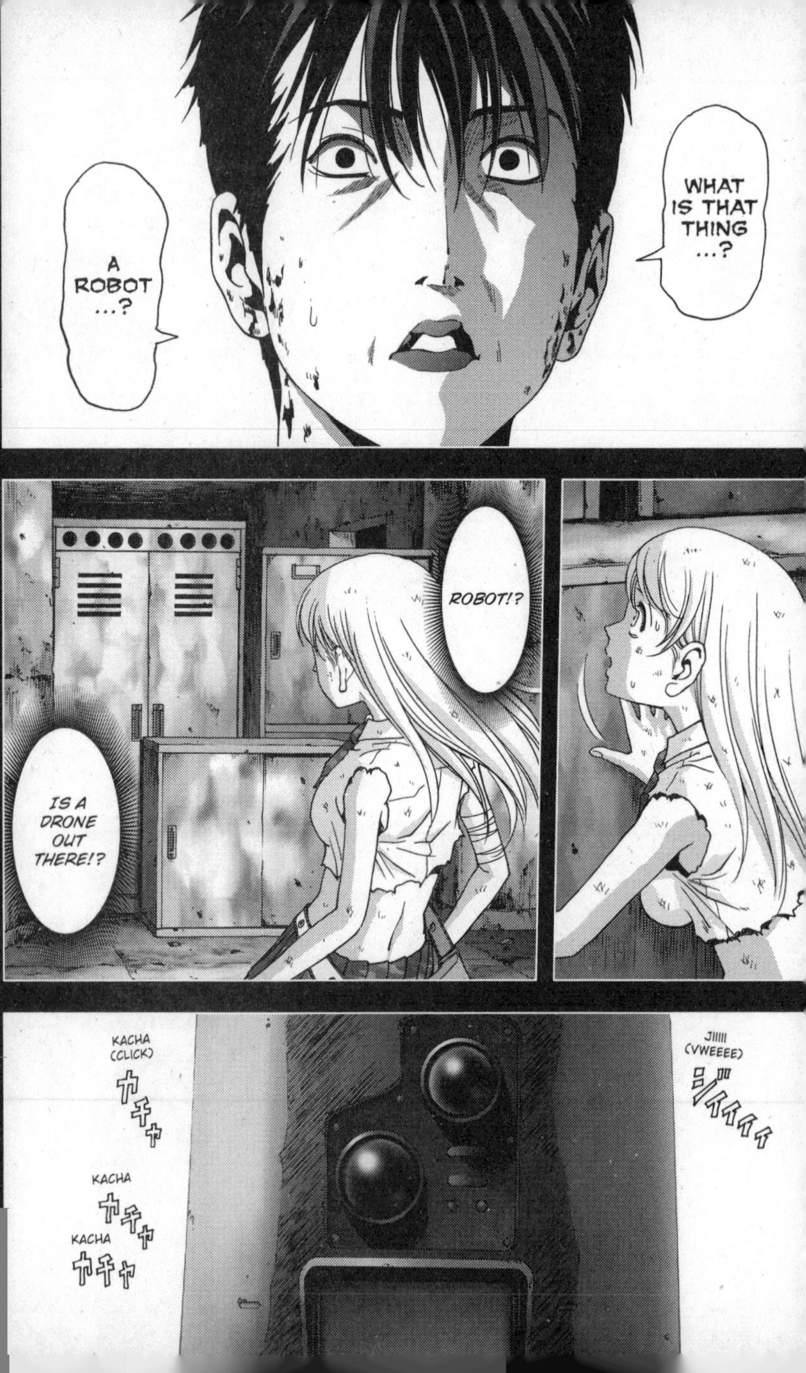
WHAT IS THAT THING ...?
A ROBOT ...?
ROBOT!?
IS A DRONE OUT THERE!?
JIIII (VWEEEE)
ジイイイイ
KACHA (CLICK)
カチャ
KACHA
カチャ
KACHA
カチャ

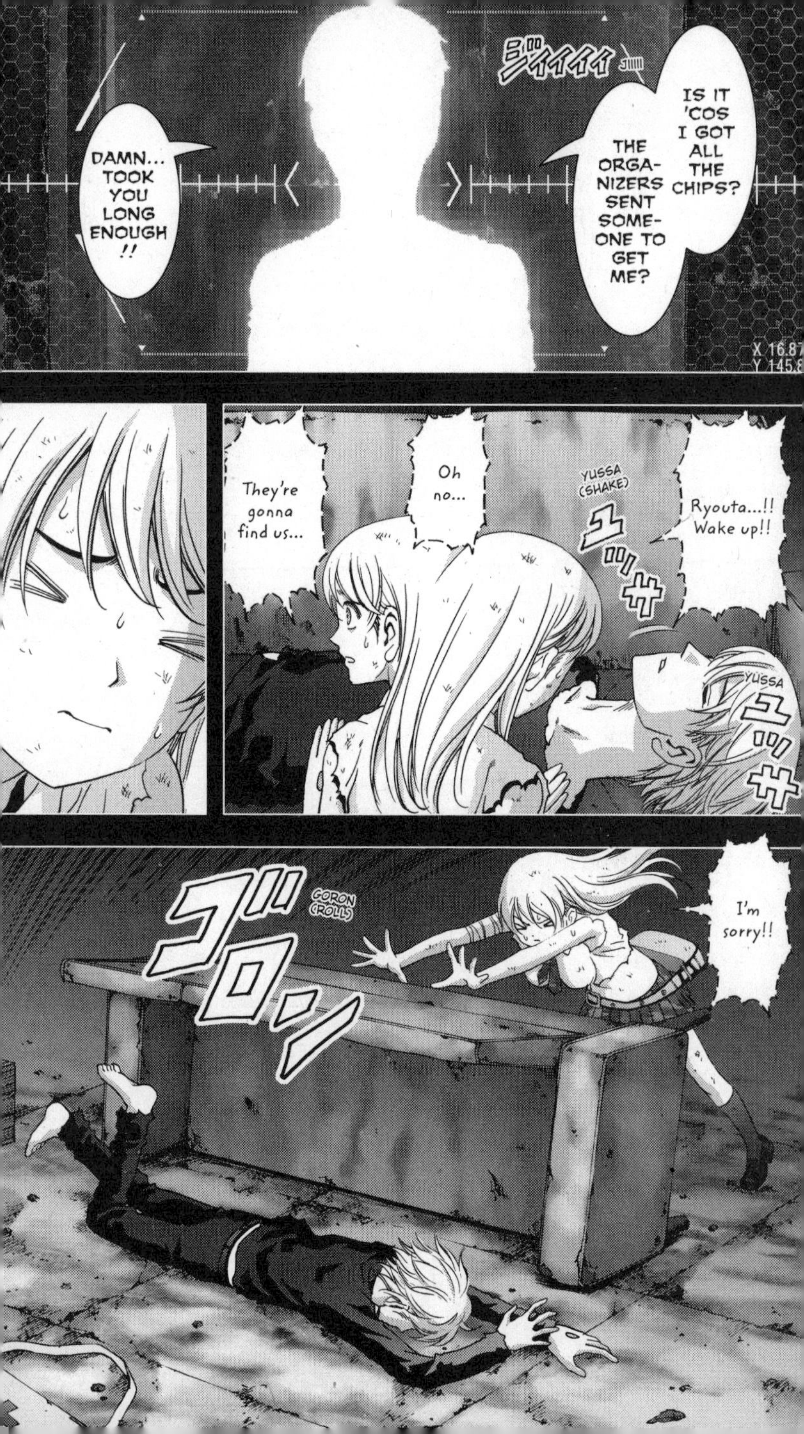

ジィイイイ
IS IT 'COS I GOT ALL THE CHIPS?
THE ORGANIZERS SENT SOMEONE TO GET ME?
DAMN... TOOK YOU LONG ENOUGH!!
X 16.87
Y 145.8
Ryouta...!! Wake up!!
YUSSA (SHAKE)
ユッサ
YUSSA
ユッサ
Oh no...
They're gonna find us...
I'm sorry!!
GORON (ROLL)
ゴロン

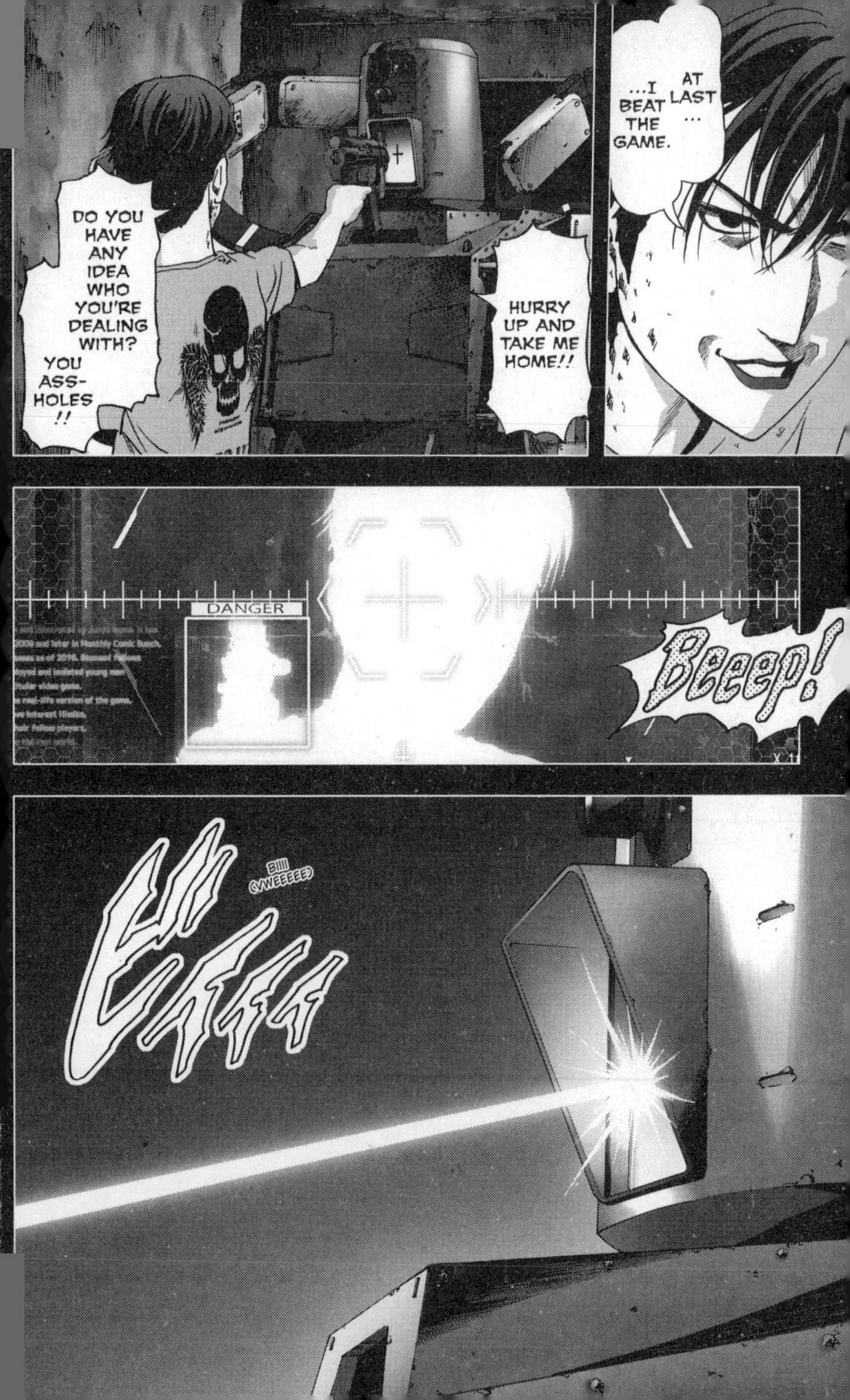
AT LAST ... ...I BEAT THE GAME.
HURRY UP AND TAKE ME HOME!!
DO YOU HAVE ANY IDEA WHO YOU'RE DEALING WITH?
YOU ASS-HOLES!!
DANGER
Beeep!
BIIII (VWEEEEE)

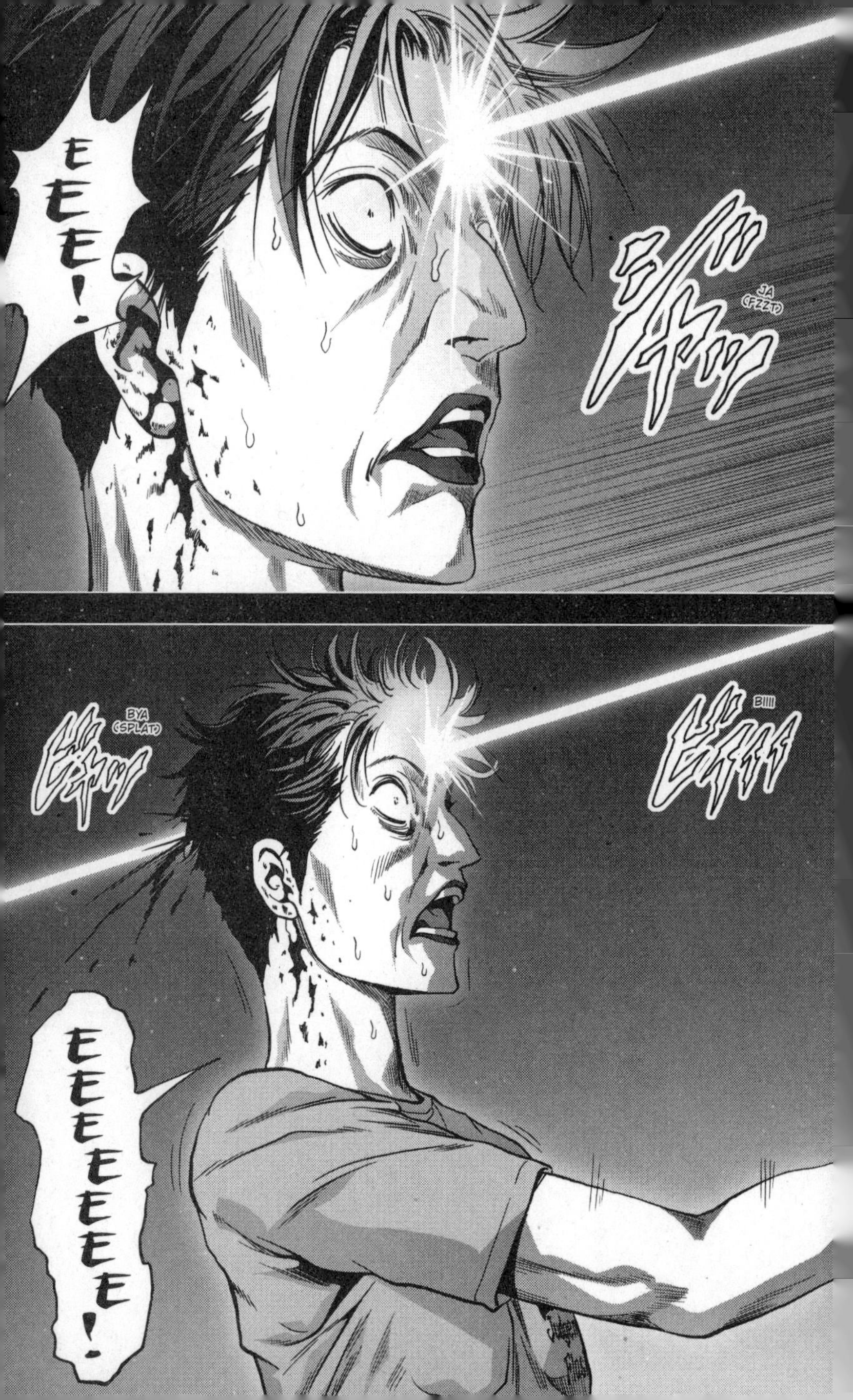
JA (FZZT)
EEE!
BIIII
BYA (SPLAT)
EEEEEEE!

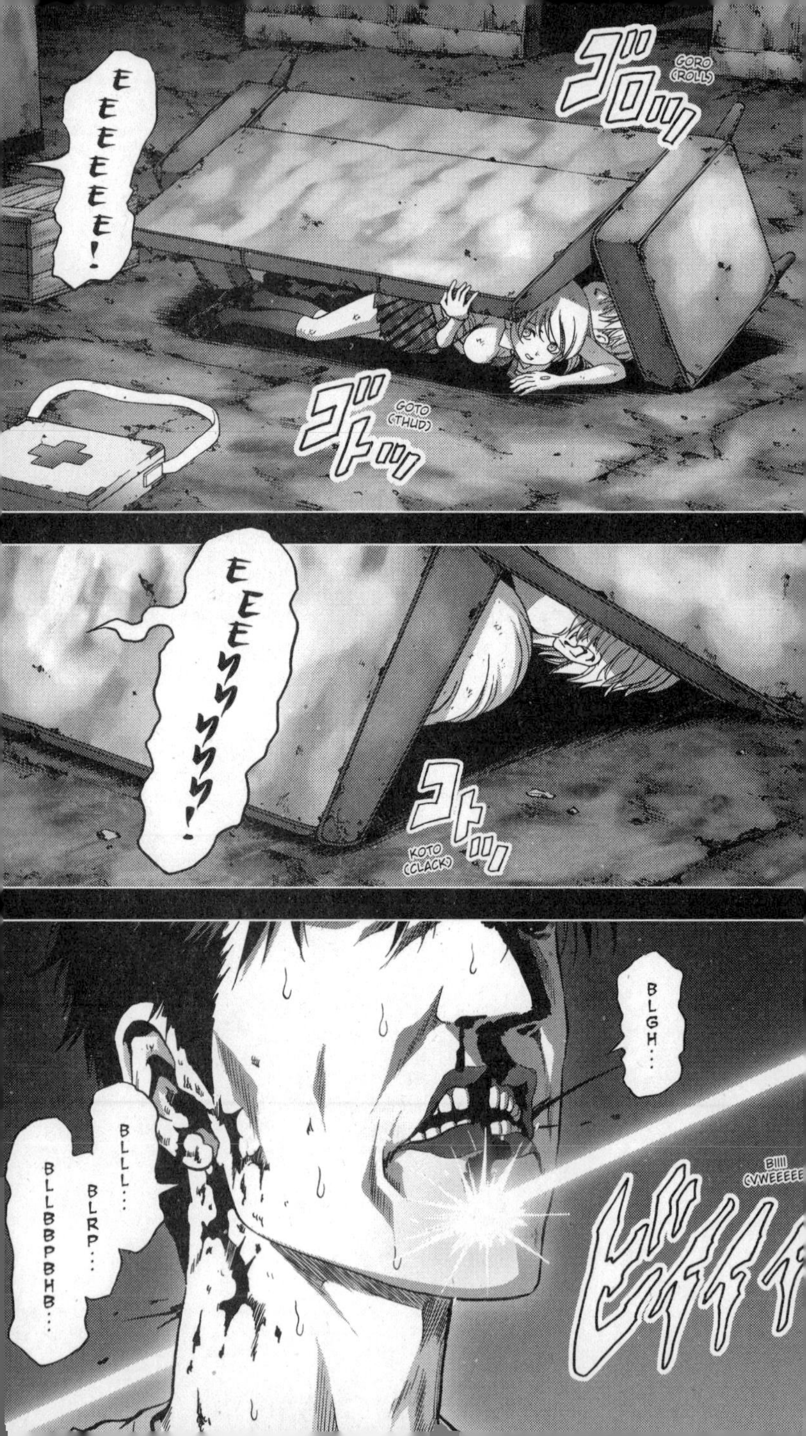
GORO (ROLL)
EEEEEEE!
GOTO (THUD)
EEE!
KOTO (CLACK)
BLGH...
BIIII (VWEEEEE
BLLL...
BLRP...
BLLBBPBHB...

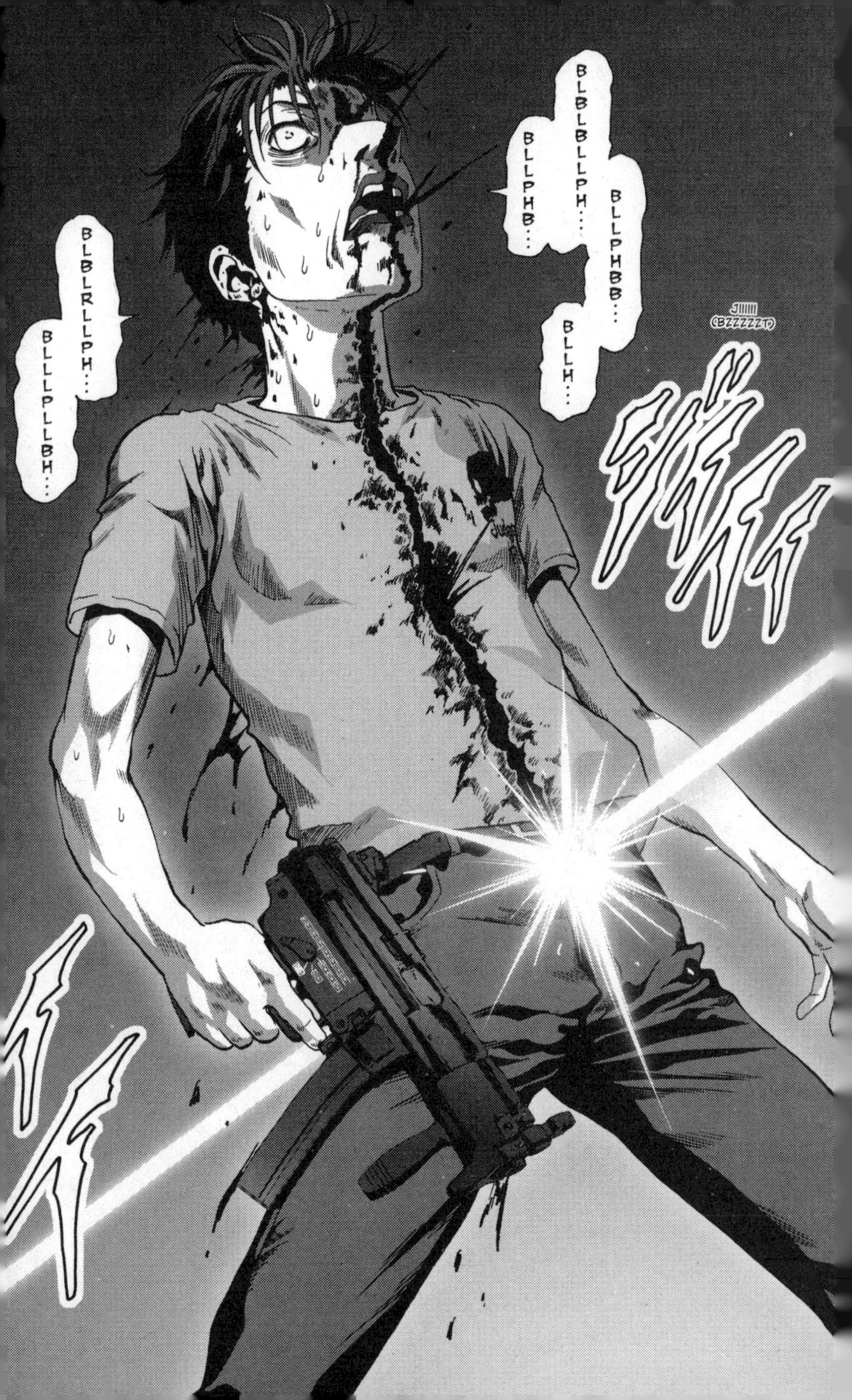

BLBLBLLPH...
BLLPHB...
BLLPHBB...
BLLH...
JIIIIII
(BZZZZZT)
BLBLRLLPH...
BLLLPLLBH...

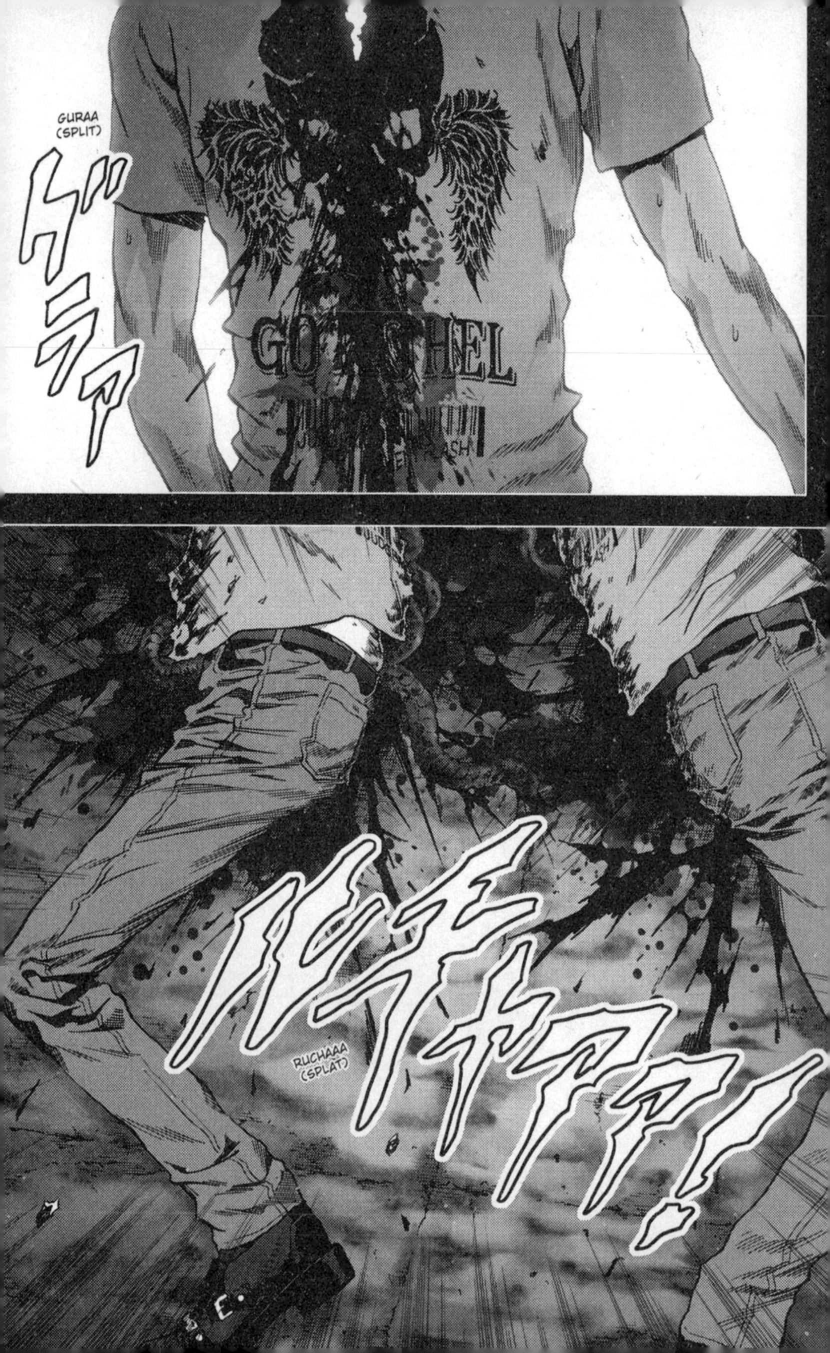
グラァ
GURAA (SPLIT)
ルチャアア!
RUCHAAA (SPLAT)

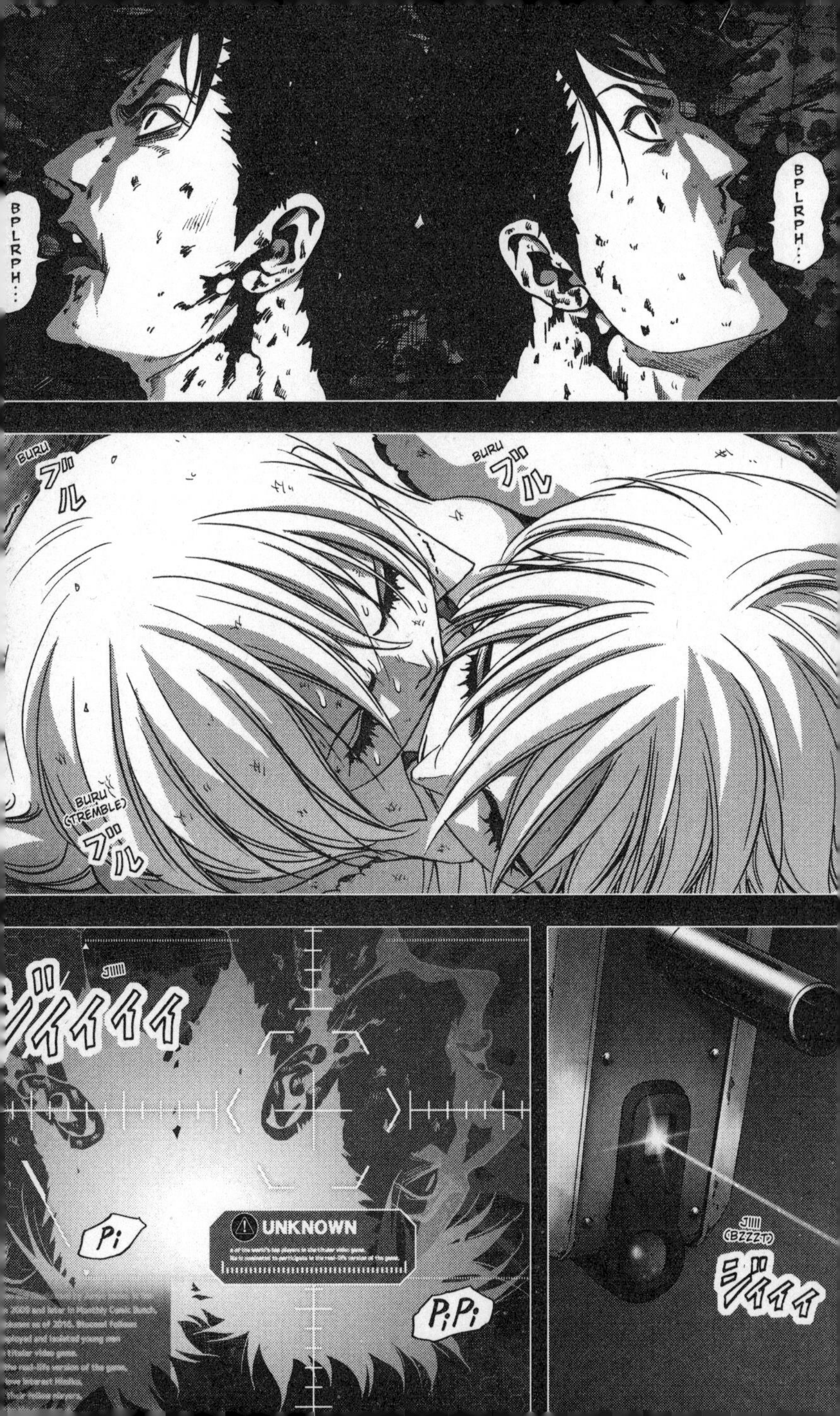
BPLRPH...
BPLRPH...
BURU
ブル
BURU
ブル
BURU (TREMBLE)
ブル
JIIII (BZZZT)
ジイイイ
JIIII
ジイイイイ
UNKNOWN
PiPi
Pi

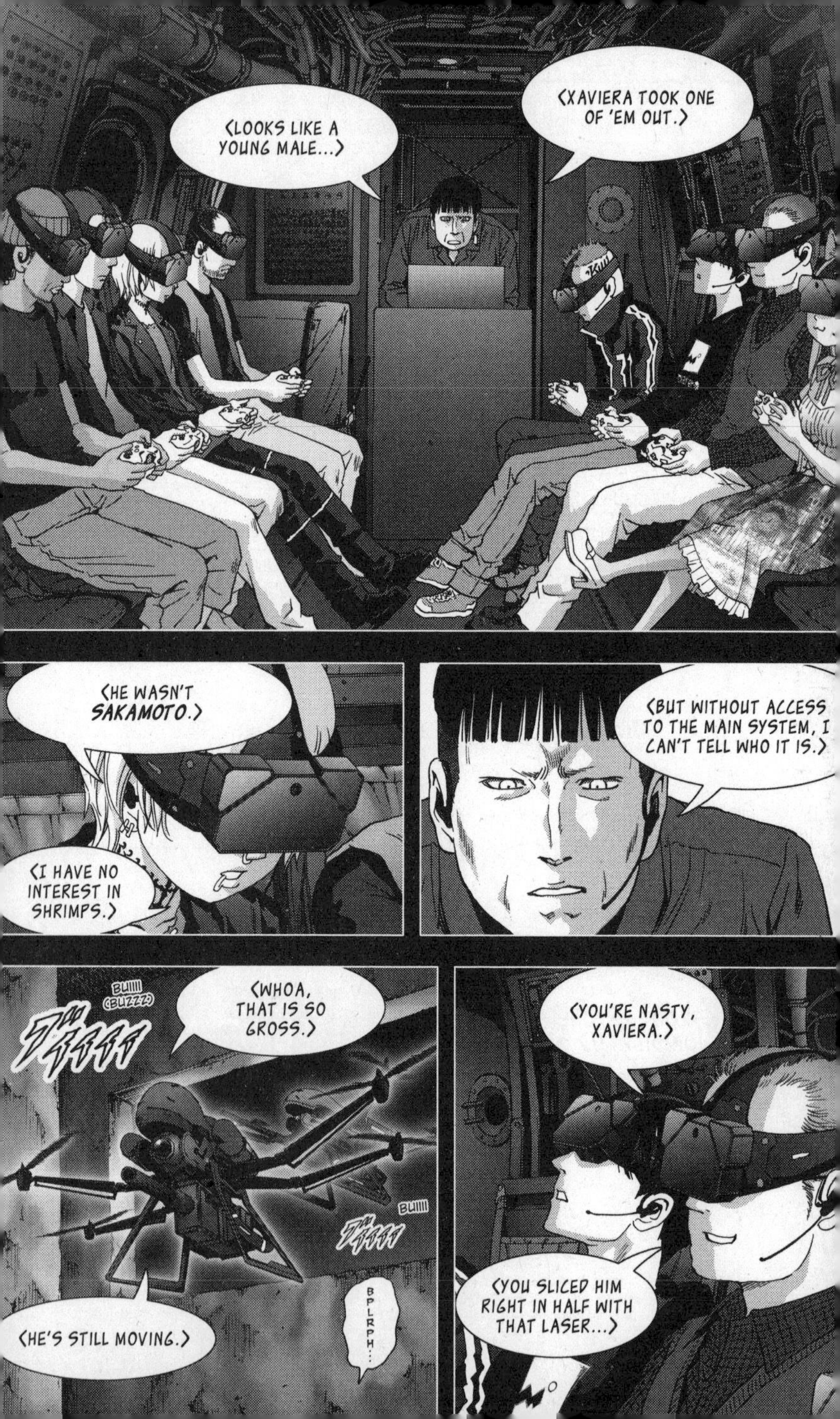
<XAVIERA TOOK ONE OF 'EM OUT.>
<LOOKS LIKE A YOUNG MALE...>
<BUT WITHOUT ACCESS TO THE MAIN SYSTEM, I CAN'T TELL WHO IT IS.>
<HE WASN'T **SAKAMOTO**.>
<I HAVE NO INTEREST IN SHRIMPS.>
<YOU'RE NASTY, XAVIERA.>
<YOU SLICED HIM RIGHT IN HALF WITH THAT LASER...>
<WHOA, THAT IS SO GROSS.>
BUIIII (BUZZZ)
BUIIII
BPLRPH...
<HE'S STILL MOVING.>

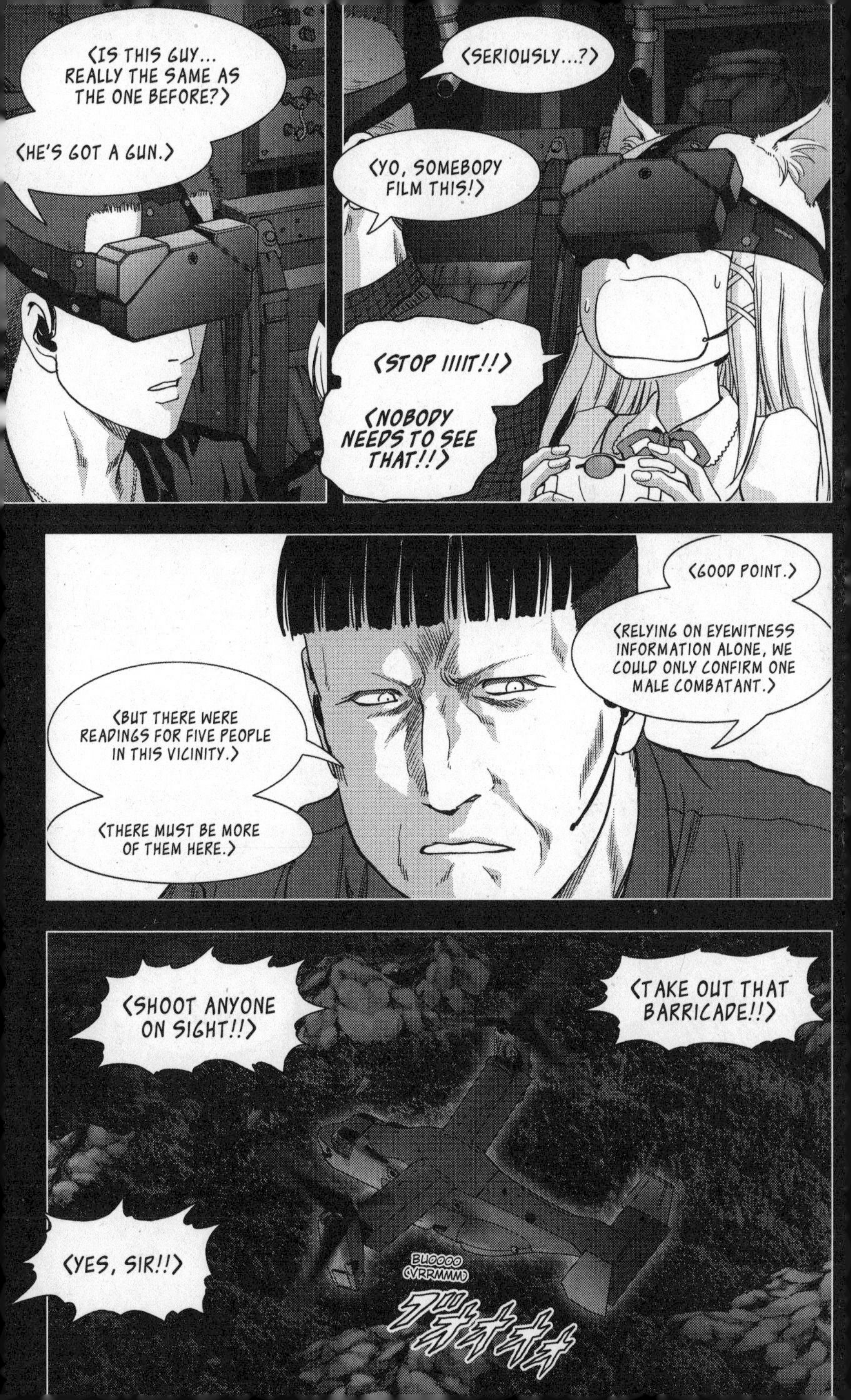
⟨SERIOUSLY...?⟩
⟨YO, SOMEBODY FILM THIS!⟩
⟨STOP IIIIT!!⟩
⟨NOBODY NEEDS TO SEE THAT!!⟩
⟨IS THIS GUY... REALLY THE SAME AS THE ONE BEFORE?⟩
⟨HE'S GOT A GUN.⟩
⟨GOOD POINT.⟩
⟨RELYING ON EYEWITNESS INFORMATION ALONE, WE COULD ONLY CONFIRM ONE MALE COMBATANT.⟩
⟨BUT THERE WERE READINGS FOR FIVE PEOPLE IN THIS VICINITY.⟩
⟨THERE MUST BE MORE OF THEM HERE.⟩
⟨TAKE OUT THAT BARRICADE!!⟩
⟨SHOOT ANYONE ON SIGHT!!⟩
⟨YES, SIR!!⟩
BUOOOO (VRRMMM)

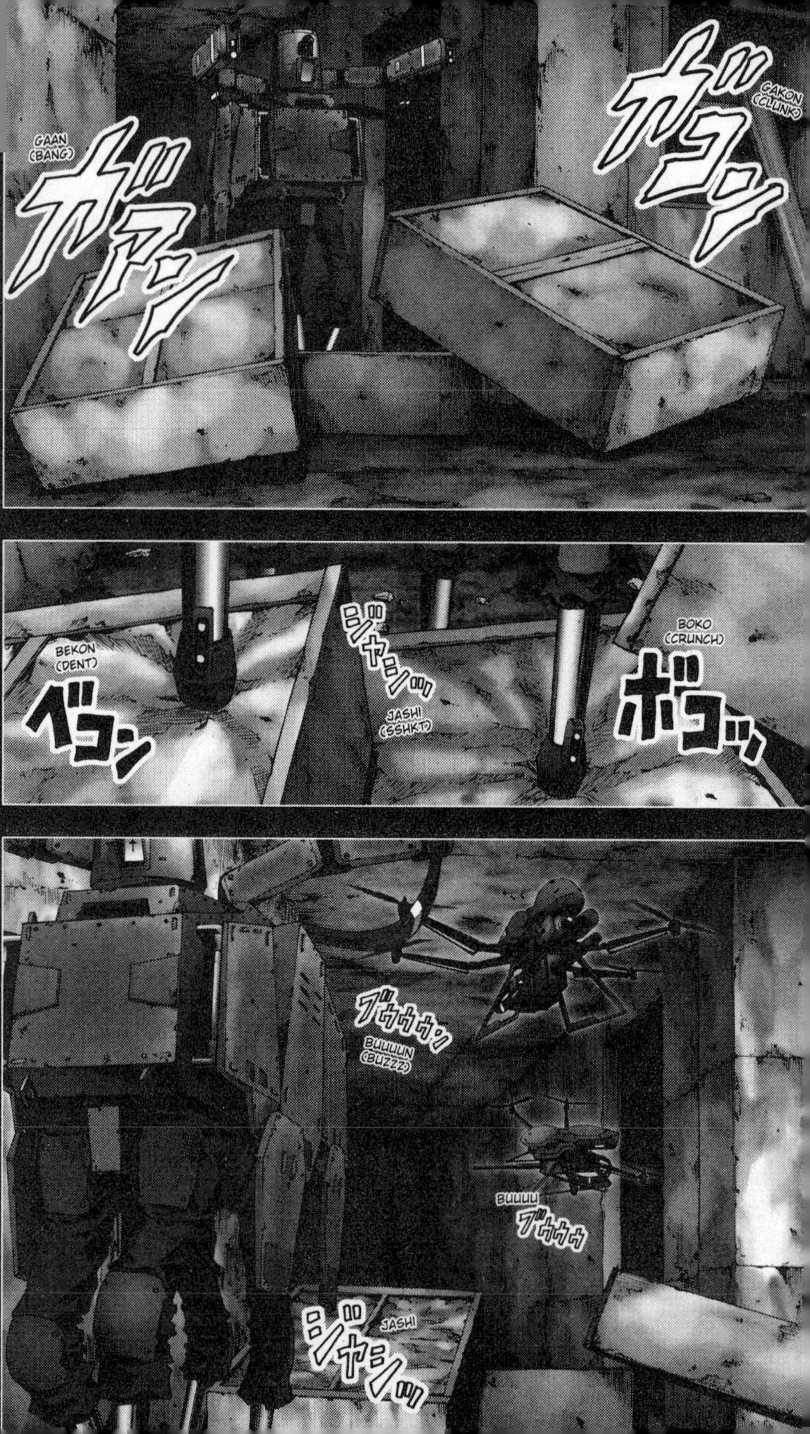
GAKON (CLUNK)
ガコン
GAAN (BANG)
ガアン
BOKO (CRUNCH)
ボコッ
ジャシッ
JASHI (SSHKT)
BEKON (DENT)
ベコン
ブウウウン
BUUUUN (BUZZZ)
BUUUU
ブウウウ
JASHI
ジャシッ

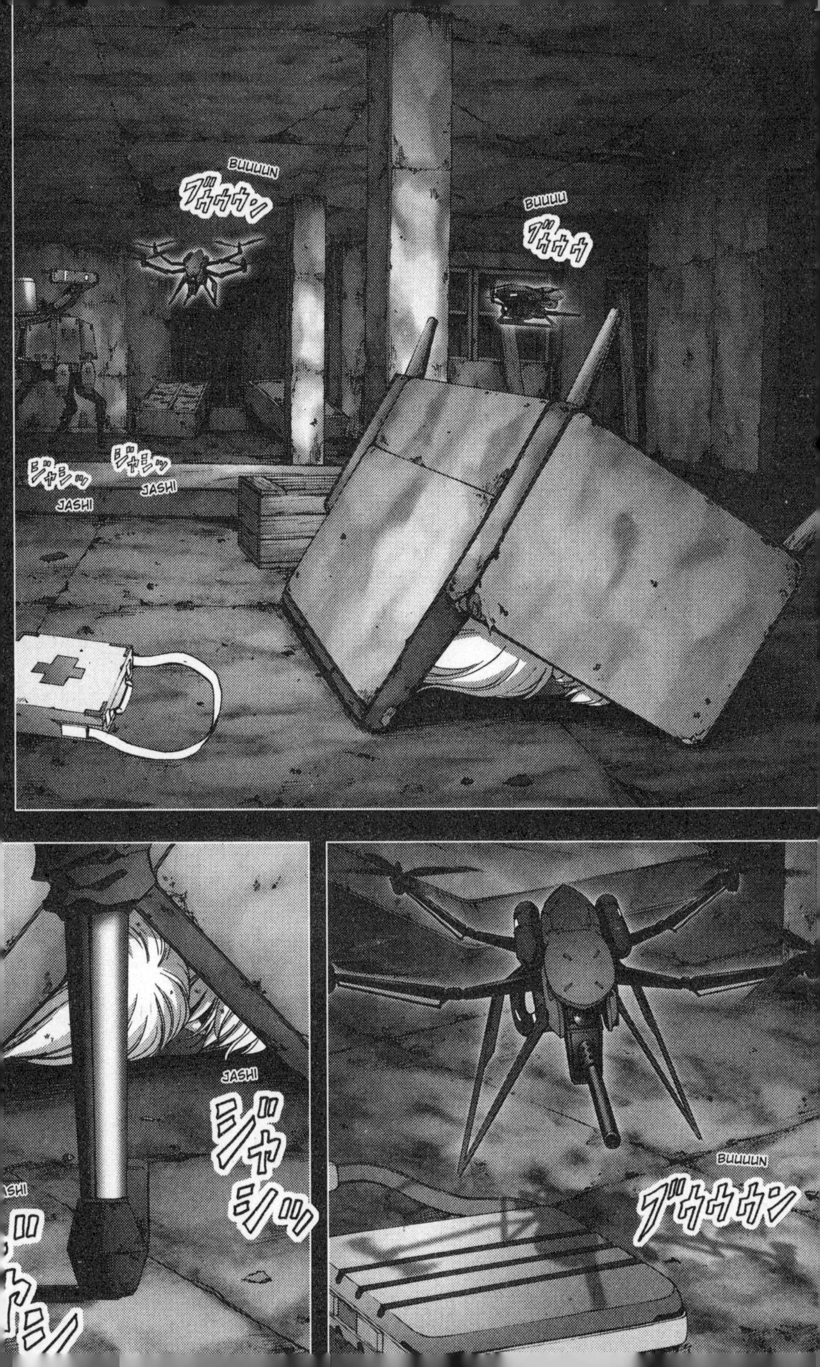
BUUUU
BUUUUN
JASHI
JASHI
BUUUUN
JASHI

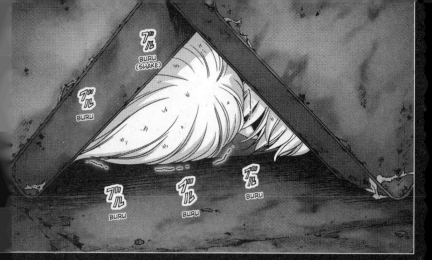

ブル
BURU (SHAKE)
ブル
BURU
ブル
BURU
ブル
BURU
ブル
BURU
BUUUUN (BUZZZZ)
ブゥゥゥン
BUUUUU
ブゥゥゥゥ
<NOBODY'S HERE. THINK THEY WENT ON AHEAD?>
<YEAH...THEY WOULDN'T BE DUMB ENOUGH TO TRY HIDING THIS CLOSE.>
<I WOULDA GOTTEN THE HELL OUTTA HERE WHILE I STILL HAD THE CHANCE.>
JAKIN (KACLICK)
ジャキン

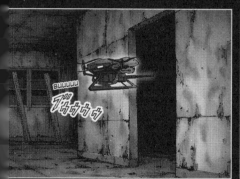

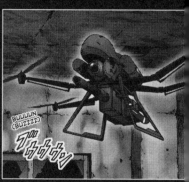

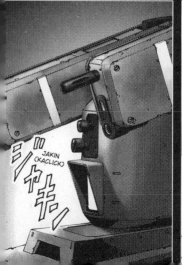

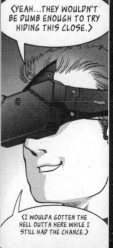

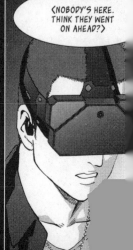

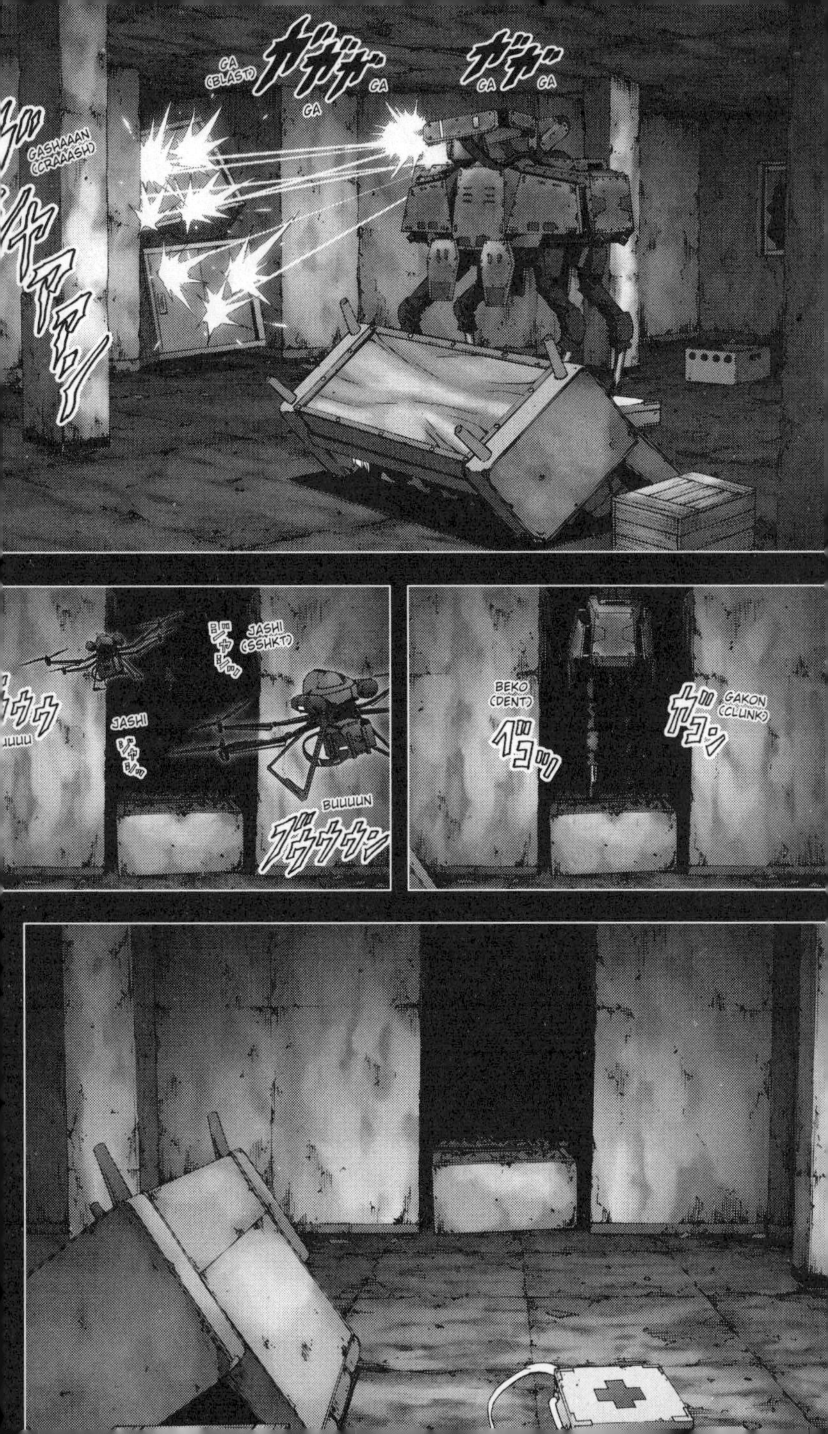
GA GA
GA (BLAST)
GA
GA
GASHAAAN (CRAAASH)
GAKON (CLUNK)
BEKO (DENT)
JASHI (SSHKT)
BUUUUN
JASHI

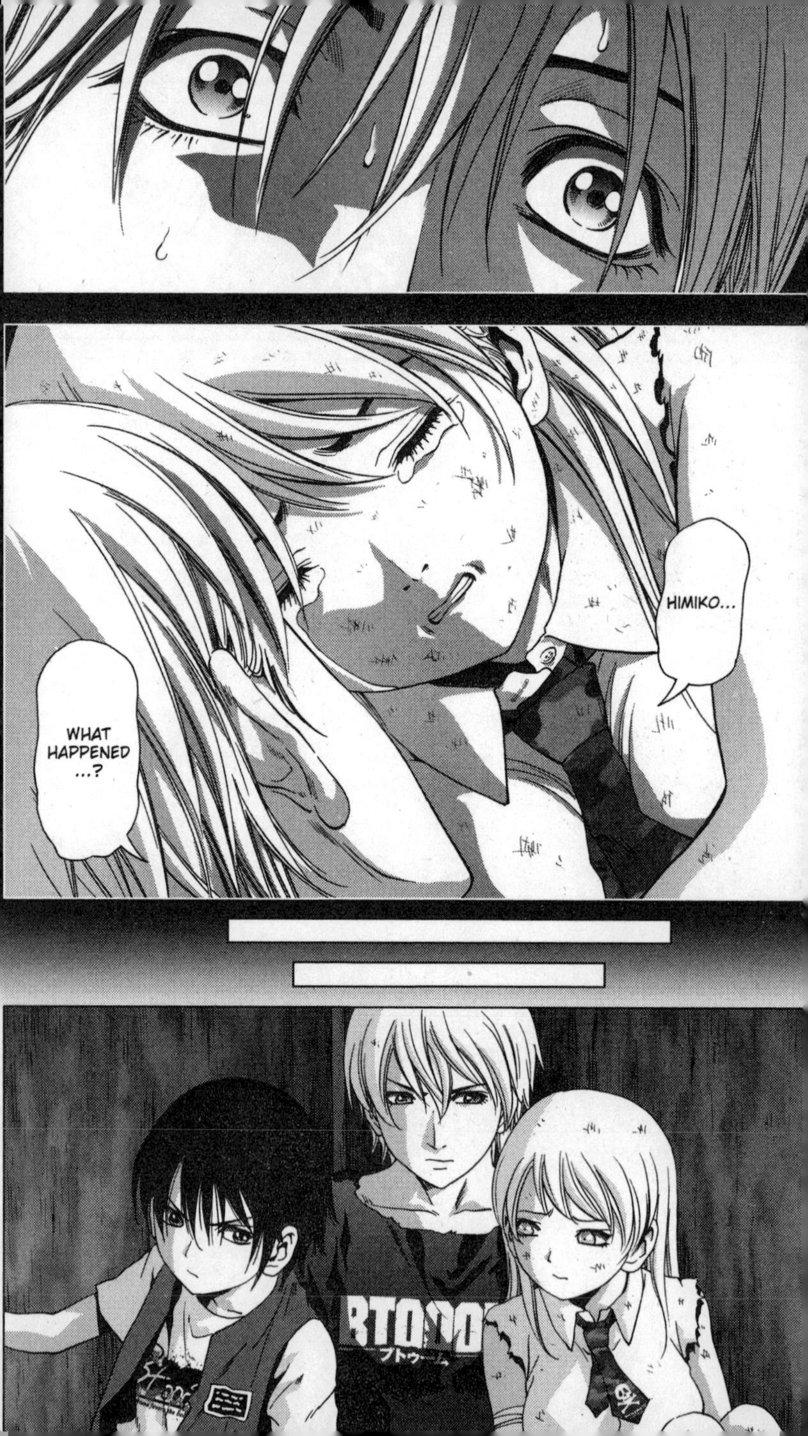
HIMIKO...
WHAT HAPPENED ...?

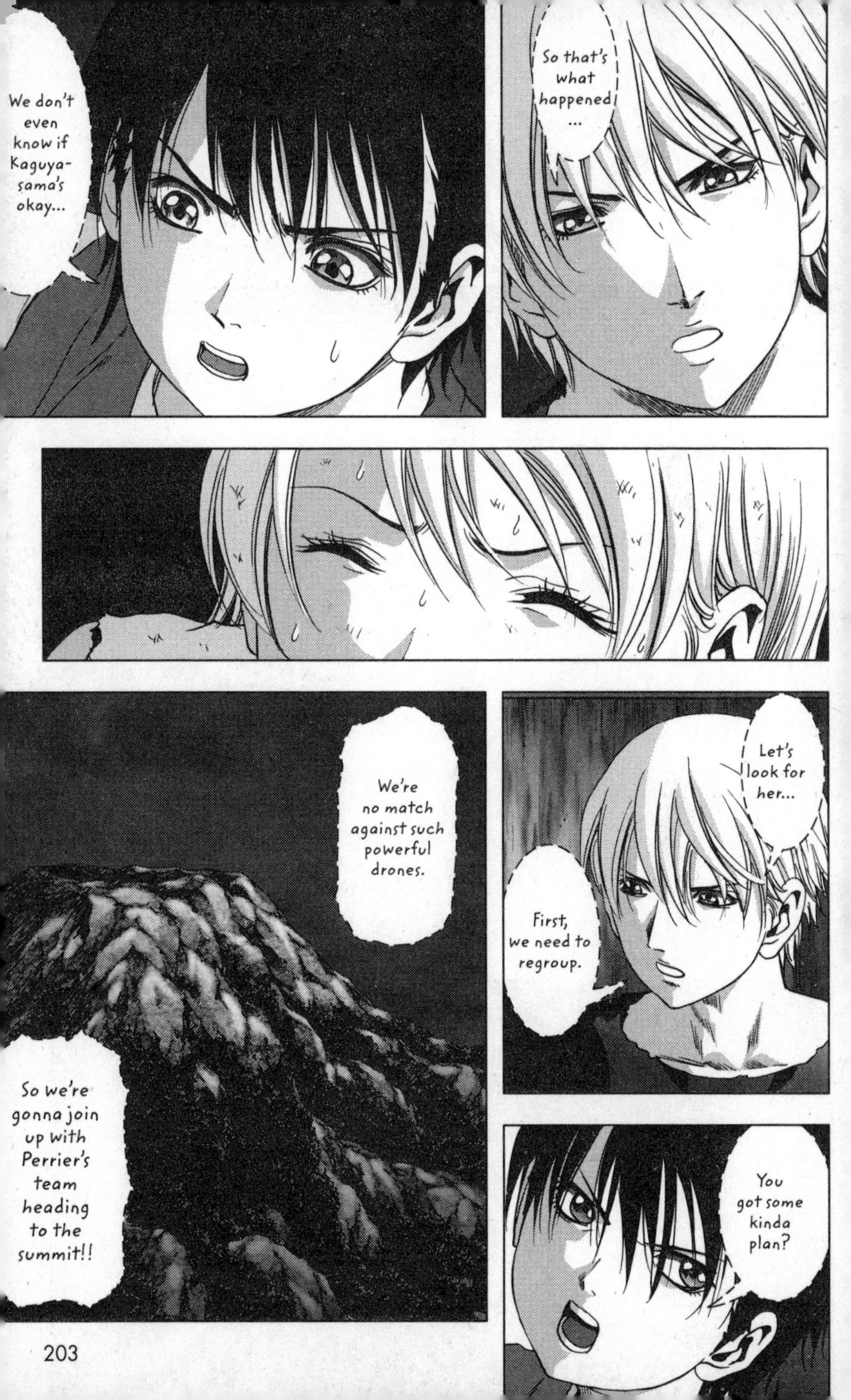
So that's what happened...
We don't even know if Kaguya-sama's okay...
Let's look for her...
First, we need to regroup.
You got some kinda plan?
We're no match against such powerful drones.
So we're gonna join up with Perrier's team heading to the summit!!

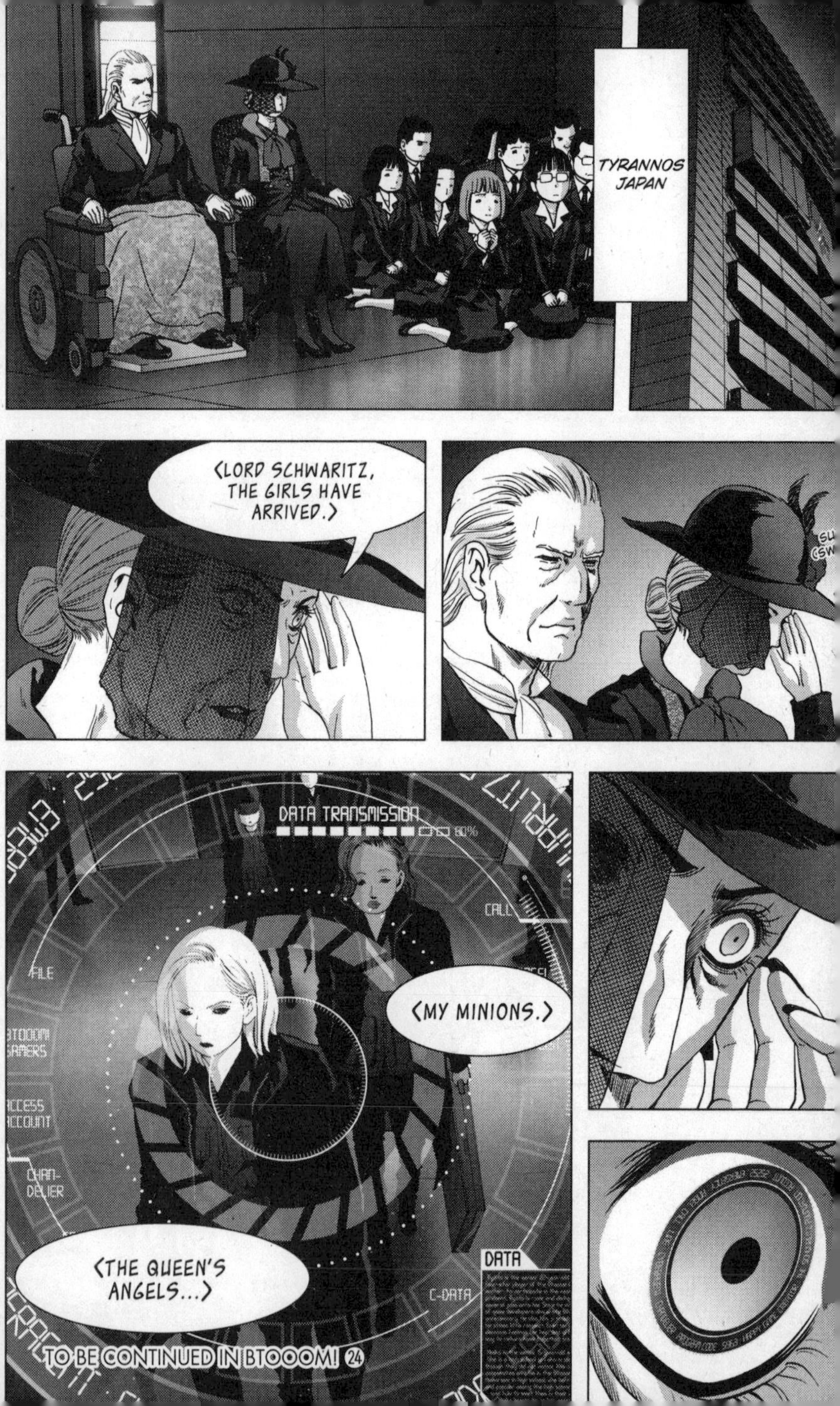
TYRANNOS JAPAN
〈LORD SCHWARITZ, THE GIRLS HAVE ARRIVED.〉
DATA TRANSMISSION
80%
CALL
FILE
BTOOOM GAMERS
ACCESS ACCOUNT
CHAN-DELIER
C-DATA
DATA
〈MY MINIONS.〉
〈THE QUEEN'S ANGELS...〉
TO BE CONTINUED IN BTOOOM! 24

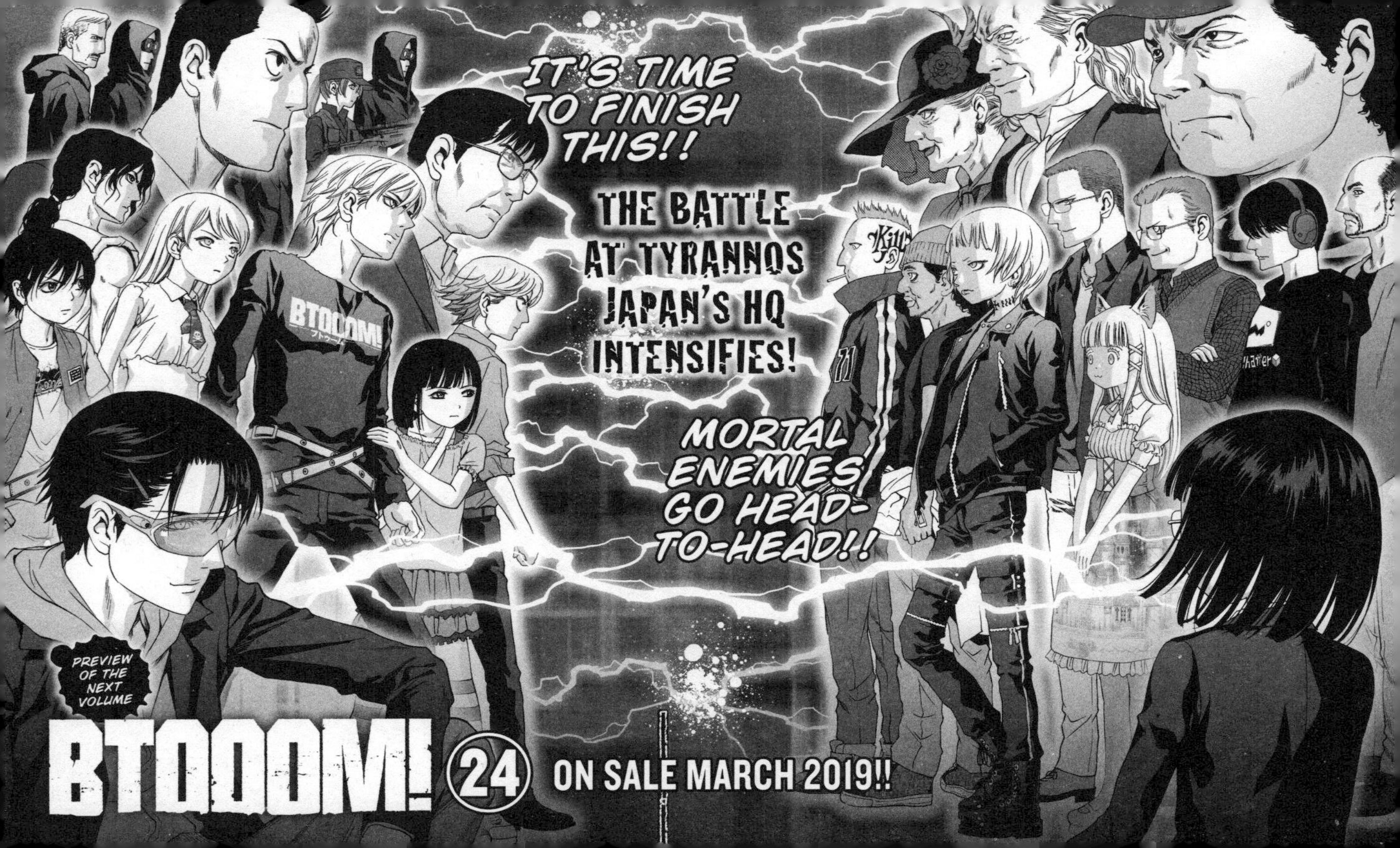

IT'S TIME TO FINISH THIS!!
THE BATTLE AT TYRANNOS JAPAN'S HQ INTENSIFIES!
MORTAL ENEMIES GO HEAD-TO-HEAD!!
PREVIEW OF THE NEXT VOLUME
BTOOOM! 24 ON SALE MARCH 2019!!

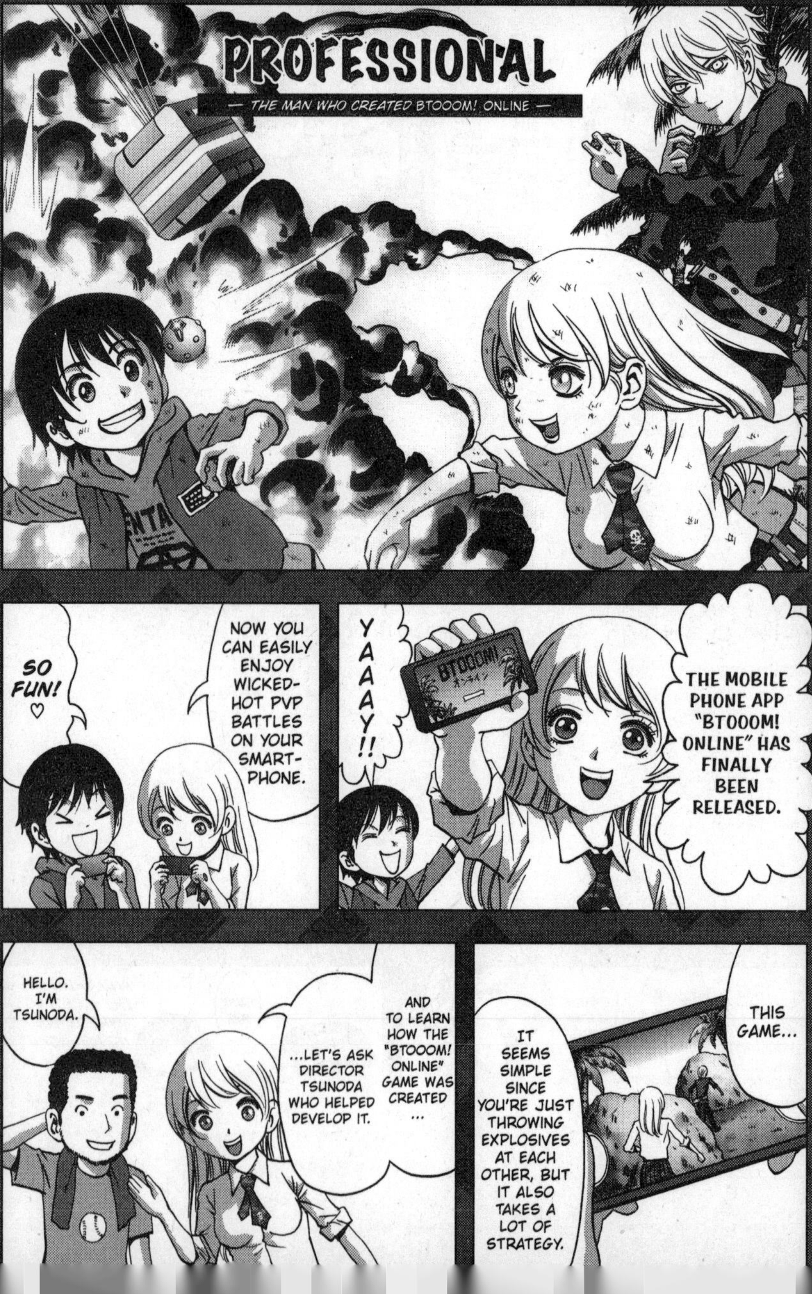
PROFESSIONAL
— THE MAN WHO CREATED BTOOOM! ONLINE —
THE MOBILE PHONE APP "BTOOOM! ONLINE" HAS FINALLY BEEN RELEASED.
YAAAAY!!
NOW YOU CAN EASILY ENJOY WICKED-HOT PVP BATTLES ON YOUR SMART-PHONE.
SO FUN! ♡
THIS GAME...
IT SEEMS SIMPLE SINCE YOU'RE JUST THROWING EXPLOSIVES AT EACH OTHER, BUT IT ALSO TAKES A LOT OF STRATEGY.
AND TO LEARN HOW THE "BTOOOM! ONLINE" GAME WAS CREATED ...
...LET'S ASK DIRECTOR TSUNODA WHO HELPED DEVELOP IT.
HELLO. I'M TSUNODA.

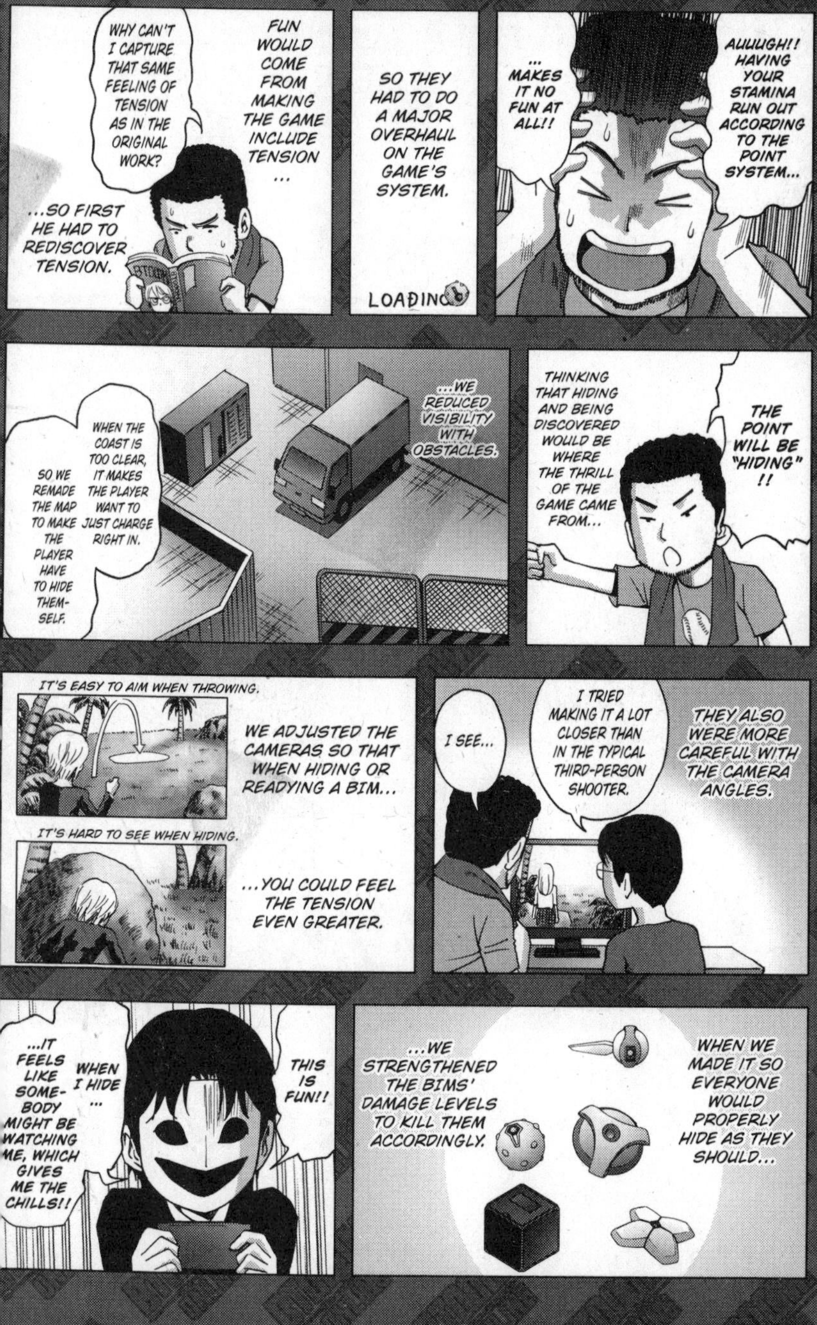
AUUUGH!! HAVING YOUR STAMINA RUN OUT ACCORDING TO THE POINT SYSTEM...
...MAKES IT NO FUN AT ALL!!
SO THEY HAD TO DO A MAJOR OVERHAUL ON THE GAME'S SYSTEM.
LOADING
FUN WOULD COME FROM MAKING THE GAME INCLUDE TENSION...
WHY CAN'T I CAPTURE THAT SAME FEELING OF TENSION AS IN THE ORIGINAL WORK?
...SO FIRST HE HAD TO REDISCOVER TENSION.
THE POINT WILL BE "HIDING"!!
THINKING THAT HIDING AND BEING DISCOVERED WOULD BE WHERE THE THRILL OF THE GAME CAME FROM...
...WE REDUCED VISIBILITY WITH OBSTACLES.
WHEN THE COAST IS TOO CLEAR, IT MAKES THE PLAYER WANT TO JUST CHARGE RIGHT IN.
SO WE REMADE THE MAP TO MAKE THE PLAYER HAVE TO HIDE THEMSELF.
THEY ALSO WERE MORE CAREFUL WITH THE CAMERA ANGLES.
I TRIED MAKING IT A LOT CLOSER THAN IN THE TYPICAL THIRD-PERSON SHOOTER.
I SEE...
IT'S EASY TO AIM WHEN THROWING.
WE ADJUSTED THE CAMERAS SO THAT WHEN HIDING OR READYING A BIM...
IT'S HARD TO SEE WHEN HIDING.
...YOU COULD FEEL THE TENSION EVEN GREATER.
WHEN WE MADE IT SO EVERYONE WOULD PROPERLY HIDE AS THEY SHOULD...
...WE STRENGTHENED THE BIMS' DAMAGE LEVELS TO KILL THEM ACCORDINGLY.
THIS IS FUN!!
WHEN I HIDE...
...IT FEELS LIKE SOMEBODY MIGHT BE WATCHING ME, WHICH GIVES ME THE CHILLS!!

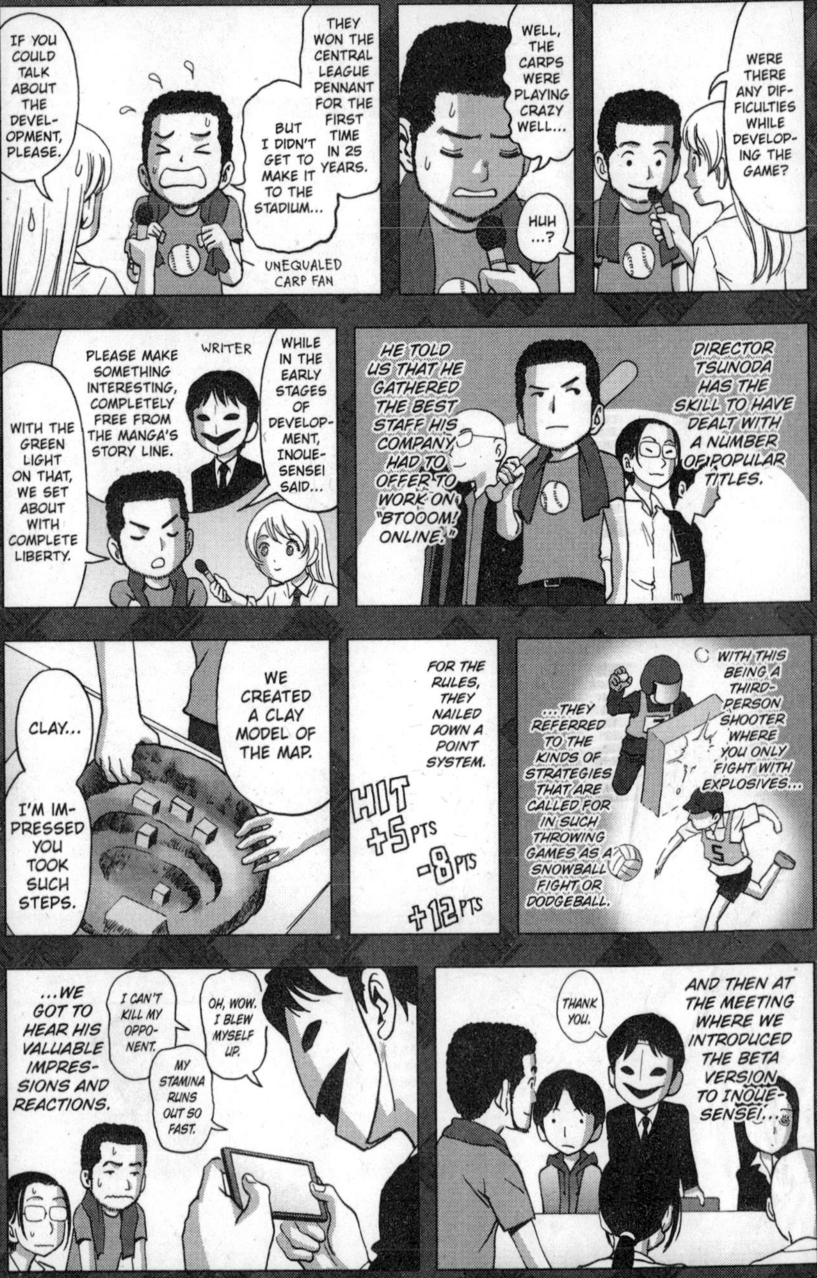
WERE THERE ANY DIFFICULTIES WHILE DEVELOPING THE GAME?
WELL, THE CARPS WERE PLAYING CRAZY WELL...
HUH ...?
THEY WON THE CENTRAL LEAGUE PENNANT FOR THE FIRST TIME IN 25 YEARS.
BUT I DIDN'T GET TO MAKE IT TO THE STADIUM...
IF YOU COULD TALK ABOUT THE DEVELOPMENT, PLEASE.
UNEQUALED CARP FAN
DIRECTOR TSUNODA HAS THE SKILL TO HAVE DEALT WITH A NUMBER OF POPULAR TITLES.
HE TOLD US THAT HE GATHERED THE BEST STAFF HIS COMPANY HAD TO OFFER TO WORK ON "BTOOOM! ONLINE."
WHILE IN THE EARLY STAGES OF DEVELOPMENT, INOUE-SENSEI SAID...
WRITER
PLEASE MAKE SOMETHING INTERESTING, COMPLETELY FREE FROM THE MANGA'S STORY LINE.
WITH THE GREEN LIGHT ON THAT, WE SET ABOUT WITH COMPLETE LIBERTY.
WITH THIS BEING A THIRD-PERSON SHOOTER WHERE YOU ONLY FIGHT WITH EXPLOSIVES...
...THEY REFERRED TO THE KINDS OF STRATEGIES THAT ARE CALLED FOR IN SUCH THROWING GAMES AS A SNOWBALL FIGHT OR DODGEBALL.
FOR THE RULES, THEY NAILED DOWN A POINT SYSTEM.
HIT +5 PTS
-8 PTS
+12 PTS
WE CREATED A CLAY MODEL OF THE MAP.
CLAY...
I'M IMPRESSED YOU TOOK SUCH STEPS.
AND THEN AT THE MEETING WHERE WE INTRODUCED THE BETA VERSION TO INOUE-SENSEI...
THANK YOU.
OH, WOW. I BLEW MYSELF UP.
I CAN'T KILL MY OPPONENT.
MY STAMINA RUNS OUT SO FAST.
...WE GOT TO HEAR HIS VALUABLE IMPRESSIONS AND REACTIONS.

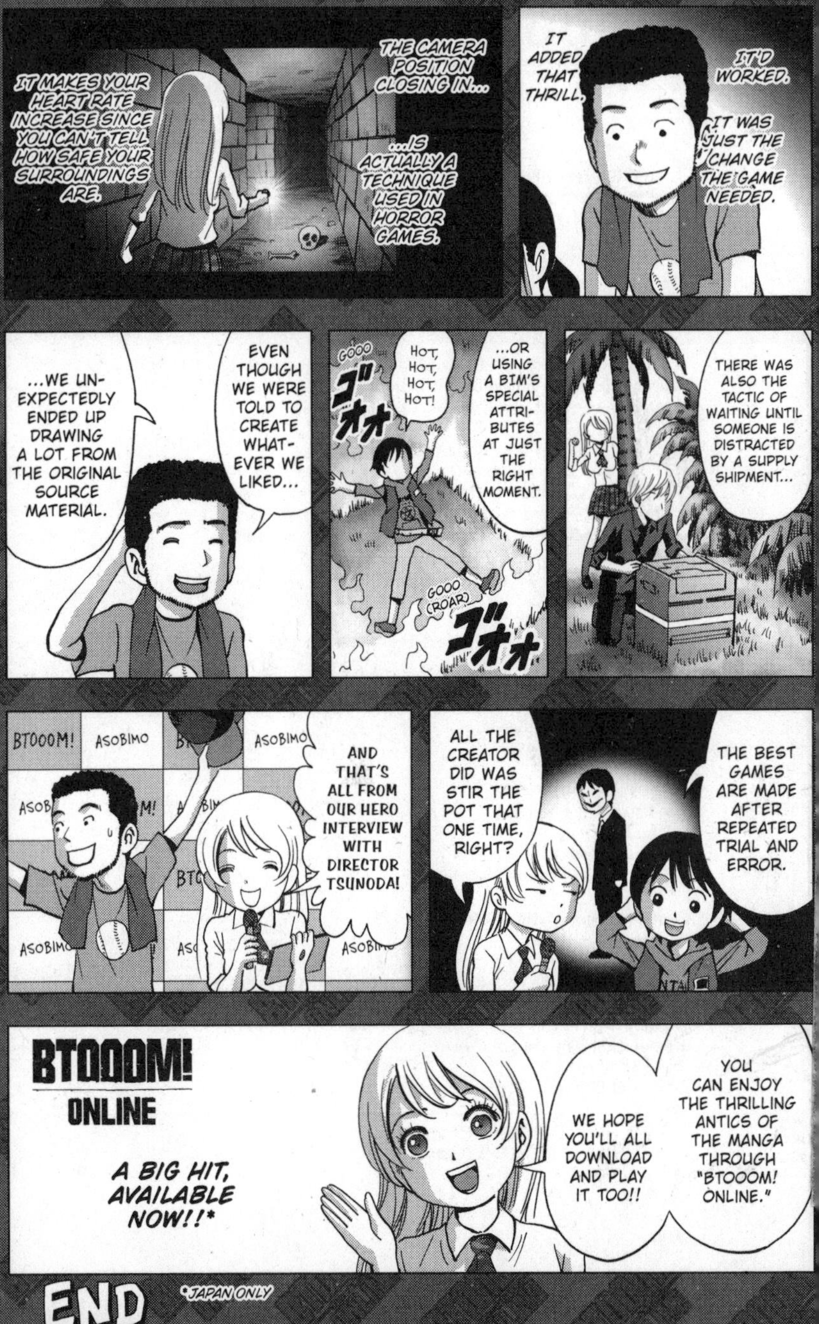
IT'D WORKED.
IT ADDED THAT THRILL.
IT WAS JUST THE CHANGE THE GAME NEEDED.
THE CAMERA POSITION CLOSING IN...
IT MAKES YOUR HEART RATE INCREASE SINCE YOU CAN'T TELL HOW SAFE YOUR SURROUNDINGS ARE.
...IS ACTUALLY A TECHNIQUE USED IN HORROR GAMES.
THERE WAS ALSO THE TACTIC OF WAITING UNTIL SOMEONE IS DISTRACTED BY A SUPPLY SHIPMENT...
...OR USING A BIM'S SPECIAL ATTRIBUTES AT JUST THE RIGHT MOMENT.
HOT, HOT, HOT, HOT!
GOOO
ゴオオ
GOOO (ROAR)
ゴオオ
EVEN THOUGH WE WERE TOLD TO CREATE WHATEVER WE LIKED...
...WE UNEXPECTEDLY ENDED UP DRAWING A LOT FROM THE ORIGINAL SOURCE MATERIAL.
THE BEST GAMES ARE MADE AFTER REPEATED TRIAL AND ERROR.
ALL THE CREATOR DID WAS STIR THE POT THAT ONE TIME, RIGHT?
AND THAT'S ALL FROM OUR HERO INTERVIEW WITH DIRECTOR TSUNODA!
BTOOOM!
ASOBIMO
ASOBIMO
YOU CAN ENJOY THE THRILLING ANTICS OF THE MANGA THROUGH "BTOOOM! ONLINE."
WE HOPE YOU'LL ALL DOWNLOAD AND PLAY IT TOO!!
BTOOOM! ONLINE
A BIG HIT, AVAILABLE NOW!!*
END
*JAPAN ONLY

BTOOOM! 23

JUNYA INOUE

Translation: Christine Dashiell

Lettering: Brndn Blakeslee

BTOOOM! © Junya INOUE 2017. All rights reserved. English translation rights arranged with SHINCHOSHA PUBLISHING CO. through Tuttle-Mori Agency, Inc., Tokyo.

English translation © 2018 by Yen Press, LLC

Yen Press
1290 Avenue of the Americas
New York, NY 10104

Visit us at yenpress.com
facebook.com/yenpress
twitter.com/yenpress
yenpress.tumblr.com
instagram.com/yenpress

First Yen Press Edition: December 2018

Yen Press is an imprint of Yen Press, LLC.
The Yen Press name and logo are trademarks of Yen Press, LLC.

The publisher is not responsible for websites (or their content) that are not owned by the publisher.

Library of Congress Control Number: 2013497409

ISBNs: 978-1-9753-2892-4 (paperback)
       978-1-9753-2893-1 (ebook)

10 9 8 7 6 5 4 3 2 1

WOR

Printed in the United States of America